GOVERNMENT AND SPORT

GOVERNMENT AND SPORT

The Public Policy Issues

Edited by
ARTHUR T. JOHNSON
University of Maryland
Baltimore County

and

JAMES H. FREY
University of Nevada,
Las Vegas

Rowman & Allanheld
PUBLISHERS

ROWMAN & ALLANHELD

Published in the United States of America in 1985
by Rowman & Allanheld, Publishers
(a division of Littlefield, Adams & Company)
81 Adams Drive, Totowa, New Jersey 07512

Library of Congress Cataloging in Publication Data
Main entry under title:

Government and sport.

  Includes indexes.
  1. Sports and state—United States—Addresses,
essays, lectures. 2. Sports—Government policy—
United States—Addresses, essays, lectures. 3. Sports—
Law and legislation—United States—Addresses, essays,
lectures. I. Johnson, Arthur T. II. Frey, James H.
GV583.G676   1985   796'.0973   85-11878
ISBN 0-8476-7371-5

85 86 87 / 10 9 8 7 6 5 4 3 2 1
Printed in the United States of America

Contents

Tables and Figures   vii

Preface and Acknowledgments   ix

1   Introduction   1
     Arthur T. Johnson and James H. Frey

PART I
PUBLIC POLICY AND THE ATHLETE

2   Balancing the Rights of Professional Athletes and Team
     Owners: The Proper Role of Government   21
     James B. Dworkin

3   The Amateur Athlete as Employee   41
     Allen L. Sack and Bruce Kidd

4   The Impact of Title IX on Women's Intercollegiate Sports   62
     Linda Jean Carpenter

5   The Regulation of Sports Agents   79
     Robert H. Ruxin

6   Violence in Professional Sports and Public Policy   99
     D. Stanley Eitzen

PART II
PUBLIC POLICY AND SPORTS ADMINISTRATION

7   Legal and Constitutional Challenges to the NCAA: The Limits
     of Adjudication in Intercollegiate Athletics   117
     Brian L. Porto

8   Professional Sports and Antitrust Laws: The Ground Rules of
     Immunity, Exemption, and Liability   140
     Phillip J. Closius

9   Property Rights in Sports Broadcasting:
     The Fundamental Issue   162
     Philip R. Hochberg

10   The Impact of Tax Policy on Sports   171
     James F. Ambrose

PART III
PUBLIC POLICY, SPORTS, AND THE PUBLIC INTEREST

11 Gambling, Sport, and Public Policy 189
    James H. Frey

12 The Sports Franchise Relocation Issue and Public
    Policy Responses 219
    Arthur T. Johnson

13 Foreign Policy in the Sports Arena 248
    James A. R. Nafziger

14 Conclusion: Sports, Regulation, and the Public Interest 261
    James H. Frey and *Arthur T. Johnson*

Indexes 265
Contributors 273

Tables and Figures

Tables

2.1	Average Player Salaries, 1970, 1980, and 1982	37
4.1	Sport Offerings for Female Intercollegiate Athletes, 1977–1984	68
4.2	Gender of Personnel in Athletic Programs' Administrative Structure, 1984	69
11.1	Nevada Sports Book Analysis	194
11.2	Gambling Economic Profile, 1983	196
11.3	Legal Gambling in America	198
11.4	Disbursement of Revenue by New York City Off-Track Betting Corporation, 1971–1979	206
12.1	Professional Sports Teams Within Standard Metropolitan Statistical Areas, 1984	220
12.2	Public Revenue and Expenditures Attributable to Professional Baseball and Football in Baltimore, 1977–1983	225
12.3	Stadium Lease Expiration Dates for Major League Baseball Franchises	229
12.4	Distance Between First Place and Last Place Teams, 1984	240

Figure

14.1	Distribution of Benefits and Costs of Various Sports Policies	263

Preface and Acknowledgments

The major purpose of this book is to demonstrate the great influence government has, and will continue to have, on the operation of professional and amateur sport in the United States. Government policy as implemented through legislation, court decisions, and bureaucratic rules and regulations is now an even more important variable in defining the nature and dynamics of American sport. For years, the practice was to ignore sports or to adopt a "hands-off" stance when it came to policy proposals. Sport was sacrosanct; it was not a "business" engaging in interstate commerce or seeking profit. Rather, it was a "game" that provided a vehicle for men and boys to live out their fantasies, to pursue their dreams, or to learn the values that were important to living and succeeding in America.

The "apple pie" approach to sport has crumbled significantly in recent years in the wake of legal and legislative challenges to what has been standard operating procedure. These challenges have come from many corners, but the most significant have originated with athletes and fans. Unions of professional athletes and individual amateur athletes have called into question labor practices that limited the individual's freedom of movement and the right to command a full measure of the worth of his or her labor. Representatives of the public interest have demanded accountability from the owners of professional sport franchises who would move their teams to another city in the name of profit and in what appears to be total disregard for the public's investment (such as tax subsidies and gate receipts) in that franchise. These issues, and many others, are addressed in this text.

In producing a book where public policy is the focus, there is the risk of being outdated, even though every effort is made to be timely. Several of the problems discussed in the following chapters are under current debate in Congress and in governing bodies such as the National Collegiate Athletic Association (NCAA). Nevertheless, the material contained in the chapters represents important updates on policy issues that have not received systematic attention by policy analysts or by academicians. The last such publication was Roger Noll's *Government and the Sport Business* (The Brookings Institution, 1974). Our text is designed to bring the reader up to date in a systematic manner on the significant policy issues in sport.

For the most part, the contributors to this text resist exotic solutions and attempt to cope with the policy problems within the existing system. We hope that the prescriptions made herein will attract serious attention from policy analysts, public officials, and others who have an interest in the organization and operation of modern sport in America. More important, we hope that this book will contribute to a more informed discussion of public policy as it relates to professional and amateur sport.

During the two years this text has been in preparation, we have received support and encouragement from many sources. First, we acknowledge the patience and the resources provided by colleagues from our respective departments and institutions—the Department of Political Science at the University of Maryland Baltimore County, and the Department of Sociology of the University of Nevada, Las Vegas.

We also thank the authors, who devoted considerable time and energy to their contributions. They were a cooperative group, and they responded in a very diplomatic fashion to our comments on drafts and to our frequent reminders of the manuscript's deadline. In addition, we appreciate the patience and encouragement of Mr. Spencer Carr, editor at Rowman & Allanheld. We must also thank Debra Duddlesten, Sandra Cueva, and Marie Ahsan for their typing assistance. Finally, we would like to thank Ms. Marjorie Barrick of Las Vegas, whose generous support of the academic programs at the University of Nevada, Las Vegas, made it possible for Jim Frey to receive a Barrick Fellowship for the fall of 1984. This award included release time to work on this manuscript.

James H. Frey
Arthur T. Johnson

1

Introduction

Arthur T. Johnson
James H. Frey

The rationale for this book, and the assumption of its essays, is that in very basic ways public policy affects the structure, operations, and future of amateur athletics and professional team sports in the United States. To understand the dynamics of the sports industry, it is necessary to recognize the relationship between government and sport and to realize that many issues in the world of sport also are issues of public policy.

The essays of this text address the substance of specific public policy issues within sport. This introduction offers a context for those articles by providing (a) a brief discussion of the relationship between sport and the state, (b) a description of the changing perceptions of sport in the United States and the subsequent legitimation of government intervention, and (c) an analysis of the process by which issues of sport become matters to be debated within government institutions. We conclude by raising three questions that speak to the proper role of government in sport and to the appropriateness and efficacy of public policy solutions to specific issues in sports.

SPORTS AND THE STATE

The recent history of professional and amateur sport reflects a chronology of legal battles, courtroom dramas, congressional investigations, and regulatory actions. The increasing attention paid by the state to sport is a reflection of sport's place in society and of several trends.

First, sport is an effective transmitter of values.[1] Through sport, the predominant values of society—fair play, rule obedience, equality—are taught to participant and fan alike. Sport also can promote a feeling of community attachment and goodwill among citizens, as well as provide the impetus for surges of patriotism and national pride in general. The performance of the American ice hockey team in the 1980 Winter Olympics and recent victories by American athletes in the 1984 Summer Olympics had this effect. It is unlikely that any state will ignore such an effective socialization agent as sport.

Second, the trend toward more government intervention has occurred within every other major social institution; there is no reason not to expect it to extend to sport. Sport is just one more arena in which activity is increasingly governed by rules, bureaucracy, specialization, rationality, and modern technology. In such arenas, disputes arise and participants appeal to legislatures and courts for satisfaction.

Third, as both amateur and professional sport have evolved into complex organizations and "big business," characterized by commercialism and hierarchy, it has become more difficult to view sport at any level as an idyllic activity safe from the scrutiny of government. Prior to the 1960s, sport entrepreneurs were the beneficiaries of tacit and overt agreements that, by granting sport a special status of being free from normal government regulation, reinforced the separation of sport and the state.[2] Today, given the great escalation of the monetary rewards of sport, all participants—players, entrepreneurs, media interests, private sector sponsors of teams, athletes, and events, and even the state itself—seek their "fair share" of the fruits of sport and tend to oppose the favored treatment of one set of interests over another. Thus, although government is less likely to enter into the explicit preferential agreements of a time past, it does become a key arbiter in distributing the material rewards of sport.

Fourth, sport has acquired the status of a *public trust*, which must be protected. As a result, public policy in the form of law or regulatory action has been implemented to guarantee the public equitable access. In recent years government action has been sought to promote parity in competition, to eliminate discrimination, to investigate athletic regulatory bodies, to gain civil rights guaranteed by law, to ensure spectator access via television, and to control the amount and level of violence in sport. This trend is augmented by the rise of "entitlement" movements, which have made it possible for lower-level participants (for example, players) to demand equal benefits from the athletic enterprise. They have pursued their demands in the legislative, judicial, and bureaucratic arenas, often successfully. The direct intervention of the state into sport suggests that governmental bodies are increasingly concerned that the operating policies of sport reflect the public interest.

It cannot be assumed, however, that the public's interest is enhanced by state intervention. Many observers assert that elite class interests, as reflected by the owners of professional franchises or the membership of amateur athletic governing boards, not the public interest, are the beneficiaries of the existing organization and practices of contemporary sport. Hoch argues, for example, that the lucrative agreements between professional sports and the state may in large part be an outcome of the ability of wealthy and powerful owners, assisted by media and business interests who benefit from the presence of sport, to influence the political process directly through their lobbying efforts.[3] At the same time as these owners are negotiating contracts that will benefit their economic position, they also are able to manipulate the general public, via the media, into adopting a false consciousness that emphasizes the integrative and character-building aspects of sport.[4] Thus the American sports creed is successfully tied to the American business creed in order to create the illusion that the public interest is being served. But in reality, it is argued, government intervention serves the class interest of owners and governing boards.

The more critical exponents of this conflict theory of sport assert that sport is simply an extension of "bourgeois rule";[5] it can even be an instrument of coercion and oppression veiling the real structure of production relations. State-capitalism exploitation is maintained as a result. Brohm asserts: "Sports systems in general appear as an 'armed apparatus of coercion' which has the ultimate function of protecting the class rule of the bourgeoisie sport, like all other institutions mediated through the structures of the state apparatus."[6] These critics see increased involvement by the state in sport as the result of an effort to promote the existing social order and value hegemony—that is, to maintain class rule.[7]

This view stands in contrast to the liberal-pluralist view of the relation of state and sport. The liberal-pluralist perspective maintains that there are no ulterior motives in the relation of government and sport. This relation reflects the natural conditions of society.

> In such theories sport would generally be seen as a voluntary set of social and cultural practices that allow for periodic release from the tension of everyday existence and which provide for collective representation of diverse community interests. The potential multiplicity of collective representations that may occur, however, is mediated by the fact that sport is seen to be institutionalized in a consensual way. That is, it is assumed that sport's main organizational structure, system of rule and collective meanings are shared by the majority of the members of society. . . .
>
> Sport is not seen to be a formal part of the state system. The state may have occasion to "regulate" some aspects of sporting practice, but sport is not generally recognized to be part of the state apparatus. [A moral corollary suggests] not only that sport *is* separate from the state system, but that it *ought* to be separate from the state system.[8]

Thus sport participation is seen as a voluntary act that provides for periodic tension release, for community identification, and for temporary personal exhilaration. Sport is also an expression of consensus shared by voluntary members. Since participation is voluntary and the sport organizations are considered voluntary associations, sport is not viewed as a formal part of the state system. The pluralists see state involvement as indirect and only accommodating or facilitating. This perspective reinforces the ideal concept of the separation of the state and sport, and it suggests that the state, when necessary, intervenes on behalf of the larger public interest, not on behalf of specific class interests.

It is our contention that separation of sport and the state no longer exists, if it ever did. It is not necessary to embrace the Marxist critique of sport to agree that sport does not have to be manipulated directly by the capitalist class in order to function on its behalf. Also, it is important to understand that sport is important not only in social reproduction, but that it has the potential to play an "oppositional role" where it is a factor in transforming capitalist society.[9]

Just as there are a variety of theories on the relation of sport and the state, so too do the actual formal arrangements between sport and government span a wide spectrum of possibilities.[10] In some nation states, such as the Soviet Union and the countries of Eastern Europe, sport is very much a part of the state apparatus. In fact, there is usually a Minister of Sport who retains a cabinet-level position. The directions and organizational forms taken by sport in these countries are very much the result of policy deliberations by governmental bodies. In countries like the United States, direct intervention, at least by the allocation of tax monies, is less prevalent. Intervention exists, but it is less obvious. For example, even though Congress chartered the United States Olympic Committee (USOC), it rarely intercedes into the USOC's daily operations, the 1980 boycott being an exception. Somewhere in between we find the British and Western European systems, which permit sport autonomy; but because they make tax dollars available to sport bodies, governments can have a direct policy impact on sport in those countries.[11]

Regardless of the model held out to a nation's citizens, sport and politics always have been institutional partners in any society, particularly where that society's reputation or national pride are at stake. Although in the United States the separation of sport and politics may be viewed as the appropriate relationship, it is not the practiced one.

Sport always has been seen as a visible and effective means to communicate national and international policy, whether it be opposition (for example, boycott) or support (such as sport exchange).[12] In the political context sport is real and it is serious. While we acknowledge the use of sport for symbolic and acculturation purposes by the state and those who hope to be its representatives, this integration has not necessarily resulted in public policy, at least in the formal sense.[13] It therefore receives little attention in this text. We are concerned more with the emergence of sports issues as the rightful concern of public policymaking bodies, with government's eventual definition of those issues, and with the likely consequences of the implementation of certain public sports policies.

Changing Perceptions of Sport and Government

Among the many factors that influence the making of public policy and its implementation are the prevailing values and norms of society, the attitudinal milieu of policymakers, the relative political power of participants in a given policy contest, and the feasibility of available policy options. Yet it is the perception of the appropriateness of government action that determines whether an issue gains agenda status; that is, whether a government institution seriously will consider acting on an issue. The perception of sport held by participants, policymakers, and the public has been the principal influence on the perceived appropriateness—and therefore probability—of government acting on matters of relevance to sport. These perceptions have changed over time and can be summarized in three statements.

1. *Historically, sports—amateur and professional—have been presented by their representatives and perceived by the public as being merely "sport" (i.e., fun and games, diversion), and this image was accepted by public officials.*

The "joy of sports" has been praised by novelists, journalists, social commentators, sports representatives, and public officials.[14] There is no question that an idyllic image of sport was held by the public and went virtually unchallenged until the 1960s. Sport has been viewed historically as simple diversion—entertainment, fun, and games. Sports were for children and for young men in college. College football held the nation's fancy in the early 1900s, until sports heroes like Babe Ruth and Red Grange popularized professional sports. Heroes always have been the stuff of sports, and many have been canonized by an adoring public and an often duplicitous press.[15]

Community leaders and public officials quickly realized that sport was a means for developing character and inculcating democratic values. Thus sport became an important element in the American educational system as well as an essential tool in the Americanization of recently arrived immigrants.[16] Further, American sports could be exported to other parts of the world to demonstrate America's democratic traditions and values.[17] Public officials believed that baseball could produce any desired state of affairs, from ending juvenile delinquency to bringing about international peace. In 1953 Senator Edwin Johnson (D–Col.) suggested that baseball was "democracy in action." "If the free world and Iron Curtain countries could compete on the baseball diamond," he asserted, "plans for war would disappear from the face of the earth like an early-morning dew." [18]

Sport, especially amateur sport, was pure. When an occasional scandal or unsavory event occurred and received public attention, such as the Black Sox scandal of 1919 and the college basketball gambling scandals of the early

1950s, citizens and officials alike first expressed shock and anger, and then sought culprits or explanations external to sport to account for these incidents.

The perception of sport as fun and games kept it insulated from serious analysis by academic or social commentators. Its close association with societal values, and in some instances government officials, ensured that its critics, when they began to attack sport, were either ignored or attacked in turn. Even in the 1960s, when social and antiwar activists began to exploit athletic events to gain publicity for their causes, they were denounced consequently for attempting to "politicize" athletics. At the same time, patriotic and nationalistic demonstrations at athletic events, such as honoring military heroes at halftime of football games, were accepted as appropriate.[19]

In sum, an image of sport evolved that depicted sport as providing innocent diversion while at the same time sport was perpetuating important social values. This idyllic image survived into the 1960s unchallenged by policymakers.

2. *Historically, public officials, accepting this idyllic image of sport, have been content to allow the sports industry—amateur and professional—to regulate itself and to remain relatively free from government intervention.*

As long as the idyllic image of sport went unquestioned, government intervention was deemed inappropriate. "Except in the suppression of gambling or illegal amusements and in the maintenance of the Puritan sabbath, Americans traditionally looked upon sport as private in nature, to be regulated by private governing bodies."[20] Congress, especially, appeared to be content with deferring to sports officials and "remaining in the grandstand" with regard to problems in the sports industry.[21] At most, legislators during this period prodded sports officials to address the more blatant problems, such as the feud between the National Collegiate Athletic Association (NCAA) and the Amateur Athletic Union (AAU).

Thus Congress rarely, if ever, recognized sport as a substantive legislative matter before 1950. More than fifty bills relating to professional sports were introduced in Congress between 1951 and 1960. None that substantively affected professional sports was passed.[22] Similarly, with regard to amateur sports, in the 1950s Congress did not adopt any legislation of consequence, with the exception of its 1950 incorporation of the U. S. Olympic Committee, which provided for the basic structure of elite sport administration in the United States.[23]

The courts also exercised self-restraint by recognizing the status quo with regard to sports. The Supreme Court surprised many in 1953 (*Toolson* v. *New York Yankees*) by upholding precedent set in 1922 (*Federal Baseball Club* v. *National League*) and by refusing to subject professional baseball to federal antitrust laws.[24] When other sports, especially football, could not gain judicial protection from those same laws in the 1950s, they sought to do so in the friendlier congressional arena.[25] Thus much of the professional sports legislation introduced in the 1950s and early 1960s was designed to protect and strengthen the leagues' power of self-regulation.

If government did threaten to intervene in an unfavorable manner, it was usually in response to dramatic events, such as the brutality of college football at the turn of the century, the college basketball gambling scandals of the early 1950s and 1960s, the poor performance of American Olympic teams as a result of the bitter NCAA–AAU feud, and the abandonment of Brooklyn and New York by the Dodgers and Giants in 1958. Even in light of these events, spokesmen for professional and amateur sports implored public officials to remain out of the sports business.

That is not to say that representatives of sports organizations were totally opposed to government enacting sports policy. The professional leagues, especially, often requested legislation, mainly for the purpose of antitrust protection. The goal was to strengthen their self-regulation authority and to protect themselves from future threats of government intervention. Amateur officials, however, had little to fear from government and at times also found themselves seeking government's favor.[26]

Clearly, during the period prior to the mid-1960s, sports representatives and public officials were in agreement that the regulation of the industry would violate prevailing norms and values and would not be justified given the public perception of sport as mere fun and games. Obviously, sports officials did not have the political power to obtain all that they sought from government, but at least in Congress they had a congenial relationship with leaders and were capable of vetoing attempts of unfriendly intervention.

3. *The dramatic changes and internal conflicts in the sports industry since the mid-1960s has undermined the idyllic image of sport and has increased the probability of resorting to government intervention to resolve specific industry problems as they arise.*

The period since the mid-1960s has been bittersweet for amateur and professional sports. Just as the nation experienced a period of growth and frenzied activity in the 1960s and 1970s, so did sports. Professional and amateur sports received new infusions of money and attracted new records of spectator interest. Nevertheless, sports officials were plagued by incessant internal disputes among themselves, as well as by new demands and challenges from increasingly militant athletes. Thus, in the midst of unprecedented popularity, sports officials periodically found themselves unable even to produce scheduled events because of the players' strikes of 1972, 1974, 1976, and 1985.

In professional sports, each established sports league was threatened with competition from leagues that emerged in three of the four major team sports (baseball being the exception). The result was intense competition for players and escalated salaries. Franchises in the new as well as the established leagues were bought and sold (or exchanged) as frequently as baseball trading cards. The tax advantages and public sudsidies associated with such deals often were more important than the franchises' viability or the community's record of fan support. The purchase of the New York Yankees by Columbia Broadcasting System in 1964 symbolized the displacement of individual ownership by corporate ownership, a trend that was to characterize the 1960s and 1970s.

Network television money became crucial to all professional sports after the 1961 Congress granted the leagues an antitrust exemption to pool television rights to all league games and to sell them as a package to the networks. A lucrative television contract, such as the current National Football League agreement, makes it possible for a franchise to be guaranteed a profit for the season before a single ticket is sold.

Athletes finally were able to organize themselves into viable labor associations. They eventually found the unity and strength to challenge successfully league labor practices and policies through lengthy court battles and bitter labor conflicts. Strikes or lockouts occurred in 1972, 1974, 1976, 1981, and 1982. The results included a temporarily alienated public, a vastly improved economic position for athletes, and union political power to rival that of the team owners. In 1976, for example, professional basketball players were able to block the National Basketball Association–American Basketball Association merger until their concerns were dealt with in good faith by the owners. The most important result, however, may have been that the idyllic image of sport was eroded and was replaced by an image of professional sport as "big business." [27]

Amateur sports also experienced growth, conflict, and intensified public scrutiny. The Soviet Union and East Germany challenged American dominance of international sports competition in the 1960s and surpassed the United States in the 1970s. Many blamed the bitter feuding between the National Collegiate Athletic Association and the Amateur Athletic Union, which reached its height in the 1960s, for the United States' decline in international athletic superiority. The rivalry suggested that organizational self-interest came before the interest of individual athletes or national pride. [28] The black-fist salute during the Summer Games in Mexico City in 1968, the massacre of Israeli athletes at the Olympics in Munich in 1972, the American-led boycott of the 1980 Moscow Olympics, and the retaliatory boycott by the Eastern Bloc nations of the 1984 Summer Games in Los Angeles, as well as many other highly publicized political events, proved that, despite the rhetoric, politics could not be separated from international sports competition. [29]

Amateur sports organizations, like their professional counterparts, also faced challenges from athletes. Amateur athletes during this period have sought a greater voice in setting organizational policies and have demanded a guaranteed right to participate in athletic competition. From little league to college, athletes, especially female athletes, have successfully challenged organizational rules and discriminatory practices that have limited participation. College sports became fully integrated in the 1960s, and Title IX of the Higher Education Act of 1972 dramatically opened locker rooms to women. The latter occurred, however, over the resistance of the NCAA, which argued in Congress and in the courts that economics made Title IX demands too burdensome.[30]

The NCAA has not only had to contend with a rival sports organization, but it has had to struggle to keep its own members in line. Recurring recruiting scandals, persistent revelations of academic abuses and transcript tampering, and conflict over the structuring of athletic divisions have proven to be embarrassing and difficult public relations problems for college athletics.[31] In 1983–84 the NCAA struggled with challenges to its authority from the American Council on Education (ACE), which stressed the need to upgrade academic concerns in college athletics, and from the rival College Football Association (CFA), which sought to break the NCAA's monopolistic grip on television rights.[32] The public reluctantly has come to accept the fact that college coaches have been forced to make academic achievement for athletes a lower priority than athletic accomplishment because of the pressure to garner the television and ticket revenues a "top-ten" team requires to exist.

In sum, the period since the mid-1960s has been a frenetic time, and one in which the economics of sports have become highly visible. Although the idyllic image of sports still may linger among some romantics, it has been replaced largely by another that depicts sport as a business—big business. At the same time, government intervention into the affairs of professional and amateur sports is no longer viewed as inappropriate, and the likelihood of continued intervention has increased dramatically.

The acceptance of such action as appropriate is due as much to the general increase in the scope of government activities since the 1960s as to the changed perception of sports. The public now expects government to control big business, and sport, especially professional sports, is now perceived as big business. The movement to privatize and deregulate notwithstanding, government now is expected to solve social problems, and sport has exhibited many of society's social problems (drugs, gambling, and violence), as well as certain problems unique to sport.

The height of government concern with professional sports occurred in 1976, when the House of Representatives created the Select Committee on Professional Sports "to conduct an inquiry into the need for legislation with respect to professional sports."[33] The committee's chairman asserted in his opening remarks that the root causes of the turmoil in the world of sports in 1976 were economic, and that the profit motive threatened the intrinsic value of athletic competition.[34]

Amateur sports received intense government attention in the early 1960s as various personalities—Robert Kennedy, Theodore Kheel, and Douglas MacArthur—were requested to mediate the NCAA-AAU feud. Government pressure, however, was greatest when President Gerald Ford issued an executive order creating the President's Commission on Olympic Sports (PCOS) in 1975.[35] The commission conducted its investigation and held hearings from 1975 to 1977. The culmination of its work was the Amateur Athletic Act of 1978, which reorganized much of American amateur sport.[36]

Agenda Setting

This evolving legitimation of government intervention in sport makes the probability almost certain that conflicts within the sports industry, problems endangering the stability of the sports world, and sports issues of public concern will find their way onto the agenda of one or more governmental institutions.

Congress is perhaps the most important policymaking institution with regard to professional and amateur sport.[37] It not only adopts policy affecting sports operations and organizations through the normal legislative process, but congressional committees exercise oversight and investigative functions as well. Often a committee will threaten to act in an attempt to prod sports organizations to correct a problem or to resolve an internal dispute. The NCAA, for example, has been the target of hearings on different occasions (1964 and 1977). The 1976 congressional inquiry into professional sports and its implied threat of imposing government regulation, was an attempt to get the sports leagues, especially professional baseball, to end the turmoil that appeared to have overtaken professional sports.

The judiciary also has become a significant policymaker, applying established public policy principles to the sports industry and its practices. Not only have the courts made public policy with regard to sport, but, as in the case of the NFL's player draft and franchise relocation rule, judges have advised sports organizations on how to manage their operations.[38] The so-called "baseball anomaly" may be the best-known example of judicial legislation in sports.[39] The courts have reviewed sports issues related to antitrust, labor, tax, broadcasting, and civil-rights policies among many other policy areas. The courts are not merely arbiters of disputes between participants of Sportsworld, but they also are active policymakers. As sports policy has evolved, so has a law of sports.[40]

Executive agencies also are active in making public sports policy. They consider and adopt rules and regulations that affect sports activities and are lobbied to support or oppose sports legislation before Congress. The former Department of Health, Education, and Welfare was primarily responsible for interpreting Title IX, and it bore the brunt of the NCAA's lobbying and litigation efforts against Title IX regulations. The Federal Communications Commission (FCC) played the central role in evaluating 1973 sports anti-blackout legislation and sought the extension of that legislation.[41] The FCC also sought to prevent the siphoning of sports broadcasts from commercial television by pay television. The courts resisted such regulations, to the joy of sports officials, who saw a financial bonanza in pay and cable television. Other agencies such as the National Labor Relations Board, the Department of Labor, the Immigration and Naturalization Service, the Internal Revenue Service, the State Department, and the Justice Department have played a role in, or currently are involved in, sports policymaking. In fact, the PCOS suggested that federal agencies increase their support for and involvement in elite amateur athletics.[42]

Before a public policy issue is debated, adopted, or implemented, however, it must gain agenda status within an institution. How does a sports issue gain the legislative, judicial, or executive agenda? Some analysts suggest that, since sport is unique, it perhaps gains agenda status in a unique manner. We would argue that whatever the uniqueness of sport, the acquisition of agenda status for sports issues can be explained adequately by existing theories and concepts.

Triggering events nearly always precede the ascent of sports issues to an institution's agenda.[43] For example, the relocation of a popular franchise (such as the Oakland Raiders, Washington Senators, or Milwaukee Braves) is guaranteed to stimulate legislative proposals to restrict such movement or to penalize the league. Similarly, in amateur sports disastrous performances in international competition by American teams will bring about congressional clamor for reform of amateur athletics.

Whenever a conflict within the private sphere results in a clear winner and loser, it is likely the latter will seek to change the results by broadening the scope of conflict with a request for govenment intervention. If the losers continue to lose, they will seek a friendlier arena.[44] Players are more likely to look to the courts for help in their struggle with sports entrepreneurs and officials rather than to Congress. Recent examples include the cases of the Rozelle Rule, player discipline, and free agency.[45] Sports officials continue to seek legislative protection from injurious court decisions as well as blanket protection from potentially harmful future government action. The attempts by the NFL since 1982 to obtain antitrust immunity for league franchise relocation rules and revenue sharing arrangements are the most recent examples.[46]

Whether organizations seek governmental assistance or resist greater industry regulation will depend upon the participants' calculation of the magnitude and distribution of a proposal's expected costs and benefits.[47] The antitrust exemption to allow pooling of television rights to professional sports contests was expected to benefit all organized interests at relatively low cost to any specific group, while the approval of a restructuring formula for the United States Olympic Committee and the specific mandates of Title IX as interpreted by HEW promised to impose significant costs on specific organized groups while benefiting less well-defined groups, such as "the public," "athletes," or "women athletes." These latter groups are likely to benefit less in the final outcome if the policy contest is decided in Congress than if it is bureaucratically or judicially determined (as in the case of Title IX).[48]

Organized Interests and Policy Outcomes

Once agenda status is gained, organization is crucial to the achievement of the policy outcomes desired. Most of the participants in the sports policy game are well organized and capable of waging strong campaigns to influence the policymaking process.

Until recently, sports administrators and officials have held the advantage of power vis-à-vis other participants. Professional team owners tend to be successful entrepreneurs in other industries, and they are very wealthy. They also not only tend to be well connected politically, but they are wise enough to hire representatives, such as their league commissioners, who have a political or governmental background. The emergence of corporate owner-ship also has increased the financial and political capacity of the leagues. As argued earlier, however, perhaps the most important advantage sports officials have enjoyed until recently has been the image of sport and the perception that sport should be free of government intervention.

Amateur sports officials especially benefited from that perception until recently. The NCAA, for example, always was assured of the political support of the education lobby and of great influence within Congress and the courts. In fact, until Title IX, the NCAA had not lost a major court decision, never faced a formal challenge to its monopolistic control over college sports broadcasting arrangements, and was able to ignore on occasion congressional demands to cooperate with the AAU and USOC.

The professional athletes' newfound wealth has provided players' associa-tions with the financial resources and political clout necessary to neutralize the team owners' power. Tough collective bargaining and the willingness to strike, combined with key judicial decisions, have won a larger share of the franchise revenues for the players. Despite this gain in power, union leaders believe they have higher probability of success in the courtroom or in the regulatory bureaucracy than in Congress. Their strategy has been to initiate action in the courts and bureaucracy while opposing and blocking potentially harmful legislative proposals. This has proven to be a successful strategy.

Amateur athletes have been struggling to increase their influence within the USOC and other amateur athletic organizations, but they have achieved only mixed success. After calling much attention to their problems during the PCOS hearings, amateur athletes played an important role in shaping the athletes' rights section of the Amateur Athletic Act of 1978 only to see it weakened considerably in final form as a result of NCAA opposition. The athletes' weakness and lack of unity were further evidenced in their abortive attempt to oppose President Carter's boycott of the Moscow Olympic Games. Advances won by women under Title IX are now being threatened by Reagan administration policies. Still, the effort to provide amateur athletes with strong political representation continues.

Finally, it is important to note that the general public, especially the sports fan, has no interest group representation. Consumer-advocacy groups remain uninterested in sports issues, and attempts at organizing sports fans, most notably Ralph Nader's FANS in 1977-78, have met with dismal failure. Because of the popularity of sports, when a significant segment of the public is somehow harmed, responsive public officials will initiate corrective action. Thus, when the 1971 and 1972 Super Bowls were blacked out, Congress was highly critical of the NFL's blackout policy. It took only eight days to pass sports antiblackout legislation after an NFL official in 1973 publicly criticized the fans' blackout complaints. Nevertheless, Congress failed to make permanent that legislation three years later.[49] The failure to act on the franchise relocation issue may be another example of the public's lack of organization and power. Without strong, organized group representation, the public and the sports fan are without a voice in sports policy debates and are powerless to influence the outcome of those debates.

CONCLUSION

In sum, amateur and professional sports are items on the agendas of various public policymaking institutions, and sports activities are affected in myraid ways by public policy decisions. This has occurred as a result of a changed perception of the nature of sport and a general change in the values and norms of society affecting public expectations of government. The former has evolved from one of fun, games, and innocent diversion to one of big business, and the latter has shifted to expectations of a more activist societal institution.

The sports industry therefore has become a legitimate area of interest for government, and sports policy is evolving into a distinct policy area analogous to housing, energy, public health, and other commonly recognized fields. As a result, government is asked to do more than settle internecine disputes within the sports industry. Those who seek government intervention propose that it play a variety of roles, including that of regulator, arbiter, subsidizer, facilitator, guardian, and reformer. Policymakers therefore must answer three questions as they develop sport policy and decide specific policy issues.

First, they must reach a consensus on the question: What is the proper role of government relative to sports? This is the most basic question, and opinions span the spectrum of possibilities. Some, believing in separation, argue that the sports industry should be self-regulating and government's only role should be to guarantee self-regulation and well-being. This implies antitrust immunity for most of the business practices of sports organizations. Others believe government should continue to grapple with issues of sports policy as they arise, forsaking any clear definition of the sport-government relation. These issues would be settled as the power relationships between groups dictate. Still others call for a more systematic and comprehensive role for government in sport. Some go so far as to call for industry-wide regulation.

The response to this first question delimits responses to a second question, which asks: Is this specific sports issue an appropriate issue for government to resolve? That is, within whatever role policymakers choose, is a particular issue appropriate to address? While consensus may evolve as to the proper role of government, intense disagreement exists as to the types of issues to be addressed. For example, should government attempt to control the degree of violence on the sports field? Unless government adopts an extreme form of regulatory action, the issue of the proper response to sports violence will remain controversial.

Finally, policymakers must decide for the issues addressed: Is government action capable of bringing about a resolution of the issue before them? Action may not be technologically or administratively feasible, legitimate values may be in direct conflict, knowledge may be lacking, or cost may be unacceptable. Thus, even if policymakers desire to act, they may defer.

Each chapter in this text applies these three questions to a specific sports policy issue. Each essay is prospective as well as retrospective. The goal is not only to increase our understanding of the substantive policy issues discussed but also to appreciate better the complexities of the sport-government relationship and more knowledgeably to ponder the future of that relationship.

NOTES

1. Theodore Lowi notes the importance of sport to the regime as an agent of socialization in "Campus, Society, and the Place of American Sport," Appendix G in George H. Hanford, *An Inquiry into the Need for and Feasibility of a National Study of Intercollegiate Athletics* (Washington, D.C.: American Council on Education, 1974). Jacques Ellul, among many others,

recognizes that sport has become "an indispensable constituent element of totalitarian regimes" in their creation of "mass man." See his *The Technological Society* (New York: Alfred A. Knopf, 1964), p. 383.

2. Michael Roberts, "The Separation of Sport and the State," *Skeptic* 21 (September/October 1977): 16–19.

3. Paul Hoch, *Rip Off the Big Game* (Garden City, N.Y.: Doubleday, 1972). For case studies at the local level that possess similar themes but less extreme conclusions than Hoch, see Steven A. Riess, "The Baseball Magnate and Urban Politics in the Progressive Era: 1895–1920," *Journal of Sports History* 1 (Spring 1974): 41–62; and Steven A. Riess, "Power Without Authority: Los Angeles' Elites and the Construction of the Coliseum," *Journal of Sports History* 8 (Spring 1981): 50–65.

4. Jean-Marie Brohm, *Sport: A Prison of Measured Time* (London: Inks Links, 1978). For an analysis of the media's promotion of baseball as the "national pastime" and the social control function of baseball in the Progressive Era, see Steven A. Riess, *Touching Base: Professional Baseball and American Culture in the Progressive Era* (Westport, Conn.: Greenwood Press, 1980).

5. Eldon E. Snyder and Elmer A. Spreitzer suggest this term to describe the various theories that speak to clashing interests in sport. See their *Social Aspects of Sport*, 2d ed. (Englewood Cliffs, N.J.: Prentice-Hall, 1983). Its roots clearly are based in Marxist thought. See, for example, the essays in Hart Cantelon and Richard Gruneau, eds., *Sport Culture and the Modern State* (Toronto: University of Toronto Press, 1983).

6. Brohm, *Sport*, p. 54.

7. For other critiques of the state's exploitation of sport, see Hoch, *Rip Off the Big Game;* Cary Goodman, "The Mind/Body Politics," *Social Policy* (January/February 1978): 60–64; and Bruce Kidd, *The Political Economy of Sport* (Ottawa: CAPHER, 1980).

8. Cantelon and Gruneau, *Sport Culture*, pp. 18–19.

9. See the thoughtful essay by Richard Gruneau, "Sport and the Debate on the State," pp. 1–38 in Cantelon and Gruneau, *Sport Culture*. See also Arthur T. Johnson, "Government, Opposition and Sport: The Role of Domestic Sports Policy in Generating Political Support," *Journal of Sport and Social Issues* 6 (Fall/Winter 1982): 22–34, for a discussion of the exploitation of sports by government and opposition forces alike.

10. For a summary and discussion of these models, see The President's Commission on Olympic Sports, *First Report to the President* (Washington, D.C., February 9, 1976), pp. 13–68. See also R. Stokvis, "Conservative and Progressive Alternatives in the Organization of Sport," *International Social Science Journal* 34 (1982): 197–208, for an analysis of the consequences for sports organizations of alternative relations with state agencies.

11. For the Canadian example, see C. E. S. Franks and Donald MacIntosh, "The Evolution of Federal Government Policies Toward Sport and Culture in Canada: A Comparison," *Sport and the Sociological Imagination*, Nancy Theberge and Peter Donnelly, eds. (Ft. Worth: Texas Christian University Press, 1984), pp. 193–209; and Kidd, *Political Economy of Sport*.

12. On the use of sport in international relations, see Andrew Strenk, "The Thrill of Victory and the Agony of Defeat: Sport and International Politics," *Orbis* 22 (Summer 1978): 453–69; and James A. Nafziger and Andrew Strenk, "The Political Uses and Abuses of Sports," *Connecticut Law Review* 10 (1978): 259–89.

13. For a discussion of the symbolic importance of sport in American political life, see Richard Lipsky, "Toward a Theory of American Sports Symbolism," *American Behavioral Scientist* 21 (January/February 1978): 345–60, and his *How We Play the Game—Why Sports Dominate American Life* (Boston: Beacon Press, 1981). New York Mayor John Lindsay's reelection has been attributed to the connection of his campaign and image to the New York Mets during their championship season in 1969. The success of such former athletes as Jack Kemp (R.-N.Y.) and Bill Bradley (D.-N.J.), and the desire of presidents and presidential candidates to identify with sport (John F. Kennedy and Richard Nixon with football; Dwight Eisenhower with golf; Jimmy Carter with softball), also suggests the importance of sport to electoral politics.

14. Michael Novak, *The Joy of Sports* (New York: Basic Books, 1976).

15. See Neil David Isaacs, *Jock Culture, U.S.A.* (New York: W. W. Norton, 1978), and Richard Crepeau, "Sport, Heroes and Myth," *Journal of Sport and Social Issues* 5 (Spring/Summer 1981): 23–31.

16. Several historians suggest that sport and recreation were exploited by community leaders for social control purposes rather than in pursuit of socially redeeming goals. See, for example, Cary Goodman, *Choosing Sides: Playground and Street Life on the Lower East Side* (New York:' Schocken Books, 1979), and Dominick Cavallo, *Muscles and Morals: Organized Playgrounds and Urban Reform, 1880–1920* (Philadelphia: University of Pennsylvania Press, 1981), for a dissenting perspective.

17. See examples cited in Strenk, "Thrill of Victory," and Nafziger and Strenk, "Political Uses and Abuses of Sports."

18. 99 *Congressional Record* 2151 (March 20, 1953).

19. See Jack Scott, *The Athletic Revolution* (New York: Free Press, 1971), Harry Edwards, *Sociology of Sport* (Homewood, Ill.: Dorsey Press, 1973), and Paul Hoch, *Rip Off The Big Game*. For a critique of these and other critical works on sport, see Christopher Lasch, "The Corruption of Sports," *New York Review of Books*, April 28, 1977, pp. 24–30.

20. John Betts, *America's Sporting Heritage* (Reading, Mass.: Addison Wesley, 1974), p. 376. See also Richard Lipsky, "Toward a Political Theory of American Sports Symbolism," pp. 345–47, on the separation of sports and politics.

21. See Arthur T. Johnson, "Congress and Professional Sports: 1951–1978," *Annals of the American Academy of Political and Social Science* 45 (September 1979): 102–15.

22. Ibid., pp. 104–7.

23. PL 91–804 (64 Stat 899).

24. Federal Baseball Club of Baltimore v. National League, 259 U.S. 200 (1922); Toolson v. New York Yankees, Inc., 346 U.S. 356 (1953). Two decades later, the Supreme Court again surprised many when it refused to subject professional baseball to antitrust laws. See Flood v. Kuhn, 407 U.S. 258 (1972).

25. See Johnson, "Congress and Professional Sports," pp. 105–7.

26. As a price for the 1961 antitrust exemption, which permits sports leagues to pool broadcasting rights and to sell those rights as a package, the National Football League had to agree not to televise its games on Friday nights or on Saturdays during the college and high school football seasons. This prohibition was written into PL 87–331 in deference to amateur sport officials.

27. One indication that a change in perception was taking place is the fact that several publications ran articles on the changing values in sports, each noting the changing economic structure of amateur and professional sports. These publications included *The Christian Science Monitor* (1978), *The Washington Post* (1978), *New York Times* (1974), and *Sports Illustrated* (1978).

28. See *The Final Report of the President's Commission on Olympic Sports, 1975–1977*, vol. 1 (Washington, D.C.: Government Printing Office, 1978), pp. 45–65.

29. The rhetoric still remains, but the reality of the political nature of international sports events is well documented. See, for example, Strenk, "Thrill of Victory," Nafziger and Strenk, "Political Uses and Abuses of Sports," Richard Espy, *The Politics of the Olympic Games* (Berkeley: University of California Press, 1979); and James H. Frey, "The U.S. vs. Great Britain: Responses to the 1980 Boycott of the Olympic Games," *Comparative Physical Education and Sport* 6 (Winter 1984): 3–13.

30. See, for example, *Sex Discrimination Regulations*, Hearings Before the Subcommittee on Postsecondary Education of the Committee on Education and Labor, House of Representatives (June 17, 1975), especially pp. 46–66, and NCAA v. Califano, 444 F. Supp. 425 (D. Kan. 1978) rev. 622 F2d. 1382 (10th Cir. 1980).

31. In October 1984 Walter Byers, executive director of the NCAA, for the first time publicly admitted that improprieties in college sports are widespread and out of control. He acknowledged that it was not uncommon for college athletes to receive more than $20,000 a year in illegal payments beyond the aid provided by their athletic scholarships. See "Some Players Get Over $20,000 a Year in Illicit Payments, NCAA Chief Says," *The Baltimore Sun*, October 12, 1984, p. 1.

32. It was not until 1977 that Congress conducted what was termed "the first serious review of NCAA internal practices." See Gordon Martin, "Due Process and Its Future Within the NCAA," *Connecticut Law Review* 10 (1978): 290. In 1982 the NCAA reportedly spent $2.3 million on legal fees, mainly as a result of its continuing challenge to Title IX and response to the

CFA challenge, and it experienced its first deficit in twenty-nine years. See *Chronicle of Higher Education* (January 19, 1983): 17.

33. H. Res. 94–1186.

34. *Inquiry into Professional Sports,* Hearings Before the House Select Committee on Professional Sports, 94th Cong., 2d sess. (1976), pp. 2–3.

35. Executive Order 11868 (6/23/75) 40 FR 26255.

36. See PL 95–606. See also Cym Lowell, "Federal Administrative Intervention in Amateur Athletics," *George Washington Law Review* 43 (March 1975): 729–90, for an analysis of an earlier effort to enact legislation affecting amateur athletics at the elite level.

37. See Roger Noll, "Alternatives in Sports Policy," in Roger Noll, ed., *Government and the Sports Business* (Washington, D.C.: The Brookings Institution, 1974), p. 427, and Arthur T. Johnson, "Congress and Professional Sports: 1951–1978," pp. 103–15.

38. Courts have offered advice in James McCoy (Yazoo) Smith v. Pro Football et al. (1976) and Los Angeles Memorial Coliseum and Oakland Raiders, Ltd. v. National Football League: Alvin Pete Rozelle, Eugene V. Klein, and Georgia Rosenbloom Frontiere et al. (1982).

39. The "baseball anomaly" refers to the fact that, of all sports, only baseball enjoys a general exemption from federal antitrust laws.

40. On the existence of a "law of sports," see John Weistart and Cym Lowell, *The Law of Sports* (Charlottesville, Va.: Bobbs-Merrill, 1979).

41. PL 93–107. See also *Third Annual Report of the Federal Communications Commission on the Effects of Public Law 93–107, the Sports Anti-blackout Law, on the Broadcasting of Sold-out Home Games of Professional Football, Baseball, Basketball and Hockey.* U.S. Senate, Committee on Commerce, Science, and Transportation, Committee Print, June 1976.

42. *The Final Report of the President's Commission on Olympic Sports, 1975–1977,* pp. 72–79.

43. For discussions of triggering events, see Roger W. Cobb and Charles Elder, *Participation in Politics: The Dynamics of Agenda-Building* (Baltimore: Johns Hopkins University Press, 1972); Robert Eyestone, *From Social Issues to Public Policy* (New York: John Wiley & Sons, 1978); and Larry N. Gerston, *Making Public Policy* (Glenview, Ill.: Scott, Foresman, 1983), pp. 22–49.

44. E. E. Schattschneider, *The Semisovereign People* (New York: Holt, Rinehart and Winston, 1960).

45. For a comprehensive and evolutionary review of relevant cases, see "Discipline in Professional Sports: The Need for Player Protection," *The Georgetown Law Journal* 60 (1972): 771–98; Lionel S. Sobel, "The Emancipation of Professional Athletes," *Western State University Law Review* 3 (Spring 1976): 1895–1922; John C. Weistart, "Judicial Review of Labor Agreements: Lessons from the Sports Industry," *Law and Contemporary Problems* 44 (Autumn 1981): 109–46.

46. The National Football League lobbied hard for passage of S.2784 in the 97th Congress (1982). See *Professional Sports Antitrust Immunity,* Hearings Before the Committee on the Judiciary, United States Senate, 97th Congress, 2d session on S.2784 and S.2821 (1982). See also Arthur T. Johnson, "Municipal Administration and the Sports Franchise Relocation Issue," *Public Administration Review* 43 (November/December 1983): 519–28.

47. James Q. Wilson, "The Politics of Regulation," in *Social Responsibility and the Business Predicament,* James W. Mackie, ed. (Washington, D.C.: The Brookings Institution, 1974), pp. 135–68, and James Q. Wilson, "The Politics of Regulation," in *The Politics of Regulation,* James Q. Wilson, ed. (New York: Basic Books, 1980), pp. 364–72.

48. Contrast, however, NCAA v. Califano, 444 F. Supp. 425 (D. Kan. 1978) rev. 622 F.2d. 1382 (10th Cir. 1980), with Grove City v. Bell, 104 Sct. 1211 (1984).

49. The House and Senate approved different versions of an antiblackout bill in 1975 to succeed the 1973 legislation that was scheduled to expire in 1976. Agreement on the bill was reached within the conference committee and the committee's report was signed by the conferees. The Senate conferees, led by Senator Warren Magnuson (D-Wash.), however, failed to file the signed conference committee report. Thus no Senate vote on the bill could be taken. Shortly thereafter, Seattle was granted an NFL franchise.

PART I

Public Policy and the Athlete

The chapters in this section provide analyses of issues and public policies—actual and proposed—that directly concern the athlete. James Dworkin examines whether public policy can achieve a balancing of interests between professional athletes and team owners. He reviews the history and current status of labor-management relations in professional sports and concludes that athletes and team owners should negotiate their differences within the framework of the collective bargaining process, rather than seek government intervention. Dworkin argues that the proper role of government simply is to ensure that the rights of both groups are balanced.

While it is clear that professional athletes are employees, there is staunch denial of such status for amateur athletes. Bruce Kidd and Allen Sack examine the distinction between leisure and work and find that the situations of scholarship athletes in American universities and Canadian elite athletes meet those criteria that define an employee-employer relationship. They argue that recognition of college athletes' status as employees of their universities will ensure them of deserved rights and fair treatment and will be a step toward ending hypocrisy and corruption within intercollegiate athletics. Kidd and Sack conclude that amateur athletes have every right to attempt to use policymaking machinery to further their interests, just as the administrators of amateur sports have done over the years.

Linda Carpenter assesses the impact of Title IX on female participation and control of administrative positions in college athletics. She discovers that unintended consequences of Title IX have been the demise of the Association of Intercollegiate Athletics for Women (AIAW) and a decline in the number of female sports administrators. She identifies an uncertain future for women in college athletics as a consequence of the *Grove City* case and calls for legislation that would reverse the interpretation of Title IX, by the Supreme Court in this case. The 98th Congress failed to do so, but it is certain that the issue will be an important one in the 99th Congress.

Robert Ruxin describes the problem that athletes, especially those young athletes about to enter the professional ranks, often experience with unscrupulous agents. He reviews several options to resolve the problem, including government regulation of agents. Ruxin argues that significant government regulation should occur only if the integrity of sports is threatened, which is not the case at present. He calls for greater cooperation among players' unions, the NCAA, and agents themselves; more education of the athlete with regard to ethical and legal obligations of agents; and enforcement of current laws to stop extreme abuse.

Finally, Stanley Eitzen explores the larger significance of sports violence and cites a need for legislation that will make clear that sport is not outside the law. This action is necessary because of the increase in the number of incidents where the violence clearly exceeds what is accepted as "normal" for the game and that would stimulate criminal investigation in any other setting. After analyzing various alternatives to direct government intervention to control sports violence, Eitzen concludes that legislation is necessary and would receive public support.

Other issues, not discussed in this volume, are of direct relevance to athletes and are about to receive agenda status within selected governmental arenas. The mandatory drug screening of college and high-level amateur athletes unilaterally imposed by coaches and ruling federations will probably become an issue of individual rights within amateur sports. Within professional sports, drug screening and disciplinary action taken for drug use will remain a collective bargaining issue. Players' associations will seek a greater share of team income if cable and pay television revenues increase as expected, and the leagues will continue to seek antitrust exemptions to protect their distribution (revenue sharing) of television revenues. Amateur athletes will continue to seek greater participation in the administration of amateur sports, and college athletics increasingly will become the subject of closer governmental examination as a growing number of athletes and sports administrators admit that payments to college athletes are not uncommon and that abuses within college athletics are out of control.

2

Balancing the Rights of Professional Athletes and Team Owners: The Proper Role of Government

James B. Dworkin

This chapter is concerned with the development of the employer-employee relationship in the professional team sports of baseball, basketball, football, and hockey. The key questions to be addressed revolve around the role that government has played and should play in regulating employer-employee relationships in the professional sports industry. What rights should players have? What rights should team owners have? Can public policy effectively strike the necessary balance between the rights of owners and players? Or, is this balancing of rights an issue best left to the private sector?

In answering these questions, the development of the employer-employee relationship will be traced to illustrate the creation of the now-famous *reserve clause,* which served to bind players to one team and thus hold down salaries. Next, various attempts made by players in the sports industry to eradicate the reserve rule will be discussed. These attempts include the creation of rival leagues, the formation of player unions, litigation, and the usage of the process of collective bargaining. Third, the current state of affairs with respect to the employer-employee relationship in the various team sports will be described. The current status of free agency rights, recent strike developments, team compensation limits, and the use of arbitration systems will be highlighted. In the light of all of the evidence presented, conclusions as to the effectiveness of government intervention in the sports industry will be presented. Finally, the future role for government in regulating aspects of the employment relationship in the professional team sports industry will be discussed.

THE DEVELOPMENT OF THE IDEA OF
PLAYER RESERVATION

In the earliest days of development of the professional sports industry, there was essentially no government regulation of the employer-employee relationship. Of course, this was true for most other industries as well. Management was free to set the terms and conditions of employment, and the worker could either accept these terms or look for work elsewhere. Management dictation of the terms of the employment relationship led to several abuses, such as long, hard hours, low pay, the employment of children in factories, no benefits, and company-sponsored towns and stores. It was these kinds of abuses that attracted government intervention in order to guarantee workers a minimum level of protection.

In professional sports much the same story can be told. That is, intervention by government came *after* the professional team owners had created a rather intolerable set of working conditions. The most potent of these working conditions was referred to as the reserve rule. What follows is an examination of how this condition developed in major team sports.

Baseball

Professional baseball dates back to the year 1876 with the formation of the National League. Prior to that time, some teams did pay players for their services. However, the concept of paying all team members began in earnest with the formation of the National League.[1]

One of the little-known facts about the early National League was that players did have complete freedom of movement from team to team. The process of switching teams at the conclusion of a season was referred to as "revolving." The players enjoyed this freedom because it allowed them to play baseball for the highest bidder; this sounds very much like the free agency system in operation today. The truth of the matter is that early baseball players had even more freedom than today's athletes. But it did not take the owners long to react to this situation. Two things were occurring that the owners disliked immensely. First, in bidding for the best players year after year, salaries were driven up in the process. The owners, of course, did not wish to pay any more for the services of a professional ballplayer than was absolutely necessary. Second, the owners argued that when the best players changed teams after every season fan loyalty was bound to suffer. If fans stopped attending the games, revenues from ticket sales would shrink dramatically.

The owners had at their disposal a perfectly good way of preventing their star players from changing teams. All they had to do was to "match" or better any offer made by another team. Most players, if offered an identical salary, would prefer to avoid a dislocating move. In more recent years, in basketball, this system of "first refusal" has been included as part of the players' collective bargaining agreement. While a basketball free agent can go out and obtain his best salary offer, he still must present this offer to his original team. If his original team chooses to match the offer, the player must stay with that team.[2]

The National League owners chose a different strategy. Meeting secretly on September 30, 1879, these officials enacted the first "reserve rule." This rule, to take effect for the 1880 season, provided that each club could protect five players from intraleague raiding. The understanding among all of the owners was that their five players would be protected from raiding *if and only if* they agreed not to tamper with any of the reserved players from the other squads. This rule worked wonderfully from the perspective of the owners. Almost overnight, a system of rampant team changes and escalating player salaries changed to one of total team control over the terms and conditions of employment. True, the other players not so reserved were still free to seek a better offer from another team. These early days of baseball, however, typically featured teams with only about eleven players. After reserving five "stars," there was typically not much talent left that was attractive to the other teams in the leagues. In fact, the club owners liked the reserve rule so much that it was amended in 1883 to include eleven players, in 1887 to include fourteen players, and soon after, to include every player on every team.[3]

This first reserve rule, established in 1879, was in effect in professional baseball until a landmark arbitration ruling in December 1975, almost one hundred years later.[4] This reserve rule allowed the owners to maintain what economists refer to as a monopsonistic labor market in baseball. A monopsony market exists where there is but one buyer of a particular item, in this case the services of a professional ballplayer. Once signed to a professional team, a player had to deal with only that team. A player might be traded, but even that move was up to club ownership. More likely, a club would offer a player a salary figure and point out that the player's contract contained paragraph 10(a), which read as follows:

On the day before December 20 (or if a Sunday, then the next preceding business day) in the year of the last playing season covered by this contract, the Club may tender to the Player a contract for the term of that year by mailing the same to the Player at his address following his signature hereto, or if none be given, then at his last address of record with the Club. If prior to March 1 next succeeding said December 20, the Player and the Club have not agreed upon the terms of such contract, then on or before 10 days after said March 1, the Club shall have the right by written notice to the Player at said address to renew this contract for the period of one year on the same terms, except that the amount payable to the Player shall be such as the Club shall fix in said notice;

provided, however, that said amount, if fixed by a Major League Club, shall be an amount payable at a rate not less than 80 percent of the rate stipulated for the next preceding year and at a rate not less than 70 percent of the rate stipulated for the year immediately prior to the next preceding year.[5]

The impact of paragraph 10(a) was devastating from the standpoint of the player. He could either accept the owner's offer or risk being "reserved" for the next season at a twenty percent cut in salary over what he had earned in the previous season. Of course, he could retire from baseball and enter any other profession for which he had the qualifications. However, if he wanted to play baseball, it had to be for the team that owned his contract. Team owners argued that these ownership rights were perpetual in nature. Thus it was that baseball management was able to hold player salaries artificially low through the creation of monopsony powers embodied in the player reservation system. The advantage in negotiations clearly resided with management.

Basketball, Football, and Hockey

Athletes in the other major professional sports found themselves in much the same position as those in professional baseball. In each case, an athlete's freedom of movement from team to team was hampered by the creation of some sort of a reservation system.

For example, in professional basketball, each Uniform Player Contract contained paragraph 22, which read similarly to clause 10(a) in the baseball players' uniform contract.[6] A player was bound to one, and only one, team. If a player refused to sign a contract for an upcoming season, team management could *unilaterally* renew his contract for the ensuing season at a wage rate not lower than that earned the previous season.

Football players were faced with a similar dilemma. Their Standard Player Contract contained paragraph 10, which bound them to their teams for an additional season (at not less than 90 percent of the previous season's rate of pay).[7] This system began in the year 1947. Prior to that time, players could never become free agents because a perpetual reservation clause was included in every contract. While the one-year reservation system enacted in 1947 may appear to have given the football player an upper hand over other professional athletes, in effect their situation was really not any better. As it developed, the first attempt by a football player actually to switch teams brought forth a host of other anticompetitive actions by the League.

Finally, the professional hockey players' contract contained the now-familiar reservation language in paragraph 17 of the Standard Player Contract.[8] This language also provided that hockey players were owned by one team and that this team had the right to the players' services into perpetuity. Later developments in this area will be reviewed in the next section.

In summary, when speaking of employment rights, we all like to think that we as employees have the freedom to choose our employer and the concomitant right to decide to change employers as we see fit. An insurance salesman who disagrees with the employment policies of Agency X is perfectly free to quit and seek a job in insurance with Agency Y. These simple rights were denied to professional athletes for many years.

Athletes were denied the right to choose which team to play for and were not allowed to switch teams if they were unhappy with the employment policies fostered upon them. The clubs had effectively devised an employment scheme that forced all professional athletes to deal with only *one* team if they wished to pursue their athletic talents. The major impact of the reservation system was to cause an extreme imbalance in bargaining power between owners and players. In an unregulated employment world, the owners prospered, while the players toiled for wages much below the level they would have received had they been bargaining in a more competitive environment. The future would not be hard to predict. Unhappy with their low salaries, professional athletes would try almost anything to lessen the impact of the reservation system. Of course, this would be the very same system that the owners sought to protect.

THE FIGHT FOR FREEDOM

Many professional athletes found the reservation system to be intolerable. But what power did the individual player have to do anything about his employment conditions? Even though they had little power, the history of professional athletics is replete with examples of player attempts to abolish or soften the blow of the reservation system. In this section four such attempts are described: the formation of unions, the formation of rival leagues, the efforts of legal prosecution under the antitrust laws, and, finally, the process of collective bargaining.

The Formation of Unions

Unions of professional athletes go back far into the history of professional sport. While there are many reasons why people join unions,[9] the previous section already has delineated the major source of dissatisfaction leading to unionization attempts on the part of professional athletes—the reservation system.

Baseball players have looked to unions on at least five separate occasions. Their first union, called the National Brotherhood of Professional Ball Players, was formed in 1885. This union had as one of its major goals the abolition of the reservation system, which had been created some five years earlier.[10] Subsequently, several associations were formed, including the

League Protective Players' Association (1900–1902), The Baseball Players' Fraternity (1912–18), the American Baseball Guild (1946), and the Major League Baseball Players Association (1954 to present). In the other major sports, the scenario is much the same. The National Basketball Players Association was formed in the early 1950s, the National Football League Players Association was formed in 1956, and the National Hockey League Players Association was formed in the late 1950s, even though formal recognition of the union by the league did not occur until June 1967.

The move toward unionism was brought about largely by the low wages produced by the restrictive player reserve systems of each professional sport. Feeling powerless to combat the system on an individual basis, players turned to group action in the hope that their unions could make some progress against the reservation system. A second and even more important fact is that these early unions, especially baseball, were largely ineffectual. The reason for their ineffectiveness was simple. These unions were *voluntary* organizations; players did not have to join a union, and, more significant, clubs and leagues did not have to deal with these unions as collective organizations. The public policy mandate granting unions the right to organize and bargain collectively and requiring management to negotiate in good faith with a union representing the majority of the workers would not be passed until 1935, with the National Labor Relations Act.[11] The future impact of collective bargaining on the player reservation system would be significant. However, prior to the passage of the National Labor Relations Act, players' unions simply did not possess the legal clout to address effectively this series of concerns.

Rival Leagues

Frustrated with their unsuccessful initial attempts at changing the reserve system through unions, players turned to other means of attack. One popular tactic was the formation or joining of a rival league.[12] The basic idea behind a rival league was to set up an alternative professional sports system within which the players could practice their trade. Very important to this system was the element of freedom of movement generated for the players. While a player might be bound to negotiate only with team X *within* the established professional league, this same restriction would not apply to an entirely different league. Thus players could jump leagues and in the process obtain a rather large increase in pay. It always has been the case that the newly formed league attempted to win players from the more established league with promises of larger salaries and better working conditions. For example, in 1890 baseball players formed their own league, called the Players League, to compete with the established National League.[13] Over the years, there have been several rival leagues in professional baseball; the last one of any significance was the Mexican League in 1946.

While jumping to a new league usually resulted in a higher salary for the player involved, it certainly did not offer him a *permanent* escape from the dreaded reserve rule. Only temporary relief was provided, since these rival leagues also adopted their own reservation rules. Thus, a player could improve his lot somewhat by jumping to a new league, but, once he had moved, he was again subjected to the same problem he faced in the original league—limited freedom of mobility. In addition, established leagues often meted out severe penalties to league jumpers who wished to return to their original league. And in some instances, players were banned for life because of their league-jumping activities. Clearly, league jumping was a risky activity.

Again, the scene in the other major sports has been similar. In basketball, the rival league was the American Basketball Association (ABA), in football the World Football League (WFL) and, today, the United States Football League (USFL), and in hockey, the World Hockey Association (WHA). Of all these, and many other rival leagues that could be mentioned, only the USFL exists today. Even its fate is in doubt as the USFL strives to compete with the NFL for television and ticket sales dollars.

From the players' perspective, the establishment of rival leagues has both positive and negative features. The most salient of these positive features are the higher salaries offered and the opportunity to circumvent the mobility-limiting reservation system practiced by the more established league. Many star players have jumped leagues to enjoy these benefits. However, these benefits may be illusory or short-lived. There is always some element of risk in joining a new league. Given the track record of the majority of these attempts, one would first have to be suspicious about the stability of a new league. It is nice to make more money, but is there any guarantee of payment should the club or league fold as a result of financial exigency? If the league does cease operation, how easy will it be to return to the older, more established league? Will the older league have "blacklisted" the outlaw players who jumped to the new league? Many of these questions have antitrust law implications and are covered in chapter 8.[14]

The conclusion with respect to rival leagues must be that they provide only a temporary solution to the players' concerns about the reservation system. The temporary relief that is provided is the result of the element of competition infused into the labor market through the creation of the rival league. Predictably, ownership in the established league typically has tried to preserve the anticompetitive nature of its operations. This has been some-what successful, since many players have not been willing to take the necessary risk involved in league jumping.

Antitrust Law Prosecution

A third major line of attack against the reservation system was through the use of antitrust law actions. Chapter 8 reviews the major cases and issues involved, but a few points need to be emphasized here first.

Frustrated by their inabilities to change the reservation system through unionization or the threat of league jumping, many players felt that the reservation system could best be challenged on the grounds that its anticompetitive nature was in violation of the spirit of our nation's antitrust laws. But baseball players quickly learned that they would get nowhere with this argument. In an early decision, the U.S. Supreme Court ruled that baseball was a sport, not a business, and thus it was not covered under the antitrust laws.[15] Many subsequent Supreme Court decisions in baseball relied on this earlier exemption.[16] It was clear that the baseball players would have to look elsewhere in their battle against the reserve system.

Events went a bit differently in other sports. In essence, the Supreme Court has refused to extend the baseball exemption to basketball, football, hockey, or any other professional sport.[17] These sports have tried in vain to obtain the same antitrust exemption that has been held by baseball since 1922. The failure to obtain such an exemption has played a major role in the demise of the player reservation systems in these sports. In finding that these player reservation systems did violate the Sherman Act,[18] the courts were opening the door for the implementation of *jointly* bargained solutions.

COLLECTIVE BARGAINING

One important piece of federal legislation that aided professional athletes in their quest to abolish or revise the reservation system was the Sherman Act. In many situations, unilaterally established reservation systems were found to be in violation of antitrust laws. A prime example is the *Mackey* case in professional football.[19] The main point of this case is that a reservation system per se does not necessarily violate the Sherman Act. Such a system can win judicial approval if it meets certain conditions. The major condition unmet in *Mackey* was that the reserve system clearly was not a product of bona fide arm's-length bargaining. Rather, it was a system unilaterally imposed upon the players by the National Football League. The court in the *Mackey* case went so far as to suggest that the parties solve this issue through the process of collective bargaining.

> It may be that some reasonable restrictions relating to player transfers are necessary for the successful operation of the NFL. The protection of mutual interests of both the players and the clubs may indeed require this. We encourage the participants to resolve this question through collective bargain-

ing. The parties are far better situated to agreeably resolve what rules governing player transfers are best suited for their mutual interests than are the courts.[20]

The second major public policy ingredient necessary to effectuate the court's request in the *Mackey* case was a federal labor law granting workers the rights to form and join unions and to bargain collectively with management. This same law would require management to negotiate in good faith with a union chosen by a majority of the employees working for the firm. The National Labor Relations Act (Wagner Act) of 1935 included these conditions.[21] It was only after the passage of the Wagner Act that unions in professional sports had the power to become officially recognized as exclusive bargaining agents for athletes[22] and to use the process of collective bargaining to negotiate wages, hours, and other conditions of employment. The stage was set for joint action on the player reservation issue. The combination of the Sherman Act with the National Labor Relations Act provided the public policy framework necessary to balance the rights of athletes and owners. Given that both sides finally were on relatively equal footing, negotiations could now proceed.

In baseball, recall that the owners did and still do enjoy antitrust exemption. Thus collective bargaining was to be the means through which the players would attack the reserve system. With the bargaining rights inherent in the National Labor Relations Act, the Major League Baseball Players Association (MLBPA) has negotiated several contracts with the National and American leagues since 1968. The 1973 contract contained two important elements. First, the owners and players agreed to a grievance-arbitration procedure. Misunderstandings or differences of opinion as to the meaning of existing contract language could now be cleared up by going to a neutral outsider, an arbitrator. Second, the players and owners incorporated the Uniform Player's Contract into the collective bargaining agreement in 1973. This contract contained the player's salary, several rules and regulations, and the reserve clause. Whether or not they knew it at the time, the owners had just "opened the barn door," in that the players now possessed the right to challenge the owners' interpretation of the reserve rule through the process of arbitration.[23]

The owners did not have to wait long for this challenge to occur. Players Andy Messersmith and Dave McNally filed grievances claiming that the reservation clauses in their contracts enabled management to reserve them for only one season after their current contracts had expired. This is exactly what their club owners did for the 1975 season. The owners argued that the reserve clause in the Uniform Player's Contract was *perpetual* in nature. That is, they claimed that Messersmith and McNally were the properties of their respective clubs for as long as these clubs wished to retain their services. An arbitrator was called in to resolve this dispute, and his historic decision was rendered on December 23, 1975.[24] Peter Seitz ruled in favor of the players and, in so doing, ended the perpetual reservation system that had existed in baseball since 1880. The Seitz decision did not say that the reserve system was illegal. It simply said that the owners' interpretation that the reservation clause existed into perpetuity was incorrect. Thus each player could be reserved, but only for one season after his contract had expired. After that one season, the player would be a free agent, able to bargain with as many clubs as were interested in acquiring his services. Arbitrator Seitz's interpretation was limited to the contract language before him, but he made a strong recommendation in his ruling that stressed the ability of the parties to mold a compromise reserve system through the process of collective bargaining:

> The parties are still in negotiation, however, and continue to have an opportunity to reach agreement on measures that will give assurance of a reserve system that will meet the needs of the clubs and protect them from the damage they fear this decision will cause, and, at the same time, meet the needs of the players. The clubs and the players have a mutual interest in the health and integrity of the sport and in its financial returns. With a will to do so, they are competent to fashion a reserve system to suit their requirements.[25]

Basketball players appeared to have more freedom of movement than was the case in baseball. This was because paragraph 22 of their player contracts said specifically that a club could renew a player's contract for a period of *one* year. After that one year, free agency was a theoretical possibility. But the basketball player faced a much more potent problem—compensation for teams losing a free agent player. Baseball did not address this issue before the Seitz decision because there were no free agents. In basketball, however, compensation for teams losing free agents was an integral part of the employment relationship. The system worked as follows: First, the two teams involved would meet to try to work out the proper compensation. If the parties failed to reach an agreement, the commissioner had the power to set the compensation award, which could include cash payments, future draft choices, or player exchanges. The major problem with basketball's free agency procedure was that teams were unwilling to sign free agents because of the compensation the commissioner might extract from them. Thus the fate of the professional basketball player, in truth, was not much better than that of the professional baseball player.

Matters improved considerably for basketball players following the out-of-court settlement of the Oscar Robertson lawsuit.[26] While this lawsuit had several purposes, the one of most interest to us was its attempt to ban further use of the option compensation system. In exchange for the dismissal of the Robertson suit, the owners agreed to a new collective bargaining pact that instituted several modifications to the reservation process. First, option clauses were no longer automatically included in player contracts. A contract could include an option clause for one year, but only if it was agreed to by both sides through bargaining. Second, the owners and players agreed to experiment with a new form of compensation system, the so-called first-refusal process. The older, commissioner-based compensation process was to stay in effect until the conclusion of the 1980–81 season. The first-refusal system was to take effect thereafter and continue at least through the 1986–87 season. This newer system should reduce the fear of signing free agents, since teams no longer will have to worry about excessive compensation awards dictated by the commissioner of the NBA. The next section briefly reviews what has occurred since the adoption of first refusal rights and, in particular, the attempt by the owners to hold down salaries through the use of a team salary cap.

Turning briefly to football players, recall that in 1947 the NFL chose to insert a one-year option rule (paragraph 10) into the Standard Player Contract. Fifteen years passed without many problems. Then, in 1962, a player from the San Francisco Forty-Niners (R. C. Owens) actually played out his option and signed with the Baltimore Colts. Never having faced this situation before, the owners had no compensation system in existence. However, it did not take them long to enact a provision that has come to be known as the "Rozelle rule."[27] This rule empowered Commissioner Pete Rozelle to make compensation awards to teams losing free agents where the teams involved could not agree on compensation through bilateral negotiations. Compensation awarded by the commissioner could consist of current roster players, future draft choices, or *both*. Obviously, the system had an extremely negative effect on player movement as team owners reacted in the same manner as did their counterparts in basketball. They would not sign free agents in fear of what it might cost them in the commissioner's compensation award.

Several players filed suit against the NFL for conspiring to restrain their freedom of movement through this option-compensation system. The major cases involved Joe Kapp[28] and John Mackey.[29] The court ruled in the Mackey case that the Rozelle rule did violate the Sherman Act. As mentioned earlier, the court laid the groundwork for the parties to use collective bargaining to resolve this difficult question of player movement from team to team. The first collectively bargained compromise in this area was agreed to on March 1, 1977. The basic elements of this system and its current problems will be reviewed later.

Finally, how did the professional hockey player rid himself of the language of paragraph 17 in his Standard Player Contract, language that bound him to his team into perpetuity? One step taken was the provision for salary arbitration inserted in 1969. Even though a player could have his salary determined through arbitration, the clubs still would argue that this player was their property into perpetuity.

The players did not have much success in fighting this system until the establishment of the rival World Hockey Association. This newer league offered much higher salaries, and several NHL stars like Gerry Cheevers and Derek Sanderson did jump leagues. The NHL's response was to go to court to try to enforce paragraph 17 and thereby forbid players from jumping leagues. The owners were thwarted in several cases, however.[30] The final blow was struck when the NHL reserve clause was stricken from player contracts as violating the Sherman Act in that the reserve clause had been imposed unilaterally upon the players and it was not the subject of arm's-length collective bargaining.[31] Again, the time was ripe for the players and owners to employ the process of collective bargaining to resolve problems associated with the player reservation system.

THE CURRENT STATE OF AFFAIRS

What is evident by now is that government need only play a rather minor role in regulating the various aspects of the employment relationship in professional team sports. Government regulation has set up an environment in which both the employer and employee are on an equal footing in terms of power. Time and again, the strong suggestion has been made that these two actors are best suited to work out the details of the employment relationship by themselves. The vehicle for establishing terms and conditions of employment has been, and will continue to be, the process of collective bargaining. Many thorny issues have arisen, but the collective bargaining process has been up to the task of conflict resolution in every case. A few examples of how collective bargaining has worked in these four sports will demonstrate this point. The key fact to remember is that government regulation has established the conditions necessary to cause the parties to negotiate in good faith; however, government does not dictate the terms and conditions of employment to the players or owners. These matters are handled adequately through private sector negotiations, without government involvement.

Baseball

In baseball, the owners and players negotiated a six-year reservation system after the Seitz arbitration decision of late 1975. A player would be reserved to his team for six seasons, after which time he could become a free agent. The monopsonistic labor market for baseball players' services thus was made much more competitive. Another important ingredient in this system was the minimal amount of compensation required to be paid to a team losing a free-agent player. This is a crucial aspect of the baseball system because, unlike basketball and football, the baseball owners did not have to worry about onerous compensation awards.

As might be expected, salaries skyrocketed, for several teams were now able to bid over player services. While the owners and the commissioner claimed that these higher salaries were ruining the game, owners kept right on offering ever higher contracts. In an attempt to reverse, or at least slow down this process, the owners entered the 1980 negotiations determined to revise the free agency system. Their goal was to enact a compensation formula that would cause owners to think twice before signing free agents. The entire story of these protracted negotiations is much too long to relate. This dispute led to a 58-day strike forcing the cancellation of 714 regularly scheduled games during the 1981 season.[32] A settlement finally was reached on a new compensation formula. While both sides claimed victory, an impartial observer would probably conclude that since player salaries have continued to climb, the new compensation formula has not done everything the owners had hoped it would do. It is certain that the compensation for teams losing free-agent players will continue to be a major issue at the bargaining table.

It also should be noted that strikes do sometimes occur in collective bargaining situations. Strikes have occurred in baseball and football, and they will probably occur again. The point is that the strike is but a part of the collective bargaining process. Strikes cause parties to reassess costs of agreement and disagreement. Strikes do not mean the death of the professional game, as many observers believe. Nobody wants a strike in baseball, but the strike is an important part of the negotiating process. More often than not, it is the mere threat of a strike that stimulates the parties to negotiate in good faith and to reach an agreement. While baseball suffered during the strike of 1981, the game has recovered and is as popular as ever.

A final issue regarding baseball is the role of salary arbitration.[33] Players have possessed the right to go to arbitration over salary disputes since 1974. The owners' major complaint has been that the arbitrators have used the huge salaries paid to free agents for comparison purposes in rendering their binding awards. Management would prefer to limit the scope of comparisons that these arbitrators can employ. The players want to keep the current system intact. Salary arbitration will continue to be a major issue at the bargaining table. Whatever the outcome, it is clear that the twin forces of salary arbitration and free agency have served to infuse competitiveness into the baseball players' labor market and thereby have caused salaries to rise to more competitive levels.

Basketball

The most pressing current issue in basketball is the owners' attempt to place a cap on total team salaries. This practice is the result of owners' concern over spiraling salaries brought on by the first-refusal free agency process.

In the years prior to first refusal, the NBA commissioner (at that time, Larry O'Brien) would rule on the compensation due to a team losing a free agent. For example, when the San Diego Clippers signed Bill Walton to a five-year, one-million-dollar-per-year contract in 1979, Commissioner O'Brien ordered players Kevin Kunnert and Kermit Washington to report to the Portland Trail Blazers. In addition, O'Brien awarded Portland $350,000 in cash and first round draft picks in 1980 and 1982 from San Diego. This kind of compensation award clearly served to destroy the owners' appetites for the free agency process. This system was replaced by a first-refusal process in the 1981–82 season. This process proved to be lucrative for the players. Reacting rather predictably, NBA club owners decided that the increase in players' salaries had to be controlled. Through the process of collective bargaining, labor and management were able to reach a new agreement covering this issue on March 31, 1983. Basically, labor received a promise that 53 percent of defined gross revenues would be earmarked for players' salaries. A salary cap per team set at approximately $3.6 million per team was implemented during the 1984–85 season.

Both sides appear to be satisfied with this compromise solution. The owners now have an ability to project future labor costs rather accurately, and they are assured that all teams will be competing on an equal basis. In other words, a richer team will not be allowed to spend an exorbitant amount on players' salaries. All teams, with minor exceptions, will be held to the negotiated salary cap. The players also have won the right to claim a fixed percentage of the defined gross revenues. As these revenues increase in the future, salary caps will increase by a set formula. Thus players' salaries will probably continue to increase. Even if this cap were to remain at $3.6 million, with eleven players per team, the average NBA player salary still would be over $327,000 per season.

Football

In football, players were concerned that even though the Rozelle Rule had been abolished free agency was still just a pipe dream. In this sport, the owners and players had agreed to a free agency compensation formula that clearly favored the clubs. In their collective bargaining pact of March 1, 1977, the two sides agreed to a first-refusal system similar to that in basketball, with one major difference. Unlike basketball, which abandoned the idea of compensation when it instituted its first-refusal plan, football owners and players agreed to maintain compensation for teams losing free agents as part of the overall procedure.[34] The exact nature of the compensation was precisely stipulated in the contract. For example, a team signing a free agent player to a salary of over $200,000 would owe that player's former team two first round draft picks as compensation. Of course, this was stiff compensation, *but* it was agreed to by the two parties through collective bargaining. As one might expect, very few players were able to employ the free agency procedure to change teams. In addition, teams now knew exactly what compensation would be due according to the collectively bargained formula. The situation was improved for the owners, but the players were no better off than they had been prior to the abolition of the Rozelle Rule.

The players had another major complaint as they entered the 1982 negotiations. They claimed that because of the revenue sharing practices employed by club owners, there was neither incentive to purchase free agents nor to pay players according to their performance. The players contended instead that their salaries were based solely on the position they played, the number of years they had been in the league, and the round in which they were drafted.[35]

In the negotiations, the players fought for the elimination of compensation for teams losing free agents and for a fixed wage scale based on seniority; 55 percent of the owners' gross revenues was to go to the players for salaries and other purposes. The old contract expired on July 15, 1982, and shortly thereafter a seven-week strike began. The strike finally was settled and the season was saved, but the players did not get what they had demanded. Compensation for teams losing free agent players remains an important element in football's free agency system. Under the current system, not much player movement is expected to occur. The players did not receive a fixed percentage of the gross revenues, nor did they receive the wage scale they demanded. What they did receive was a series of minimum salaries tied to years of seniority with the league. Even though football players seem to be at a disadvantage compared to their counterparts in baseball and basketball, it must be remembered that the system they now operate under was the result of bilateral negotiations.

Hockey

Professional hockey players also used the collective bargaining process to carve out a system to replace the former perpetual-player-reservation model. In 1975, after the landmark decision in the *Philadelphia World Hockey Club* case,[36] the owners and players reached mutual agreement on a compromise free agency system.[37] They agreed to affirm the right of the players to become free agents after playing out an option season. However, hockey clubs were able to retain the element of compensation for teams losing free agents; this is referred to as "equalization." This process is similar to others described earlier, but with one significant difference: The final decision on the equalization payment is made by an *arbitrator* if the two sides cannot agree bilaterally to the proper amount of this payment.

The concept of equalization still exists in the current collective bargaining pact between owners and players. However, the nature of the compensation process was changed somewhat in the 1982 collective bargaining agreement. Neither side was satisfied with the arbitration process. The players desired total free agency without compensation. They did achieve this for players age 33 and above. The only condition is that the player's current club does have the right of first refusal. However, no compensation is involved in situations involving players in this category.

For all other players, there is a compensation formula much like the one found in football. The formula stipulates that there will be no compensation for a free agent's former team if he signs a free agent contract for less than $85,000. The compensation due to a player's former team increases to two first round draft picks for players signed to contracts in excess of $200,000. This steep compensation formula probably will not have a much different impact upon player movement than did the former arbitration system. Uncertainty has now been replaced with certainty. However, the price of certainty may be very steep for many NHL clubs.

CONCLUSION

Professional athletes possess unique abilities to throw baseballs, score goals, shoot baskets, and throw touchdown passes. Professional athletes also have extremely short careers by typical standards. Of a population of well over 200 million persons in the United States, the four major professional sports employ a very small proportion—approximately 3,000. Given the scarcity of such talent and the shortness of careers, it is to be expected that the remuneration for such athletic services would be high.

As we have seen, however, professional owners have established rules and regulations designed to lessen the bargaining power of their athletes. The player reservation systems have created monopsonistic labor market conditions that enable the club owners to hold player salaries at levels far below competitive market rates.

Athletes view this situation as being unfair. Why should they be denied the same right granted to all other workers, rights designed to protect the worker's freedoms to join unions and bargain collectively with management? The obvious answer to this question is that there is not a good reason why these rights should be denied to a person just because he happens to be a professional athlete. Similarly, why should professional sports leagues be treated any differently from all other businesses when it comes to our nation's antitrust laws? The baseball exemption discussed earlier makes no sense. Professional sports leagues are businesses and, as such, should be subject to the laws of our nation that were passed to regulate certain types of business activities.

There has never been a need for any special governmental regulation of the employer-employee relationship in professional sports. Professional sports should be treated the same as any other business when it comes to labor relations. The only role for government in this area has been, and will continue to be, one of balancing the rights of players and owners. Applying the Sherman Act and the National Labor Relations Act to professional athletics was all that was ever needed. Once power had been balanced, and both sides were willing to come to the negotiating table in good faith, the process of collective bargaining was to be the method for resolving all kinds of disputes. The parties resolve their problems by themselves. There is an absolute minimum level of governmental intervention in the employer-employee relationship in professional sports today.

Government merely has set the ground rules for the implementation of the process of collective bargaining. As we have seen, the outcomes of collective bargaining have not been the same in each sport. All athletes have wanted higher salaries. In each sport, collectively bargained solutions have changed the nature of the formerly monopsonistic labor market to one that is more competitive. The exact extent of the competitiveness allowed is a subject to be determined through collective bargaining. Table 2.1 illustrates the different outcomes that are consistent with a system of free collective bargaining.

One can gain interesting insights into the workings of the process of collective bargaining by studying the data presented in Table 2.1. Note first that nominal salaries have increased a great deal in each sport since the inception of collective bargaining. Real salaries, however, are another matter. Note particularly the slow increase in real-salary dollars for the professional

Table 2.1 Average Player Salaries, 1970, 1980, and 1982 (in dollars)

		Baseball	Basketball	Football	Hockey
1970	Nominal	$ 29,000	$ 40,000	$ 34,000	$ 25,000
	Real	24,936	34,394	29,751	21,496
1980	Nominal	150,000	190,000	70,000	110,000
	Real	60,728	76,923	28,340	44,534
1982	Nominal	235,000	215,000	95,000	120,000
	Real	81,006	74,112	32,747	41,365
1982	Gross revenues	$400 million	$120 million	$550 million	$120 million

Note: Nominal wages refer to money received in the paycheck. Real wages correct nominal wages for the influence of inflation. Thus real wages are a better reflection of the purchasing power of the dollars received.

Source: Salary data from Business Week, February 22, 1982. Real salaries are in 1967 dollars. Gross revenue estimates from U.S. News and World Report, October 11, 1982.

football player over the twelve-year period represented in the table. This slow growth in salary was one of the major reasons for the football strike of 1982.[38]

It also is interesting to examine the row labeled gross revenues for 1982. Simple arithmetic will bring these dollar figures into clearer perspective. By 1982 baseball players' salaries accounted for approximately 38 percent of the gross revenues generated by the sport (650 players multiplied by $235,000/ $400 million). That is, for every dollar of revenue brought in by the teams, thirty-eight cents were spent on player salaries. In basketball, this figure was around 45 percent, and it is pegged at 53 percent beginning with the 1984–85 championship season. Of course, note how basketball generates far fewer revenue dollars than does baseball. The richest sport in terms of revenue, football, pays out the smallest fraction of said revenue for salary purposes (approximately 22 percent). Finally, in hockey the percentage of total revenues going for salary purposes is nearly 45 percent.

These agreements made through collective bargaining have been translated directly into player salary dollars. The richest professional athletes, baseball and basketball players, operate in an environment with great player freedom of movement. Baseball players can become free agents after six years, and there is no compensation penalty to deter a team from acquiring a free agent's services. Thus, by 1982, average nominal salaries for baseball players had increased to $235,000.

Basketball players also were able to do away with compensation for teams losing free agent players with the implementation of the first-refusal system in the 1981–82 season. These players have been able to change teams, and their average salary in 1982 was quite high—$215,000. Of course, the average salary of basketball players in the future will be determined through the negotiated formula that granted the players 53 percent of defined gross revenues for salary purposes.

The two sports that still employ free agent compensation systems have witnessed a rather slow growth in player salaries and the concomitant lack of player ability to switch teams. The average salary of a football player was $95,000 in 1982, while his counterpart in hockey toiled for an average salary of $120,000. Teams are not willing to pay huge amounts of money for free agents and, in addition, be forced to suffer large compensation payments to the free agent's former team.

The conclusion is obvious. While collective bargaining works very well, it certainly does not work the same in all cases. Different sets of bargainers will reach different agreements, which in turn will lead to different salary outcomes. The degree of competitiveness in the athletes' labor market has increased, but this increase varies depending upon the nature of the bargaining in each sport.

The key fact to remember is that collective bargaining has proven to be a viable alternative to governmental regulation of the employer-employee relationship in professional sports. It is a process that works well in that it enables the parties directly involved in the disputed situation to work out an agreement by themselves instead of having to turn to government for an imposed solution. For those of us who believe in a minimum of governmental interference in the workings of our economic system, the use of the process of collective bargaining is indeed a welcome situation.

NOTES

1. For a fuller discussion of this issue, see James B. Dworkin, *Owners Versus Players: Baseball and Collective Bargaining* (Boston: Auburn House, 1981).

2. See *National Basketball Players Association Agreement*, April 29, 1976, signed by the National Basketball Association and the National Basketball Players Association, pp. 28–41.

3. Mark Goldstein, "Arbitration of Grievance and Salary Disputes in Professional Baseball: Evolution of a System of Private Law," *Cornell Law Review* 60 (August 1975): 1045–74. See also Paul Gregory, *The Baseball Player: An Economic Study* (Washington, D.C.: Public Affairs Press, 1956).

4. *Professional Baseball Clubs*, 66 LA 101 (December 23, 1975).

5. *Basic Agreement Between The American League of Professional Baseball Clubs and The National League of Professional Baseball Clubs and Major League Baseball Players Association*, effective January 1, 1973, p. 37, paragraph 10(a).

6. See *National Basketball Association Uniform Player Contract*, paragraph 22.

7. See *Standard Player Contract for The National Football League*, paragraph 10.

8. See *Standard Player Contract for The National Hockey League*, paragraph 17.

9. The literature in this field is far too voluminous for any one citation to do it justice. However, a beginner should start with the following pieces: Joel Seidman, Jack London, and Bernard Karsh, "Why Workers Join Unions," *Annals of the American Academy of Political and Social Science* (March 1951): 75–84; William Whyte, "Who Goes Union and Why," *Personnel Journal* 23 (December 1944): 215–30; Henry Farber and Daniel Saks, "Why Workers Want Unions: The Role of Relative Wages and Job Characteristics," *Journal of Political Economy* 88 (April 1980): 349–69.

10. For a detailed account of this union and other attempts in baseball, basketball, football, and hockey, see Dworkin, *Owners Versus Players*, pp. 10–39.

11. 49 Stat. 449 (1935), as amended by Pub. L. No. 101, 80th Cong., 1st sess. (1947), and Pub. L. No. 257, 86th Cong., 1st sess. (1959); 29 U.S.C. 151–68, 29 F.C.A. 151–68.

12. Of course, the creation of rival leagues is not a phenomenon of solely historical interest. In recent years fans have witnessed the development of the United States Football League (USFL), a challenger to the National Football League. A 1984 announcement by USFL officials indicates that they have decided to go "head-to-head" with the NFL in the traditional fall season, rather than continue their "off-season" schedule. It remains to be seen how successful this head-on conflict will be.

13. For a fuller discussion of the Players League, see David Voigt, *American Baseball: From Gentlemen's Sport to the Commissioner System* (Norman, Okla.: University of Oklahoma Press, 1966), pp. 161–69.

14. See Chapter 8: Philip J. Closius, "Professional Sports and Antitrust Law: The Ground Rules of Immunity, Exemption, and Liability."

15. Federal Baseball Club of Baltimore, 259, U.S. 200 (1922).

16. Examples are Toolson, 346 U.S. 356 (1953) and Flood v. Kuhn, 407 U.S. 258 (1972).

17. For an example, see Radovich v. National Football League, 352 U.S. 4456 (1957).

18. 15 U.S.C., section 1 and 2.

19. Mackey v. National Football League, 543 F.2d 606 (8th Cir. 1976).

20. Ibid.

21. Public Law 101, 80th Cong. (1947).

22. For one example of how the National Labor Relations Board exerted its jurisdiction in the professional sports arena, see The American League of Professional Baseball Clubs and Association of National Baseball League Umpires, 180 NLRB 190 (1969).

23. For a much more detailed account of this series of events, see Dworkin, *Owners Versus Players*, pp. 41–82.

24. See note 4 above for the citation to this case and Dworkin, *Owners Versus Players*, pp. 72–80, for a detailed description of this arbitration ruling.

25. See *Professional Baseball Clubs*, pp. 117–18.

26. Robertson v. National Basketball Association, 389 F. Supp. 867 (S.D.N.Y., 1975).

27. See Constitution and Bylaws for the National Football League, 1975, Article 12, Section 1(H).

28. Kapp v. National Football League, 390 F. Supp. 73 (ND. Cal. 1974).

29. Mackey v. National Football League, 352 U.S. 4456 (1957).

30. See Boston Professional Hockey Club v. Cheevers, 348 F. Supp. 261 (D. Mass.), remanded, 472 F. 2d 127 (1st Cir. 1972). Also see Nassau Sports v. Hampson, 355 F. Supp. 733 (D. Minn. 1972).

31. See Philadelphia World Hockey Club, Inc. v. Philadelphia Hockey Club, Inc., 351 F. Supp. 462 (E.D. Pa. 1972).

32. For a thorough account of this strike and the resulting agreement, see Dworkin, "Results of the Professional Baseball Players' Strike of 1981," *Texas Business Review* 55, no. 6 (November-December 1981): 268–71.

33. For a description of this process, see Dworkin, *Owners Versus Players*, pp. 136–73.

34. See the *Collective Bargaining Contract Between the National Football League and the National Football League Players Association*, effective March 1, 1977, Article XV.

35. See "Why a Percentage of Gross? Because We Are the Game," A Report to Members of the National Football League Players Association, (September 1981), 64 pp.

36. Philadelphia World Hockey Club, Inc. v. Philadelphia Hockey Club, Inc., 351 F. Supp. 462 (E.D. Pa. 1972).

37. See *National Hockey League–National Hockey League Players Association Collective Bargaining Agreement*, effective September 15, 1975, pp. 34–37.

38. Since the establishment of the United States Football League, the average NFL salary increased to $130,000 in 1983 and to $160,000 in 1984.

3

The Amateur Athlete as Employee

Allen L. Sack and Bruce Kidd

What is widely known as "amateur" sport is becoming increasingly commercialized. The United States Supreme Court ruled in 1984 that the National Collegiate Athletic Association's (NCAA) control over televised intercollegiate football is a *per se* violation of the Sherman Antitrust Law.[1] By defending the universities' right to negotiate directly with networks over the sale of football broadcasts, the court underscored the fact that college sport is a business like any other. This same trend can be seen in international "amateur" sport. The television rights to the Olympics and other international games are sold for millions of dollars, while the Olympic symbol is sold to advertise everything from soft drinks to children's dolls.

"Amateur" sport has been increasingly professionalized as well. Most athletes at major athletic universities in the United States receive athletic scholarships, which pay for room, board, tuition, and other expenses. In the Olympic sports, the rules now permit athletes to accept living and training grants, endorsement fees, and in some cases prize money, as long as these funds are administered by their sports governing bodies. As a result, Los Angeles Olympic stars like Edwin Moses and Carl Lewis have become millionaires.[2]

In the face of these radical transformations, the notion that athletes competing at this level are "amateurs" has shown remarkable resiliency. There are, of course, occasional allegations that athletes receive extra benefits "under the table," and athletes periodically are sanctioned for violating amateur regulations. However, the activity itself still carries the expectation that in some way it differs significantly from "professional" sport—that is, the salaried training and competition performed for corporations like the National Football League. It would appear that the consequences of the wholesale, and officially sanctioned, commercialization and professionalization of elite "amateur" sport generally have escaped close critical scrutiny.[3]

This chapter will examine the objective conditions of athletic activity in "amateur" sport today. The first task will be to identify the conditions that distinguish sport as an amateur or leisure activity from sport as employment. This analysis will be applied to two highly visible forms of "amateur" sport in North America—the "restricted" sphere of American intercollegiate competition and the "open" sphere of international or Olympic competition. It is our contention that the continued application of the term "amateur" to what is essentially athletic employment can lead to serious violations of athletes' rights.

AMATEUR SPORT: WORK OR LEISURE?

There is no agreement on what is meant by the term leisure. Scholars such as Pieper, DeGrazia, Dumazedier, and Kraus would argue that the essence of leisure is freedom.[4] Leisure can be viewed as activity pursued during free, discretionary, or unobligated time. According to Charles Brightbill, "leisure is time in which our feelings of compulsion should be minimal. It is discretionary time.[5] Sociologist Bennett Berger correctly points out that the notion that leisure is free or unobligated activity is in need of qualification. Berger argues that no human activity is ever totally free of normative constraint.[6] Even leisure activities are shaped by the norms, values, and group relations of society and culture. Thus, for Berger, neither work nor leisure is free from obligations. Rather, the key distinction between work and leisure "should be a distinction between the kinds of norms which constrain them or a distinction regarding the extent to which norms have been internationalized."[7] Leisure, like work, is constrained, but in a different way.

Amitai Etzioni identifies two types of control that parallel the kinds of constraints discussed by Berger.[8] When a coach exhorts his team to "win one for the Gipper" or elicits conformity by suggesting a player is somehow "letting down the team," he is using what Etzioni calls normative control. Normative control appeals to values and norms that have been deeply internalized. Leisure for Berger refers precisely to those activities that "we want to do for their own sake . . . or that we feel ethically (as distinguished from expediently) constrained to do."[9] Constraints on leisure are always normative.

One major defining characteristic of work, on the other hand, is that employers always have recourse to what Etzioni calls utilitarian, instrumental, or remunerative types of control. Employers, especially those schooled in human relations, will of course utilize normative controls whenever possible. When all else fails, however, wages can be docked, fines can be imposed, and an employee can be threatened with termination. Utilitarian control utilizes material rewards and punishments that are related intimately to the pragmatic concerns of making a living. Work may or may not be normatively constrained, but utilitarian constraint always is lurking in the background.

Amateur sport is a type of leisure activity. As such, it is free from instrumental or utilitarian constraint. An amateur can walk away from sport without economic loss.[10] An amateur, to use legal terms, has no material interest in sport, and sport participation does not constitute a property right. Professional athletes, on the other hand, may or may not feel normative constraints. This depends on how much intrinsic satisfaction they get from sport or on their need for prestige or other symbolic rewards. Nonetheless, the professional athlete ultimately must comply with demands imposed by economic expediency.

Sport in the late twentieth century has become a lucrative form of commercial entertainment in which profit maximization is enhanced by winning. Successful athletic teams also have become an instrument nations use to garner international prestige and to enhance feelings of national pride. Therefore, it is not surprising that a concern for winning has taken precedence over providing developmental and intrinsic rewards for athletes. To win games, sport has been subjected to extensive rationalization. The trend toward greater rationality is manifested in such things as systematic training and recruitment of players, extensive specialization, management control of athlete's behavior both off and on the field, and expansion of time devoted to training and preparation for contests.[11]

Professional athletes are expected to accept some of the most alienating aspects of this rationalization as conditions for their continued employment. In return for financial compensation, the professional sacrifices a great deal of control over how the game will be played and over how his body and skills will be utilized.[12] Although amateur sport is not immune to the power of rationality, its freedom from instrumental obligations gives players considerable autonomy to direct their own lives and sporting activity. The amateur coach must cajole and convince; the professional coach can demand.

It is undeniable that what the public identifies as professional sport is a highly rationalized form of work. However, professionalism and rationalization also have penetrated the upper levels of what generally is regarded as amateur sport. Given the high stakes (millions of dollars in revenue and/or international prestige), those who control amateur sport simply cannot trust the destiny of their teams to athletes who pursue sport unsupervised in their leisure or spare time. Thus a class of highly skilled amateur athletes has emerged for whom sport has taken on characteristics not unlike employment.

The problem with this development is not that athletes who receive financial support have somehow sullied or tarnished the amateur ideal. On the contrary, it would be unfair and probably unsafe not to compensate these athletes for their investment of time and labor. The real problem is that the confused legal status of these athletes can lead to violations of their rights. The imposition of the amateur label on athletes who labor under the same working conditions as professionals raises two major concerns with regard to legal rights.

The first is that as long as athletes are defined as amateurs, it is assumed that they have no material interest in their athletic participation. Because of this, the athlete cannot claim an economic loss as a result of unfair disciplinary action. What this means, at least in the United States, is that amateur athletes are unlikely to be protected by the due process clauses of the Fifth and Fourteenth amendments of the Constitution, which provide that "no person shall be deprived of life, liberty or property without due process of law." Before the recent liberalization of International Olympic Committee (IOC) regulations, Donald Shuck wrote that "some courts have recognized the substantial economic value of amateur participation but have generally viewed this interest as far too speculative to be considered a property right which would merit constitutional protection."[13] One wonders how long it will take the courts to recognize the property interests of Olympic athletes who now receive substantial yearly stipends and place millions into trust funds.

The second concern raised by the misrepresentation of athletic employees as amateurs is that it implies a degree of freedom and autonomy that elite athletes, such as those on athletic scholarships, generally do not possess. The notion that sports participation is voluntary and gratuitous rather than a *quid pro quo* contract denies athletes protections that attach to contractual or exchange transactions.[14] The amateur label also justifies exclusion from basic employee rights like worker's compensation, collective bargaining, or the right to negotiate independently for higher wages.

In summary, amateur sport is a leisure activity that is free from utilitarian or economic constraint. When the term is applied to parties involved in an employer-employee relationship, exploitation and the denial of rights are the inevitable result. The remainder of this chapter will examine college sport in the United States and international Olympic competition to determine the appropriateness of the amateur label in these contexts. The section on college sport will address the issue of whether an athletic scholarship constitutes a contract for hire. The section on Olympic sport will examine the impact of current IOC regulations concerning compensation on high-performance athletes. Close attention will be given to the formal agreement between athletes in Canada and the Canadian national sports organization to determine whether it constitutes a contract of employment.

ARE SCHOLARSHIP ATHLETES EMPLOYEES?

Big-time college sport in the United States provides an excellent context within which to examine the legal dimensions of many of the issues raised above. The issue of worker's compensation for injured scholarship athletes is especially relevant because decisions in such cases cannot be reached without first determining whether college sport constitutes employment. There generally are two criteria that must be met before a claimant in most worker's compensation cases can recover benefits. First, the worker must qualify as an employee. Second, the worker must suffer a personal injury by accident arising out of and in the course of employment.[15]

One of the most recent cases in which a scholarship athlete sought worker's compensation is *Coleman* v. *Western Michigan University* (1983).[16] Coleman was on a football scholarship at Western Michigan in 1974 when he suffered a disabling injury during practice. It is undisputed that Coleman could no longer play football after his injury. NCAA regulations permitted Coleman to keep his scholarship until the end of the year. In the following fall, however, his scholarship aid was reduced and he had to leave school because he could not afford to continue there. Coleman was denied compensation by the Workmen's Compensation Appeals Board in Michigan and later lost again in the Michigan Court of Appeals.

This case deserves special attention because it attempts to define employment by examining the objective conditions under which athletes carry out their activity. The State of Michigan requires application of an "economic realities" test for determining the existence of an employment relationship. This test, based on criteria developed in *Askew* v. *Macomber* (1976), sets forth certain factors that Michigan courts must consider in determining whether there exists an expressed or implied contract for hire.[17] A discussion of each of these factors provides an excellent framework for examining the legal status of athletic scholarships and will allow a comparison of *Coleman* with other worker's compensation rulings.

The first *Askew* factor is whether the proposed employer has the right to discipline or fire the proposed employee. The Michigan Court of Appeals argued that the NCAA rules do not allow an institution to condition financial aid on a student's ability as an athlete. Thus it concluded that athletes cannot be fired for poor performance or disciplined for failure to follow management dictates. The NCAA Constitution does, in fact, say that "institutional aid may not be gradated or cancelled during the period of its award on the basis of . . . a student athlete's ability or his contribution to a team's success."[18] However, the fact that the period of the award is one academic year weakens the court's position significantly.

The granting of a one-year "no-cut" scholarship does not negate the reality that athletes must perform to a coach's expectations in order to qualify for another year of compensation. Before 1973 the argument advanced by the Michigan court would have been much more convincing. Before 1973 athletic scholarships were awarded for four years and could not be removed for poor athletic performance or injury. A school that recruited an athlete who failed to make the grade in athletics had no choice but to pay for the athlete's four-year education. The main conditions were that the athlete not withdraw from sports voluntarily, fail to meet minimum academic requirements, or engage in serious misconduct or fradulent misrepresentation of application information.

In 1973 all this changed. The rationale for one-year scholarships, according to Charles Neinas, Director of the College Football Association, was to eliminate the practice of "brutally running off" inferior athletes in order to free their scholarships for those with greater promise.[19] In other words, the NCAA actually was saying that it is far more humanitarian to fire athletes than to force them to quit. The 1973 rule change gave coaches significantly more control over personnel decisions. Giving athletes nine months or less to find another job or alternate sources of funding in no way alters the fact that financial aid is tied directly to evaluations of athletic performance.

A case in point is James Mosier, a basketball player at the University of Massachusetts. In 1981 the university decided not to renew Mosier's basketball scholarship for the 1981–82 academic year. Mosier appealed this decision to the University Scholarship Committee, which reached the following conclusions: "NCAA rules were adhered to in the decision not to renew. . . . Mr. Mosier is not a basketball player of sufficient calibre to play at the level at which this university engages in sport. . . . There was insufficient reason to attribute the denial of the award renewal to any reason other than the athletic department's evaluation of Mr. Mosier's athletic ability."[20] Unfortunately, this case never went to court, but it is fairly certain that the University of Massachusetts was well within its rights.

The second *Askew* factor is whether the proposed employer has the right to control or dictate the activities of the proposed employee. The position of the Michigan court was that sports activity always gives a coach considerable control over an athlete, "whether or not an athlete had the benefit of a scholarship."[21] In taking this position, the court did not appear to be sensitive to the distinction between normative and utilitarian constraints raised earlier in this chapter. It certainly is true that coaches at all levels tend to make broad demands on athletes who play for them. However, scholarship athletes like Coleman receive room, board, tuition, and books in return for their athletic participation. Because athletic scholarships are awarded for one year only, and because performance is a condition for renewal in a subsequent year, coaches have recourse to economic constraints when appeals to pride, team loyalty, and other types of normative symbols are ineffective. The fact that Coleman had to leave school when his aid was reduced underscores how dependent many athletes are on their scholarships. Given the knowledge that coaches make renewal decisions on the basis of athletic performance, few athletes are likely to risk insubordination.

It would be an error to underestimate the kinds of demands that legitimately can be made on scholarship athletes as a condition for retaining their scholarships. Carolyn Thomas states that "the managers of sport ask the athlete to change diet. They ask the athlete to change patterns of weight gain and loss. They ask the athlete to run anaerobic training patterns. They ask the athlete to play with injury. They ask the athlete to think certain kinds of things, to behave in certain ways."[22] It should be added that in some sports athletes are asked to risk serious injury almost every day. It is undeniable that some athletes subject themselves to this kind of regime voluntarily. The fact remains, however, that coaches who control financial compensation have considerable power to dictate such activities.

The third *Askew* factor is the extent to which the proposed employee is dependent on the payment of wages or other benefits for daily living expenses. Given the *Coleman* court's position on the first two factors, it is surprising that it found that the payment-of-wages factor weighs in favor of the finding of an employment relationship. Citing *Morgan* v. *Win Schuler's Restaurant* (1975), the court defined wages as "items of compensation which are measurable in money or which confer an economic gain upon the employee."[23] In return for his services as a football player, Coleman received room, board, tuition, and books. The court ruled that Coleman was dependent on his scholarship to pay his daily living expenses. The plaintiff testified that "he could not have met all of his expenses without scholarship aid."[24]

The issue of payment of wages also played an important role in the case of *Rensing* v. *Indiana State University Board of Trustees* (1983).[25] In this case, Rensing, an Indiana State University football player, was rendered a quadriplegic as a result of an injury suffered in spring football practice. Rensing applied for worker's compensation on the grounds that he was a university employee. An Indiana appeals court ruled in favor of Rensing, arguing that the evidence "clearly demonstrates that the benefits received by Rensing were conditional upon his athletic ability and team participation. Consequently, the scholarship constituted a contract for hire . . . and created an employer-employee relationship between the Trustees and Rensing."[26] This decision was later reversed by the Indiana Supreme Court.

The Indiana Supreme Court argued that the primary consideration in determining the existence of an employer-employee relationship is that there be intent that a contract for employment exist. "In other words, there must be a mutual belief that an employer-employee relationship did exist."[27] The court used the issue of payment of wages to illustrate that neither party believed he was involved in a contractual relationship. According to the court, the university could not have viewed Rensing's scholarship as payment for services rendered because the NCAA expressly prohibits athletes from accepting pay.[28] Indiana State University had no intention of paying Rensing; rather, Rensing was given what the NCAA calls "unearned financial aid."[29]

The major problem with this argument is that it presents a characterization of scholarship aid that obviously serves the interests of the defendant and assumes that the defendant actually believes this characterization to be valid. It is quite possible that Indiana State University intended that Rensing's scholarship constitute pay and was well aware that the relationship was contractual. Yet, to evade worker's compensation liability, the university and the NCAA may have found it expedient to mask the objective reality of this relationship by developing their own definition of what constitutes or does not constitute pay. In the same vein, neither the university nor the athlete is likely to embrace openly a definition of scholarship aid as pay, if as a result the Internal Revenue Service treats scholarships as taxable income. In both of these instances the parties may have an interest in masking their true intentions and beliefs.

Mark Alan Atkinson criticizes approaches to defining employment that rely primarily on definitions offered by the contesting parties. According to Atkinson, "Workmen's compensation law does not blindly accept characterizations made by employers or employer organizations. For example, if an employer calls himself an independent contractor in an attempt to evade workmen's compensation liability, the courts will look past mere titles to realities."[30] Had the Rensing court followed this logic, it would have looked beyond NCAA or its member institutions' definitions of pay to assess the intentions of the contesting parties. A close examination of what Rensing actually had to do as a condition for continued financial aid would yield far better inferences as to contractual intent than taking at face value the university's presumed commitment to a particular definition of scholarship aid.

The fourth *Askew* factor is whether the task performed by the proposed employee was "an integral part of the proposed employer's business." The *Coleman* court placed considerable weight on this factor in ruling against the plaintiff. According to the court, "the primary function of the defendant university was to provide academic education rather than conduct a football program."[31] Furthermore, the court argued that the plaintiff's football playing was not essential to the defendant university's business, which even the plaintiff recognized as education and research. The university, it was argued, could operate effectively even in the absence of an intercollegiate football program.

There is no doubt that education, not football, is the primary purpose of a university. Yet it also is obvious that a university employs a variety of people who are not directly engaged in the educational function. Security guards ensure that crime on campuses is kept to a minimum; custodians trim shrubs, paint hallways, and otherwise maintain the physical plant. The fact that security and ground maintenance are not the primary business of a university makes these jobs no less integral than classroom teaching.

The real issue is whether Coleman performed a function that was at least as integral to the business of the university as jobs performed by other nonacademic personnel. As a football player, Coleman participated in what has become one of higher education's most effective public relations instruments. College sport also has become a valuable source of revenue. At many schools, including Western Michigan, revenue from football helps support the entire athletic program. So important has college football become as a commercial venture that schools have sought court action to defend what they view as their athletic property rights.

When the United States Supreme Court ruled that it is a violation of antitrust law for the NCAA to monopolize negotiations with networks over football television rights, Justice White, in his minority opinion, underscored the Court's view that college football is a business much like any other. According to White, "the court errs in treating intercollegiate athletics as a purely commercial venture in which colleges and universities participate solely, or even primarily, in pursuit of profits."[32] It seems safe to say that, at least as far as the majority of Supreme Court Justices is concerned, playing football is an integral part of a university-run business.

After closely examining the four factors that comprise the economic realities test, the *Coleman* court rendered the following decision. On the first two factors the court granted that the defendant had at least some right to control the plaintiff's activities and to discipline the plaintiff for nonperformance, but these rights were limited. The third factor, the payment of wages, supported existence of an employment relationship. On the fourth factor, relating to the employee's activities being integral to the employer's business, the court went against the plaintiff. Because all four factors had to support an employer-employee relationship, Coleman lost the case.

Although the Coleman case has provided a framework for discussing several dimensions of college sport as a kind of employment, one other argument relating to the legal status of athletic scholarships must be raised. In both *Rensing* and *Coleman*, the argument was made that the plaintiffs were not employees under contract, but students who had received educational grants. The question was raised as to how athletes on scholarship differ, if at all, from other students receiving financial aid. This distinction is a crucial one and deserves some attention here.

The Implications of Viewing Scholarship Athletes as Employees

Weistart and Lowell present two very different views on the legal status of an athletic scholarship.[33] In the first view, the one that Weistart and Lowell much prefer, an athletic scholarship can be treated as an academic grant that helps a deserving student further his or her education. The scholarship is a gift. Of course, as with any academic scholarship, certain conditions, such as maintaining a minimal grade-point average, must be met. In this view, college sports are educational, and making athletes attend practice and play games to retain aid is no different from the condition that other academic scholarship holders must attend class and pass exams. The strength of this construction is that it does not force one to take the somewhat absurd position that athletic scholarships are not contingent on athletic performance.

The second position that can be taken on athletic scholarships is that they are *quid pro quo* contracts. This is the position developed throughout this chapter. In this view, an athlete offers to play sports in return for room, board, tuition, and fees. The scholarship is not an educational grant, but compensation for services rendered. Unlike academic scholarship holders, athletes must meet two often contradictory conditions to retain their aid. Like other students, they must meet minimal academic requirements. At the same time, they must engage in athletic activities for which faculty senates are unwilling to grant academic credit and which often make it much more difficult to meet academic demands. In reality, scholarship athletes are working their way through school by playing sports.

Both views have their merits as intellectual constructs, but it is in their practical impact for political interests that we see their full significance. Weistart and Lowell warn of the "dire consequences" of treating an athletic scholarship as *quid pro quo* relationships.[34] Clearly, what they mean is that acknowledging that scholarship athletes are employees opens a veritable Pandora's box of athletes' rights. As employees, athletes would be protected by worker's compensation and would have a right to other employee benefits. Athletes could form unions, bargain over salaries, and demand fair grievance procedures. In short, the college sports industry would no longer have access to a cheap and docile labor supply.

Far from viewing these consequences as "dire," we recognize them as necessary and predictable responses to the professionalization of college sport. Athletes who shoulder the responsibilities of employees must have concomitant rights and protections. If schools find it too costly to offer athletes basic employee rights and protections, they should abandon the professional sports business and adopt an amateur sport model more in line with their stated academic missions. Going into business always entails costs. A court ruling that recognizes scholarship athletes as employees would simply make it clear that labor costs in the college sports industry no longer can be wished away. In our opinion, the consequences of such a ruling would be overwhelmingly positive.

By forcing schools to consider the costs of transforming athletes into paid entertainers, a court ruling in favor of plaintiffs like Rensing and Coleman would do more to resurrect amateur college sport in the United States than any action likely to be taken by such organizations as the NCAA or the American Council of Education. Faced with the prospect of paying athletes according to their market value, offering benefit packages comparable to those of other workers and having to recognize players' unions, the majority of schools would do well to restructure their athletic programs so that athletes are free from utilitarian constraints, which are the essence of professionalism. The elimination of scholarships based on athletic ability would be a logical first step. When sport is not a kind of employment, athletes are free to give their academic roles top priority and can be expected to meet the same academic demands as other students.[35]

Even though Coleman and Rensing lost, there is evidence that these cases have generated enough concern among college administrators to elicit significant proposals for athletic reform. It is probably no coincidence that the NCAA took under consideration in 1984 the adoption of catastrophic injury insurance for athletes and a return to four-year scholarships. Both of these proposals can be viewed as attempts to prevent future court actions like Rensing and Coleman. If the mere threat of future court action can move the NCAA to consider such proposals, an actual court victory for an injured athlete would virtually guarantee rule changes in the direction of amateurism. In schools that choose to retain the professional sports model, even after legal recognition of athletes as employees, the exploitative and hypocritical aspects of present-day big-time college sports would quickly disappear.

A major conclusion to be drawn from all of this is that court action in the area of amateur sports can be a powerful stimulus to social reform. Of course, it would be better if organizations like the NCAA would initiate reforms on their own before it became necessary to turn these matters over to judges. As Brian Porto correctly points out in Chapter 7, judges often lack the knowledge of sport that would allow them to assess relevant facts. One could certainly argue that the judges who ruled against Rensing in the Indiana Supreme Court had little knowledge of the objective realities of big-time college sports. The conclusion we draw from this is not that there is a need for "judicial restraint," but that judges must be better educated. It seems fairly certain that in the matter of worker's compensation for college athletes, an informed judiciary is far more likely to recognize the rights of athletes than are those in the college sports industry, whose economic survival might well depend on the denial of such rights.

OLYMPIC AND INTERNATIONAL COMPETITION AS EMPLOYMENT

It would not be an exaggeration to say that the last decade has witnessed a revolutionary change in the rules governing eligibility for competition in the Olympic sports. For most of the century entry was restricted to those who abided by a strict amateurism, and who did not accept any payment other than limited expenses for their participation in the sport. Even "scholarships dependent upon athletic prowess" were considered to be in violation of Olympic rules.

This changed in 1974, when the International Olympic Committee dropped the term "amateur" from its eligibility code and permitted athletes to receive payment for their living and training expenses for an unlimited period. Further liberalization occurred in 1982, when the IOC legalized endorsement and prize income as long as it was placed in a trust fund administered by the athlete's national federation. Essentially, the IOC now allows each international federation to set its own eligibility rules.[36] The new system has created its own contradictions, however. For example, prior to the 1984 Winter Olympics, the IOC ruled that an athlete who had played a single game in the National Hockey League was ineligible as a "professional," while another who had played 323 games in the now-defunct World Hockey Association was eligible.[37] Even though the Eastern bloc countries bitterly opposed this ruling,[38] the changes have been welcomed as a progressive step. For those athletes who have been able to earn money from "amateur" sport, the new rules usually have meant more time to train, longer careers, and in some cases immense wealth.

Has the payment of "amateur" athletes made them employees in the sense of NHL hockey players or "scholarship" athletes in American universities? Those American athletes who have received endorsement fees and prize money are best considered independent businesspersons or self-employed professionals, rather than employees, because they draw their income from a variety of sources. They also retain control over their day-to-day training and competition. They may be dependent upon or subordinate to a coach, but it is not usually the coach who remunerates them: The coach's control mechanisms are normative rather then instrumental. Even where the athlete is obligated contractually—say, to a shoe company—the contracts are not usually contracts of employment where the "employer has the right to control or dictate the activities of the employee," but contracts for service, where the athlete is bound to provide the service (such as wear a particular brand), but not in the way he or she performs athletic labor.

In England an important source of income for many athletes is the Sport Assistance Fund (SAF), a private foundation that provides outstanding athletes, upon application, with living and training grants. Yet the athlete–SAF relationship bears little resemblance to the model of employment we have outlined. While renewal of the grant usually depends upon performance, the SAF does not control the athlete's day-to-day activity in any way, nor can it punish or discipline him or her for failure to perform to expectations. The SAF, for example, cannot have an athlete removed from a national team. The situation in Canada, however, is quite different. In Canada, virtually all athletes who compete in international competition on national teams are remunerated by the federal government. Thus one finds a much clearer case of Olympic athletes who have been transformed into employees.

The Canadian Carded-Athlete System

With the passage of the Fitness and Amateur Sport Act in 1961, the Canadian Government made the provision of opportunities for high-performance sport a matter of public policy. Grants were made to the national sports organizations (NSOs), such as the Canadian Track and Field Association, for sending athletes to national and international competitions, training coaches, and conducting demonstration events. The government encouraged the NSOs to bring international competitions to Canada and inaugurated (and wholly subsidized) its own multisport event, the Canada Games, as a developmental project. These efforts were accelerated early in the 1970s, when the responsible agency, Sport Canada, increased its financial aid, extended administrative and technical assistance to the NSOs, developed a national coaching-certification scheme, and encouraged the creation of permanent national teams and training centers, presided over by full-time national coaches. These initiatives transformed the NSO from a volunteer-financed and controlled regulatory body into a heavily subsidized, professionally led programming agency, whose chief concern has become the preparation of successful national teams. The Canadian Government now provides 80 percent of NSO funding. In fiscal 1984–85, Sport Canada will spend $45 million on high-performance sport. Although the system ultimately is dependent upon political will, it seems well established. The new Conservative government has promised to maintain and improve it.[39]

An essential component of the system is the athlete assistance or "carded athlete" program. Athletes receive financial assistance from the program according to a ranking or carding system based upon performance. An "A card" is awarded to an athlete ranked in the top eight in his or her event in the world (in the top four for teams); a "B card" is awarded to one in the top sixteen (in the top eight for teams); and a "C card" is awarded to athletes who "have demonstrated the potential to achieve A or B card status." An A card entitles the holder to support for two years; B and C cards must be renewed annually. The base 1984–85 allowance is $650 per month for A cards, $550 for B cards, and $450 for C cards. To that may be added a monthly supplement, paid on the basis of demonstrated need, for extraordinary training costs, day care, special equipment, moving and travel expenses, and facility rentals. In addition, the program pays for university and college tuition, books, and instruments. Some athletes have received as much as $1,500 a month in total award. After they retire, athletes who have been carded for at least three years are eligible for a final living stipend of $450 a month for eight months, plus two semesters' tuition. Cards are granted by Sport Canada upon NSO nomination, and checks usually are mailed directly by Sport Canada to the athlete. In 1983–84, 750 athletes received assistance, at a total cost of $3.6 million.[40]

There is no doubt that the changes introduced by Sport Canada have significantly improved training and competitive opportunities. Canadian high-performance athletes now enjoy better coaching, better facilities, and better support programs than ever before. It is instructive that 88 percent of the 1984 Winter and Summer Olympic teams, which took home more medals than ever before, benefited from carded-athlete assistance. The system has been much more equitable than the market in distributing financial assistance, for it helps all international athletes who make the standards, not just those whose gender, race, and physical appearance meet the advertising needs of a particular corporation, nor only those who compete in sports like distance running or skiing, where a mass market for equipment induces manufacturers to pay endorsement fees. The retirement assistance plan gives veteran athletes some chance to readjust to "civilian life" and to prepare for a subsequent career.

The issue here, however, is whether the carded-athlete system constitutes a form of employment. Under Canadian law, there are four main indicators of the presence of an employment relationship: (a) the master's power of selection of his servant; (b) the payment of wages or other remuneration; (c) the master's right to control the method of doing the work; and (d) the master's right of suspension or dismissal.[41] It should be apparent that these indicators closely resemble the Askew factors used to define employment in the state of Michigan.

In the case of carded-athlete assistance, we believe each of these indicators is present. The NSO has the power to select an athlete for membership on a national team, with which nomination for assistance usually is commensurate, and the power to suspend or dismiss the athlete. It controls the method directing athletes' performance, through training requirements set down by the national coach or technical director, the requirement that athletes attend specified camps and competitions, and the general instruction that athletes conduct themselves for the "benefit" of the program. Lest there be any doubt, these obligations are enumerated in an "NSO/athlete agreement," which Sport Canada requires both parties to sign as a condition of carded-athlete assistance. According to the 1984–85 agreement, athletes are obliged to:

- provide an annual training chart and monthly updates to the national coach
- participate in all mandatory training camps and competitions
- dress in the required uniform while traveling as a member of the team
- avoid intoxication at training camps and competitions
- submit to random doping control testing upon request
- avoid competitions in which South Africans are participating
- participate in up to two days of "reasonable non-commercial promotional activities as requested by Sport Canada"
- refrain from airing complaints to the media until all established grievance procedures are exhausted.

If the athlete fails to maintain satisfactory training or to honor these commitments, the NSO may recommend withdrawal of card status and benefits.[42]

The only point at issue is whether the payments made under the program constitute a form of remuneration. Analysis of the objective conditions suggests that they do. Those coaches who supervise national team athletes on a daily basis openly use the powers of card nomination and withdrawal as an instrumental control. "We're paying them, so we have every right to demand a rigorous training commitment from them," Canadian Women's Field Hockey Coach Dr. Marina van der Merve has said.[43] Athletes, too, understand the system as a *quid pro quo*. An estimated 60 percent depend on carding for their livelihood, having no other income except family contributions. These circumstances, plus the presence of the three other indicators, lead us to conclude that carded-athlete assistance meets the established tests of employment. Given that Sport Canada sets the general conditions and performance standards and pays the athletes, it would suggest that Sport Canada, and not the NSO, is the effective employer.

To date, however, Sport Canada and the NSOs deny that what they call "financial aid" constitutes remuneration. In fact, although that portion of "aid" paid toward living costs approximates the minimum wage (for a forty-hour week) in most provinces, Sport Canada has obtained an understanding from the Department of National Revenue that carded-athlete assistance not be taxed. It may well be argued that this designation benefits athletes by protecting them from the tax collector and possible investigation by Olympic authorities for "open professionalism." Defenders of the status quo also can point out that several "natural justice" protections recently have been added to the system in response to athletes' complaints. NSOs now are required to publish the criteria for card nomination at least ten months prior to the commencement of the eligibility cycle and to provide an appeal mechanism consistent with "natural justice" or "due process" for athletes who believe they have met the criteria but are not nominated for cards. The same requirements govern discipline and the withdrawal of cards. At the same time, Sport Canada has made a concerted effort to clarify the language of the "NSO/Athlete Agreement" and other regulations governing athletes' lives in order to reduce the potential for the infringement of rights inherent in undue discretion.[44]

Despite these advantages, the interests of athletes would be better served if the designation of carded-athlete assistance were brought into line with its objective conditions and recognized that the program creates athletic employment. First, the change would give athletes the additional protection of minimum standards legislation and the possibility of seeking coverage for worker's compensation. Second, it would give athletes the common-law safeguard that prevents employers from dismissing an employee summarily without cause, and a ready remedy in court should that occur. There is still no guarantee that every NSO will establish the "natural" justice procedures required by Sport Canada. Third, it would give athletes a much better chance to influence, through negotiation with Sport Canada and the NSOs, the payments they receive and the conditions under which they train and compete. While individual and collective bargaining theoretically are possible under the present system, they are discouraged by the denial of the employment relationship. The present arrangement helps characterize Sport Canada as a philanthropic benefactor that is challenged only by the uninformed and ungrateful. Even if athletes were to initiate proposals for change, there is no requirement that Sport Canada and the NSOs have to listen: Athletes could not enjoy the protections of labor legislation without first being recognized as employees.

Not every reader will agree, but we believe individuals and public policy are best served if the terms and conditions of human labor, even athletic labor performed for the state in the name of the community, are determined mutually by employee and employer. For example, a monthly stipend of $650 plus expenses seems princely to those of an earlier generation who vied for Olympic honors with no financial assistance whatsoever, but in terms of the importance the Canadian Government now places on winning performances and the salaries commanded by athletes in the private sector, it is arguably a niggardly sum. It compares unfavorably to the $1,000 and $1,500 monthly stipends the Canadian Government pays to graduate students and artists, respectively, and in these cases the government has made no effort to control recipients' activity. In the absence of a well-established labor market and widely accepted criteria for salary determination, it is essential that the payments for carding be negotiated by athletes and Sport Canada rather than unilaterally imposed.

Whether it is done by voluntary association under the present system or by an athletes' union operating within the framework of federal labor legislation, there is some precedent for collective bargaining by Canadian "amateur" athletes. In 1975 the carded athletes banded together to seek higher living grants, threatening political action and a possible boycott of the 1976 Olympic Games in Montreal if their demands were not met. The campaign won them an additional $1.6 million in benefits.[45] In 1984 track-and-field athletes formed their own union. Although it has not sought negotiations with either Sport Canada or the CTFA, its very formation led to several significant improvements in CTFA-athlete relations.[46] In addition, Canadian athletes can draw on the experience of university faculty, graduate students, and artists, as well as professional athletes in commerical sport who, despite the highly individual, creative nature of their work, have bargained collectively and formed unions to enhance their lives.

In this chapter we have argued that athletes on athletic scholarships in the United States and on carded-athlete assistance in Canada are employees, although their employers refuse to acknowledge this reality. In the former case we recommended that colleges either return to a truly amateur model, thereby giving athletes freedom to control the degree and the nature of their athletic involvement, or be prepared to grant athletes the full range of rights and protections available to other employees. Among these rights is the right to negotiate individually or collectively over financial compensation. We view Olympic reforms that have allowed athletes to benefit financially from their athletic labor as the wave of the future in high-performance sport. The NCAA schools that intend to continue to employ athletes to produce sports spectacles would do well to follow the IOC's lead.[47]

The situation of carded athletes in Canada is in some respects less exploitative than college sport in the United States. In terms of both due process and financial support, Canadian athletes have been able to establish rights and protections that are unheard of in American colleges and universities. Nonetheless, by clinging tenaciously to the amateur myth, Sport Canada is able to insist that athletes shoulder the responsibilities of employees while being denied concomitant rights and protections. Thus we would support efforts to gain legal recognition of the employment status of Canadian carded athletes. That the objective conditions of employment exist already seems to us to be undeniable.

CONCLUSION

It remains for us to consider how these proposals for expanding athletes' rights can be implemented and to position ourselves in the debate on the role of government. Athletes' rights can be implemented by employer initiative, collective bargaining, court decision, legislation, and government regulation. Ideally, they should be established by mutual employer-athlete agreement so that both parties can influence directly the form and substance they will take. But if agreement cannot be obtained by negotiation, it may well be necessary for athletes to seek relief in court or pursue legislative change, which raises the question of the role of the state. Many in the sports community oppose the intervention of judges and politicians into "the private world of sport" on the ideological grounds that "politics and sport do not mix" and "the government which governs least, governs best."[48] We do not agree. While we hold no illusions about either the neutrality or the competence of the state, we can only describe as a mystification the notion that government has no place in sport. In both the United States and Canada, elected federal, state/provincial, and local governments allocate millions of dollars to sports, and they privilege the activity in a number of other ways, from special legislation to award ceremonies. In short, sports are a significant *public* enterprise and athletes (as well as coaches, officials, and other sport participants) have every right to explore all the avenues of public policy determination in pursuing their goals.

So the question for us is essentially strategic. As we already have discussed, a favorable court ruling can have a salutory effect on a regulatory body like the NCAA. A legislative bill often provides opportunity for bringing problems before a wider public. Senator Ernie Chambers of the Nebraska State Legislature has had some success with this latter strategy. Chambers introduced Legislative Bill 764, which would prohibit state colleges and universities from discontinuing the scholarship of an injured athlete if he or she is making satisfactory academic progress.[49] He also proposed that the state extend worker's compensation coverage to injured athletes.[50] Not only did his efforts attract national media attention, but the Nebraska Legislature ultimately passed an amended version of Bill 764, which guarantees that scholarships cannot be taken away from injured athletes and provides college athletes with additional disability protection. In this instance, legislative action has won protections for athletes that NCAA regulation had previously denied them.

Another example of a relatively successful legislative intervention in the area of sports is the Amateur Sports Act of 1978.[51] After years of bitter jurisdictional conflict between the NCAA and the AAU over control of international competition, the Congress was compelled to intervene. The resulting legislation addresses issues ranging from the "eligibility of individual athletes for international competition to procedures for complaints, challenges and arbitration."[52] Before the passage of this act, athletes often were torn between their desire to compete internationally and the threat that doing so would lead to their being declared ineligible by one or another governing body. The Amateur Sports Act, by eliminating most jurisdictional disputes, has helped to protect the amateur athlete's interest in participating. Although the act has been criticized for not directly providing for an Athlete's Bill of Rights,[53] it does demonstrate that even small gains often require government intervention.

Admittedly, no single strategy is sufficient in itself. Athletic disputes rarely lend themselves to judicial test cases, and even when they do the costs may be prohibitive. A well-publicized legislative hearing can certainly enhance public awareness, but given the bread-and-butter priorities of most elected officials, sports bills rarely get to the point of final decision.[54] The responsiveness of each of these mechanisms can also vary significantly from jurisdiction to jurisdiction. Nonetheless, we would encourage athletes to pursue each of these avenues simultaneously and not be deterred by those who would manipulate the amateur label to suit their economic and political interests. Only by careful and energetic efforts to dispel the amateur myth can athletes and those who attempt to defend athletes' rights expect to get a fair hearing, regardless of the forum in which this debate is carried out.

NOTES

1. Board of Regents of the University of Oklahoma v. National Collegiate Athletic Association, 52 LW 4928.

2. Carl Lewis, for example, is in high demand for track meets all over the world. He may be offered $10,000 for one meet to run a 60-meter dash. Money is paid to his agent and deposited in a trust fund. Lewis's expenses are paid out of this fund. Lewis, Billy Olsen, and Dwight Stones have bought homes with money from these expense accounts and may draw all of the remaining money out of the trust funds when amateur competition is completed. See Blackie Sherrod, "Our Phony Athletics Code Abets Dishonesty," The NCAA News, vol. 18 (April 18, 1984), p.2.

3. Exceptions to this can be found in the "jockraker" literature published during the youth radicalization of the late 1960s and early 1970s. See, for example, Jack Scott, The Athletic Revolution (New York: Macmillan, 1971); David Meggyesy, Out of Their League (Berkeley: Ramparts Press, 1971).

4. Joseph Pieper, Leisure: The Basis of Culture (New York: New American Library, 1963); Sebastian deGrazia, Of Time, Work and Leisure (New York: Anchor Books, 1964); Joffre Dumazedier, Toward a Society of Leisure (New York: The Free Press, 1967); Richard Kraus, Recreation and Leisure in Modern Society (New York: Appleton-Century-Crofts, 1971).

5. Charles Brightbill, The Challenge of Leisure (Englewood Cliffs, N. J.: Prentice-Hall, 1963), p. 3.

6. Bennett M. Berger, "The Sociology of Leisure: Some Suggestions," in Erwin O. Smigel, ed., Work and Leisure (New York: College and University Press, 1963); pp. 21–40; see also Richard Gruneau's discussion of "the paradox of play" in Class, Sports and Social Development (Amherst: University of Massachusetts, 1983), pp. 20–23.

7. Ibid., p. 29.

8. Amitai Etzioni, Modern Organizations (Englewood Cliffs, N.J.: Prentice-Hall, 1964), p. 59.

9. Berger, "The Sociology of Leisure," p. 29.

10. Although amateurs cannot be said to have economic rights vested in their athletic participation, there is a growing belief that opportunities to sport and physical education should be considered basic human rights, available to all. See the International Charter of Physical Education and Sport, proclaimed by UNESCO in 1978.

11. David L. Westby and Allen L. Sack, "The Commercialization and Functional Rationalization of College Football," Journal of Higher Education 47 (November-December 1976); 625–47.

12. For an excellent discussion of the rationalization of sport and its relationship to industrialization, see Jean Marie Brohm, Sport: A Prison of Measured Time (London: Ink Links, 1978).

13. Donald L. Shuck, "Administration of Amateur Athletics: The Time for an Amateur Athlete's Bill of Rights Has Arrived," Fordham Law Review (October 1979): 66–67.

14. John C. Weistart and Cym H. Lowell, The Law of Sports (New York: Bobbs-Merrill, 1979).

15. W. R. Dillmar, State Workman's Compensation Laws (New York: Oceana Publications, 1959), pp. 12–21.

16. Coleman v. Western Michigan University, 336 N.W. 2d. 224 (1983).

17. Askew v. Macomber, 398 Mich. 212, 247 N.W. 2d. 288 (1976).

18. National Collegiate Athletic Association, NCAA Manual, Article 3, Section 4, Part b–1 (Shawnee Mission, Kansas: National Collegiate Athletic Association, 1982), p. 19.

19. Charles Neinas, Statement during panel discussion, "College and University Athletics: The Legal Impact of Financial Aid," Law and Amateur Sports II, Conference Sponsored by Indiana School of Law, Bloomington, February 10–11, 1983.

20. Decision of the George H. Barber Subcommittee of the University Scholarship Committee in the Case of James R. Mosier, January 7, 1982.

21. Coleman v. Western Michigan University, 336 N.W. 2d. 226 (1983).

22. Carolyn E. Thomas, "The Golden Girl Syndrome: Thoughts on a Training Ethic," NAPEHE, Annual Conference Proceedings, vol. 2 (1980), p. 139.

23. Morgan v. Win Schuler's Restaurant, 64 Mich. App. 37, 234 N.W. 2d. 885 (1975).

24. Coleman v. Western Michigan University, 336 N.W. 2d. 226 (1983).

25. Rensing v. Indiana State University, 444 N.E. 2d. 1170 (1983).

26. Rensing v. Indiana State University, 437 N.E. 2d. 78 (1982).

27. Rensing v. Indiana State University, 444 N.E. 2d. 1170 (1983).

28. National Collegiate Athletic Association, *NCAA Manual*, Article 3, Section 1, Part a–1.

29. Ibid. Article 3, Section 4, Part d.

30. Mark Alan Atkinson, "Worker's Compensation and College Athletics: Should Universities Be Responsible for Athletes Who Incur Serious Injury?" *Journal of College and University Law*, no. 2 (Fall 1983–84):203.

31. Coleman v. Western Michigan University, 336 N.W. 2d. 226 (1983).

32. Board of Regents of the University of Oklahoma v. National Collegiate Athletic Association, 52 LW 4937.

33. Weistart and Lowell, Law of Sports, pp. 8–9.

34. Ibid., p. 18.

35. It is clear that this nonprofessional model works with considerable success at Division III schools and in the Ivy League. Athletes in these schools often are highly recruited and they devote many hours to their sport, but when conflict emerges between sport and the demands of the classroom, athletes can give up sports and retain financial aid.

36. The developments to 1974 are summarized by former IOC president Lord Killanin in "Eligibility and Amateurism," in Killanin and Rodda, eds., *The Olympic Games* (New York: Collier-Macmillan, 1976), pp. 143–53. The present rule is stated in International Olympic Committee, *Olympic Charter 1984*. For the background to most recent changes, see IOC, *The Official Report of the 11th Olympic Congress*.

37. James Christie, "Five Canadians Ineligible, IOC rules," *The Globe and Mail* (February 7, 1984).

38. See, for example, the Final Document of the Annual Conference of the Sports Leaders of the Socialist Countries, P'yongyang, North Korea, September 1983.

39. These developments are summarized by Eric F. Broom and Richard S. P. Baka, *Canadian Governments and Sport* (Calgary: CAHPER, 1979); see also William Hallett, "Federal Involvement in the Development of Sport in Canada," and Donald MacIntosh, "Bill C-131 Revisited," papers published in *Proceedings of the 5th Canadian Symposium on the History of Sport and Physical Education* (Toronto: University of Toronto, 1982).

40. Sport Canada, *The Athlete Assistance Program: A Guide . . .1984–85.* (Ottawa: Supply and Services, 1984). We are grateful to Abby Hoffman, director, Sport Canada, and John Brooks, manager, Athlete Assistance Program, for their help.

41. Marine Pipeline and Dredging Ltd. v. Canadian Oil Ltd. (1964), 46 D.L.R. (2nd) 495, 502 (Alta, S.C., Appellate Division per Kane, J. A.).

42. Sport Canada, "1984 NSO/Athlete Agreement."

43. Interview with Dr. van der Merve, April 28, 1984.

44. Sport Canada, *The Athlete Assistance Program*; and Bruce Kidd and Mary Eberts, *Athletes' Rights in Canada* (Toronto: Ministry of Tourism and Recreation, 1982).

45. See Abby Hoffman and Bruce Kidd, "Time is Up," *SWIM* (May 1975); and Doug Gilbert, "Our Olympic Athletes Broke and Embittered," and "COA Boosts Aid to Olympians," *The Gazette* (June 4 and June 13, 1975).

46. Interview with Ann Peel, executive member, Canadian Track and Field Athletes' Association (September 10, 1984).

47. In a recent *Sports Illustrated* article, Walter Byers, Executive Director of the NCAA, acknowledged a growing public acceptance of the relaxation of amateurism in the Olympics. Byers argues that some "big-time" sports schools might well decide to go "the Olympic way. They'll say 'Look, we can't police this thing, and there's nothing wrong with it. Let's take off the cap and let the players get what's needed and let's go.'" Walter Byers, quoted in Jack McCallum, "Why Is This Man Saying Things He's Saying?" *Sports Illustrated* (September 17, 1984).

48. Thomas D. McIntyre, "Sport and the State: A Liberal Perspective," *Proceedings of the 1980 Annual Conference of the National Association for Physical Education in Higher Education* (Champaign, Ill. Human Kinetics, 1981), pp. 251–55; or Bruce Kidd, "The Canadian State and Sport: The Dilemma of Intervention," ibid., pp. 239–50.

49. John Whitesides, "Bill Would Protect Grant of Hurt Athlete," *Omaha World Herald* (January 25, 1984), p. 37.

50. Ibid., "Athletes Compensation Bill Is Advanced to Legislature," *Omaha World Herald* (January 26, 1984), p. 35.

51. James A. R. Nafziger, "The Amateur Sports Act of 1978," *Brigham Young University Law Review* (1983), pp. 47–100.

52. Ibid., p. 98.

53. Shuck, "Administration of Amateur Athletics."

54. Arthur T. Johnson, "Congress and Professional Sports: 1951–1978," *Annals of the American Academy of Political and Social Science* 445 (September 1979), p. 114.

4

The Impact of Title IX on Women's Intercollegiate Sports

Linda Jean Carpenter

In 1972 it appeared that only feast and plenty would abound in the future of women's intercollegiate athletics. The Association for Intercollegiate Athletics for Women (AIAW) had emerged as the national governing body for intercollegiate sport for women. There was a sense of being in the first surge of a continuing wave of enthusiasm, participation, and acceptance of women's intercollegiate athletics.

The 1972 image of a bright future for women's athletics was made even brighter by the passage of Title IX of the Education Amendments of 1972, which barred sex bias in "any education program or activity receiving federal financial assistance."[1] Title IX's language closely paralleled that found in Title VI of the 1964 Civil Rights Act, which barred discrimination on the basis of race, religion, and national origin. Title IX's antidiscrimination intent reflected a continuing congressional policy that was expanded to the handicapped a year later in Section 504 of the Rehabilitation Act of 1973 and to the aged in the Age Discrimination Act of 1975. It is undeniable that 1972 was a signal year of good promise for women's intercollegiate athletics. More than a decade later, however, we find that women's athletics has evolved quite differently than predicted.

During the years since 1972 the three main forces in women's intercollegiate athletics—the National Collegiate Athletic Association (NCAA), the AIAW, and Title IX—demonstrated an unusually malleable interrelationship. None was a proponent of inequity. None was an opponent of sports participation. Yet, it is doubtful that any other mixture of forces could have effected so much change, both positive and negative, in women's intercollegiate athletics. The change effected was not only on women's athletics, but upon each of the three acting forces as well.

GOVERNANCE AND LEADERSHIP

The congressional policy of encoding various civil rights guarantees and using the potential withdrawal of federal funds as enforcement muscle has had massive impact upon the policies and, ultimately, the existence of the governance structures of intercollegiate athletics. Before Title IX, the mostly-male NCAA seemed disinterested in assuming any major leadership role in women's athletics.[2] The AIAW grew from a membership of 278 institutions in its charter year of 1971–72 to 508 two years later, and to a peak of 970 in 1979–80.[3]

Soon after its passage, Title IX's impact began to be felt by both the NCAA and the AIAW. This was true even though the regulations for the implementation of Title IX were slow in coming,[4] and once they were formulated they seemed to raise more questions than they answered. Did Title IX mandate the merger of previously separate men's and women's departments of athletics? Did it mean that for every dollar spent on men's basketball a dollar needed to be spent on women's basketball? Did it mean coed teams must exist in all sports or, perhaps, did it require separate but equal teams? Did it require that a female must be allowed to try out for a male team and vice versa? Did Title IX require that the NCAA enter the governance of women's athletics?

Even in the face of so much uncertainty, Walter Byers, the NCAA executive director, reflected the fears of many when he said that Title IX would mean the "possible doom of intercollegiate sports."[5] The fear was grounded on the notion that bringing equity to women's programs would mean extracting funds from men's budgets. In response to this fear, the NCAA adopted a sequence of alternating, seemingly inconsistent policies that produced a strong lobbying effort on behalf of the position that Title IX did not apply to athletic programs.

Early in 1974, the NCAA assistant executive director and a group of male athletic directors visited the Department of Health, Education and Welfare (HEW) lawyer Gwen Gregory, whose responsibility it was to design the Title IX physical education and athletics guidelines. At the same point, the NCAA Committee on Women's Athletics, which had some of its members serving on an NCAA special committee lobbying against the inclusion of athletics in Title IX, was reconstituted. At a March 1974 meeting, the following lobbying efforts were reported:

> The steps the NCAA had taken after their meeting with [HEW attorney] Gwen Gregory [were reported]. Byers indicated that they had substantial input to [Secretary] Weinberger and that there had been enough heat generated by NCAA presidents so that Weinberger had instructed Gregory . . . to reconsider certain sections of the draft copy [of the regulations]. . . . In addition, the NCAA has been in contact with Ann Armstrong and Dave Mead in the White

House . . . who evidently will have the responsibility for screening the guidelines before Nixon signs. . . . The point the NCAA is making [in its lobbying efforts] is that athletics are outside [Title IX]. . . . The NCAA is frank to admit the tremendous lobbying effort they have been making to have athletics removed from the Guidelines because they feel they cannot exist with the present interpretation.[6]

The NCAA Joint Legislative Committee on Athletics and Education also described lobbying efforts. In its report to the NCAA Executive Committee in May of the same year, the committee reported:

The Association (NCAA) is working diligently toward changes in Title IX regulations as they pertain to women's sports on college campuses. Seemingly, a majority of senators and congressmen agree with the NCAA position that the basic law was not intended to give the Department of Health, Education and Welfare control over the intercollegiate athletic programs. Confusion appears to reign within HEW regarding interpretations of the legislation, and various women's activist groups have complicated the issues by disseminating false and misleading information.[7]

When it became generally accepted that Title IX in fact would apply to athletics, the NCAA launched a strong campaign supporting the "Tower Amendment," which sought to exclude revenue sports, such as football, from the jurisdiction of Title IX. Not only had Title IX legislation affected the NCAA, but the NCAA was now making an effort to affect the legislative expression of public policy by offering interpretations of Title IX. The Tower Amendment, introduced on May 20, 1974, passed the Senate, but it died in the House-Senate Conference Committee on June 11, in part because of the lobbying efforts of the AIAW and various women's groups. The NCAA urged the House-Senate Conference Committee to reconsider its decision by noting:

Draft regulations of HEW would severely damage intercollegiate athletic programs of the nation's colleges which are already sorely pressed with financial problems. HEW is proposing an unwarranted and deep intrusion of government into institutional management and the imposition of arbitrary rules unnecessary to assure equal opportunity in sports for men and women. NCAA colleges are developing sound intercollegiate programs for women based upon the extent of their desire to participate and attempts to manage the intercollegiate programs of our 700 members through Federal directives can only lead to chaos for men's and women's athletics.[8]

From this point through the issuance of the final regulations for Title IX on July 21, 1975, the NCAA continued to pursue strenuous lobbying efforts directed at HEW as well as at Capitol Hill.[9] Emotions ran high, and the amplitude of the lobbying effort was felt. Gwen Gregory of HEW charged that "the NCAA is determined to sabotage Title IX. . . . [T]hey're throwing in red herring, asking us to be arbitrary. A good deal of the reaction so far to Title IX has been panicky and alarmist, and some of it deliberately distorted."[10]

Following the failure of the Tower Amendment, the NCAA pursued its advocacy activities to protect its constituency from the perceived harm of Title IX. It did so not only by continued lobbying, but also through the courts. In *NCAA* v. *Califano*,[11] for instance, the NCAA argued the inapplicability of Title IX regulations to athletics based on several constitutional issues.[12]

In apparent contradiction to the arguments put before the courts and Congress, the NCAA decided to enter the realm of women's athletics governance. Its justification was that such a move was mandated by Title IX and to do less would be to violate its responsibilities under Title IX.[13] Some have intimated that the NCAA adopted this posture because to do so would at least guarantee the NCAA control over women's athletics if in fact it was inevitable that Title IX would apply to athletics. Whatever the motivation, this new posture of the NCAA was the beginning of the end for the AIAW. The demise of the AIAW, which had experienced substantial growth in membership and television revenue, found itself in competition for both with the financially superior NCAA. Soon the AIAW lost both to an attractive NCAA strategy that included such things as offering to pay travel expenses for championship participants and encouraging buyers of broadcast rights to the popular men's basketball games to purchase also the broadcast rights to women's events through the NCAA.

The AIAW filed an antitrust suit against the NCAA[14] in a final effort to retain control of women's athletics programs within an organization mostly made up of women. Upon the filing of the suit, the AIAW ceased operations, and upon the denial of its appeal in the Spring of 1984, the AIAW ceased to exist.

Thus the growth of women's athletics and the subsequent fear of substantial drain on the budgets of men's programs to fund that growth set in motion a series of events that led to the demise of the AIAW. Certainly the death of the AIAW was not consistent with either the spirit or letter of Title IX. Indeed, it is possible that the AIAW would have met its demise even in the absence of Title IX, a victim of budgetary constraints, of external pressures from agencies such as the NCAA, and of internal pressures born of impatience for growth and confusion about the future identity of women's sports.

The AIAW since its inception faced a sequence of events that had a power and momentum that would have swept away all but the most securely anchored organizations. If Title IX had not been one of those events, however, the AIAW would no doubt have had a greater longevity, and thus perhaps it would have enjoyed sufficient time to explore more fully the possibility and advisability of a unique identity for women's athletics.

The notion that men's athletics is the quintessential paradigm on which all athletic programs should be designed by all right-thinking groups is difficult to support. Women might have designed a program that reflected a commitment to a broad base of participation, a great variety of sports, and several levels of participation. It is possible that a program designed for women by women would have been able to develop a program of scholarships and a system of recruitment that would have encouraged integrity rather than dishonesty. Perhaps women would have adopted a personnel policy that would acknowledge the importance of women athletes being able to have sufficient role models of women as leaders in the administration of athletic programs. With time, it is possible that female leaders would have identified and developed solutions for problems (such as illegal recruiting) that remain unresolved today.

However, if the AIAW had survived the effects of Title IX, its programs might have become a mirror image of the commercialized and professionalized men's variety. In reality, Title IX functioned to produce women's programs that were similar to, rather than uniquely distinct from, the organization and administration of men's programs. Part of this similarity can be attributed to the organizational nature of the NCAA, but another part is the result of the desire of some women athletes and coaches to use Title IX to follow the NCAA scholarship model. For instance, one group of women students threatened a Title IX lawsuit against the infant AIAW if it continued to adhere to its initial nonscholarship stance.[15] Thus, because of Title IX rather than because of a philosophical decision, the AIAW took its first step toward a sameness with the NCAA on the scholarship issue. Title IX also has brought about a sameness in the leadership of both men's and women's programs by providing the means for men to enter and dominate leadership positions within women's programs. In addition, the variety of sport offerings and access to junior-varsity experiences, which long characterized women's programs, was to some degree abandoned in the face of budgetary pressures partly induced by the desire to maximize competitiveness rather than participation in women's programs.[16]

It is true that the historical design of women's programs reflects a lack of access to financial and facility support. However, it also is true that the historical design was in part the result of philosophical, gender-related decisions. It is difficult to deny the possibility that with the access to support promised by Title IX and a freedom from the external pressures for sameness imposed in the infancy of the AIAW, the design of women's athletics would not have been molded in the NCAA's image; rather, it would have evolved in a new image developed by women for women.

TITLE IX PLUS TWELVE YEARS

Participation Opportunities

Aside from whatever effect Title IX has had on the governance and design of intercollegiate athletics, has it accomplished its purpose of equity of participation for women? Certainly the opportunity for women athletes to participate in intercollegiate sports has increased markedly since 1972. For example, data from a longitudinal study by Acosta and Carpenter show that in 1977, one year before the Title IX compliance date, the number of sports offered women was 5.61 per school. In 1980 the number had grown to 6.48, and in 1984 it had grown to 6.9 in NCAA schools. Indeed, the number of intercollegiate women participants has grown from 16,000 in 1966–67 to more than 150,000 in 1983–84. This represents a growth of nearly 1,000 percent.[17] Table 4.1 reports the changes in sport opportunities for college women between 1977 and 1984.

Although participation opportunities have grown, leadership positions held by women have decreased. Although unclear at the beginning, Title IX has been determined by judicial decisions to apply to employment as well as participation access. Despite this, the percentage of women's teams coached by a female is less now than before Title IX. Between 1977 and 1984, nearly 4.5 percent of female coaches were replaced by males. In 1984 only 53.8 percent of women's teams were coached by a female head coach compared to 58.2 percent in 1977–78. The loss of female coaches is particularly striking when it is realized that prior to Title IX studies have variously reported that 80 to 90 percent of the coaches were female, while few, if any, women were found in the coaching ranks of men's teams.[18] In fact, it makes news even in 1984 when a female is appointed as coach over a Division I men's team.

The decrease is not limited to coaching positions. In 1984 more than 86.5 percent (80 percent in 1980) of women's intercollegiate athletics programs were under the supervision of a male head athletic director, and 38 percent (30 percent in 1980) had no female involved in the administration at all (Table 4.2). This is a dramatic change from the pre-Title IX era, when most women's programs had female leadership.[19]

It is difficult to find public support for inequity. Surely most would lend support to the notion that equity of access to educational programs is an American ideal and as such is a proper area of national concern. Pragmatically, whether governmental intervention is appropriate is determined in part by the nature of the results of that intervention. Without intervention, girls and women would have continued to find facilities and financial support for athletics generally inaccessible. In contrast, it might be argued that in the areas of campus leadership and national governance of sports Title IX's spirit of equity has been circumvented by creative uses of the letter of the law.

Table 4.1 Sport Offerings for Female Intercollegiate Athletes, 1977–1984

	Percentage of Schools Offering Each Sport						
	83/84	82/83	81/82	80/81	79/80	78/79	77/78
	N=738	N=738	N=664	N=664	N=609	N=609	N=609
Archery	1.2	1.6	1.8	2.2	2.8	3.3	3.0
Badminton	1.9	2.2	3.6	4.4	5.4	6.1	5.9
Basketball	95.7	93.8	97.3	95.9	97.5	96.4	90.3
Bowling	1.9	1.9	2.9	3.3	3.6	3.6	3.4
Crew	6.9	7.0	7.4	7.7	7.2	6.9	6.9
Cross Country	64.0	59.9	59.5	54.0	46.6	39.6	29.4
Fencing	8.0	8.0	10.4	9.8	9.6	9.5	9.8
Field Hockey	30.2	30.3	34.6	36.1	37.1	38.2	36.3
Golf	20.5	19.8	19.7	18.5	24.1	20.8	19.9
Gymnastics	18.6	20.0	22.1	23.0	25.6	28.2	25.9
Ice Hockey	2.8	2.4	2.9	2.9	1.8	1.5	1.3
LaCrosse	13.5	13.3	13.5	13.7	13.9	13.8	13.0
Riding	2.6	2.4	2.4	2.2	3.1	2.5	2.0
Riflery	2.8	2.7	1.8	1.9	3.4	3.3	3.8
Sailing	2.7	2.8	2.7	2.4	1.9	2.5	2.3
Skiing	4.9	5.0	5.7	5.4	5.2	4.6	3.6
Soccer	18.7	16.4	16.4	12.5	8.2	4.6	2.8
Softball	65.5	65.6	67.1	65.6	62.3	58.9	48.4
Squash	2.0	2.0	2.9	2.7	2.8	2.5	2.3
Swimming-Diving	44.8	42.5	49.1	48.6	46.9	44.8	41.0
Synchronized Swimming	1.5	1.3	2.7	3.3	3.2	3.4	3.3
Tennis	82.6	82.6	85.5	85.4	88.6	86.5	80.0
Track	58.7	57.2	62.0	59.3	58.6	54.3	46.1
Volleyball	84.0	83.6	85.7	84.9	87.8	85.9	80.1

Note: The return rate for 1982/83 and 1983/84 was 69 percent of all NCAA and previous AIAW members (N=1076). The return rate for 1980/81 and 1981/82 was 71 percent (N=937). The return rate for 1977/78, 1978/79, and 1979/80 was 66 percent (N=915).

Regardless of the appropriateness of governmental intervention in this case, it cannot be denied that the face of women's intercollegiate athletics has been drastically and irrevocably changed by it.

Judicial Interpretation

Even though drastic changes have been wrought in the name of Title IX, in 1984 its very jurisdiction over athletics is still in doubt as a result of the decision in *Grove City* v. *Bell*,[20] which culminated a series of widely discussed and sometimes inconsistently decided cases. Among them is *North Haven Board of Education* v. *Bell*,[21] which affirmed the applicability of Title IX to employment practices. In *North Haven* the Supreme Court also noted that Title IX was "program-specific," but it declined to define "program." The "program-specific" question asks if the Department of Education's office of

---

Table 4.2   Gender of Personnel in Athletic Programs' Administrative Structure, 1984

I.   In 86.5 percent of all coed colleges and universities, women's athletic programs are
     under the control of a male athletic director (83 percent if all-female schools are added).

     Percentages by subgroupings:

     86.5 percent of coed NCAA schools have male head directors (84.2 percent including
     all-female schools have male head athletic directors).

     86.5 percent of coed ex-AIAW schools have male head directors (79 percent if all-female
     schools are added).

     90 percent of NCAA *Division 1* schools have a male head athletic director (no difference
     whether coed or coed plus all-female).

     85.2 percent of coed NCAA *Division 2* schools have a male head (84.1 percent if all-
     female schools are added).

     83 percent of coed NCAA *Division 3* schools have a male head (78.8 percent if all-
     female schools are added).

II. In 37.9 percent of all coed college and universities, no female is involved in the
     administration of the women's athletic programs (36.4 percent if all-female schools are
     added).

     Percentages by subgroupings:

     32.4 percent of coed NCAA schools have no female in their athletic administration (31.6
     percent if all-female schools are added).

     58.8 percent of coed ex-AIAW schools have no female in their athletic administration
     (53.7 percent if all-female schools are added).

     21.4 percent of coed NCAA *Division 1* schools have no female in their athletic
     administration (21.4 percent if all-female schools are added).

     37.4 percent of coed NCAA *Division 2* schools have no female in their athletic
     administration (36.9 percent if all-female schools are added).

     39.2 percent of coed NCAA *Division 3* schools have no female in their athletic
     administration (36.9 percent if all-female schools are added).

Source: R. Vivian Acosta and Linda Jean Carpenter, "Changing Status of Women in
Intercollegiate Athletics, 1977–1984," paper presented at the AAHPERD National Convention (1984).

Civil Rights is limited in its enforcement jurisdiction to the specific subunit of
the college actually receiving federal funds or if the jurisdiction is institution-
wide.

Other cases have supported the "program-specific" notion, including
Othen v. *Ann Arbor School Board*[22] (even though the case was limited to a
consideration of attorney's fees); *Hillsdale* v. *Department of HEW*[23] (college's
receipt of federal student financial aid does not subject the entire college to
Title IX, but rather only the college's federal financial aid program); and
University of Richmond v. *Bell*[24] (in the absence of direct aid to the athletics

department, evidence of indirect aid, such as student athletes' receipt of federal financial aid, and a substantial percentage of student aides in the athletic office receiving salaries from federal college work-study funding was insufficient to trigger Title IX jurisdiction). Thus the exemption of substructures within an institution seemed to rule.

On the other hand, *Haffer* v. *Temple University*[25] suggested that indirect aid received by athletics was sufficient to trigger jurisdiction. Temple University decided not to appeal, and thus it is unclear if the institution-wide jurisdiction of Title IX would have been upheld in this instance.

The progress through these and other cases involved an evolution of argument from the "institutional approach" found in Title VI cases, such as *Board of Public Instruction of Taylor County* v. *Finch*,[26] to the "infected" theory, where discrimination found in one non-federally funded area infects a federally funded area elsewhere; to the "benefit" theory, where federal money may benefit the entire institution by relieving the university from the burden of committing its funds; and finally, to the "free-up" theory, which states that any infusion of federal money frees up the institution's general fund. This was the finding in *Bob Jones University* v. *Johnson*.[27]

Each of these theories was formulated to support a broad enforcement capability by the Department of Education. However, following the government's failure to appeal the *Richmond* case in 1982 and the almost immediate dropping of its investigation at the College of William and Mary, it became apparent that the Department of Education had changed its enforcement policy. This change in policy would be seen in the latter stages of the *Grove City* case in 1984.

Grove City College is a small, private institution that accepts no direct federal assistance. The only federal dollars found on its campus arrive in the form of federal grants (BEOG-Pell) received by about 10 percent of its students. The Department of Education held that those dollars were within the meaning of "federal funds" and, thus, the college was required to sign a letter assuring its compliance with Title IX. The college refused to do so.

The Department of Education then moved to enforce compliance by withdrawing the student grants, even though all agreed there was no evidence of discrimination. Several affected students and the college administration joined in a suit for the reinstatement of the grants. Justice Powell's opinion in the case notes that "One would have thought that the Department [of Education], confronted as it is with cases of national importance that involved actual discrimination, would have respected the independence and admirable record of this college. But common sense and good judgment failed to prevail."[28]

As the *Grove City* case traversed the path to the Supreme Court, the enforcement policy changed. Even granting that the extent of violation committed by Grove City College could be only the tiniest molehill on the mountain of discrimination, the Department of Education allowed—indeed, encouraged—a narrow, precedent-setting reading of Title IX when the case arrived at the Supreme Court. This urging was not for the benefit of Grove City College but rather was an expression of the newly formed policy against vigorous enforcement of antidiscrimination legislation. Thus a change in how the words of Title IX were to be *defined* was instituted.

Regardless of the appropriateness of governmental intervention in the area of civil rights, if government does intervene, the meaning of black letter (statutory) law should remain constant between and within administrations. Even though the strenuousness of enforcement might vary according to who or what political party is in office, as long as a statute is on the books, the definitions of its terms should be unambiguous. How else can those finding themselves under the jurisdiction of such a statute act in ways that are predictably within guidelines of compliance?

Despite the lack of magnitude of Grove City College's noncompliance, the case has been heralded as a turning point for Title IX as well as for the entire family of civil rights legislation. The Supreme Court found it necessary to address two main questions in *Grove City*. First, can indirect funds such as BEOG-Pell grants trigger jurisdiction under Title IX? The Supreme Court unanimously answered in the affirmative. Second, when jurisdiction has been triggered, is enforcement institution-wide or specific to the program receiving those funds? The Court responded in a 6–3 decision with multiple and somewhat dissimilar opinions that enforcement is specific to the program and, in this case, to the financial aid office only. The Supreme Court's *Grove City* decision rejected the series of arguments (benefit, free-up) proposed in earlier days when the Department of Education's policy was toward more vigorous enforcement.

It is important to note that even though we know now (post-*Grove City*) that Title IX is "program-specific," we still lack a judicially defined interpretation of "program." Whatever the definition of "program" turns out to be, any "program-specific" interpretation of Title IX is unlikely to reach athletic departments. Two possible avenues for retaining Title IX jurisdiction over athletics in the post-*Grove City* era have been suggested: These suggestions have been made in an effort to tie federal funds to the specific program of athletics. It is unlikely that either method of tying funds to program will trigger Title IX jurisdiction over athletic programs.

First, few stadiums and gymnasiums have been built by federal funds. In those few instances where federal funds were involved, it appears that the Office of Civil Rights will not, in its current nonenforcement posture, stretch its jurisdiction to a program taking place within the walls of a federally funded building. To obtain jurisdiction successfully, the Office of Civil Rights would need to decide that the building and the program carried on within it were the same. This is unlikely.

Second, within weeks following the *Grove City* decision, the Office of Civil Rights closed a number of cases for lack of jurisdiction. Where discrimination was found in the area of scholarships, jurisdiction was retained. However, enforcement of Title IX's antidiscrimination demands was limited solely to the administration of the scholarship and was not extended to any specific program in which the scholarship student might participate.

In the few months before and after the *Grove City* decision, activity has been high on topics related to Title IX. A month before the February 1984 decision, the Commission on Civil Rights changed its composition and rules of operation. Within the changes can be seen a policy alteration consistent with the change in the Department of Education's policy change toward less vigorous enforcement. After voting to remain free of the policies of the previous commission, the new Commission on Civil Rights differentiated between civil rights policy and social/economic policy (not within the commission's jurisdiction). Commissioner John H. Bunzel indicated that research efforts of the commission would evaluate the extent to which discrimination explains disparities among groups rather than assuming that such disparities are the result of discrimination. Further, although affirmative action is not part of Title IX, the commission's altered policy on the issue supports the general change. Affirmative action, the commission says, should now be directed to creating a qualified pool of applicants rather than to a quota system for hiring.[29]

In March 1984 the Commission on Civil Rights voted to urge Congress to make an entire institution subject to federal laws forbidding discrimination. At the same time, however, the commission also recommended that sanctions (removing federal funds) should not be made institution-wide, but only in the specific programs in which discrimination takes place. Thus on the surface it appears that the Commission on Civil Rights is advocating an expansion to institutional applicability of civil rights legislation, in contrast to the program-specific results of *Grove City*, while at the same time limiting the enforcement muscle to specific programs. The effect of the commission's recommendation is to encourage Congress to maintain the Supreme Court's narrow interpretation of Title IX.

The commission has also asked Congress to consider the issue of whether a particular action must have been pursued with the *intent* of discriminating or only with the *effect* of discriminating in order to fall under the Department of Education's jurisdiction.

The question of discriminatory intent is a relatively new addition to the controversy surrounding Title IX. When sex discrimination exists at a college *and* the Office of Civil Rights decides to pursue Title IX enforcement *and* the discrimination is in a program specifically receiving federal funds, the additional requirement of proving discriminatory intent rather than merely discriminatory effect will make picking up the gauntlet of Title IX enforcement all the more difficult. The Supreme Court has decided to consider the question as it applies to Title IX's companion antidiscrimination legislation in *TWA, Inc.* v. *Thurston*,[30] which considers whether the plaintiff must prove intent to discriminate on the basis of age, and in *Alexander* v. *Jenning*,[31] which considers whether a rule having disparate impact is sufficient to show a violation of Section 504 (Handicapped).

Within three weeks after the *Grove City* decision, the Department of Education's Office of Civil Rights dropped a number of enforcement actions against athletics programs that had been found to use discriminatory practices. Among these was Auburn University, where the Office of Civil Rights dropped its claim against the athletics program even though discrimination was found to exist in many areas. The Office of Civil Rights did, however, maintain jurisdiction in the area of scholarships, finding that Auburn failed to award its athletic scholarships and grants-in-aid so as to provide reasonable opportunities for such awards to students of each sex in proportion to the number of students of each sex participating in intercollegiate athletics.

The Office of Civil Rights also dropped its enforcement action against the University of Maryland–College Park, where, although the athletics program was found to violate Title IX regulations, the financial aid to athletes was in compliance. It appears, therefore, that an institution is free to pursue a course of discrimination in its athletics program without fear of complaint as long as its scholarships are dealt with on a more even-handed basis.

Congressional Reaction to the "Program-Specific" Interpretation

In November 1983, before the *Grove City* case was decided by the Supreme Court, the House of Representatives made a minor attempt via House Resolution 190 (passed 414 to 8) to express its desire that Title IX be broadly interpreted. Quickly after the *Grove City* decision was handed down, numerous multisponsored bills were put forth in both the House and Senate to clarify or alter (depending on one's interpretation of its original legislative history) Title IX's institution-wide applicability.[32] None, however, was adopted before the close of the 98th Congress.

Clarification means that Congress would spell out in very specific terms what it intended when it originally passed the antidiscrimination legislation. Legislative intent is crucial to the judicial interpretation of statutory wording that has been claimed to be ambiguous. If Congress passes clarifying legislation for Title IX, it would mean that the institution-wide jurisdiction denied in *Grove City* was in fact the intent of Congress. Thus the judiciary would no longer be able to misinterpret the meaning of that portion of Title IX, and jurisdiction in the future would include athletics programs (even if they specifically received no federal funds) at any institution receiving federal funds.

An omnibus bill, S.2568, sponsored by 56 senators in the 98th Congress, would apply the institution-wide clarification to the entire family of civil rights legislation. Basically it would replace "in programs or activities" with "recipient." Recipient would be defined as "any state or political subdivision thereof, or any instrumentality of a state or political subdivision thereof, or any public or private agency, institution or organization or other entity . . . to which federal financial assistance is extended (directly or through another entity or person)."

Those in favor of the omnibus bill argue that if clarifying legislation applied only to Title IX, it might be interpreted later by the courts that Congress intended to limit its institution-wide concept to sex discrimination. In addition, they argue, the language in several members of the family of civil rights legislation is similar and thus all should be clarified identically. Furthermore, a unified effort by all those affected by discrimination is likely to be more effective.

Those who prefer to clarify only Title IX argue that Title IX and its antidiscrimination relatives are sometimes reviewed by different House and Senate committees. In addition, they view the passage of clarifying legislation for Title IX alone more likely than finding agreement in the House and Senate for all of the related legislation at this point.

Some are not only against the omnibus bill, but against any clarifying legislation at all. George C. Roche III, President of Hillsdale College in Michigan testified at a May 1984 joint hearing of the House Education and Labor and Judiciary Committees that "Title IX reflects no truth in labeling" because both public and private colleges would be subject to vague antidiscrimination expeditions by federal enforcement officials operating in a climate of perpetual suspicion.[33]

Still others express the view that Title IX already has completed its mission indirectly by highlighting the issue of sex discrimination, and thus no clarifying legislation is necessary. They argue that college administrators have become sensitized to the problems of sex discrimination and consequently have put into place written guidelines against such activities to demonstrate their commitment. They note that the administrators' goodwill is ensured, at least within large schools, by the difficulty of tracing federal funds to identify those departments and programs in which the college might feel free to discriminate. Local laws in many areas prohibit discrimination. Others add to their argument against clarifying legislation that vocal women's groups now exist that would act as watchdogs against sex discrimination. Still others suggest alternative means of pursuing a claim of sex discrimination, such as suing under contract law for a college's breach of antidiscrimination promises made in its manuals and bylaws.

Goodwill and issue sensitivity often become ephemeral banners in the winds of decreasing budgets and reduced enforcement pressures. On one campus the goodwill vanished within days of the *Grove City* decision, and women's athletic scholarships were reduced as a result. On another campus the college attorney had to work to convince the administration that *Grove City* did not mean he could tear up the college's conciliation agreement arrived at with the Office of Civil Rights in response to past discriminatory practices in the athletics program. A number of administrators already have used *Grove City* to question the right of the Office of Civil Rights to investigate complaints on campus at all.[34]

The goodwill of college administrators is unlikely to be any more effective as a barrier to sex discrimination in athletics now than it was before Title IX. Nor are assurances from the NCAA particularly heartening. The NCAA calmed many fears held by women when it adopted a several-year plan to equalize the number of men's and women's teams at each campus. This action demonstrated a commitment to the expansion of women's teams to meet the desires of women athletes. However, in the spring of 1984 the NCAA issued an interpretation of its own equalization plan that completely altered its effect. Under the new interpretation, if a school fails to comply with the NCAA mandate to equalize the number of teams offered for men and women in the prescribed time, that school's women's program will be barred from championship play. The men's program will remain unaffected.

The interpretation of the equalization plan removes any incentive, except an individual concern for fairness, to expand the offerings for women. By its interpretation, the NCAA treats the men's and women's athletics programs as two separate programs on campus. However, each institution is still allotted only a single vote in NCAA decisions, and that vote in most instances is cast by a male.

The NCAA interpretation of its own rule destroys the hope some women had for even-handed treatment by the NCAA. It is clear that without a clarified Title IX, women's intercollegiate athletics participation is unlikely to grow to meet the needs of the nation's girls and women. Title IX was the instrumentality that allowed the drastic reduction in the percentage of women in leadership positions, but the loss of Title IX's applicability to athletics would do nothing to correct the problem. Although it is counterintuitive, a clarified Title IX offers the only means of assuring the future possibility of women's reentry into leadership positions within women's athletics. Currently, there are too few women in leadership positions for their call for equity in the hiring process to be easily heard. A clarified Title IX would add strength to their voices and ultimately a fuller opportunity for women to benefit from and contribute to America's intercollegiate athletics programs.

The best prescription for a bright future in women's athletics is simple: Adopt policies that allow women the freedom to enjoy athletics. The passage of legislation that clarifies Title IX will be a step toward that freedom. Its effect on the participant would be to keep the doors of the gym open. Its potential effect on the leadership is less certain, but it would at least provide an avenue to overcome the massive decline in female representation.

If no clarifying legislation is passed, the future of women's athletics will be determined by women's ability to put pressure on the power structure of the NCAA. Because of the NCAA's immersion in the financial politics of sport, women who want to change women's sports must develop strategies that have an impact on the money and politics of the NCAA. Women and men committed to women's sports must place pressure on the sources of the NCAA's financial and political power, such as television networks, campus presidencies, and athletic events of high interest. Pressure also must be exerted from within by female college presidents, female executives, and all those who realize the negative aspects of having women's athletics programs totally controlled by men.

Women athletes are not demanding separate governance structures. They rightfully are demanding opportunities to escape chauvinistic attitudes that say "The NCAA knows best." Women are no longer, if they ever were, bemused by the resources and leadership experience of the NCAA. They have seen that power and money do not guarantee correct choices and, in fact, often mandate tainted choices. They now know that without Title IX there is no incentive for the NCAA or its member colleges and universities to commit resources to the development of women's athletics. Without such commitment even small changes such as mentorship programs for women coaches, job data banks, and equal voting privileges for women's programs will not be developed by the NCAA.

Without such commitment, there will be no development of effective roles for women of independent thought within the NCAA administrative structure from which to design a women's program that is not necessarily in the image of the men's.

NOTES

1. P.L. 92–318.
2. In January 1964 at the NCAA Convention, representatives of Division of Girls' and Women's Sports (DGWS) and American Association for Health, Physical Education and Recreation (AAHPER) urged the NCAA to remain uninvolved in women's sports. Their introduction by NCAA officers included the statement: "I would like to point out clearly that there is no attempt to move into the activities [of women's sports] which are very well handled by competent leadership. . . . I think we have enough to do in solving some of our own problems without attempting to solve the problems of the women." *1963–64 NCAA Yearbook*, p. 144.

In response to an inquiry of Richard C. Larkins, president of the National Association for College Directors of Athletics, concerning the NCAA position in regard to women's athletics, Charles M. Neinas, assistant to the NCAA executive director responded in a letter dated March 8, 1966: "The NCAA limits its jurisdiction and authority to male student-athletes. In fact, the Executive Regulations of this Association [NCAA] prohibit women from participating in National Collegiate Championship events. Also, the NCAA's Constitution and By-law provisions concerning recruitment of athletes and conduct of intercollegiate athletics relates to the programs sponsored by our member institutions for male students. Consequently, a national organization assuming responsibility for women's intercollegiate athletics would not be in conflict with this Association."

3. *Chronicle of Higher Education* (December 8, 1980), p. 9. The *Chronicle* article reiterated the statement of the AIAW, stressing its founding principles, which included: (1) to provide a national championship program for female athletes and (2) to develop a governance system that served, rather than exploited, student athletes while avoiding the excesses that were typical of the men's programs. The AIAW stressed that it followed much less expensive recruitment rules and possessed a more flexible competitive structure (unlike the division structure faced by women under the NCAA, which basically would require women's teams to compete in the division in which the men's teams held membership, unless a petition to do otherwise was granted to each school).

4. The regulations were finally issued on July 21, 1975.

5. Bart Barnes and N. Scannell, "No Sporting Chance: The Girls in the Locker Room," *The Washington Post*, May 12, 1974, p. A–14.

6. Carol E. Gordon, Memorandum to the AIAW Executive Board, March 20, 1974, pp. 2–4.

7. National Collegiate Athletic Association, *1973–74 NCAA Annual Reports*, p. 38.

8. Alan Chapman, Memorandum to Chief Executive Officers, Faculty Athletic Representatives and Athletic Directors of NCAA Member Institutions, June 14, 1974, p. 2

9. See, for example, *Sex Discrimination Regulations*, Hearings Before the Subcommittee on Postsecondary Education of the Committee on Education and Labor, House of Representatives, 94th Cong., 1st sess. (1975), and *Prohibition of Sex Discrimination*, 1975, Hearings Before the Subcommittee on Education of the Committee on Labor and Public Welfare United States Senate, 94th Cong., 1st sess. 1975.

10. Barnes and Scannell, "No Sporting Chance," p. A–20.

11. 622 F2D 1382 (10th Cir. 1980).

12. The NCAA's argument is summarized by:

> The regulations regarding athletic programs exceed the authority delegated to the Department of Health, Education and Welfare by Title IX, and are not rationally related to the objectives of Title IX and are not supported by fact in that they fail to provide and seek to prohibit programs, procedures and classifications which have a rational basis in fact and are not discriminatory on the basis of sex. (Comments of the National Collegiate Athletic Association to the Department of Health, Education and Welfare on the Proposed Regulations on Nondiscrimination on the Basis of Sex in Education Programs and Activities Receiving Federal Financial Assistance [September 27, 1974], p. 2.)

13. Soon after the 1974 defeat of the Tower Amendment, the NCAA's staff prepared a recommendation that the NCAA "take 'affirmative action' in meeting the anticipated Title IX guidelines by offering championship competition for women immediately." See NCAA, *1974–75 NCAA Annual Reports*, p. 63.

14. AIAW v. NCAA, 558 F. Supp. 487 (1983).

15. Marymount College (Fla.) AIAW Minutes November 4–6, 1973 Delegate Assembly, p. 5.

16. R. Vivian Acosta and Linda Carpenter, "Changing Status of Women in Intercollegiate Athletics, 1977–1984," paper presented at the AAHPERD National convention (1984).

17. Ibid.

18. See the works of Carolyn Lehr, including "Women Coaches: Endangered Species," paper presented at the 1982 AAHPERD Convention; Donna Pastore and Sue Whiddon, "The Employment of Males and Females in Athletics and Physical Education in the State of Florida," *Physical Educator* (December 1983): 207–10; and the unpublished works of Sharon Mathes, Iowa State University, Ames, Iowa. Also of interest is "More Hurdles to Clear," Clearinghouse

Publication 63, (July 1980), which is a compilation of data from other studies concerning women and girls in competitive athletics. See Milton Holmen and Bonnie Parkhouse, "Trends in the Selection of Coaches for Female Athletes: A Demographic Inquiry," *Research Quarterly for Exercise and Sport* 52 (1981): 9–18.

19. Catherine M. Mathison, "A Selective Study of Women's Athletic Administrative Settings Involving AIAW Division I Institutions," unpublished paper, University of Pittsburgh (February 1980).

20. 104 S. Ct. 1211 (1984).

21. 102 S. Ct. 1912 (1982).

22. 507 F. Supp. 1376 (E.D. Mich. 1981).

23. 696 F. 2d 418 (6th Cir. 1982).

24. 543 F. Supp. 321 (E.D. Va. 1982).

25. 688 F. 2d. 14 (3rd Cir. 1982).

26. 414 F. 2d. 1068 (5th Cir. 1969).

27. 396 F. Supp. (D.S.C. 1974). For a more complete description of this evolution, see Eva S. Tashiran-Brown, "Title IX: Progress Toward Program-Specific Regulation of Private Academia," *Journal of College and University Law* 10 (1983–84): 1–62.

28. 104 S. Ct. 1219 (1984).

29. United States Commission on Civil Rights, *Civil Rights Update*, March 1984.

30. TWA Inc. v. Thurston, Supreme Court Case 83–727.

31. Alexander v. Jenning, Supreme Court Case 83–727.

32. Among the clarifying legislation on the floor of the House and Senate at the time of this writing were S. 2363, S. 2412, and H.R. 5011, S. 2568, and the corresponding H.R. 4590.

33. "Notepad," *Chronicle of Higher Education* (May 23, 1984): 17.

34. Cheryl Fields, "Strong Anti-Sex Bias Policies of Universities and States Are Seen Dampening the Effect of Grove City Ruling," *Chronicle of Higher Education* (March 14, 1984): 21.

5

The Regulation of Sports Agents

Robert H. Ruxin

From the Orange Bowl to the inner-city playground, sports agents have become omnipresent, if not omnipotent. As their role and influence increased over the years, various schemes for monitoring, influencing, and controlling the quality of agents' services have been suggested. These proposals range from the education of athletes about how to select and work with a player-agent to the registration and bonding of agents by the state. This chapter describes and analyzes four of the more significant efforts to address the "agent problem." They are: (1) state regulation; (2) union regulation; (3) registration by the National Collegiate Athletic Association (NCAA); and (4) self-regulation backed by government sanction. This chapter considers what aspects of athlete representation could be regulated and what interests are at stake. After discussing the various approaches to regulation, this chapter examines alternatives to regulation and concludes with consideration of the philosophical basis for and against government regulation of agents.

THE ROLE OF AGENTS

Agents have represented athletes since Red Grange hired C. C. ("Cash and Carry") Pyle in 1925. Player representatives did not become an acknowledged part of the professional sports scene, however, until the advent of the bidding wars between the National Football League (NFL) and the upstart American Football League in the 1960s, nor did they become an accepted part of pro sports until the early 1970s after each of the major sports unions obtained the right for its members to have agents negotiate their salaries. In 1982 the NFL Players Association (NFLPA) went a step further and retained the right to negotiate individual contracts and to certify any agent selected by a veteran player. At the 1984 Olympics even many of the "amateur" participants had retained agents to negotiate product endorsements and identify other financial opportunities that might be available as the result of their athletic achievements.

When the median salary was $17,000—as it was for major-league baseball players in 1967—few athletes needed an agent; most players had very little bargaining power. The rise of agents has coincided with undreamed-of increases in players' salaries. By 1985 average salaries were projected to exceed $300,000 in baseball and in the National Basketball Association (NBA), $200,000 in the NFL, and $140,000 in the National Hockey League (NHL).[1] High-level amateur athletes such as Carl Lewis and Mary Decker also could expect considerable reward from their athletic pursuits.

The drastically increased bargaining power of the athletes, not their agents, makes most of the financial gains possible. The United States Football League did not offer Herschel Walker a million dollars a year because of his agent, Jack Manton, but rather because the league believed luring Walker from Georgia before his senior year would bring the new league instant credibility.

Competition from new leagues is one of the three major factors that have accelerated salary increases. The second is the opportunity to enter the open market as a free agent. This right, won by collective bargaining, strikes, lawsuits, and arbitrators' decisions, gives players the threat of an alternative to accepting the owner's final offer. In baseball, the only major team sport not to face competition from a new league, much of the salary increase and the erosion of owners' control over salaries can be traced to the salary arbitration process established in the early 1970s. Finally, multimillion- and even billion-dollar television contracts enable the owners to offer higher salaries and guaranteed multiyear contracts.

Agents help athletes take advantage of their bargaining power. They push the limits of the going rate and they shape the package. Manton, for example, obtained an all-cash deal for Walker. Dave Winfield's ten-year contract with the Yankees includes annual payments to the David M. Winfield Foundation, a charitable organization.[2] Third-baseman Bob Horner receives bonuses for not exceeding a certain weight each week of the season. Dave Butz earns $3,500 for each quarterback sack.

All agents, by definition, negotiate playing contracts. Many provide additional services themselves, through associates or by referral to affiliated entities. These services include financial planning, investment advice, money management, tax and estate planning, and tax return preparation. Some agents, such as Mark McCormack's International Management Group, manage the athletes funds, including paying all the bills. Many use a team of specialists within their firm to assist athletes in finding endorsement and speaking opportunities.

One of the most important personal roles for an agent is to help prepare his clients for a second career. In addition to assuring that the client receives adequate financial planning assistance, a good agent guides his clients into off-season education and employment. As playing salaries increase and the athletes' financial need to work in the off-season diminishes, this function becomes more important. Some agents have even negotiated an off-season job for their client in an owner's nonfootball business as part of a playing contract. Another reason many agents keep in close touch with their clients is to try to prevent losing a client to another agent. Finally, a close relationship also puts the agent in a good position to detect signs of drug use or gambling and helps the athlete cope with any such problems. Unexplained expenditures from a financial management account may tip off an alert agent to a problem. In sum, the wide range of professional and personal services an agent provides is a significant factor in evaluating the manner and degree of the regulation of agents.[3]

WHAT COULD BE REGULATED AND WHY

The Lessons of Gary Anderson

The adventures of Gary Anderson in the six months after he played his last game for Arkansas in the 1983 Bluebonnet Bowl illustrate many of the problems associated with agents. *Sports Illustrated* described the Gary Anderson affair as "a study in manipulation."[4] More than 100 agents contacted Anderson. In November of his senior year a "recruiter" for Dr. Jerry Argovitz, a dentist turned agent, approached Anderson in Fayetteville. Soon afterward Anderson received a two-page letter from Argovitz extolling the virtues of "the Argovitz family." A few days after starring in the Bluebonnet Bowl, Anderson signed with Argovitz. The 630-word contract appointed Argovitz as Anderson's exclusive business manager and provided for a 7 percent agent's fee. That fee turned out to be $96,250, all of it paid upon signing a pro contract even though Anderson signed a four-year contract with the Tampa Bay Bandits. Actually Anderson was required to pay only 4 percent up front, but Argovitz's corporate accountant suggested there would be tax benefits for Anderson if he paid all of it up front.

Argovitz, to his credit, flatly rejected a very modest contract offer from the New Jersey Generals, whose coach, Chuck Fairbanks, suggested that Anderson would be only a low second- or third-round NFL pick. After the Chargers drafted Anderson on the *first* round, Tampa obtained his USFL rights. In the meantime, Anderson dropped out of school, and Argovitz formed a partnership to buy a USFL expansion franchise, but he never mentioned his USFL ownership role to Anderson.

After Argovitz reached a handshake agreement with Tampa for a $1,375,000 deal, he sent Anderson into virtual hiding and lied (by his own admission) when the NFL's Chargers tried to find Anderson to make a counteroffer. Anderson signed the Tampa contract, bought his mother—widowed for twenty-one years—a four-bedroom house, furniture, and a $14,000 car, and got married. He also made a new friend. A Houston sportswriter curried the favor of Anderson with gifts and gladhanding. By the summer Anderson had hired Lloyd C. A. Wells as his second agent after Wells promised to get him a better deal from San Diego, including a potential movie role. Wells would receive a 6 percent fee.

Wells borrowed $30,000 at no interest and with no payback terms from the Chargers, the team seeking his client's services. He negotiated four one-year NFL contracts totaling $1.5 million, but with $800,000 deferred beyond 1986 and, contrary to Anderson's understanding at the time, with only very limited guarantee clauses.

Anderson then sued Argovitz and the Tampa Bay Bandits. A federal judge refused to grant an order allowing Anderson to play in the NFL. He refused after his attorney asked Anderson to read his contract to the court in order to show that Anderson could not read and was susceptible of being duped at any time.[5]

The Anderson case illustrates many of the problems surrounding agents:

- *The pressure of solicitation.* It is extremely difficult for a young athlete to choose among hundreds of agents, many of whom offer inducements such as loans, cash, jewelry, and even cars, women, and drugs.
- *Excessive fees and upfront collection.* Although competition among agents generally has pushed fees down from 8 to 10 percent of a contract's value to 3 to 5 percent, the real cost of an agent's services still varies because of factors such as timing of payments, whether expenses are included, and the extent of services provided.
- *Conflicts of interest.* Argovitz's USFL ownership and Wells's acceptance of loans from the team against whom he was negotiating are examples. These arrangements raise the possibility that the agent may be unduly influenced by factors other than the client's best interests.
- *Multiple agents.* Agents constantly are telling athletes they can do a better job than the athlete's present agent. Often the jilted agent's only recourse is to respond in kind.
- *Lack of preparation.* Athletes are not prepared to cope with the business side of being a professional, although many colleges are beginning to address this shortcoming.

Some of these problems directly relate to the competence and integrity of the agent, especially the solicitation method, the fee charged, and the presence of a conflict of interest. Other agent abuses include misappropriation of athletes' funds, poor investment advice, uninformed tax counseling, and negotiating contracts with excessive deferred compensation or, more generally, less compensation than the athlete could have obtained—although occasionally a lower annual salary may extend a fringe player's career.

Some of the problems, particularly those faced by college athletes, relate to other factors. Young athletes lack the preparation, education, and information to make informed decisions about agents and to make related decisions such as when to sign a professional contract. The rules of the various professional leagues as to when an athlete is eligible to be drafted and how and when teams may contact athletes and their advisers complicate the decision-making process. Moreover, the interplay between the NCAA rules relating to eligibility and amateurism and the professional leagues' rules reduce the athlete's bargaining power. The combination of these problems makes the amateur athlete more susceptible to the unscrupulous agent.

The lack of effective regulation of agents allows the same agents, both perennials and drifters, to take advantage of athletes. For some observers the question is not whether to regulate agents, but how to do it. Regulation could be credential-oriented, requiring the agent to demonstrate and maintain certain qualifications and skills. Alternatively, regulation could address the practice of sports agentry, such as solicitation, fees, and conflicts, and such specific functions as the handling of athletes' funds.

For others, the regulation of agents is neither desirable nor feasible. The abuses of some agents do not merit the burden on other agents or the expenditures of government resources. It may be that regulating agents is the wrong solution. An alternative approach might be directed at reforming NCAA and professional league rules that impede a college athlete's access to full information and advice. The focus should be on better preparation of the college athlete for the business aspects of life as a professional athlete.

Why Regulate?

The obvious reason to regulate is to protect the athlete. However, while the athlete's interest is usually the stated reason for regulation, other motivations underlie the interest of various parties in regulating agents. Attorneys who cannot directly solicit clients would benefit if regulation similarly handicapped nonattorney agents or, as a California assistant attorney general has suggested, if it exempted athlete solicitation from the proscription of solicitation. Solicitation certainly goes too far. Scores of agents hounding athletes at bowl games and tournaments benefits few athletes and annoys many. Neither is it desirable, however, for athletes to turn only to established agents who can afford not to solicit because they can rely on other clients or friendly coaches for referrals.[6] Solicitation restrictions do discourage many lawyers from competing with agents who are not similarly restricted. Solicitation is just one issue. Some agents and sports attorneys view regulation as a means to restore credibility and respect to their business and to establish athlete representation as a profession.

Some politicians support the concept of regulation in order to meet prominent athletes and obtain publicity. Merely chairing a legislative hearing on agent abuses guarantees television and sports-page coverage. Some legislators are former athletes who may feel a genuine need to help the athlete, especially those whose professional careers are unlikely to last beyond the first contract they sign. But legislators must also face the issue of whether the public interest demands protection for well-paid athletes.

Sports unions are obligated to protect their members' best interests. Ensuring that each athlete has at least the opportunity to receive adequate assistance in negotiating individual contracts is certainly part of that duty. Regulating agents may well be an appropriate mechanism for a particular union, but there is a danger that regulation is a means to aggrandize power and influence.

The NFLPA lobbied effectively for the California agent statute and made NFLPA control over agents an important point in the 1982 negotiations with the NFL.[7] Since the right to individual representation during contract negotiations was a significant collective bargaining victory for sports unions in the early 1970s, the NFLPA's assertion of jurisdiction over agents could portend a new era of union-controlled collective *and* individual negotiations. A pool of contract negotiators retained by a union might well be more effective and cost each athlete less. But the benefits are unlikely to outweigh the potential loss of access to the personal services and guidance many agents provide—including advice about union issues. Both the athlete and the agent need the union. Well-informed and thoughtful agents can be an important resource for a union. Any effort to credential, regulate, or assist agents requires a balancing of a trade union's traditional role in negotiating all aspects of the employer-employee relationship and the special role of individual representation in professional sports.

Professional leagues can benefit from regulation if it reduces the opportunity for agents to undermine the integrity of the game with drugs and gambling. An agent may use drugs to attract clients and even introduce a client in need of drugs to gambling interests, or he, himself, may serve as a conduit of information to gamblers. Most teams prefer to deal with honest and competent (though not necessarily the most competent) agents because their clients are less likely to be distracted by off-the-field problems. In times of interleague competition, however, some teams will act aggressively to influence less scrupulous agents to deliver certain players to them. Finally, states with successful university football programs protect their investment and ability to earn bowl and TV revenue if regulation diminishes the opportunities for client-hungry agents to convince college athletes to leave school early.

In sum, the motivations for regulation are a mixture of genuine concern for the athlete and varying degrees and forms of self-interest, some of which coincide with the athlete's best interest. Ideally, regulation should protect the athlete as consumer, protect the integrity of sports, and encourage ethical, competent persons to be involved. The question is not so much whether a problem exists, but how to address it.

FOUR APPROACHES TO THE AGENT PROBLEM

State Regulation: The California Model

In September 1981 California became the first state to enact a law intended to regulate all agents for professional team athletes. All agents (with the significant exception of any member of the California bar when "acting as legal counsel") must register annually with the state, pay substantial filing and license fees, deposit a $10,000 surety bond, file a copy of the form of contracts they offer athletes, and receive the Labor Commissioner's approval for such contracts. Agents also must file their fee schedules and may not change fees prior to filing a revised schedule.[8]

To protect amateur athletes, the agency contract must state prominently that an athlete will jeopardize his or her amateur standing by signing the contract. To discourage agents from inducing student athletes to violate amateur eligibility rules, the law requires an agent to file a copy of his registration statement with a student's school before contacting a student *in any manner* about an agency contract or a professional sports contract. If an agency contract with a student is not filed within five days of execution, it is void and unenforceable. The law also includes a dispute resolution process, which is mandatory unless the contract provides for a comparable arbitration of disputes.

Violation of the law is a misdemeanor punishable by a fine of not less than one thousand dollars, not more than sixty-days imprisonment, or both. Any agency contract negotiated by an unregistered agent is void and unenforceable.

In the three years after its enactment the law had very little impact; most agents ignored it. Of an estimated 250 to 300 agents doing business in California, only 24 had registered. Regulations were proposed and revised but not formally adopted. What went wrong? Why weren't the regulations adopted and the law enforced in any meaningful way?

First, a fundamental problem was the lack of funding. The legislature intended the law to be self-supporting and did not appropriate any funds for enforcement. The only source of funding was registration fees. But until a substantial number of agents paid the $100 filing fee and $500 "main office license fee," there would never be sufficient money to enforce the law.[9]

Second, many agents did not register because they did not believe the law applied to members of the California bar. The California Senate Select Committee on Licensed and Designated Sports focused on this issue during an informational hearing on the law in July 1983. A lawyer with athlete clients, an NFL player, and a state official presented three contrasting viewpoints. Margaret Leonard, a California attorney who represented professional golfers (a sport not covered by the law), told the committee that she no longer represented football players because she would not comply with the law:

> I went through a lot of rigorous training to become an attorney . . . I've handled all kinds of negotiations for [business] clients . . . It has involved a lot more money than any of these football players that I've represented . . . I've never been required to be bonded . . . it's insulting to me to have to post a $10,000 bond to handle somebody's $30,000 to $40,000 contract when I'm handling a million dollar supermarket escrow and am not regulated . . . The incentive for me to be a good attorney and to be ethical and to take care of my clients is the threat of disbarment.[10]

Gene Upshaw, then president and later executive director of the NFL Players Association, presented the athletes' perspective to the committee:

> Athletes . . . had no protection . . . They were just sitting ducks . . . Most of them are getting money from agents, and now attorneys seem to be, in one sense saying that they are attorneys and they really don't have the right to solicit, but as an agent they can wear two hats. They can solicit . . . That's the only way they can get clients. We really thought the attorneys would embrace this legislation because . . . [it] would help, not only the non-attorneys, but the attorneys.[11]

Ronald Russo, an assistant state attorney general who represents some forty state licensing authorities, took a middle ground:

> Nothing in the State Bar requires an attorney when he's representing an athlete to do anything about refunding fees or tell them . . . about arbitration [rights] . . . and it isn't the State Bar that's being focused on when those rights are provided. And so, the idea that an athlete is protected by an attorney from the abuses of an attorney because there is this other large organization that proceeds very slowly . . . doesn't solve the problem. That just says that if that lawyer misbehaves, that lawyer will be punished, but meanwhile what happens to the athlete?[12]

Russo suggested that rather than exempt attorneys from the entire law, they should be exempted from certain provisions of the law, such as bonding, if they have malpractice insurance.

The California law provides for registration of agents and sets certain requirements for agency contracts; it does not specify credentials as would a licensing statute. Its applicability to attorneys is just one of several significant ambiguities. For example, if the law applies to an attorney-agent, the requirements to notify an athlete's school of intended contact and to file an executed agency contract may violate the athlete's right to seek counsel on a confidential basis. On balance, however, the overall benefits to athletes should outweigh any potential loss of confidentiality for a few athletes.

Although the Labor Commissioner may reject a registration, no standards are specified. It will be difficult to defend a rejection without statutory guidance. The reach of the state's jurisdiction is unclear. Arguably, it applies to a New York agent who does not maintain an office in California but who meets a potential client at the Rose Bowl. However, what happens if New York enacts similar legislation? The sensible approach would be a uniform agreement on priority of jurisdiction and reciprocal enforcement. Finally, there is the serious policy issue of whether or not the state should expend general funds to protect well-paid athletes. A more pragmatic approach would be a start-up budget with a repayment mechanism.

Despite the law's ineffectiveness, it seems likely to remain on the books. At least until after the California legislature considers amendments early in the 1985 session, no regulations were to be implemented. The impact of the present law will be minimal without funding of an enforcement test case or some other form of inducement for agents to register. A starting point would be for the NFLPA to require all agents doing business in California to register as a prerequisite to NFLPA certification.

Union Certification: The NFLPA System

As part of the collective bargaining agreement negotiated during the 1982 strike, the National Football League Players Association obtained the right to negotiate individual contracts for veteran players or to authorize a player's agent to negotiate his contract.[13] Armed with this authority, the NFLPA instituted a certification process as a prerequisite to negotiating for a veteran.[14] The key elements required for certification as a "contract adviser" are:

- The filing of an application, which includes educational and occupational information, disclosure of convictions for or allegations of professional misconduct, and a list of current NFL clients.
- A limitation on fees for contract negotiation based on a sliding-scale percentage *above* the minimum applicable salary for up to three years— 10 percent of the first year, 5 percent of the second year, and 2 percent for the third year—with an additional 2 percent for the second year and 1 percent for the third year for guaranteed contracts. For a minimum

salary contract, the maximum fee is $125 per hour up to $1,000, but it is payable only if the player makes the active list for at least one regular season game.
- Submission of the NFLPA's standard form representation agreement to the union for each client.
- Binding arbitration of any dispute over the representation agreement.
- Lack of any ownership interest in a professional football team, and prohibition against engaging in any activity that creates an actual or potential conflict of interest with effective representation.
- Informing NFLPA regularly of developments in negotiations for new contracts.
- Not soliciting athletes in five respects:
  1. Providing anything of significant value to a player to become his agent.
  2. Providing anything of significant value in return for a personal recommendation of the agent's selection by a player.
  3. Misleading or lying in the process of obtaining a client.
  4. Using titles or business names that falsely imply a professional credential.
  5. Asking for or accepting anything of value from any NFL club or management personnel for personal use or benefit.

- Attendance annually at an all-day seminar sponsored by the NFLPA at three locations.[15]

At the start of the 1985 season more than 1,250 agents had been certified or provisionally certified for one year because of a lack of experience in representing NFL players. Only about one-third of those certified actually represented an NFL player. Although no applicant had been denied certification, the NFLPA warned approximately 150 agents who had not attended a briefing session that they would forfeit their certification if they did not attend a future session, and denied renewals to several other agents.

The league and the union had implemented a system of notification and verification to ensure that no agent would negotiate for a veteran without union approval. However, the union lacked jurisdiction over rookies, the players most vulnerable to agent abuses. This is a significant omission, especially considering that the average NFL career is about four years and that most rookies sign a multiyear package. The union expressed optimism throughout 1983 and 1984 that it would expand coverage to rookies either by negotiations with the NFL or by petitioning the National Labor Relations Board. In the meantime, the league tried to encourage rookies to retain certified agents.

It is difficult to evaluate the success of the certification program apart from another union gain in the 1982 agreement—the right to receive copies of all player contracts. With these contracts and the current negotiating information that agents must provide the NFLPA, the union has generated extensive and timely contract data. For example, the union's economist told agents at the 1984 briefings that sixth-year reserve running backs who had gained 500 to 600 yards the previous season averaged $200,000 in salary, that 46 contracts included low-interest loans averaging $109,000, and that 90 percent of all contracts included some form of bonus, most commonly an honors clause (typically $5,000 to $10,000 for making an all-conference team).

The NFLPA encourages certified agents to use these data in their negotiations. The availability of current data should mitigate one major source of poor representation—negotiations premised on a lack of market knowledge. An obvious result of unequal knowledge is low salaries. Sometimes the result is quite different—outrageous demands by new agents that lead to hard feelings, holdouts, and even shortened careers. A variation is a seemingly lucrative contract, but one that is actually below the going rate because of substantial deferred compensation or overvalued in-kind payments.

In essence, the immediate benefits of the NFLPA certification system will not lie so much in keeping out unqualified or unscrupulous agents, since the system imposes no substantive qualifications or encompasses any significant investigation; rather, certification's greatest benefit will be as a mechanism to achieve closer cooperation, particularly sharing information, between the union and the agents for the mutual benefit of the players. In the longer term the system may make it more difficult for unscrupulous agents to prosper. Unless the union is able to devote additional resources to investigating the accuracy of information submitted by agents, however, unscrupulous agents will continue to circumvent the certification system and use this credential to attract clients.

One of the most controversial elements of the system is the compensation scale. Consider a third-year special teams player who is a free agent. His agent identifies teams who might be interested in him, contacts the general managers, and finally determines that the best alternative is to negotiate an NFL contract at the minimum level with performance and honors bonuses. Since the agent's compensation is based only on salary above the minimum (and signing and reporting bonuses), he gets only $1,000, unless the athlete successfully applies to the union for an "exceptional services" exception to the compensation formula.

If the union applies this system to rookies, it will need to rework the compensation formula in order to prevent competent agents from resisting representation of lower-round draft choices and free agents, who can really benefit from an agent's "placement" services. The principle behind the system's requirement that the agent gets paid as the player receives the fruits of the negotiation is sound and responds to some gross abuses by agents who collected large sums up front. But the agent who works diligently to get an athlete a chance at making a team deserves some compensation even if the athlete is cut.

Finally, the legality of the NFLPA certification system is not entirely certain. There is some question as to whether the National Labor Relations Act, Section 9, gives the union the right to bargain exclusively on behalf of individual members (and nonmembers in right-to-work states). Furthermore, the plan may be subject to antitrust challenge,[16] although the NFLPA believes that a Supreme Court case upholding a comparable actors' agent-certification plan would apply to the football plan.[17]

In summary, the NFLPA agent-certification plan is the most aggressive internal effort by any sport to police agents. It is a registration system, not a licensing process. Its scope is limited primarily to contract negotiation for veteran players. The most significant regulatory aspect is the compensation scale. The system's most significant contribution may be to educate and inform agents, especially about current going rates for particular talent and experience. In this respect, the baseball union plays a similar role, although without the fanfare and zeal of the NFLPA.[18] The Major League Baseball Players Association pioneered the right to obtain complete and current contract information through collective bargaining. This service does more to facilitate the ability of an agent to serve the athlete than any other service offered by a sports union to its members.

If the NFLPA succeeds in extending its coverage to rookies and to United States Football League (USFL) players through its affiliated players association, it can eliminate many of the worst agent abuses. If it is to succeed, however, it must maintain the support, and not undermine the position, of its members' "contract negotiators." The best way to serve its members and their agents is to provide timely and relevant contract information.

NCAA Registration

College athletes are an obvious target for agents or would-be agents. Their vulnerability to abuse is exacerbated by the strictly defined but irregularly enforced boundaries of amateurism established by the National Collegiate Athletic Association (NCAA) and further by the way in which the draft eligibility rules of the various professional leagues relate to NCAA rules.[19] For example, under NCAA rules a college coach may not negotiate on behalf of one of his athletes, but he may help him determine his professional worth. When John Thompson attempted to do just that after Pat Ewing's junior year, the NBA fined the Portland Trailblazers $250,000 for violating a league rule that bars contacts with undergraduates who have not entered the draft.[20]

For many years the NCAA stayed away from any involvement in the selection of an agent by student athletes. The only exception was to bar an eligible athlete from agreeing, in writing or orally, to be represented by an agent. Finally, in the early 1980s, as agents and tales of agent abuses proliferated, the NCAA gradually changed its position. After indirectly funding the publication and distribution of a pamphlet intended to introduce student athletes to issues relating to agent selection in 1982-1983,[21] the NCAA formed a special committee on player agents in 1983.

The special committee made several recommendations intended to assist student athletes in selecting an agent. They included publication of a revised pamphlet, and they authorized universities to set up panels of three university employees from outside the athletic department to advise athletes about agent selection. The NCAA approved these recommendations at its 1984 convention. In August 1984 the NCAA Executive Council recommended for approval at the 1985 convention a proposal to facilitate the purchase of insurance against injuries that could prevent or hamper a professional career.[22] The availability of such insurance would reduce the pressure to leave school early and limit the influence of agents who help undergraduates obtain insurance at the cost of entering into an agreement with that agent.

In addition, in the fall of 1984, the NCAA initiated a voluntary agent registration system that called for agents to file an information form with the NCAA headquarters in Shawnee, Kansas. Registered agents must agree to notify the athletic director prior to contacting an eligible athlete or a coach. Many coaches and athletic directors encourage athletes to deal only with registered agents. The NCAA distributes the names and office location of registered agents to its members. Schools can obtain other information about an agent only by specific request. The NCAA keeps registered agents informed of its rules relating to amateurism and professional sports. It intends to remove from the list agents who fail to notify an athletic director prior to a contact or who do anything to jeopardize an athlete's eligibility.[23]

The NCAA's recognition that it has a responsibility to help prepare student athletes to cope with the transition to professional sports, including agent selection, is long overdue. Certainly, more education, information, and counseling are appropriate and beneficial, although even these are not a total solution. A better-informed consumer should be less susceptible to abuses initiated by agents.

Until the NFLPA certification system is extended to rookies, the NCAA registration plan fills an important void. Rather than duplicate the efforts of the unions, the NCAA should focus on working with the player unions. Already, NCAA staff participates in NFLPA agent seminars and provides information about the NFLPA plan to its members' athlete counseling panels. The NCAA uses the NFLPA agent list for its mailing of registration forms, and it helps the college athlete contact the unions for information and advice about agents and professional contracts.

A voluntary registration system that cannot verify credentials is unlikely to affect the most flagrant abusers. It might further give agents inside tracks at particular schools. The concept of notifying the athletic director prior to any contact may be more of an intrusion on the athlete's ability to obtain outside advice than a beneficial screen. A notification requirement would be justified if college athletes were allowed to retain agents. Legalizing agents, as Penn State coach Joe Paterno suggested in testimony before Congress,[24] would enable the university to assist its athletes in selecting an agent and determining whether to turn professional early. As long as retaining an agent makes an athlete ineligible, many coaches will be reluctant to discuss an undergraduate's options with an agent and the athlete.

The NCAA, however, seems to be moving in the opposite direction. In May 1984 it reinterpreted its constitution so as to limit the services an attorney may provide an undergraduate. Since 1974 the NCAA has allowed an athlete to retain an attorney to evaluate professional contract offers, provided the attorney does not negotiate for a contract. Thus attorneys could contact professional teams (particularly in baseball, where many college juniors are drafted), discuss the terms of an offer, and reject an offer, as long as the attorney did not "negotiate." Under the revised rule a lawyer may not be present during discussions of a contract offer with a pro team or have any direct contact (in person, phone, or mail) with the team on behalf of the athlete. The NCAA explained the basis for the new interpretation:

> More and more agent-attorneys have used the language to become involved actively in actual contract discussions with professional sports organizations concerning student-athletes. Some lawyers have asked [teams] to communicate all contract offers . . . through them while, at the same time, insisting that they are not representing the student in contract negotiations.[25]

No one can question that the former rule was ambiguous on what constituted "negotiating." Some baseball teams used the rule to trap undergraduates into accepting their offer by notifying the NCAA that an attorney was negotiating for an athlete. Rather than trying to preclude any opportunity for an athlete to benefit from a lawyer's ability to discuss an offer with a pro team, the NCAA should reassess the fundamental question of why retaining someone to negotiate makes the athlete a professional.

In sum, this type of restrictive rule, coupled with the varying ways in which each professional league's draft system relates to the NCAA rules, is one major reason that agents move surreptitiously in soliciting college athletes. As long as these rules remain in place, any NCAA registration system is doomed to be of limited benefit to most student athletes. The NCAA's and its members' initiatives in counseling and educating athletes about agents promises to improve the athlete's ability to obtain better representation.

Government-Sanctioned Self-Regulation: The Sports Lawyers Association Proposal

A special congressional committee nearly a decade ago recommended a joint effort by players' unions, bar associations, and other industry participants to establish professional standards for agents.[26] Until recently, the only serious effort at self-regulation by a group of agents was the formation by the NFLPA of the Association of Representatives of Professional Athletes (ARPA). The organization drafted a voluntary code of ethics and offered seminars for agents. The code proved to be ineffective, and the organization faded after its association with the NFLPA fell apart.

The Sports Lawyers Association (SLA), an organization that predates ARPA and which has a history of educating lawyers practicing in the sports industry, developed a self-regulatory proposal in 1984. The plan, patterned after the "college" approach used by a number of medical specialties, outlined a certification structure backed by state authorization. A draft bill, using the SLA concept, was submitted to the Illinois legislature. The SLA program suggested the establishment of a national Academy of Sports Agents. Certification by the academy would be mandatory for all agents. The academy's curriculum would encompass lessons in contract negotiation, endorsement solicitation, and the management of athletes' funds. The academy would set rules for review of applicants and ultimately establish testing procedures for certification. It would sanction seminars required for continued membership and establish a code of ethics. In essence, the proposal was to establish sports agentry as a profession.[27]

Under this proposal, no one could serve as a sports agent without certification. Each state would authorize the academy as the exclusive licensing body for sports agents. The state would conduct hearings on appeal of an academy decision to deny or revoke certification. All professional teams performing in the state, including visiting teams, would be required to notify the state of all agents who represent members of their teams. Sanctions for violations, such as falsely indicating status as certified, obtaining certification by fraudulent means, and violation of the rules of the academy, would include:

- A civil fine of up to $20,000 per violation
- Contracts between an athlete and an agent who commits a violation voidable by the athlete
- Repayment of fees to the athletes
- Suspension or provisional certification with mandatory disclosure to all clients of the agent's status.

Before reaching the fundamental question of the appropriateness of state involvement, two issues need be noted. One is jurisdiction. If more than one state adopts the academy concept, which state has jurisdiction over which agents? (Not to mention the international aspect in hockey, soccer, and baseball). The second issue, and one that killed the proposed Illinois bill, relates to federal constitutional problems. Unless all states simultaneously implemented the plan, the lack of similar standards for engaging in a particular profession would raise serious equal-protection concerns. Also, the proposal may impermissibly assign state powers to a private entity.

Both issues would be resolved by federal legislation. However, is the regulation of sports agents a worthy use of federal resources? One member of the SLA board of directors thinks not. John Wendel, an attorney for many baseball minor leagues and teams, believes that athletes should rely on the courts and their union's bargaining ability pursuant to federal law to redress any problems with agents. "The position of the athlete in these precincts is over-rated and should not be further protected by preferential legislation guaranteed only to put them on a larger pedestal in an even more unreachable position," Wendel stated in a letter to SLA President Lloyd Shefsky. In his view, any proposal also should protect the agent from the athlete who "capriciously switches agents without adequate notice or proper compensation."[28]

The stated public interest in the academy concept is that the practice of sports agentry merits and receives the confidence of the public and that appropriate safeguards assure honesty, professional responsibilities, educational and ethical standards, and high levels of service for clients. Lloyd Shefsky responded:

> Many agents have gone broke before anybody could have obtained recourse through the courts; others are so financially well-fixed they could withstand a suit, especially since the courts would be reluctant to go after an agent where there are no established guidelines for behavior by agents. This proposal establishes those guidelines, so that anyone who fails to comply with the guidelines could be subjected to civil suit with a meaningful result. A second purpose is to attempt a prophylactic solution and hopefully keep some of these abusive agents out of the business before they do any harm.[29]

To avoid the jurisdictional and constitutional infirmities of the state-by-state approach, the SLA has begun to seek federal legislation. Congress would grant the Secretary of Commerce broad jurisdiction to empower a voluntary organization (presumably the Academy of Sports Agents or a similar entity) to regulate the practice of sports agentry. An established governmental entity or new commission would be designated to oversee the private regulatory entity and to serve as an appeals board. The legislation would be similar to the enabling act that led to the sanctioning of the National Association of Securities Dealers (NASD) as a regulatory body for securities dealers.

Although the SLA's proposal has received informal support from the leadership of the four major players' unions, enactment of the necessary legislation will require the endorsement and active support of the unions. Support from the leagues and the colleges would be very helpful, as would help from the agents who represent a majority of the players. Such a coalition will have to presuade members of Congress that a group whose average salary exceeds $200,000 needs special protection. With every increase in player salaries and ticket prices, the likelihood of legislation decreases. Furthermore, if the NFLPA system reduces agent abuses, Congress will be even more reluctant to intrude. An alternative to government-backed self-regulation would be for unions to obtain agent-certification authority through collective bargaining and sanction the Academy of Sports Agents as the certifying body.

ALTERNATIVES, PHILOSOPHY, AND A PROGNOSIS

In discussing four models of regulation—state, union, NCAA, and self-regulation—this chapter has noted various alternatives to federal regulation. The theory behind these alternatives is either that agent abuses can be reduced by preventive measures (education and information) or redressed and possibly deterred by generally applicable legal rights and processes (litigation).

In economic terms, educating and informing the athlete-consumer seeks to make the market for agent services more perfect. That is, if the athlete knows what he needs and who is capable of fulfilling those needs, he is more likely to pick a qualified agent (or at least he would be less likely to select an incompetent or dishonest agent). Colleges, the unions, and organizations of agents can assist.

From the supply side of the market, educating and informing agents and prospective agents raise the quality of service available. For example, as the baseball experience demonstrates, union cooperation with agents in explaining the implications of collective bargaining agreements and distilling and distributing salary data is invaluable.

Resorting to litigation will not always be satisfactory. After an athlete signs a contract, it is difficult to prove that an agent was negligent because he did not obtain a "good enough" contract. (Sometimes renegotiation is an option.) When an agent mishandles funds, legal remedies are certainly available. But litigation is futile if the agent has vanished or is broke. In any case, litigation is expensive and time-consuming. Meanwhile, the athlete may face bankruptcy, especially if he discovers the problem at the end of his career.

Should the government, state or federal, assist the athlete? California has, with lots of fanfare and little impact. Several other states and Congress have considered agent problems. The area of greatest concern is the relationship of agents to young athletes. One of the few abuses uncovered by California in administering its agent law involved a would-be agent who advertised nationally a football tryout camp. For a minimal fee ($50 to $75), athletes would be evaluated by professional scouts, and the "agent" would represent them and reimburse their travel expenses. When athletes arrived in California from all over the country, they found no one—no scouts, no agent, no registration fees, and certainly no reimbursement.[30] These are not the overpaid veteran free agents. Many of these athletes will last only a few years, if that, in the pros. Their case for protection from agents who overpromise, overcharge, and disappear overnight is the strongest.

Is this justification strong enough? Even if it is compelling, what kind of meaningful, cost-effective regulation is feasible? Is it complete licensing (the Academy of Sports Agents) or simply a registration system (California)? The California system has not received a fair test because of the lack of funding for enforcement. That lack of funding itself may signify a lack of public interest in spending tax dollars to protect athletes. What is the public interest in regulating agents? It is not to make it more difficult for agents to persuade football players to leave Penn State early, even if the defection of a star running back to the pros could cost the state taxpayers hundreds of thousands of dollars in lost television revenues. Successful regulation of agents could even add to salary escalation by benefiting the most skilled agents. Would higher ticket prices be in the public interest?

If agents threaten to undermine the integrity of a sport, there is a significant public interest in regulation. For example, some agents or their cohorts attempt to recruit college athletes through gifts and favors that create a sense of obligation. If they are able to force the athlete to repay the debt by associating with gamblers or any way that affects their performance, certainly the public interest demands a response. Federal action is most likely if more evidence is uncovered of a link between agents and drug abuse by young athletes.

One response short of government regulation as discussed is to allow some sunshine into the agent-selection process. The first step is a thorough congressional investigation of the agent business and the various approaches to regulating agents, particularly self-regulation. An appropriate response from Congress would be strong encouragement to the NCAA to modify its restrictions on undergraduates retaining agents and attorneys.

Significant government intervention is unlikely. The prospects of legislative intervention diminish as athletes' salaries escalate. Moreover, the efforts by the unions, colleges, and agents to improve the ability of athletes to select suitable professional advisers and the capability of those advisers to serve the athletes give legislators more reason to stay on the sidelines. A few states may adopt a variation of the California law, but, regardless, more action is likely in the courts than in the legislatures.

NOTES

1. *New York Times*, September 2, 1984, p. 8E; *Sports Illustrated*, July 2, 1984, p. 64.

2. This provision, which commits Yankee owner George Steinbrenner to pay $3 million over ten years, caused several legal disputes, which are now settled, in which Steinbrenner alleged that the foundation lacked accountability. *Sports Industry News*, August 29, 1984, p. 140.

3. For a more complete discussion of the business of the agents, see Robert H. Ruxin, *An Athlete's Guide to Agents* (Bloomington: Indiana University Press, 1983).

4. This subsection is based on the facts as presented by Bill Brubaker in *Sports Illustrated*, August 29, 1983, pp. 24–31.

5. Although the number of lawsuits against agents seems to be increasing, most are settled prior to appellate-level judicial review. Thus there are few reported decisions. See, for example, Zinn v. Parrish, 644 F.2d 360 (7th Cir. 1981); *Sports Industry News*, August 29, 1984, p. 140 (alleging that an agent embezzled a client's funds); *National Law Journal* (August 13, 1984): 6 ($2.4 million lawsuit against investment broker for embezzlement and racketeering). See also John Weistart and Cym Lowell, *The Law of Sports* (Indianapolis: Bobbs-Merrill, 1979), pp. 319–33; John Barnes, *Sports and the Law in Canada* (Toronto: Butterworths, 1983), pp. 274–78.

6. The highest court of each state establishes the rules under which attorneys practice. The states have begun to conform their codes of conduct with the Model Rules of Professional Conduct adopted by the American Bar Association on August 2, 1983. Rule 7.3 forbids solicitation by mail or in person, or otherwise, unless the lawyer has a prior professional or family relationship. The Model Rules are available from the ABA, 750 North Lake Shore Drive, Chicago, IL 60611.

7. Ed Garvey, *The Agent Game: Selling Players Short* (Washington, D.C.: Federation of Professional Athletes, 1984), pp. 16–21.

8. California Labor Code sections 1500–1547, reprinted in Ruxin, *Athlete's Guide to Agents*, pp. 148–55.

9. California, Senate, Select Committee on Licensed and Designated Sports, Licensing of Sports Agents, Interim Hearing on AB440, 1981, July 22, 1983, pp. 27–33.

10. Ibid., pp. 15–20.

11. Ibid., pp. 5–8.

12. Ibid., pp. 44–49.

13. *Collective Bargaining Agreement between National Football League Players Association and National Football League Management Council*, Art. XXII, Section 2 (Washington, D.C.: National Football League Players Association, 1982), pp. 32–33.

14. NFLPA Regulations Governing Contract Advisors (Washington, D.C.: National Football League Players Association, 1983).

15. Ibid.

16. Lionel S. Sobel, "The Regulation of Player Agents," 5 *Entertainment Law Reporter* 10 (March 1984): 3–9.

17. Garvey, *The Agent Game*, p. 21. Garvey has no doubts of its validity; Professor Sobel is less certain (p. 8). Garvey relies on two Supreme Court cases: H. A. Artists & Associates v. Actors' Equity Association, 451 U.S. 704 (1981), holding immune from the antitrust laws a union's unilaterally imposed system of regulating theatrical agents, but barring the union from collecting a registration fee; and American Federation of Musicians of U.S. and Canada v. Carroll, 391 U.S. 99 (1968), holding immune from the antitrust laws unilaterally adopted union regulation of orchestra leaders and booking agents for "club dates" because their activities had a direct and substantial effect on union members' wages.

Although these cases form a strong basis for arguing that the NFLPA regulations are valid under the antitrust laws, they are not dispositive. Several factual differences are evident. For example, the actors' agents significantly increase their clients' chances of finding work, and the union enforces the regulations by disciplining its members. Moreover, the regulations are not a result of collective bargaining. The NFLPA's regulations themselves are unilateral, but the union bases its authority to impose them on the collective bargaining agreement. Whether any of these factors would be determinative in any challenge to a particular aspect of the regulations is beyond the scope of this chapter. For a thoughtful analysis of court review of collective bargaining agreements in sports, see John C. Weistart, "Judicial Review of Labor Agreements: Lessons from the Sports Industry," 44 *Law and Contemporary Problems* 109 (Autumn 1981).

For discussions of the agent's role in two related fields—entertainment and television news—see *Entertainment, Publishing and the Arts Handbook*, M. Meyer, ed. (1983), pp. 247–54 (Analysis of amendments to California law regulating entertainer's personal managers); pp. 255–63 (regulation of talent agents in California); and Monica Collins, "Anchors, Agents and Angst," *Boston Magazine*, April 1984, pp. 81–82.

18. Like the NFLPA, no baseball union staff represents individual players. Both the baseball union and the NBA Players Association hold briefings for agents who represent athletes in their sports. The NBA releases salary data only to players, not to agents. The general counsel of the NBAPA and executive director of the NHL Players Association also represent individual players. For an extensive report on potential conflicts of interest in hockey, see "The Man Who Rules Hockey," *Sports Illustrated*, July 2, 1984, pp. 60-74.

19. Robert H. Ruxin, "Unsportsmanlike Conduct: The Student Athlete, The NCAA, and Agents," 8 *Journal of College and University Law* 3 (1981–82): 349–53; reprinted in *Law and Amateur Sports* (Bloomington: Indiana University Press, 1982), pp. 193–96. One such rule is that of pro football leagues against drafting most undergraduates. A federal court recently held the USFL rule to be a group boycott and therefore a *per se* violation of the antitrust laws. The plaintiff, former University of Arizona punter Bob Boris, subsequently agreed to settle the case. Boris v. United States Football League, 1984–1 Trade Cases (CCH) 66,012 (D.C.D. Cal. Feb. 28, 1984). For discussion of cases in which the NCAA regulations intended to preserve amateurism and fair competition have been upheld as reasonable restraints in an antitrust context, see *Justice* v. *National Collegiate Athletic Association*, 577 F. Supp. 356, 382 (D-AZ, 1983).

20. *The Washington Post* (May 31, 1984), p. C2.

21. Robert H. Ruxin, *A Career in Professional Sports: Guidelines That Make Dollars and Sense* (Collegiate Commissioners Association, 1982). The NCAA published a revised edition in the fall of 1984.

22. *NCAA News*, August 20, 1984, p. 16.

23. Ibid.

24. U.S. Congress, Senate Committee on the Judiciary, Collegiate Student-Athlete Protection Act of 1983, Hearings on S.610, 98th Cong., 1st sess., March 17, May 23, 1983, pp. 13–26. The hearings present the views of various groups and individuals on agents and issues relating to undergraduates signing professional contracts.

25. *NCAA News* (9 May 1984), p. 7. To be printed in *NCAA Manual 1985–86* (published annually in March).

26. *Inquiry into Professional Sports: House Select Committee on Professional Sports*, Final Report H.R. Rep. No. 94–1786, 94th Cong., 2d sess. 70–77 (1977).

27. *Sports Lawyers Newsletter* (Spring 1984), pp. 1-2.

28. *Sports Lawyers Newsletter* (Summer 1984), pp. 1–2.

29. Ibid.

30. 15 U.S.C. 780—1,2,3.

6

Violence in Professional Sports and Public Policy

D. Stanley Eitzen

An observer of sport has charged that "crimes are being committed regularly on ice-rinks and playing fields."[1] Consider the following examples:

- 1965: Juan Marichal of the San Francisco Giants hit John Roseboro, the catcher of the Los Angeles Dodgers, with his baseball bat.
- 1969: Wayne Maki of the St. Louis Blues used his hockey stick to hit Ted Green of the Boston Bruins, giving him a serious concussion and massive hemorrhaging that required two brain operations.
- 1979: Steve Luke of the Green Bay Packers struck Norm Bulaich of the Miami Dolphins in the face, breaking his jaw and splintering the bones around one eye and ending his football career.
- In the first two months of the 1980 baseball season, there were nine bench-clearing melees following alleged deliberate knockdown pitches.
- 1984: In a hockey game between the Montreal Canadians and the Quebec Nordiques, there were two bench-clearing brawls, a total of 257 minutes in penalties, and ten players ejected. At one time there were fourteen separate fights occurring, among them one between Louis Sleigher and Jean Hamel. Sleigher hit Hamel in the head, putting him motionless on the ice for several minutes. He was helped from the ice, spitting blood and with his right arm hanging limp.

These examples have a common element: aggressive behavior outside the rules that injures in the context of professional sport. Concerning such conduct, two questions arise: Is this issue of gratuitous violence in sport a serious social problem? And, if so, how should it be controlled?

The assumption underlying this chapter is that excessive violence in sport

I want to thank Richard B. Horrow, Chris J. Carlsen, and Congressman Thomas Daschle for their colleagueship in providing background materials on this complex subject.

is a significant problem because athletes are not immune from the laws that
govern conduct in society; and since the professional sports are major
spectacles observed by millions, willful acts to maim other players, if left
unpunished, glorify violence and set deplorable examples for youth and
adults alike. "When moral rules are bent, more than sport is mangled. In the
end it is not the players who are cheapened and injured, nor even the event
itself. It is the children and adults who watch and then repeat what they see
on the playground and in the stands—and perhaps in their lives."[2]

The second question—how should excessive sports violence be controlled?—is the subject of this chapter. More specifically, it addresses
whether such violence can be resolved by government and, if so, by what
mechanisms.

THE PROBLEM

Few would deny that a basic function of government is to protect people
from behavior that disregards their rights, safety, and welfare. It is unclear,
however, whether the government should intervene in sports to ensure that
the participants are protected from the malevolent actions of other players.
Traditionally, sports teams and leagues have policed themselves (with little
success or enthusiasm) when occasional acts of violence have occurred. In
those few instances when the criminal justice system has become involved in
prosecuting instances of sports violence, the laws have been applied un-
evenly, leaving the impression that, for the most part, athletes are exempt
from the laws that govern behavior elsewhere in society. Thus the relevant
question: Should sport be a special case where participants are exempt from
the laws that protect citizens from the flagrant assault of others? And, if not, a
second major question: What is the appropriate mechanism in society to
control such excesses? Inherent in this second question is the issue of whether
or not government intervention is appropriate. To initiate this discussion, the
issue of what is flagrant aggression in an already aggressive activity is
addressed.

Types of Sports Violence

Many sports involve aggressive body contact within the rules: blocking,
tackling, body checking, collisions, shoving, and the like. Not only is it legal
in many sports to aggress against opponents, but it is approved by coaches,
peers, and spectators. It is taken for granted that when one participates in
these sports there is a probability of being injured, even seriously. In college
football, for example, a government study of the 1975–76 school year found
the injury rate was 929 per 1,000 participants, including a rate of 105 per
1,000 for "major" injuries, where players could not participate for at least

three weeks.[3] The injury rate for professional football players exceeds 1,000 per 1,000 annually.[4] In terms of seriousness, playing football at all levels results in 90 neck fractures a year.[5] But while the chances for injury are relatively high and participants in effect consent to the possibility of injury, they do not consent to being injured intentionally outside of the rules.[6] This suggests that there is a difference between normative violence (aggressive acts that are within the rules of sport) and illegitimate violence, which involves the intentional use of force to harm an opponent outside the rules of sport.[7]

This chapter focuses on "illegitimate violence," which is defined as physically assaultive behavior that is intended to and does injure another person.[8] This definition is consistent with that of Richard Horrow, who has defined excessive (illegitimate) sports violence as "force having no reasonable relationship to the competitive goals of sport, is unreasonably violent and could not be reasonably foreseen or consented to by the person affected."[9]

This definition is important because it recognizes that aggression is part of the sport, but that some acts go beyond this "normal" part of the game. While seemingly an easy distinction, the line between legitimate and illegitimate violence is not always apparent. Most injuries actually occur from aggressive acts that are within the rules of the sport. Some "extracurricular" hitting is intended to intimidate opponents by inflicting pain and punishment and is demanded by some coaches and expected by peers. Is that type of physical contact, then, normative? Since knockdown pitches are part of baseball, should such behavior be excused even if someone is injured? Participating in fights is expected of hockey players, as evidenced by the incident in 1982 when Paul Mulvey of the Los Angeles Kings refused his coach's demand to leave the bench and participate in a fight on the ice. His coach told Mulvey that he would never play again for the team because of his cowardice. Is Mulvey the deviant or is his coach? Apparently the hockey world considered Mulvey the deviant because after the incident he was sent to the minors and rejected by the other NHL teams.

The leagues have not placed severe sanctions on players for their flagrant violent acts. For example, when Juan Marichal felled John Roseboro with a baseball bat, he was fined only $1,750 by the league. If that act had occurred outside the sports arena, it likely would have resulted in a prison sentence. Precisely because the leagues have been ineffective in policing violence and because of the difficulties in establishing what is inappropriate aggression in sport, we must consider how to define it, how to control it, and the proper role of the courts and legislatures in the process.

THE ALTERNATIVES

At issue is identifying the appropriate social control mechanism to curb what might be termed "criminal violence" in professional sport. The alternatives

that have been tried or suggested fall into three categories. Sports violence
can be controlled internally by the efforts of the leagues without government
interference, in the criminal and civil courts, as are other forms of interper-
sonal violence, or, as most recently considered by Congress, it can be
controlled by arbitration panels mandated by the law within the league
format.

League Control

Typically, the constitution and bylaws of a professional sports league give the
league commissioner the responsibility to investigate and penalize excessive
violence by players with fines and/or suspensions. The proponents of internal
control by the leagues have several arguments that appear compelling. First,
league officials, unlike judges, attorneys, and juries, have an understanding
of the rules and customs of their sport, thus knowing when an aggressive act
exceeds the norms. "They know better than anyone what conduct is reasonable and what risks the players do, in fact, assume."[10] Second, since contact
sports are emotional and physical, with acts of aggression permitted, it is
inappropriate for the courts to apply the laws on assault and battery that
apply to the rest of society inside sports arenas. The argument is that contact
sports are similar to certain other occupations, such as law enforcement,
where force is sometimes expected in the line of duty. To impose the regular
laws on assault and battery on the police or on athletes, it is argued, would do
grave damage to these occupations.[11]

Third, theoretically, internal controls should provide a powerful deterrent
against further violence. The judgment by a league can be swift, certain, and
severe—precisely those qualities that make punishment most effective. The
league should be able to act more rapidly than the courts and, because of a
thorough knowledge of the game, be more able than the courts to impose
uniform and predictable sanctions. Most important, the leagues have the
authority to suspend guilty players, thereby depriving them of their liveli-
hoods (and in the short careers of athletes, every month and season are
precious). Since this also negatively affects the competitive edge of these
players' teams, the teams will use their power to curb excessive violence.

There are several problems, however, that minimize or negate the argument that the leagues are the best enforcers of negligent player conduct.
Foremost, it is inappropriate for a body that regulates a sport to deal with
criminal behavior that arises in that sport. As two lawyers familiar with
sports violence have argued:

> To suggest that the governing body of a particular sport determine appropriate
> sanctions for a quasi-criminal or a criminal act would be tantamount to granting
> the board of directors of General Motors jurisdiction over the determination of
> guilt or innocence and the appropriate punishment for one of their employees

who, while on the job, killed his foreman. It would seem that if violence in sports is to be curtailed, the only effective remedy lies with the state, where the capability of meting out effective deterrent sanctions exists.[12]

A second problem, and one related to the first, is that the internal disciplinary procedures of the leagues amount to a private system of criminal law that gives the commissioner in each league immense powers as accuser, judge, and jury. This private system places the players at a tremendous disadvantage, since they are denied the procedural safeguards found in the public sphere.[13]

Third, commissioners have tended to punish excessive violence of athletes rarely, minimally, inconsistently, or not at all. Three examples from professional football make this point:

- When George Atkinson leveled Lynn Swann with a vicious forearm, causing Swann to suffer a serious concussion and miss part of the 1976 season, Commissioner Pete Rozelle imposed a fine of $1,500 on Atkinson.
- When Darryl Stingley was paralyzed by Jack Tatum's vicious hit, which Tatum admitted was overly aggressive in order to intimidate his opponent,[14] not even his team was penalized in yardage, since the blow was within the rules.
- When linebacker Stan Blinka was suspended for one game in 1982 by Rozelle for a "cheap shot" against receiver John Jefferson, it marked only the second time in the 63-year history of the league (the first was in 1977) that a player had been suspended by the league for an unnecessarily violent act.

In contrast to the nominal fines and rare suspensions that league officials have given to violent athletes, penalties have been far more severe and uniformly given to athletes involved in gambling or for even associating with known gamblers. Apparently the leagues perceive gambling as a much greater offense than athletes maiming one another.[15]

Another set of problems center on the arbitrary decision by a league on what type of conduct it will and will not tolerate. Professional hockey, for example, is the only team sport in which players who fight are not automatically ejected from that contest. (International and collegiate hockey have ejection rules, so it cannot be argued that fighting is necessary to play hockey at a competitive level.) Clearly, fighting is an accepted part of professional hockey. This policy is reflected in the token penalties for fighting—a two-minute period in the penalty box—and in the statement by National Hockey League President John Ziegler, who testified before a congressional subcommittee that the league viewed spontaneous fighting as a justifiable "outlet for the frustration in hockey."[16]

On first reading, these criticisms appear to be surmountable at the league level. The hockey editor of *Sports Illustrated*, Mark Mulvoy, in an open letter to President Ziegler of the NHL, argued that the problem of stopping hockey violence can be solved easily: "The solution to on-ice violence is simple. The first time a player drops his gloves or swings his stick, kick him out of that game and the next five; also, don't allow teams to replace suspended players on their roster. For the second such incident, kick the player out of that game and the next ten."[17] Similar sanctions could be applied consistently in the other sports as well. Most important, violence could be deterred if the punishment was swift, certain, and meaningful to *the offending player, his coach, and the owner of his team.* Then coaches and owners would not encourage intimidation, such as when a pitcher was fined $250 by his manager for not throwing at a batter as instructed.[18] Nor would they hire and use players in "enforcer" roles. Each team in the NHL, for example, tries to have at least one player in this role. His job is to intimidate opponents with excessive physical play and to start fights deliberately to give teammates a psychological lift.

But despite these optimistic claims, solutions to thwart excessive violence within the league family will not likely be forthcoming. Simply put, this is because the incentives for the players, coaches, owners, and leagues encourage violence rather than minimize it. Violence is believed to have commerical value: It is box office. The media sensationalize violence in their coverage of sports events and in advertising upcoming contests. Spectators are thrilled by violence, especially that which is linked to heroic action— athletes "confronting one another, putting their physical well-being on the line for the sake of achieving a legitimate and valued goal: victory."[19] Violence by athletes confirms for spectators that the players are committed totally to achieving victory at whatever cost. The commercial value of a team and its players is enhanced with success. Thus intimidation and violence are used to gain a competitive edge. This aspect cannot be overemphasized: "Since winning is viewed as the sole criterion for success, the means to achieve that end become less scrutinized."[20] Some marginal athletes also have employed a strategy of being overly aggressive as a means for them to participate.

In sum, the common belief that violence makes sports more profitable for athletes, coaches, team owners, and the television networks means that the leagues are confronted with a fundamental contradiction: Violence is the means for achieving winning and financial benefit. At the same time, the leagues insist that they are the ones to police excessive violence. Is there any wonder, then, why the efforts of the leagues are too weak to destroy the financial incentives to engage in violent conduct? This conflict of interest that the leagues face negates any genuine attempt by them to curtail excessive violence. Since league officials apparently remain convinced that sports violence is more entertaining than illegal, the effective sanctioning of sports violence must be found in some other agency and/or mechanism of social control.

Sports Violence and the Courts

An alternative to the leagues' efforts to control violence are the courts—criminal and civil.

Criminal sanctions. The criminal courts have jurisdiction over sports violence because of the laws prohibiting assault and battery. The argument advanced by proponents of criminal sanctions for the perpetrators of sports violence is that criminal behavior is criminal whether or not it is inside a sports arena.

> The mere act of putting on a uniform and entering the sports arena should not serve as a license to engage in behavior which would constitute a crime if committed elsewhere. If a participant in a sporting event were allowed to feel immune from criminal sanction merely by virtue of his being a participant, the spirit of maiming and serious bodily injury, which at present occurs all too frequently in a sport such as hockey, may well become the order of the day. It is ludicrous to think that anything short of criminal sanctions will deter conduct that is criminal in its character.[21]

As logical as this argument is, in actuality the criminal courts rarely have been used for sports violence, and then without success. Only one criminal prosecution for an alledged act of sports violence has occurred in the United States. In *State* v. *Forbes* (1976), David Forbes of the Boston Bruins was charged with assault when he hit Henry Boucha of the Minnesota North Stars over the head with the butt of his hockey stick, jumped on him, and pounded his head onto the ice. As a result of this savage attack, Boucha had three operations to repair his eye socket, twenty-five stitches, and a recuperation period of eight months to recover from double vision. The jury was unable to reach a verdict, however, and a mistrial was declared.[22] Three Canadian trials of defendants charged with sports-related criminal violence also have resulted in acquittals.[23]

There are several reasons for the paucity of criminal cases involving sports violence and why prosecutors have been unsuccessful in obtaining convictions. First, there is the widespread belief that contact sports are unique because violence is intrinsic to them. Moreover, proving intent (a criminal mind—*mens rea*) is difficult when players are engaged in an emotionally charged activity, moving at high speeds, making quick decisions, and hitting each other in the normal course of the activity. It may be clear to a prosecutor that "any blow struck in anger or which is intended or likely to do corporal hurt is a criminal assault,"[24] but jury members have proven less likely to accept a criminal definition of such action. Also, given the special nature of contact sports, many believe that the sports would be changed significantly if criminal sanctions were applied to overly aggressive acts. Players fearful of criminal prosecution may become tentative, reducing their effectiveness. If this assumption is correct, then the use of criminal sanctions may "eliminate some desirable conduct necessary to the continued vigor and popularity of the game."[25]

Criminal justice officials tend to ignore sports violence because it is so widespread. This is the "community subgroup rationale," whereby illegal conduct is overlooked because everyone is doing it. By this reasoning, it would be unfair to punish a few for what almost everyone in the group is doing.[26]

Another legal problem that inhibits prosecutors in sports violence cases is the so-called assumption-of-risk doctrine. When people voluntarily consent to participate in a high-risk activity such as coal mining or professional hockey, they cannot recover damages from another participant if injured. If, however, it can be proven that the injury resulted from something other than good-faith competition—that is, the intentional effort to do harm—then the injured party can sue for damages and the perpetrator is guilty of a crime. As Hechter has argued: "Historically, a player's consent to participate in the sport cannot take away the basic criminal nature of the act as the consent can in no way affect the rights of the public, and as the assault was a breach of peace the consent of the person struck is immaterial."[27] Once again, the prosecutor is faced with the difficult task of convincing a jury that the injury occurred outside the normal bounds of competition.

Richard Horrow surveyed twenty U.S. county prosecutors in whose jurisdictions most of the professional teams operate, and he found them to be averse to prosecuting sports violence. In addition to the problems already cited, the prosecutors gave these reasons for their reluctance: (1) they were already too busy prosecuting "real" criminals; (2) the grievances should be initiated by the athletes in civil courts; (3) most lawyers do not have the expertise to handle sports violence cases; and (4) it is too difficult to get a guilty verdict.[28] These problems have kept public prosecutors from prosecuting all but the most flagrant instances of sports violence, and usually not even them.

The tort suit. Most legal experts tend to agree that the most effective use of the courts to control excessive sports violence is not in the criminal courts, but in civil courts, where the injured party seeks remuneration from the assailant. The tort suit has several advantages over criminal prosecution.[29] Foremost, there is a greater chance of a ruling against the perpetrator. Tort law is more flexible than criminal law, with a lesser burden of proof required. A major advantage of the civil suit is that, because of the doctrine of *respondeat superior*, employers—owners, administrators, and coaches—can be held liable for the tortious conduct of their employees committed in the scope of their employment.[30]

These advantages of tort cases have important deterrent value. To require compensatory damages strikes at the heart of the financial incentive that is a major source of sports violence. Criminal courts do not provide compensation to the injured parties, but civil courts do. If players are held financially liable for their egregious acts, then their excessive acts may be tempered. Most important, if coaches and owners are held accountable, morally and financially, for the overly aggressive actions of their players, then they may work to curb such socially undesirable activities.

Three civil court cases have shown that offending athletes, and on occasion their employers, are financially liable for their excessive violence on the sports field. In the case of *Nabozny v. Barnhill* (1975), a participant in an amateur soccer match kicked the goalie in the head, causing severe injuries. The act took place while the perpetrator was in the penalty area, where the rules specifically prohibit contact. The court ruled that the defendant was "reckless and negligent" and was liable to the victim because he broke a safety rule designed to protect players from serious injury.[31] This ruling is especially significant because it negates the "assumption-of-risk" defense.

The case of *Hackbart v. Cincinnati Bengals, Inc.* (1979) is also significant. In the course of a professional football game, Charles "Booby" Clark of Cincinnati hit Dale Hackbart of the Denver Broncos from behind, away from the action, and seconds after the play was over, causing Hackbart to suffer a serious neck fracture. Hackbart sought damages of $1 million in the district court. The judge, however, ruled against Hackbart, arguing that the level and frequency of violence in professional football are such that participants must recognize and accept the risk that they may be injured. This decision was reversed, however, by the Tenth Circuit Court of Appeals. The judiciary ruled it appropriate for an athlete to recover for personal injuries suffered in an athletic event. The court also ruled that not only can the perpetrator be sued, but so, too, can the violent player's employer—a team—be sued for damages. In 1979 the Supreme Court upheld this ruling.[32]

The first awarding of a huge settlement occurred in the case of *Tomjanovich v. California Sports, Inc.* (1979). The plaintiff was hit in the face by Los Angeles Laker Kermit Washington during a professional basketball game, resulting in severe fractures of the nose, jaw, and skull. Tomjanovich asked for $2.6 million in damages, citing that Washington's punch was malicious and intentional assault and battery, and that the plaintiff's earning capacity was severly curtailed as a result. The jury returned a verdict calling for $1.8 million in actual damages and $1.5 million in punitive damages—remarkably, $600,000 *above* what the plaintiff had requested. This case is meaningful because it held that (1) individual acts of violence are not part of the game of professional basketball; (2) that when conduct exceeds the rules and customs of the game, resulting in injury, the injured party should be compensated; and (3) that Washington's employer was negligent because the team did not train and supervise him and because they allowed him to play after they were aware of his tendency to be violent.[33]

Despite these rulings and the advantages of tort suits over criminal cases, the civil suit has some disadvantages that have made it, too, a relatively weak control device over excessive violence in professional sports. For example, most of the players have been reluctant to bring charges against another athlete. Richard Horrow surveyed nearly 1,400 professional athletes in football, hockey, and basketball and found that they were reticent to bring charges against other players for two reasons. First, such an act would violate the "macho code" among playing peers whereby players who are victims of exceptionally violent behavior believe that they and their teammates should settle the dispute personally on the field of play. Second, the players fear being labeled troublemakers by the league owners, thereby threatening their livelihood.[34]

A second problem negating the power of the civil courts is the determination of what is and what is not acceptable violence. Some instances are obvious, but others are not. There are the problems of the variation in interpretation by judges, the unequal skills of the attorneys for both sides, and the varying composition of the juries.

Last is the problem of athletes in the course of a season playing in a multiplicity of jurisdictions. States vary in their laws. Some jurisdictions apply the doctrine of *respondeat superior* narrowly, while others have a liberal construction. The Tomjanovich case, for example, occurred in California, a state where the liberal view of this doctrine prevails, thus resulting in a favorable ruling for the plaintiff. A much different ruling might have occurred in another jurisdiction.[35] Carlsen and Walker have argued that this plurality of jurisdictions makes the tort system impractical:

> The multiplicity of jurisdictions and the corresponding multiplicity of tort doctrines to which a traveling sports participant is subject renders the tort system impractical for use as a deterrent. This multiplicity of legal standards makes it almost impossible for professional sports participants to know the applicable standard of care as they move from jurisdiction to jurisdiction. Without a clear standard to which their behavior should conform, players are less likely to exercise self-restraint. Certainty of standard would enable professional athletes to conform more precisely to the required standard.[36]

In sum, the use of criminal and civil courts to control criminal violence in sports has been minimal and sporadic, since a number of issues make criminality and/or culpability difficult to determine. What is the line between "normal" and "illegal" violence? Is sport a separate realm with different criteria for assessing violence than are used in other sectors of society? Are there differences among sports? Added to these issues are the differences in court decisions based on variations in the law by jurisdiction, jury composition, and judicial discretion.

Richard Horrow has summarized the situation:

> Realistically, there are a number of significant and serious problems every time the courts become involved in litigating sports violence. In fact, the sports establishment is probably correct when it argues that *most* disputes should be "kept within the family." However, courts, must stand ready to intervene, dispite the problems, when an act of during-the-game violence is excessively severe or when the league's fine or suspension is not severe enough. Organized athletic competition does not exist in a vacumm. The operation of law does not stop at the ticket gates of any sporting event. No segment of society can be licensed to break the law with impunity. Armed with experience gained from the *Forbes, Hackbart,* and *Tomjanovich* trials, prosecutors should formulate appropriate guidelines for bringing charges. The legislation should be drafted that clearly defines the line between aggressive play and excessive, illegal contact. The leagues need to cooperate with prosecutors, legislators and others in order to create clear standards acceptable to all concerned.[37]

Legislative Action

We have seen that internal league control and the courts have been ineffective in curbing excessive violence in professional sports. The leagues are neutralized by a basic conflict of interest, and the courts are hampered by ambiguous laws, differences in interpretation, inconsistencies in application, sporadic and haphazard interventions, and the uniqueness of professional sports— ranging from the "normal" aggressiveness intrinsic to some sports to the interstate nature of the occupation. A third alternative for controlling excessive violence is legislative action at the national level. What is needed is a rational system with clear guidelines that transcends the various court jurisdictions and with the power to impose sanctions that are fair and capable of deterring "criminal" violence. A federal solution appears appropriate, since professional sports involve interstate commerce, national communication networks, and national interest. Moreover, as the presiding judge in *Hackbart* v. *Cincinnati Bengals, Inc.* argued, there are certain "industries of extreme danger," such as coal mining and railroading, where the rapidity and specificity of legislative action is required.[38] Sport is such an industry; it's an industry where excessive violence is a problem that begs for a solution. Two bills in Congress have proposed federal intervention to control excessive violence in professional sport.

The Sports Violence Act of 1980 (H.R. 7903). Congressman Ronald M. Mottl of Ohio introduced a bill, written with the aid of attorney Richard Horrow, that would have imposed a uniform criminal sanction for exceptional acts of violence in sports. The bill called for penalties of up to a year in prison and a $5,000 fine for professional athletes who knowingly use excessive physical force. A player would be liable if the alleged illegal act met these six criteria: (1) it is inflicted in circumstances that showed a definite resolve to harm another, or demonstrated negligent, reckless, deliberate, or willful disregard for the safety of another; (2) it is in violation of a safety rule of the game designed to protect players from injury; (3) it occurs either after play is stopped or occurs without any reasonable relationship to the competitive goals of the sport; (4) it is unreasonably and excessively violent and beyond the generally accepted nuances and customs of the particular sport; (5) it could not reasonably have been foreseen by the victim as a normal risk in playing the sport; and (6) it results in contact that causes a significant risk of injury to the victim.[39]

The bill did not pass, having met resistance by many athletes, sports fans, and especially from the administrators of professional leagues, who argued that such a bill, if passed, would change the nature of contact sports. It would be an unnecessary intrusion of the federal government into an area generally unregulated but able to police itself. Moreover, opponents argued that the bill imposed criminal penalties and criminal labeling that in many cases would be too servere because the violent conduct was not the product of an evil state of mind.

The Sports Violence Arbitration Act of 1983 (H.R. 4495). Congressman Tom Daschle of South Dakota, drawing on the expertise of lawyers Richard Horrow, Chris J. Carlsen, and Matthew S. Walker, introduced legislation that included a new concept for the investigation of alleged instances of exceptional violence in sport and that increased the power to impose monetary penalties and suspensions on the perpetrators. Daschle's bill differs from the Sports Violence Act of 1980, which from the viewpoint of the legislators imposed a too severe and criminal-like punishment on athletes.[40] Instead of using the criminal justice system, the Daschle plan employs a different mechanism for control—an impartial arbitration panel.

Under the conditions of the bill, each league would be required by law to set up an independent arbitration panel through its collective-bargaining agreement. Thus the players and owners must agree on the composition of the panel, using, if necessary, the already existing procedures employed by the National Labor Relations Board. Any player or team sustaining an injury as the result of excessively violent conduct may bring a grievance before this panel. The panel would investigate the incident and hold proceedings in accordance with the Federal Mediation and Conciliation Service. The decision of the panel would be binding on the parties. If the conduct in question was found unnecessarily violent, outside the rules, and intentional, any of the following sanctions could result: an award of compensation paid by the employer of the violent player or the imposition of disciplinary sanctions against the offending player and his team (fines, suspension from play without pay, and loss of a draft choice).[41]

This proposed legislation has several strengths: (1) it places the responsibility for policing violence within each league; (2) it permits each league to determine what is excessive violence in its unique context; (3) it holds players *and* owners responsible for violence, and the more that owners are sanctioned, the greater the likelihood that players and coaches will be curbed in their excessive behavior; (4)it removes the criminal penalties and the criminal justice system from the process; and (5) it combines a federal policy decision, initiated to protect the safety of citizens involved in interstate commerce, with localized control.

The proponents of federal legislation argue that their solution provides an effective social control mechanism for the protection of athletes in each sport from intentional efforts by others to harm. As attorney Chris Carlsen, arguing for the sports court concept, has concluded: "A crumpled Darryl Stingley should have been enough to show the NFL and society that the ugliness and staggering costs cannot go on unheeded much longer or possibly justify any financial value violence has. The player's physical health, the owners' financial health and the fans' emotional health demand the establishment of the sports court now."[42]

While federal intervention to control excessive violence in professional sport appears to be the most appropriate solution, the major questions are whether such legislation will be enacted in the near future and, if so, in what form? The Daschle bill died in committee (the House Subcommittee for Labor Management Relations) because the legislative term elapsed before a hearing could be held. Efforts are underway, however, to revive the bill in the next session of Congress with additional sponsors. Richard Horrow, a major nonlegislative force behind the proposal, remains optimistic that eventually Congress will enact a Sports Violence Act.[43] That remains an empirical question, and so for the present we are left with the occasional efforts of the leagues and even less occasional attempts by the courts to sanction criminal violence in professional sports.

CONCLUSION

The three alternatives to curb excessive sports violence in professional sports examined here have been ineffective. The internal solution of league control has, for the most part, not only been weak but also has condoned and even encouraged violence by action and inaction. For a different set of reasons, the civil and criminal courts also have been relatively impotent vehicles to control the hostile violence by athletes.

The legislative alternative has, to date, not resulted in any laws to limit violence. The lack of legislation in this area is the result of a long tradition of leaving the regulation of sport to the leagues. The leagues lobby against the various bills, and legislators perceive the public as being apathetic to sports violence. Some recent public opinion data suggest that this perception of apathy by the members of Congress may be a misreading of the public. A Louis Harris poll of sports fans conducted in 1983 revealed that: (1) half felt that sports in general are too violent; (2) 80 percent felt that hockey is too violent and 70 percent believed football to be; and (3) 69 percent believed that football players who commit deliberate acts of violence on the field should be banned for a full season, and 25 percent would ban the offender for life.[44]

These data indicate that the public is not only concerned with excessive sports violence but also that it accepts severe sanctions for the perpetrators. Since experience shows that the leagues and courts are ineffectual agents for controlling such violence, the solution lies elsewhere. With public support, Congress should finally act, for if this problem is to be controlled, "society must intervene and enforce a level of conduct which is reasonable."[45]

NOTES

1. William Hechter, "The Criminal Law and Violence in Sports," *Criminal Law Quarterly* 19 (1979): 425.

2. Cited in Cameron Jay Rains, "Sports Violence: A Matter of Societal Concern," *The Notre Dame Lawyer* 55 (June 1980): 809.

3. Health Education and Welfare report, *Athletic Injuries and Deaths in Secondary Schools and Colleges, 1975-76*. Cited in Lorenzo Middleton, "Million Injuries in Year Reported in School Sports," *The Chronicle of Higher Education* (March 5, 1979): 1, 15.

4. John Underwood, *The Death of an American Game: The Crisis in Football* (Boston: Little, Brown, 1979), p. 98.

5. Robert C. Yeager, *Seasons of Shame: The New Violence in Sports* (New York: McGraw-Hill, 1980).

6. Michael D. Smith, *Violence and Sport* (Toronto: Butterworths, 1983), p. 10.

7. John Schneider and D. Stanley Eitzen, "The Structure of Sport and Participant Violence," *Arena Review* 7 (November 1983): 1.

8. Smith, *Violence and Sport*, p. 7.

9. Cited in Associated Press release, "Anti-Violence Bill That's Aimed at Pro Sports Gaining Support," *The Los Angeles Times*, March 15, 1982, p. 1.

10. Rains, "Sports Violence," p. 797.

11. Lyle Hallowell and Ronald I. Meshbesher, "Sports Violence and the Criminal Law," *Trial* 13 (January 1977): 28.

12. Gary W. Flakne and Allen H. Caplan, "Sports Violence and the Prosecution," *Trial* 13 (January 1977): 33–34. Mr. Flakne, county attorney for Hennepin County, Minnesota, was the prosecutor in the famous sports violence case of State v. Forbes; Mr. Caplan was his assistant prosecutor.

13. See M. Schneiderman, "Professional Sport: Involuntary Servitude and the Popular Will," *Gonzaga Law Review* 64 (1971); and D. I. Shapiro, "The Professional Athlete: Liberty or Peonage?" *Alberta Law Review* 218 (1975).

14. Jack Tatum with Bill Kushner, *They Call Me Assassin* (New York: Everest House, 1979), p. 223.

15. Stephen J. Gulotta, Jr., "Torts in Sports: Deterring Violence in Professional Athletics," *Fordham Law Review* 48 (1980): 768–69.

16. Cited in Jerry Kirshenbaum, "It's Time for the NHL to Stop the Hooliganism," *Sports Illustrated* March 9, 1981, p. 9.

17. Mark Mulvoy, "Hockey 1980–81," *Sports Illustrated*, October 13, 1980, p. 50.

18. Cited in Don Atyeo, *Violence in Sports* (New York: Van Nostrand Reinhold, 1981), p. 270.

19. Jay J. Coakley, "The Sociological Perspective: Alternative Causations of Violence in Sport," *Arena Review* 5 (February 1981): 45.

20. Richard B. Horrow, *Sports Violence: The Interaction Between Private Lawmaking and the Criminal Law* (Arlington, Va.: Carrollton Press, 1980), pp.38–39.

21. Flakne and Caplan, "Sports Violence and the Prosecution," p. 35.

22. State v. Forbes, No. 63280 Minn. Dist. Ct., 4th Dist. (August 12, 1975). For the details of this case, see Flakne and Caplan, "Sports Violence and the Prosecution."

23. Regina v. Green, 16 D.L.R. 3d 137 Provincial Ct. Ottawa-Carleton (Crim. Div.), Ontario (1971); Regina v. Maki, 14 D.L.R. 3d 164 Provincial Ct. Ottawa-Carleton (Crim. Div.), Ontario (1970); and Regina v. Maloney, No. S-461-76 Jud. Dis. of York, Toronto (Crim. Ct.), (1976).

24. Hechter, "Criminal Law," p.429.

25. Note, "Consent in Criminal Law: Violence in Sports," *Michigan Law Review* 148 (1976): 176. Cited in Horrow, *Sports Violence*, p. 123.

26. W. Kuhlman, "Violence in Professional Sports," *Wisconsin Law Review* 3 (1975): 771–90.

27. Hechter, "Criminal Law," p. 429.

28. Horrow, *Sports Violence*, pp. 110–27.

29. For an elaboration of the rationale for the superiority of civil suits in sports violence cases, see Candyce Beumler, "Liability in Professional Sports: An Alternative to Violence?" *Arizona Law Review* 22 (1980): 919–38; Gulotta, "Torts in Sports," pp. 764–93; and Dale J. Lambert, "Tort Law and Participant Sports: The Line Between Vigor and Violence," *Journal of Contemporary Law* 4 (1978): 211–17.

30. Gulotta, "Torts in Sports," pp. 777–87.

31. Nabozny v. Barnhill, 31 Ill. App. 3d 212, 334 N.E. 2d 258 (1975).

32. Hackbart v. Cincinnati Bengals, Inc., 435 F. Supp. 352, 354 (D. Colo. 1977), rev, d. 601 F. 2d 516 (10th Cir.), cert. denied, 444 U.S. 931 (1979).

33. Tomjanovich v. California Sports, Inc., No. H-78-243 (S.D. Tex., 1979); and Rick Horrow, "The Legal Perspective: Interaction Between Private Lawmaking and the Civil and Criminal Law," *Arena Review* 5 (February 1981): 12.

34. Horrow, *Sports Violence*, pp. 50–51.

35. Gulotta, "Torts in Sports," pp. 782–85; and Chris J. Carlsen and Matthew Shane Walker, "The Sports Court: A Private System to Deter Violence in Professional Sports," *Southern California Law Review* 55 (January 1982): 413–14.

36. Carlsen and Walker, "The Sports Court," p. 413.

37. Horrow, "The Legal Perspective," pp. 18–19.

38. Ronald Mottl and Rick Horrow, "The Legislative Perspective: The Sport Violence Acts of 1980 and 1981," *Arena Review* 5 (February 1981): 21.

39. Timothy S. Robinson, " 'Sport Nut' Lawyer Seeks Legal Curb on Violence by Professional Athletes," *The Washington Post*, July 21, 1980, p. D1; "An Assault on Violence," *Sporting News*, August 23, 1980, p. 14; Robert J. Boyle, "Ending the Immunity," *Sports Illustrated*, September 8, 1980, p. 18; Andrew C. Miller, "Miami Lawyer Thinks They Should Pass a Law Against It—Literally," *The Kansas City Star*, October 27, 1980, pp. 1C, 4C; and Mottl and Horrow, "The Legislative Perspective," pp.19–21.

40. Charlie Nobles, "Rich Horrow Fights the Violence of Pro Sports," *The Miami News*, June 11, 1983, p. 3B.

41. For the details of this bill, see Thomas A. Daschle, "Sports Violence Arbitration Act of 1983," *Congressional Record* 129, 98th Cong., 1st sess. (November 18, 1983); for the background to this use of a sports court, see Carlsen and Walker, "The Sports Court"; Chris J. Carlsen, "Deterring Players' Violence on the Field," *New York Times*, December 19, 1982; Chris J. Carlsen, "If You Think the NFL Has Enough Problems," *The Los Angeles Herald Examiner*,

September 12, 1982; and Richard B. Horrow, "How to End Violence? Pass a Law with Bite," *The Miami Herald*, November 20, 1983.

42. Carlsen, "If You Think the NFL Has Enough Problems."

43. Communication with Richard Horrow, July 10, 1984.

44. Reported in Erik Brady, "USA Sports Fans Decry Violence." *USA Today*, April 26, 1983, pp.B-1, B-2.

45. Rains, "Sports Violence," p. 810.

PART II

Public Policy and Sports Administrators

The chapters in this section examine policy issues that directly affect sports administrators and sports organizations. Challenges to the economic and organizational arrangements employed in sports are perceived by league representatives, team owners, and college officials as a threat to their control of sport. Others see these challenges as an attack on unjustified monopolistic practices that neglect the interests of the athlete and public in order to maximize the sports entrepreneur's financial interests.

Brian Porto examines recent judicial challenges to NCAA control of intercollegiate athletics and the suitability of the courts as arbiters in struggles between athletes and their schools and in conflicts between schools and the NCAA. He concludes that if the NCAA will not share its role with educators, the courts will continue to impose their logic upon intercollegiate athletics. Porto argues that courts are ill suited for such a role and may create policy that will adequately serve neither the NCAA nor its members.

Phillip Closius provides a comprehensive review of the antitrust issue in professional sports and warns against extending further the antitrust immunity of sports leagues. He especially opposes legislative granting of antitrust immunity that would confer upon all professional leagues a status equal to that of professional baseball. Closius argues that the leagues should reform their practices to comply with the "business purpose" of sport that the courts defined in the 1970s in rejecting unilateral control of sport by league administrators. League representatives, however, are reluctant to implement such reform and relentlessly continue to seek exemption for specific practices from the courts and Congress.

Philip Hochberg discusses the significant issue of the ownership of broadcast rights. Since determination of the ownership question will affect the distribution of millions of dollars in sports broadcasting revenues, this issue is certain to be the center of future labor negotiations in professional sports, and already has caused conflict among colleges and universities. Hochberg provides the necessary background for understanding this important future policy issue.

James Ambrose shifts the focus away from the more highly publicized issues of antitrust immunity and broadcasting policy to the less visible and more complicated issue of tax policy. Ambrose argues that tax policy can be a stabilizing influence on the sports industry. He asserts that sports should not be identified for special tax treatment, either positive or negative. Owners should be allowed reasonable depreciation allowances similar to those enjoyed by entrepreneurs in other industries. In so doing, responsible owners will be attracted to sports, while those who seek only financial gain from franchise ownership will look elsewhere for advantageous tax breaks.

This section clearly reveals that much of the administration of modern sports—amateur as well as professional—has to do with concerns unrelated to on-the-field activities. Sports administration today is more concerned with the business aspects of sports-broadcast contracts, tax treatment of players' contracts, and labor relations. Sports administrators attempt to make a case that such business considerations are integral to managing the "sports" side of sports, and on that basis seek special treatment for public policy purposes. The authors of the articles in this section resist that position and argue that sports should not be granted special treatment under the law.

7

Legal and Constitutional Challenges to the NCAA: The Limits of Adjudication in Intercollegiate Athletics

Brian L. Porto

Increasingly, it seems as if the most interesting collegiate sports news is made not on the fields of play, but in the courts of law. This conclusion comes from observing the steady stream of litigation concerning intercollegiate athletics that has flowed into state and federal courts in recent years. Since 1982, for example, judges have been asked to decide: (a) whether possession of an athletic scholarship renders an athlete an employee of the university that conferred the award, thereby entitling the player to worker's compensation when injured, (b) whether an athlete has a constitutionally protected property right to attend a university, when attendance is desired for the purpose of securing a professional basketball contract, and (c) whether the National Collegiate Athletic Association's (NCAA) mission to preserve intercollegiate football as an amateur activity justifies the restraints that its television plan imposes upon competition in the sports broadcasting trade.[1]

These diverse legal disputes possess a noteworthy common feature. That is, they are a part of a large group of challenges to NCAA control of intercollegiate athletics that have been initiated in recent years by many different elements of the college sports community. These challenges have been brought by members of the association, as well as by organizations that are not a part of the NCAA but are significantly affected by its policies and procedures.

THE NCAA UNDER ATTACK: A STEADY STREAM OF LITIGATION

Within the NCAA's immediate family, challenges have been brought by predominantly black colleges, universities with big-time football programs, administrators of intercollegiate athletics programs for women, university presidents, coaches, and most frequently, scholarship athletes (sometimes with their universities filing suit on their behalf). The black colleges have challenged the NCAA to devise educationally responsible academic requirements for incoming freshman athletes that also are sensitive to the educational disadvantages typically experienced by black students. In particular, these colleges have criticized the NCAA for its adoption in 1983 of Proposition 48, which requires that, beginning in 1986, entering freshman achieve specified minimum scores on the Scholastic Aptitude Test or the American College Test in order to be eligible for intercollegiate competition.[2] Black educators argue that as a result of their typically inferior elementary and high school preparation the majority of black athletes entering college are unlikely to satisfy this requirement. This assertion was in fact supported by the NCAA's own study of the impact of Proposition 48. These athletes will therefore be punished for the deficiencies of their home and school environments, for which they are not responsible, by being declared ineligible for athletics as freshmen. The presidents of the black colleges have discussed filing suit to prevent the new rules from going into effect and withdrawing their schools' NCAA memberships.

Universities that operate successful big-time football programs have challenged the NCAA to relinquish its control over the televising of college football, thereby allowing individual schools to make their own arrangements for televising their games. In this way, the highly successful schools, most of whom have joined the College Football Association (CFA) in order to press this issue, would be able to appear on television as many times as the market would permit. The universities of Oklahoma and Georgia, both CFA members, have argued successfully in federal court that NCAA control over the televising of college football violates the Sherman Antitrust Act. An appeal by the NCAA was rejected by the United States Supreme Court.[3] In a larger but related issue the CFA and the universities with big-time sports programs in general have challenged the association to reduce the ranks of Division I, the top rung on its competitive ladder, in order to restrict membership to those institutions with ambitious programs in both football and basketball.[4] At the same time, institutions in Division IA, the top competitors in football only, have demanded the right to pass rules for their division at a separate annual convention.[5] These last two challenges have taken the form of legislative proposals introduced at NCAA conventions.

Administrators of intercollegiate athletics programs for women also have been critical of the NCAA, most notably for allegedly forcing out of business the Association for Intercollegiate Athletics for Women (AIAW) in June 1982. The NCAA offered the AIAW member schools a program of women's championships at no additional cost to the schools. The AIAW could not match this offer, since it did not have financial or political power equal to that of the NCAA. The AIAW challenged the NCAA in court, arguing that this action constituted a "predatory pricing" arrangement that violated the Sherman Antitrust Act.[6] On a larger, related front, women athletic administrators and coaches, backed up by members of Congress and the former Department of Health, Education, and Welfare (HEW), challenged the association, both in and out of court, to provide equal opportunities for men and women in intercollegiate athletics programs. This challenge resulted largely from HEW's interpretation of the language of Title IX of the Education Amendments of 1972, which expressly prohibits discrimination on the basis of sex "under any education program or activity receiving federal financial aid." According to HEW, this prohibition applied not only to specific programs receiving federal aid but also to all educational activities carried on by a school that received financial aid, whether or not the particular program that featured discrimination received any federal money.[7]

Finally, athletes and coaches have challenged the NCAA on constitutional grounds. Assistant coaches in basketball and football have filed suit against the association in attempts to overturn its Bylaw 12–1, adopted in 1975, which limits the number of assistant coaches who may be employed in Division I schools. The plaintiffs charged that they possessed a constitutionally protected property right to continued employment, which was denied to them without due process by the NCAA because the NCAA had not allowed them to participate in the debate that preceded the bylaw's adoption. By denying them access to this debate, the coaches argued, the NCAA failed to accord them their right to be heard, a minimal due process requirement under the Fourteenth Amendment where a property or liberty interest has been demonstrated.

One head coach, in a successful suit against his university and the NCAA, challenged the association's claimed right to order a university to suspend a coach who has been found by the association to have violated its rules. In arguing successfully in 1979 for a temporary court order to block his suspension, and that is now permanent, he charged that the NCAA's enforcement procedure had been arbitrary and capricious and, if carried out, would deny without due process of law his property interest in earning a living.[8]

Student athletes who have been declared ineligible for competition as a result of violating NCAA regulations also have sued the association on Fourteenth Amendment grounds. In nearly a dozen suits filed during the past decade, ineligible athletes have used various rationales in claiming that they possessed a property right to participate in intercollegiate athletics that was protected by the Fourteenth Admendment and that the NCAA had violated their rights by declaring them ineligible without observing due process requirements.[9]

Other athletes, whose collegiate sports careers have been ended prematurely by injury, have challenged their universities and the NCAA in court. Using a statutory rather than a constitutional basis for their arguments, these plaintiffs have contended that their possession of athletic scholarships at the time of their injuries made them university employees who were eligible for worker's compensation under the terms of the worker's compensation laws in their respective states.[10] These suits have challenged universities to assume responsibility for financially assisting those who are seriously injured while representing them. In addition, they have in effect also challenged the NCAA either to abandon its historic view that scholarship athletes are amateurs who do not receive "pay" for their performances or to devise a means of aiding seriously injured athletes other than by worker's compensation.

The NCAA also has been confronted on governance issues by the mass media. The media have thrown down the gauntlet by reporting the numerous scandals that have plagued college athletics in recent years. Abuses in recruiting, antagonisms between participation in big-time college sports and the completion of an undergraduate education, and suggestions for reforming the existing system have been brought to the public's attention by the mass media.[11]

Of late, national education organizations, especially the American Council on Education (ACE), also have challenged the NCAA. Their aim has been to increase the power of educators within the association in order to foster academic integrity in intercollegiate athletics. The ACE's Committee on Division I Intercollegiate Athletics originally proposed the creation of a board of college presidents that would have power to veto rules and procedures of the NCAA and to impose new rules of its own creation on member institutions. The board's actions could be overruled only by a majority of presidents of NCAA institutions. In response to criticisms that it was undemocratic, the proposal was modified subsequently to permit NCAA convention delegates to overrule the actions of the proposed board by a two-thirds vote.[12] In addition, the Educational Testing Service has entered the fray, agreeing with many black leaders that the association's new minimum test score requirement for freshmen discriminates against blacks, and offering the NCAA assistance in considering alternatives that would not be discriminatory.[13]

Finally, a considerable amount of criticism of NCAA enforcement procedures has come from professors of law, who have challenged the NCAA to clarify its system of rules and penalties, and to build into its enforcement program procedural safeguards that would ensure that athletes are treated fairly in disciplinary cases.[14]

This spate of challenges to NCAA authority during the 1970s and 80s is in part a response to the substantial expansion of that authority that began in the early 1950s and hit its stride during the 60s. Specifically, the expansion of authority involved the establishment of a system of enforcing association rules, which grew from a few general principles in the early years to a detailed code requiring a 335-page manual by 1984.[15] Most important, the growth in power transformed the NCAA from a purely legislative organization with no enforcement or adjudicative mechanisms to an organization that not only drafts rules but also administers and resolves disputes concerning those rules. As the NCAA's capacity to establish and enforce penalties for rule violations has increased, so has its susceptibility to challenge. The increased rate of challenges to the NCAA also is a reflection of the recent growth in awareness of rights by American society generally and by women and members of minority groups in particular. The expansion of NCAA authority and the growth of feminism, civil libertarianism, and racial pride in America could not remain on parallel tracks indefinitely; sooner or later, the irresistible force would meet the immovable object, with the result that NCAA hegemony in college athletics would be challenged.

Recent events support these contentions. Clearly, the federal courts have indicated their belief that the scope of NCAA authority has expanded greatly since the organization's early days as a purely legislative agency. The best evidence of this is that federal courts around the country have concluded that NCAA activities are "state action" within the meaning of the Fourteenth Amendment. This is an important conclusion because without it a coach or athlete could not bring a constitutionally based due process claim against the NCAA; only state action is subject to Fourteenth Amendment protections. It is also a conclusion that derives in part from the view that the NCAA performs legislative, administrative, and adjudicative functions that are governmental in nature and that would have to be performed by a government agency if the NCAA did not exist.[16] The determination by the federal courts that the association's football television plan is a *per se* violation of the Sherman Antitrust Act also reflects a conviction that the NCAA has expanded its original mission considerably. Those rulings held the association to an antitrust standard typically applied only to purely commercial organizations.[17]

In light of the fact that so many of the challenges have been framed in legal terms and presented in court, it seems appropriate for students of judicial policymaking to inquire how well equipped our judiciary is to resolve policy disputes in college sports. More to the point, it is necessary for judicial scholars to warn educators and athletic administrators that the judiciary's peculiar weaknesses as a policymaker are likely to hinder its efforts to resolve such disputes in a manner that serves the educational needs of student athletes without imposing unreasonable burdens upon university resources.

THE LIMITATIONS OF JUDICIAL POLICYMAKING

In order to appreciate the limits of judicial policymaking in college athletics, it is necessary to be familiar with the constraints under which policymaking by judges ordinarily operates. Prominent among these is the habit of focusing attention upon the circumstances of a particular case rather than upon the larger social problem that the case may present.[18] Unlike legislators, who are free to investigate a problem in all its nuances and dimensions, and who therefore can fashion a remedy designed to counteract its most frequent and troublesome manifestations, judges are concerned principally with resolving the specific case at hand. If the case presents unusual circumstances, the court's decision may result in a policy that fails to respond to the overarching social problem, but that solves the specific problem presented by that case. In intercollegiate athletics this means, for example, that instead of producing rulings designed to eradicate employmentlike conditions in the lives of scholarship athletes, judges are content to determine whether or not particular athletes were employees of their universities when they sustained career-ending injuries. It also means that when a scholarship athlete in a relatively low-pressure athletic program is found not to be a university employee, his or her counterparts from athletically ambitious schools likely will be subjected to the same ruling despite their considerably different circumstances.

Judicial concentration upon specific cases rather than the societal dilemmas that they underscore derives largely from the fact that America's judicial institutions were formed in the eighteenth and nineteenth centuries, when the prevailing conception of the nature and purpose of a lawsuit was vastly different from that which exists today. According to the traditional view, a lawsuit is invariably (a) "bipolar," namely, subject to the participation of only the two parties named in the case, (b) "retrospective" or concerned only with an identified set of completed events, and (c) "self-contained," meaning that its final judgment will affect the lives and/or behavior of only one of the parties most directly involved.[19] This model, observes Harvard law professor Abram Chayes, is no longer a realistic one. Today's "public law litigation" is calling upon trial judges to create "complex forms of on-going relief, that have widespread effects on persons not before the court and that require the judge's continuing involvement in administration and implementation."[20] Under these circumstances, in which the judge is less of an arbiter than a policy planner and manager, the traditional concept of litigation as a mechanism designed merely for the settlement of private disputes fails to keep pace with reality. Unfortunately, while judges are increasingly being asked to act as planners and administrators of public policies that profoundly affect many diverse interests in society, judicial institutions have retained a structure and set of procedures that are designed to resolve private disputes. In the case of intercollegiate athletics, judges are being asked to make major policy determinations concerning relationships between athletes and universities, athletic departments and academic personnel, and universities and professional sports leagues. However, the judges' training and institutional guidelines equip them only to decide whether or not a specific student athlete has been denied due process by university officials.

A closely related problem is the judiciary's tendency to frame issues in terms of rights rather than policy alternatives. In keeping with the traditional view of the lawsuit as a private conflict, judges have long viewed their responsibilities as limited to the identification of the litigants' rights and duties, but not to the fashioning of policies for society. As a result, the adjudication process has an unfortunate tendency to assign rights and duties without having carefully assessed all of the costs—whether financial, administrative, or psychological—that might be associated with a particular right or duty.

Even when the judicial process attempts to weigh the implications of a prospective decision, its capacity to respond quickly and effectively to social problems is hindered by the inherently piecemeal character of policies made through litigation. Since different cases emphasize different pieces of the social-problem puzzle, judicial policymaking is inclined to respond to one portion of that problem at a time, thus separating and isolating issues that are intimately connected. Judges are by no means incapable of constructing remedies for any social malady, but the remedies they suggest are likely to be "too little, too late" as a result of the gradualism imposed by the litigation process. Therefore, a judicial response to a social problem often is characterized by fits and starts, moving too rapidly at one point and too slowly at another. Under these conditions policymaking proceeds at a pace dictated by the litigants and by the court calendar.

In intercollegiate athletics this means, for example, that each athlete who files a worker's compensation suit will attempt to distinguish his or her case from those wherein the plaintiff was declared not to be a university employee. These distinctions may be insignificant, but they will be offered nonetheless; if they are accepted by a court, the plaintiff is likely to win the suit. Therefore, permanently disabled former college athletes are likely to file worker's compensation suits indefinitely or until all available rationales for claiming employee status have been presented in litigation. As a result, the judicial process may resolve assorted disputes between disabled athletes and their universities, but it is unlikely to produce imaginative remedies for the larger problems of professionalism in intercollegiate athletics.

Finally, judicial policies suffer from their authors' frequent lack of familiarity with the subjects contained in much of today's public law litigation. This lack of expertise derives largely from the fact that judges are assigned to rule upon such a wide variety of subjects that it is virtually impossible for them to become experts in any. In light of their rotation from problem to problem, argues Donald Horowitz, "On most of the important social policy problems that come to them, judges are bound to be novices."[21] At the same time, because of limitations imposed by the rules of evidence and by the finite human capacity for independent research, judges must rely for information regarding social problems upon secondary interpretations, chiefly those of partisan expert witnesses.[22] Under these circumstances, it is not difficult to understand why "the adjudication process conspires in a dozen small and large ways to keep the judge ignorant of social context."[23]

Judges often choose to respond to a serious social problem by ignoring or emphasizing policy alternatives with a retreat into the familiar world of rights and duties. This generally is done by focusing the investigative process upon "historical facts," or events that have transpired between parties to a lawsuit. This is done at the expense of "social facts" or recurrent patterns of behavior upon which public policy decisions are typically based.[24] This misplaced focus is not necessarily the mark of a lazy judge. Rather, it results from the fact that the adversary process is designed for the resolution of individual disputes rather than the formulation of general social policies. Unfortunately for the consumers of these policies, the judges' preference for history over sociology (that is, antecedent facts over consequential facts) results in the declaration of a single rule that works beautifully in a narrow set of circumstances but is irrelevant in the vast majority of circumstances.

In college athletics this tendency has produced rulings that the college athlete has a constitutionally protected property right to participation derivative of the fact that intercollegiate athletics are an integral component of the process of higher education. Since at many schools big-time athletic programs hinder their participants' academic progress, it is naive to base a property interest in intercollegiate competition upon a perceived nexus between athletics and education. While some athletes undoubtedly could show that such a nexus exists in their particular cases, many others, if called upon to do so, would be hard pressed to satisfy this requirement. By emphasizing rights and duties and ignoring social realities, federal courts on several occasions have predicated a constitutionally protected right upon a premise of questionable credibility.[25]

JUDICIAL LIMITATIONS AND COLLEGE ATHLETICS: THREE CASE STUDIES

Worker's Compensation

Each of the weaknesses in judicial policymaking discussed above was present in decisions handed down in *Rensing* v. *Indiana State University* and *Coleman* v. *Western Michigan University*. Each case concerned the eligibility of athletic scholarship recipients for worker's compensation.[26] These decisions illustrate the inability of narrowly drawn legal rules to identify and remedy the troublesome larger problem of professionalism in college sports.

The first of two rulings in *Rensing*, handed down by the Indiana Court of Appeals in June 1982, responded favorably to Fred Rensing's appeal of a decision by the Industrial Board of Indiana that denied his request for permanent total disability benefits and for reimbursement for medical and hospital expenses arising from a football injury. Rensing, who was attending Indiana State University (ISU) on an athletic grant-in-aid, became a quadriplegic with an estimated disability of 95 to 100 percent as a result of a spinal fracture suffered while tackling a teammate in a punting drill during spring practice in 1976. He had been unable to convince either a hearing examiner or the full Industrial Board that he deserved worker's compensation because of a failure to show that his relationship to ISU was that of employee to employer, as defined by Indiana's worker's compensation statute.

The Court of Appeals concluded that Rensing and the Board of Trustees had negotiated an exchange of his football talents for their financial assistance during the four years of his athletic eligibility. This clearly placed the parties in the relationship of employee to employer. This conclusion was based largely on the terms of Rensing's athletic scholarship, which stipulated that if an injury ended his playing career he would be expected to perform alternative duties for the athletic department in order to continue receiving aid. In addition, the terms of the scholarship enabled the trustees to end their relationship with Rensing if he failed to satisfy academic requirements, quit the football team, misrepresented information on his application to the institution, or engaged in serious misconduct warranting disciplinary action. For these reasons and because the Indiana legislature recognized college scholarships as "pay pursuant to a contract of hire in the analogous context of unemployment benefits," the court reasoned that the trustees' view of an athletic scholarship as a gift or "grant" rather than an employment contract was erroneous.[27]

The Indiana Supreme Court, in a subsequent appeal by the trustees, did not agree that Rensing had been an employee of Indiana State at the time of his injury. Since the NCAA outlawed the payment of athletes for their services and the Internal Revenue Service did not regard the benefits derived from scholarships as income, it was inconceivable that Rensing's scholarship agreement could have been perceived by either of the signatories as a contract of employment. Moreover, an athletic scholarship recipient, who is not expected to hold a campus job in return for benefits, cannot be considered a university employee. He or she is simply a student whose talents have enabled him or her to receive financial assistance in the pursuit of higher education. Finally, because NCAA rules prohibit the withdrawal or reduction of athletic scholarships during an academic year as a result of poor performance or an insubstantial contribution to team success, the ISU trustees lacked the "ordinary employer's right to discharge on the basis of performance."[28]

Less than three months after the Indiana Supreme Court denied Fred Rensing's claim, Willie Coleman, a former football scholarship recipient at Western Michigan University, told the Michigan Court of Appeals that at the time of his career-ending wrist injury in 1974 he had been a university employee. The court concluded that Coleman's relationship with Western Michigan satisfied only one component of the four-part "economic reality" test, which it used to determine whether an "express or implied contract of hire" existed between the parties. Western Michigan had paid Coleman "wages" upon which he depended in order to pay daily expenses. However, because the NCAA prohibited the revocation of a scholarship during the year for which it had been awarded and the dismissal of an athlete from a team during a school year as a result of poor performance, Western Michigan's capacity to discipline athletic scholarship recipients like Coleman for unsatisfactory performances was viewed as insufficient to suggest the existence of an employment relationship. In addition, the athletic task that Willie Coleman had performed was not an "integral part" of the "business" of Western Michigan University; the university's "business" was educating students and conducting scholarly inquiry. The football program was not essential to those purposes. Willie Coleman was denied compensation under Michigan's Worker's Disability Compensation Act, as his appeal failed to clear three of the four hurdles established by the economic reality test.

The *Rensing* and *Coleman* decisions share much more than rulings unfavorable to the plaintiffs. The decisions exhibit the judicial propensity for focusing upon only one component of a large social problem: whether or not an athletic scholarship is a contract of employment. As a result, the relationship between big-time intercollegiate athletics and employment is forced to take on a "yes-or-no" simplicity that belies the murky status that the athletic scholarship recipient actually possesses. The scholarship athlete's unique dual role of student and entertainer cannot be placed into exclusive categories such as "student" or "employee." On the one hand, the athlete has been recruited by the university and given access to an undergraduate education with financial aid in return for providing athletic entertainment to the public. On the other, he or she, like every full-time student, is expected to register for a specified minimum number of academic credits per term, maintain a certain minimum grade-point average in order to ensure eligibility for athletics, complete a predetermined number of courses in a major field, and satisfy an array of general education requirements in order to graduate. In choosing to focus upon whether or not the athletic scholarship is a contract of employment, the Indiana and Michigan courts largely overlooked the contradictions and inconsistencies that derive from this dual role. As a result, they were unable to fashion or even suggest remedies for the educational, medical, and financial problems produced by the employmentlike environment of big-time college sports.

Rensing and *Coleman* also illustrate the judicial inclination to frame complex social issues in terms of rights and duties while disregarding the social implications of the rights and duties that have been assigned to the parties. In the initial *Rensing* decision, for example, the Indiana Court of Appeals ignored the considerable financial, administrative, and educational implications of assigning employee status and disability compensation rights to athletic scholarship recipients.

The financial consequences of such a decision include the rapidly escalating premiums for liability insurance, the likelihood of unemployment compensation for permanently disabled players, and the prospect of unionization by athletes in pursuit of salary and benefit packages comparable to those enjoyed by other unionized university workers. Administrative implications include the likely use of a university's employee grievance procedures by athletes to question decisions of team management that traditionally have been the prerogative of coaching staffs. This could generate complaints that might only be resolvable by experts who are not members of the institution. The educational consequences of the first Rensing decision include the designation of scholarship athletes as semiprofessionals who might be permitted to decide for themselves whether they wanted to be students as well as athletes. While such a freedom-of-choice plan might represent a recognition of the extraordinary time demands associated with playing a college sport and the unwillingness of many athletes to meet even minimal academic requirements, it also would represent a statement by the universities that they consider the preparation of athletes for professional sports careers to be one of their principal missions.

In both *Rensing* and *Coleman*, framing the issues presented in terms of rights and duties also caused the courts to ignore imporant social facts that should have been evaluated beforehand. In *Coleman*, for example, the court observed that the plaintiff's athletic scholarship did not subject him to any greater degree of control by university authorities than was experienced by any other student or athlete. That observation contradicts a large body of evidence that suggests that the demands of participation in sports prevent many athletes from obtaining degrees during the customary four-year period.[29]

Since the court determined that Coleman's scholarship constituted wages upon which he depended in order to pay living expenses, its conclusion that the university subjected him to no greater control than any other student is baffling as well as unrealistic. How could he have been both a wage-earner dependent upon his income from the university and a student subject to no greater degree of university control than any other student? In the court's eyes, apparently, it was possible for Coleman to have lost his income and educational opportunity by virtue of injury yet still not be a university employee because the school lacked sufficient disciplinary power over him to warrant his designation as an employee.

The court again ignored important social facts when it argued that Western Michigan's capacity to dismiss an athlete for unsatisfactory performance was limited significantly by the NCAA prohibition against revoking scholarships during the academic year. Since the bachelor's degree customarily takes four years to complete, annually renewable scholarships are a powerful disciplinary tool for university athletic departments. The athlete who is serious about earning a degree and who cannot do so without a scholarship must perform to the satisfaction of the coaching staff each year in order to maintain continual access to educational opportunities.[30] For this reason, the athlete is subject to a degree of university control that is not experienced by those who do not hold athletic scholarships.

Coleman and *Rensing* also concluded that football was not an integral part of the business of the defendant university. This suggests that neither court understood the important position of intercollegiate athletics in contemporary university life. The interpretation of the role of big-time intercollegiate athletics presented in these decisions fails to recognize that while universities would continue to deliver educational services in the absence of big-time athletics, many schools believe that under such circumstances they would not be able to deliver those services as effectively or to as many people as they presently do. This argument suggests that successful athletic programs mean increased student enrollment, national and regional visibility for the school, television revenue, and donations from boosters and alumni.

Finally, *Rensing* and *Coleman* reflect the judicial tendency to make policy in response to the peculiar circumstances presented by litigants. In these cases the characteristics of the athletic programs at Indiana State and Western Michigan are significant. These schools have not traditionally fielded nationally ranked, highly visible football and basketball teams; their athletic budgets are not among the largest in college sports; and they do not compete in the most prestigious athletic conferences. Under these conditions, Fred Rensing and Willie Coleman may not have been the most appropriate plaintiffs to contend that their scholarships were contracts of employment. Perhaps if similar claims were made by athletes from traditional athletic powers where the pressure for victory is more intense, where athletics are very profitable for the university, and where athletes are routinely groomed for professional leagues, judicial sensitivity to the employmentlike features of big-time college sports would have been more realistic. This discussion will remain speculative unless and until a suit is filed against the likes of Nebraska, Kentucky, Arizona State, or Alabama. Unfortunately, the plaintiff in that suit will face not only the institutional limitations of the judiciary but also the judicial affinity for following established precedents like *Rensing* and *Coleman*.

The Athlete's Property Interest in Intercollegiate Participation

Hall v. *University of Minnesota*[31] involved the efforts of a student athlete at the University of Minnesota to recover his rights to matriculate and to participate in varsity basketball. He had lost these rights because he was not enrolled in any degree-granting program. The Big Ten Conference, to which Minnesota belongs, requires that athletes at its member schools be enrolled as candidates for degrees in order to be eligible for intercollegiate competition.[32] The plaintiff claimed that his two applications to Minnesota's *University Without Walls*, a degree-granting program, were evaluated in an arbitrary and capricious manner and this deprived him, without due process of law, of his property interest in attending the university. In finding for the plaintiff, Federal District Judge Miles W. Lord observed that Hall had been singled out by two successive directors of the *University Without Walls* for unusually harsh application reviews without Hall ever having been informed of the allegations that precipitated these unprecedented measures or having been afforded an opportunity to rebut the charges against him. Judge Lord concluded that Hall indeed had been denied property without due process.

That conclusion resolved the immediate issue of Mark Hall's athletic eligibility, but it did not determine the legitimacy of Hall's peculiar interpretation of that property right. Mark Hall did not see his property interest in the earning of a degree that would prepare him for employment in a business or a profession. Rather, his interest was the exhibition of his athletic talents in order to warrant selection in an early round of the National Basketball Association draft and to receive a potentially lucrative professional contract.

Hall's interpretation of a property interest in attending a university presents this question: Can an athlete whose eligibility has been revoked for academic reasons successfully sue a university on the grounds that, since that athlete was recruited primarily to participate in its athletic program, his or her progress toward a professional athletic contract should not be impeded by academic requirements tangential to career goals and about which he or she was not informed adequately during the recruiting process? That is, could a university's academic suspension of an athlete be construed as the denial of a property right—the pursuit of a professional contract—without due process of law? Moreover, even if athletes are informed of their academic responsibilities, can they realistically be expected to fulfill those responsibilities in the face of their often inadequate preparation and motivation for college-level studies and the time demands of their sport? Most important, can an athlete be expected to meet academic requirements when his or her claimed property interest is athletic eligibility?

Hall is notable because it is one of nearly a dozen recent suits filed by high school and college athletes that claim that the plaintiff possessed a constitutionally protected property right to participation in athletics. This fact protected him against a declaration of ineligibility without benefit of a hearing.[33] Collectively, these cases illustrate the limitations of piecemeal, litigant-initiated policymaking by a highly decentralized federal judiciary. Some courts have recognized a constitutional right to participation in intercollegiate athletics while others have rejected such a concept, and still others have skirted the issue and based their decisions on alternative grounds. No clearcut policy has been articulated, and the status of the property right remains uncertain after a decade of litigation.

It is likely that student athletes will continue to go to court to assert a property right to participation in intercollegiate athletics. Some will argue that college athletics are a training ground for professional athletics; hence, the college athlete has an economic interest in maintaining eligibility for competition because collegiate participation is a prerequisite for a career in the professional ranks. Others will argue that intercollegiate sports are an integral part of the total undergraduate educational experience and, therefore, to declare an athlete ineligible for competition without due process is to deny that athlete an educational opportunity. Still others will contend that their athletic scholarships are contracts that confer upon them legally enforceable "entitlements" to participation in athletics, to the economic benefits specified in the scholarship agreement, and to freedom from the arbitrary and capricious revocation of those entitlements.[34]

The contractual rationale is the one most likely to succeed, for it lacks both the dangers of the economic argument and the flawed assumptions of the educational justification. Unlike the economic rationale, it cannot be used to exempt athletes from academic requirements because such requirements are perceived as antagonistic to a property interest in preparing for a career in professional sports. Unlike the educational notion, it recognizes that big-time intercollegiate athletics are not necessarily an integral part of the mission of higher education, but are frequently detrimental to that mission. At the same time, the athletic scholarship clearly confers upon the recipient an obligation to participate in athletics plus material benefits, such as free room, board, tuition, and a book allowance during the period for which the grant has been awarded. These would seem to satisfy the "entitlement" requirement for establishment of a property right.

The NCAA's Football Television Plan and the Antitrust Laws

The limits of adjudication also are reflected in the decision by the Tenth Circuit Court of Appeals in *Board of Regents of the University of Oklahoma* v. *National Collegiate Athletic Association*.[35] This suit challenged the NCAA's football television regulations as *per se* restraints of trade in violation of Section One of the Sherman Antitrust act.[36] The plaintiffs contended that the regulations prevent individual schools from negotiating independently with networks for the televising of their teams at prices determined by the school and the network. They also argued that the NCAA would expel and boycott institutions that violated its regulations.

The language of the majority opinion indicates that these arguments were persuasive.

We affirm the district court's conclusion that the television plan is unreasonably restrictive of competitive conditions and therefore unlawful. It increases concentration in the marketplace; it prevents producers from exercising independent pricing and output decisions; it precludes broadcasters from purchasing a product for which there are not readily available substitutes; it facilitates cartelization. Against this array of antitrust injuries, the NCAA's justifications are insufficient.[37]

Unfortunately, this language derives from the erroneous assumption that intercollegiate football can be singularly defined as a commercial enterprise and that the NCAA can therefore be viewed solely as a mechanism of business regulation. While big-time college football can be financially lucrative, it also is an extracurricular activity for full-time students who possess amateur standing.

As long as college football retains the foundation of amateurism, the NCAA can be viewed not merely as a business-regulating entity but also as an instrument for promoting and protecting football competition as an amateur activity within the university context. It is arguable that the NCAA has neglected its duty to foster athletic excellence without sacrificing academic integrity, but it cannot be asserted that the association's sole function is commercial. The NCAA performs economic and educational functions, but only the economic role was acknowledged by the judiciary.

Significantly, the U. S. Supreme Court has held since 1975 that self-regulating organizations that engage in economic activities but do not exist primarily for commercial purposes are permitted to engage in restraints of trade that are prohibited to commercial organizations.[38] Under these less stringent standards, restraints such as price-fixing, prominent in the NCAA's football television plan, would not be struck down automatically as *per se* violations of the Sherman Act, but would be examined in the light of their noncommercial justifications. If found to be essential to a reasonable policy goal, these actions would be upheld. If the federal courts applied this rule of reason to the NCAA, they likely would approve regulatory schemes, such as the football television plan, that are necessary to the preservation of amateur, intercollegiate competition, but which, if undertaken by a commercial enterprise, would violate the *per se* rule.

The "rule of reason" standard was the basis for the conclusion in Judge James D. Barrett's dissenting opinion that these restraints employed by the NCAA are fully justified, since they are necessary to maintain intercollegiate football as amateur competition. According to that opinion:

The restraints upon Oklahoma and Georgia and other colleges and universities with excellent football programs insure that they confine those programs within the principles of amateurism so that intercollegiate athletics supplement, rather than inhibit, academic achievement. As thus measured, the restraint is not unreasonable in its effect on competition; its procompetitive effect clearly outweighs the anticompetitive effect.[39]

Subsequently, Judge Barrett added: "I conclude that the district court erred by subjugating the NCAA's educational goals to the purely competitive commercialism of the 'every school for itself' approach to television contract bargaining."[40] Just as the *Hall* decision illustrated adjudication's inclinations toward narrowness and slowness, the *Oklahoma* decision has illustrated the tendency of adjudication to disregard social facts that must be recognized and appreciated if realistic, enlightened rulings are to be produced.

The U. S. Supreme Court, in its June 27, 1984, decision in *Oklahoma*, showed no more sensitivity to the NCAA's dual function than did the Tenth Circuit Court of Appeals. In a 7–2 decision, the Court upheld the appellate court's ruling, arguing that the NCAA's football television plan severely restricted both the price and the availability of televised college football. Such restrictions on price and output, said Justice John Paul Stevens's majority opinion, "are the paradigmatic examples of restraints of trade that the Sherman Act was intended to prohibit."[41] In Stevens's view, neither the need to achieve a competitive balance among member schools nor the need to ensure large live audiences for college football could justify the "naked restraint on price and output" that characterized the NCAA plan.[42]

The dissenting opinion of Justice Byron White, joined by Justice William Rehnquist, echoed the words of the earlier dissent by Judge Barrett of the Tenth Circuit. Referring to the NCAA as "an educational association" that engages in some more-or-less commercial activities," Justice White wrote: "Although some of the NCAA's activities, viewed in isolation, bear a resemblance to those undertaken by professional sports leagues and associations, the Court errs in treating intercollegiate athletics as a purely commercial venture in which college and universities participate solely, or even primarily, in the pursuit of profits."[43]

In rejecting Justice White's analysis and refusing to apply the rule of reason standard to the NCAA football television plan, the Supreme Court has helped to create an environment wherein pressures for longer seasons, weeknight games during prime viewing hours, and contests between geographically distant powers are likely to increase. Within such an environment, the challenges facing educators, who would like to see a deprofessionalization of college athletics, and athletes, who genuinely are interested in completing degrees, also are likely to increase. At a time, then, when intercollegiate athletics was beginning to make important strides toward academic integrity, the Supreme Court may well have forced the college game to take a major step in the opposite direction.

THE IMPLICATIONS OF JUDICIAL LIMITATIONS: RECOMMENDED ROLES FOR JUDICIAL AND NONJUDICIAL POLICYMAKERS IN COLLEGE ATHLETICS

The Role of the Courts

In light of their numerous weaknesses as architects of public policy, it seems appropriate to ask what role, if any, should courts play in the shaping of intercollegiate athletics policy? Certainly, it is possible for courts to be catalysts for necessary change in college sports in the years ahead if they confine themselves to issues that call for judicial scrutiny. Judicial resolution is required by questions of due process or procedural fairness. For example, the NCAA's refusal to permit the athlete's interest (restoration of eligibility) to be presented independently of the school's interest (regaining access to television appearances and postseason competition by paying the penalty imposed) during regulatory proceedings necessitates judicial vigilance. Given the NCAA's exclusive control over big-time college sports and its ability to influence profoundly a student athlete's eligibility for future grants-in-aid and opportunities for a professional sports career, the integrity of such proceedings is a fitting subject for judicial review.

Similarly, due process protection through judicial diligence is called for when the NCAA attempts to punish a coach by forcing a school to suspend or fire that coach for alleged violations of the association's rules. If the school refuses to carry out the NCAA's orders, which may have resulted from a wholly inadequate investigation, the NCAA may counter by imposing additional penalties upon the institution. Just as the NCAA's exclusive authority over intercollegiate athletics enables it to influence an athlete's eligibility for scholarships and a professional career, so that authority enables the association to influence a coach's employment future in college athletics. In either case, the association's regulatory proceedings ought to be subject to judicial review in the interest of ensuring fairness. Moreover, judges are ideally suited to scrutinize NCAA disciplinary processes, since due process issues concerning rights and duties, rather than substantive questions of educational policy, are the stuff of judicial life.

There is no better support for these statements than the litigation in which University of Nevada–Las Vegas basketball coach Jerry Tarkanian successfully sued the NCAA for due process violations by showing that its investigation of him had failed to produce adversary witnesses, documentation of violations, or any evidence more credible than hearsay.[44] The *Tarkanian* case graphically illustrates both the power of the NCAA to influence the lives of its members and their employees and the need for judicial attention to due process in NCAA regulatory activities.

Judicial scrutiny also is warranted where the NCAA has made a plainly commercial decision that cannot be justified on the basis of its role as the monitor of academic integrity and the guardian of amateurism in intercollegiate athletics. The NCAA was not intended to be, and should not be treated as, a commercial sports enterprise comparable to the National Football League or the National Basketball Association. Hence, the judiciary need not defer to association decisions motivated by a desire to promote competitive balance among schools so that spectator support and revenues might be maximized.

However, judges should defer to other policymakers on subjects that possess substantial implications for the athlete's likelihood of earning an undergraduate degree. Judges must give the NCAA and educators leeway to make educationally beneficial decisions that possess important commercial consequences. In matters such as the football television plan, where educational and commercial implications exist, the courts should have exercised restraint and permitted the higher education community to counter the creeping professionalism in college athletics, even if that requires hindering economic competition. In cases with important educational implications, judicial restraint would produce decisions that would recognize that college athletics possess employmentlike features and would admonish educators either to remove those features or designate scholarship athletes as university employees. That important choice and its implementation would be the responsibility of educational authorities.

Finally, the judiciary can be a significant force for constructive change in college athletics by serving as a reminder to a reluctant NCAA that the likely result of its failure to respond legislatively to its critics will be protracted, expensive, and potentially embarrassing litigation. At this writing, the NCAA, in an attempt to preclude more suits like *Rensing* and *Coleman*, is studying the possibility of awarding athletic scholarships for four or five years instead of annually and of offering catastrophic injury insurance to its members for the 1985–86 academic year.[45]

The Role of Educators

Given the judiciary's limitations and the NCAA's preoccupation with public entertainment, national organizations of educators must investigate the relationship between big-time college athletics and educational integrity, speak out about the antagonisms between them, and prod the NCAA to remove from collegiate sports employmentlike features. Since 1982, the American Council on Education, acting through its Committee on Division I Intercollegiate Athletics, has attempted to do all of those things, and with some success. To date, the ACE's most visible accomplishment has been the institutionalization of an advisory role for university presidents within the

NCAA through the establishment of a 44-member Presidents' Commission. The commission is empowered to propose legislation, advise the NCAA and its governing council, commission studies, establish the sequence in which convention proposals are considered, force roll call votes on controversial proposals at conventions, and call special meetings of the NCAA.[46]

The ACE's Athletics Committee also convinced the delegates to the 1984 Convention to tighten both the existing definition of "satisfactory progress toward a degree" and the academic prerequisites for immediate eligibility upon transferring to a Division I school from a two-year college.[47] The major ACE agenda item for the near future, which the Athletics Committee is pushing the Presidents' Commission to endorse, is a reduction in the number of games and the length of the season in Division I basketball and the proposal of such limits for other sports in which no limits presently exist.[48]

The NCAA has been responsive to these recent efforts by educators to participate more actively in the governance of college athletics and to toughen the academic requirements for athletic eligibility. Certainly, the educators' victories have been partial ones, since neither the presidents' panel nor the academic rules established by the 1984 Convention contain the "teeth" that the ACE would have preferred. However, complete victory is rare in any large, diverse legislative body; incremental change, often grudgingly produced, is the norm. Hence, the changes adopted by the 1984 NCAA Convention are neither cause for despair nor reason for jubilation; they are, nonetheless, positive steps in a desirable policy direction.

The Role of Legislators

The void left by NCAA inaction also needs to be filled by legislative action, as it has begun to be regarding the compensation of permanently injured athletes and the number of years for which athletic scholarships should be awarded. In April 1984 the Nebraska Legislature passed a law requiring the state's public colleges and universities to buy insurance against catastrophic injuries and to continue the scholarships of permanently injured athletes who are no longer able to participate in athletics.[49] Also in the spring of 1984, Senator Howard Metzenbaum of Ohio held hearings concerning whether colleges should be required to continue athletes' scholarships until they either receive their degrees or stop making progress toward earning them. The purpose was to decide if legislation was necessary to force the colleges to guarantee financial aid to injured athletes who could no longer play or to those who needed an additional year in which to earn a degree once their four years of athletic eligibility were completed.[50]

CONCLUSION

The gravity of the problems discussed in this chapter and the shortcomings of the NCAA necessitate careful oversight of intercollegiate athletics policy by educators, legislators, and in a limited way, judges. Support and assistance from the mass media, student organizations, state and federal departments of education, and the attentive public also will be required. Clearly, this network of actors has much work to do if employmentlike conditions are to be removed from college sports and if due process is to be extended to athletes and coaches. However, increased legislative scrutiny and the threat of litigation have induced the NCAA to consider offering catastrophic-injury insurance and four-year scholarships and to adopt increased, although still insufficient, due process protection for the student athlete.[51]

If this cooperative effort is expanded, with each actor playing the role for which it is best suited, the weaknesses of judicial policymaking will not be inflicted upon intercollegiate athletics, and the NCAA will be given every opportunity to shape the future of college sports. At the same time, the often sluggish, self-satisfied association will be prodded into greater sensitivity to the problems of the existing system, while its critics will be encouraged to cease relying on the judiciary and to devote more energy to reforming that system.

NOTES

1. Hall v. University of Minnesota, 530 F. Supp. 104 (D. Minn. 1982); Rensing v. Indiana State University, 444 N.E. 2d. 1170 (1983); Coleman v. Western Michigan University, 336 N.W. 2d. 224 (1983); Board of Regents of the University of Oklahoma v. National Collegiate Athletic Association, 546 F. Supp. 1276 (W.D. Okl. 1982); 707 F. 2d. 1147 (1983).

2. Charles S. Farrell, "Black Colleges Threaten Court Action to Alter N.C.A.A.'s New Academic Rules," *Chronicle of Higher Education* (April 20, 1983): 13.

3. For an excellent journalistic discussion of this issue, see N. Scott Vance, "NCAA's Control of Football Games on T.V.: In Doubt After Court Ruling," *Chronicle of Higher Education* (May 25, 1983): 1.

4. N. Scott Vance, "NCAA Delegates Defeat Plan to Remove up to Forty Colleges from Top Division," *Chronicle of Higher Education* (January 19, 1983): 17, and "NCAA Trying to Pare Division I," *Chronicle of Higher Education* (May 18, 1983): 23.

5. "NCAA Council Endorses Six Proposals from Committee on College Sports," *Chronicle of Higher Education* (November 9, 1983): 29.

6. Cheryl M. Fields, "Appeals Court Rejects Charge That NCAA Forced Women's Group out of Business," *Chronicle of Higher Education* (May 30, 1984): 27.

7. The broad interpretation of Title IX employed by H.E.W. was recently rejected by the United States Supreme Court in Grove City College v. Bell, 52 U.S.L.W. 4283 (1984). The Court held that the receipt of Basic Educational Opportunity Grants (B.E.O.G.) by some of Grove City's students does not justify application of Title IX's nondiscrimination provision to all of the educational programs of Grove City College. However, since the B.E.O.G. grants provide federal assistance to the college's financial aid program, that program, as a direct recipient of federal aid, may properly be regulated by the nondiscrimination provision of Title IX. At first blush, it would seem that this means that since intercollegiate athletic programs do not typically

receive federal funds they are not required to abide by the nondiscrimination provision in allocating resources to men's and women's teams. Yet, the preliminary conclusion of lawyers close to college athletics is that *Grove City* said too little to shed light on Title IX's relationship to athletic programs. Some lawyers claim that *Grove City* appears to leave athletic scholarships under the jurisdiction of Title IX, since the NCAA requires that such scholarships be administered as part of a college's overall financial-aid program. No authoritative determination can be made at this point. It is also too early to tell what the implications of federal aid in the building of campus sports arenas and the employment of students receiving financial work-study funds in university athletic departments might be for the future relationship between Title IX and college athletics. See N. Scott Vance, "Sports Scholarships May Still be Covered by Title IX, NCAA Cautions Members," *Chronicle of Higher Education* (March 7, 1984), p. 1.

8. For a discussion and analysis of the suits filed by the assistant coaches, see John Terrell McElheny, "Judicial Review of the NCAA's Bylaws 12–1," *Alabama Law Review* 29, no. 3 (Spring 1978): 547–62. The long-standing legal battle between University of Nevada–Las Vegas Basketball Coach Jerry Tarkanian and the NCAA may be winding down after a decision by the Nevada District Court on June 25, 1984. The judge concluded that Tarkanian had indeed been denied due process. The NCAA failed to provide witnesses or documentation to support its allegations that UNLV players had received "extra benefits" prohibited by association rules. Hence, the court granted Tarkanian's request that the 1979 order blocking his suspension from coaching be made permanent. The NCAA's cause was not aided by the fact that the university, also a defendant in the suit, argued at trial that it complied with the NCAA's 1977 order to suspend Tarkanian for fear that its refusal to do so would result in the imposition of additional penalties by the association. The NCAA planned to appeal the decision to the Nevada Supreme Court.

See University of Nevada v. Tarkanian, 594 P. 2d. 1159 (1979); Tarkanian v. University of Nevada et al., Civ. L.V. 79–170–R.D.F. (D. Nev.), Filed August 6, 1979; Charles S. Farrell, "Nevada Coach's Lawyers Try to Prove That NCAA Was 'Out to Get' Him," *Chronicle of Higher Education* (June 20, 1984): 21; and "Tarkanian Wins Case, Says Fight Left Mark," *Minneapolis Star and Tribune*, June 26, 1984, sec. D. p. 3.

9. See Colorado Seminary (University of Denver) v. NCAA, 417 F. Supp. 885 (1976); Hunt v. NCAA, G 76–370 C.A. (W.D. Mich. 1976); Regents of the University of Minnesota v. NCAA, 560 F. 2d. 1028 (1975); McDonald v. NCAA, 3700 F. Supp. 625 (1974); Albach v. Odle, 531 F 2d. 983 (1976); Mitchell v. Louisiana High School Athletic Association, 430 F. 2d. 1155 (5th Cir. 1970); Behagen v. Intercollegiate Conference (Big Ten) of Faculty Representatives, 346 F. Supp. 602 (D. Minn. 1972).

10. The most recent worker's compensation suits filed by former college athletes are Rensing v. Indiana State University, 444 N.E. 2d. 1170 (1983) and Coleman v. Western Michigan University, 336 N.W. 2d. 224 (1983). For a discussion of several such suits that were litigated in the 1950s and 1960s, see *Cleveland State Law Review* 19 (September 1970): 521–27.

11. In the past few years, the print media have been especially vigorous in their investigations of problems in intercollegiate athletics. Two notable examples of this growing trend are Bart Barnes, "Athletics and Academics: Making the Grade but Failing to Learn," *The Washington Post*, May 23, 1982, sec. D. p. 4; and Neil Amdur, Jane Gross, Malcolm Moran, and Gordon S. White, Jr., "College Athletics: Is Winning Everything?" *Minneapolis Star and Tribune*, April 5–8, 1982, sec. D.

12. N. Scott Vance, "Plan to Give President More Power 'Undemocratic,' NCAA Officer Says," *Chronicle of Higher Education* (September 14, 1983): 1; and "Plan to Give Presidents Control of NCAA Modified by American Council's Panel," *Chronicle of Higher Education* (October 19, 1983): 29. The NCAA eventually adopted a plan to increase presidential influence, but only via established means, such as legislative convention vote.

13. N. Scott Vance, "Testing Service Head Hits NCAA's Academic Rules," *Chronicle of Higher Education* (February 2, 1983): 1.

14. See Burton F. Brody, "NCAA Rules and Their Enforcement: Not Spare the Rod and Spoil the Child—But Rather Switch the Values and Spare the Sport," *Arizona State Law Journal* 1982, no. 1 (1982): 109–31; Roy D. Duckworth III, "The Student-Athlete and the NCAA: The Need for a Prima Facie Tort Doctrine," *Suffolk Law Review* 9 (Summer 1975): 1340–71; David F. Gaona, "The National Collegiate Athletic Association: Fundamental Fairness and the

Enforcement Program," *Arizona Law Review* 23 (1982): 1065–1102; G. Preston Keyes, "The NCAA, Amateurism, and the Student-Athlete's Rights upon Ineligibility," *New England Law Review* 15 (1979–80): 597–625; Donald L. Shuck, Jr., "Administration of Amateur Athletics: The Time for an Amateur Athlete's Bill of Rights Has Arrived," *Fordham Law Review* 48 (October 1979): 53–82; Felix J. Springer, "A Student-Athlete's Interest in Eligibility: Its Context and Constitutional Dimensions," *Connecticut Law Review* 10 (Winter 1978): 318–49; and John C. Weistart, "Legal Accountability and the NCAA," *Journal of College and University Law* 10, no. 2 (Fall 1983): 167–80.

15. See National Collegiate Athletic Association, *NCAA Manual*, 1983–84 ed. (Mission, Kan: National Collegiate Athletic Association, 1983).

16. Howard University v. NCAA, 510 F. 2d. 213 (1975), presents this rationale most clearly.

17. Board of Regents of the University of Oklahoma v. NCAA, 546 F. Supp. 1276 (W.D. Okl. 1982); 707 F. 2d. 1147 (1983).

18. Donald L. Horowitz, *The Courts and Social Policy* (Washington, D.C.: The Brookings Institution, 1977), p. 34.

19. Abram Chayes, "The Role of the Judge in Public Law Litigation," *Harvard Law Review* 89, no. 7 (May 1976): 1281–1316.

20. Ibid, p. 1284.

21. Horowitz, *Courts and Social Policy*, p. 30.

22. Ibid., p. 49.

23. Ibid., p. 31.

24. Ibid., p. 45.

25. See Behagen v. Intercollegiate Conference (Big Ten) of Faculty Representatives, 346 F. Supp. 602 (D. Minn. 1972) and Regents of the University of Minnesota v. NCAA, 422 F. Supp. 1158 (1976); 560 F. 2d. 352 (1977).

26. Rensing v. Indiana State University, 44 N.E. 2d. 1170 (1983); and Coleman v. Western Michigan University, 336 N.W. 2d 224 (1983).

27. Rensing v. Indiana State University, 437 N.E. 2d. 78 (1982).

28. National Collegiate Athletic Association, *NCAA Manual*, article 3, sec. 4, pt. b–1, *Principles Governing Financial Aid* (Mission, Kan.: National Collegiate Athletic Association, 1982), p. 19. The applicable rule states: "Institutional aid may not be gradated or cancelled during the period of its award on the basis of a student-athlete's ability or his contribution to a team's success, because of an injury which prevents the recipient from participating in athletics, or for any other athletic reason."

29. For the results of a recent survey of the graduation rates of seniors who saw regular action on college basketball teams during the 1981–82 season, see Mike Douchant, "Restoring Academic Integrity," *The Sporting News*, October 25, 1982, p. 57.

30. For recent evidence of this, see N. Scott Vance, "North Dakota Coach Cuts Scholarships," *Chronicle of Higher Education* (May 18, 1983): 24.

31. Hall v. University of Minnesota, 530 F. Supp. 104 (D. Minn. 1982).

32. The Big Ten Handbook states that in order to be able to practice and to represent a Big Ten member university in intercollegiate athletics, one must be "bona fide matriculated, registered, and regularly enrolled as a resident candidate in courses applicable to a baccalaureate degree." Intercollegiate Conference of Faculty Representatives, *Handbook of the Intercollegiate Conference*, pt. 2, rule 1, sec. 1A, *Rules of Eligibility* (Schaumberg, Ill.: Intercollegiate Conference of Faculty Representatives, 1982), p. 19.

33. See note 9.

34. The definitive decision concerning the "entitlement" criterion for asserting a property right is Board of Regents v. Roth, 408 U.S. 564 (1972).

35. Board of Regents of the University of Oklahoma v. National Collegiate Athletic Association, 707 F. 2d. 1147 (1983).

36. Ibid.

37. Ibid.

38. Goldfard v. Virginia State Bar, 421 U.S. 773 (1975).

39. Board of Regents of the University of Oklahoma v. National Collegiate Athletic Association, 707 F. 2d. 1147 (1983).

40. Ibid.

41. See *New York Times*, June 28, 1984, p. 23.

42. Ibid.

43. Ibid.

44. The NCAA also refused to let Tarkanian and the university know what procedures would be followed at the hearing and subsequently taped telephone conversations with Tarkanian and a representative of UNLV, respectively, in which they requested guidance in preparing for the hearing. See "Tarkanian Wins Case, Says Fight Left Mark," *Minneapolis Star and Tribune*, June 26, 1984, sec. D, p. 3, and "Finally, the N.C.A.A. Is Shown in Court for What It Can Be," *Las Vegas Review-Journal*, June 27, 1984, sec. B, p. 6.

45. See N. Scott Vance, "NCAA May Soon Alter Rules, Permit Four-Year Athletic Scholarships," *Chronicle of Higher Education* (May 18, 1983): 24.; regarding the NCAA's investigation of the possibility of providing insurance for 1985–86, see "Notes on Sports," *Chronicle Of Higher Education* (April 25, 1984): 23.

46. The original proposal for a Presidents' Commission, Number 35, would have empowered the panel to veto rules and procedures of the association and impose new rules of its own creation on NCAA institutions. The commission's decisions could be overruled only by a two-thirds vote of NCAA convention delegates. This proposal was soundly defeated by the delegates to the 1984 Convention. However, Number 36, a substitute, did pass. Number 36 confers upon the commission the advisory powers discussed in the text. See "A Summary of the Proposals Approved at the NCAA's Annual Convention," *Chronicle of Higher Education* (January 18, 1984): 36.

47. The original proposal regarding the "satisfactory progress" rule, which was defeated, defined "good academic standing" as "not on academic probation." It also included a section that would have required college presidents to certify to the NCAA that their athletes were in good academic standing and would have authorized the association to conduct "spot checks" to determine if schools were complying with the rule. The substitute proposal that passed requires athletes to earn each year a specified number of credits that are acceptable toward a bachelor's degree in a particular academic program and maintain a grade-point average high enough to be in "good academic standing" at their respective schools. See "A Summary of the Proposals Approved at the NCAA's Annual Convention," *Chronicle of Higher Education* (January 18, 1984): 36.

48. N. Scott Vance, "A.C.E. Sports Panel to Ask NCAA Presidents to Seek Shorter Playing Seasons," *Chronicle of Higher Education* (May 16, 1984): 28.

49. "Note On Sports," *Chronicle of Higher Education* (April 18, 1984): 30.

50. N. Scott Vance, "Senate to Probe College Rules on Sports Scholarships," *Chronicle of Higher Education* (March 28, 1984): 27.

51. As a result of a 1978 House of Representatives investigation of the NCAA, conducted by the Subcommittee on Oversight and Investigations of the Committee on Interstate and Foreign Commerce, the NCAA moved to increase protections for athletes at disciplinary hearings. Specifically, the association decided to allow the student athlete to appear at his or her school's hearing before the Infractions Committee, represented by counsel. However, the athlete who is found by the NCAA to have violated one of its rules must still be punished by the school, whether or not the institution agrees with the finding or approves of the NCAA's investigatory procedures. See David F. Gaona, "The National Collegiate Athletic Association: Fundamental Fairness and the Enforcement Program," *Arizona Law Review* 23 (1981): 1065–1102.

8

Professional Sports and Antitrust Law: The Ground Rules of Immunity, Exemption, and Liability

Phillip J. Closius

Professional sports began in America in 1876 with the organization of the National League of Baseball. From that date until approximately 1972 the legal system regarded professional sports as games or amusements rather than businesses. Professional leagues were therefore not subject to the same degree of legal scrutiny and liability applicable to commercial endeavors. The United States Supreme Court, in its resolution of *Federal Baseball Club of Baltimore, Inc.* v. *National League*,[1] typified this attitude by deciding that baseball was not engaged in interstate commerce, and therefore it was entitled to an immunity from the proscriptions of the Sherman Act.[2] Other courts applied a similiar attitude in examining contract disputes between teams and players.[3] Congress, at the request of the leagues, passed legislation immunizing certain league practices from the reach of the antitrust laws.[4] In the absence of viable player unions to counterbalance their desires, team owners in all sports took advantage of their practical immunity from the legal obligations of antitrust law to implement practices and structures that served their own interests in ways that frequently restrained trade. Public policy during this period dictated that the games be kept on "higher ground" than the world of commercial and profit considerations.[5]

The decline of professional sports' "nonbusiness" status began with increased television exposure that transformed professional athletes into personalities recognizable outside their respective home cities. Televising games was also a clear exploitation of interstate commerce by sports management. This high-profile media exposure established professional leagues as a national presence and eliminated the league argument that any game was merely a local exhibition. Reflecting this change, the federal government, empowered to control interstate commerce and regulate the broadcast media, began to replace the states as the appropriate tribunal for resolving legal disputes within professional sports. The federal system was more insulated than local governments from the political pressures and influence of a particular sport. Congress and the federal courts were more likely to perceive sports as a business to be regulated rather than a local interest to be protected. Finally, the sheer magnitude of the media dollars earned by professional sports made its "not-for-profit" image less believable.

As professional sports leagues increased their wealth and national prominence, the federal judicial system became uncomfortable with its characterization of sports as something other than a business. The Supreme Court reflected this change in policy in the 1950s by refusing to extend baseball's antitrust exemption to other sports.[6] The application of the Sherman Act to all nonbaseball sports established the foundation for the forceful imposition of antitrust constraints on team owners in the sports litigation of the 1970s. These "revolutionary" decisions substantially eliminated the status of sports as a game or amusement insulated from the legal obligations of profit-making industries. Public policy now called for professional sports to be accorded the same legal treatment as other commercial endeavors. This alteration of the judicial system's perception of the nature of professional sports was employed by players and their unions to destroy management's unilateral control over professional sports and to substitute in its place a collectively bargained equilibrium in which owners and players shared control of a league's structure. This new balance also allowed the players to participate more fully in the increased revenues being furnished by the broadcast industry. In this sense, the courts applied the antitrust laws to give players' unions leverage at the bargaining table that they had never before possessed. The major remaining judicial vestige of the old public policy view of sports is the antitrust immunity still enjoyed by baseball pursuant to the Supreme Court's ruling in *Flood* v. *Kuhn*.[7]

Team owners in the other sports have tried to mitigate the effects of this change in judicial attitude by obtaining some variant of judicial or legislative immunity from the full effects of the antitrust laws. This chapter analyzes the three major forms of immunity sought by team owners since the advent of the modern sports litigation era. These are (1) the nonstatutory labor law exemption to shelter restraints contained within collective bargaining agreements, (2) the single-entity defense to render inapplicable to sports leagues Section 1 of the Sherman Act, and (3) the direct grant of a congressional immunity to foreclose antitrust litigation regarding designated league practices. The chapter then examines the principles of substantive antitrust liability by courts to professional sport practices that are not included within an appropriate exemption.

EXEMPTIONS AND IMMUNITIES

The Nonstatutory Labor Law Exemption

The first exemption to be litigated extensively in the professional sports context was the judicially created nonstatutory labor law exemption. This immunity from antitrust liability emanates from the policy decision that federal labor concerns can, in certain circumstances, outweigh antitrust interests when the restraint at issue is the product of collective bargaining. In professional sports litigation, the exemption was invoked by leagues and team owners when a plaintiff, usually a union or a class of players, challenged a restraint embodied or incorporated within an existing collective bargaining agreement.

The concepts and policy considerations at the core of the exemption were delineated originally by the Supreme Court in the nonsports context. However, before the judiciary created the nonstatutory exemption, Congress established a balance between federal labor and antitrust interests by granting a specific statutory exemption from the antitrust laws to *unilateral* union activity.[8] This statutory exemption reflected congressional policy that the Sherman Act was not intended to be used against a union for practices that primarily influenced the labor market, even if such actions produced ancillary effects in a product market.[9] Therefore, union activity cannot be the basis of antitrust liability if "a union acts in its own self-interest and does not combine with non-labor groups."[10] In order to effectuate fully the statutory immunity granted to unilateral union activity, the Supreme Court realized that at least some bilateral agreements also must be granted an exemption. Failure to extend the statutory immunity to at least some management/union agreements would produce the incongruous result of protecting a union from antitrust liability in its unilateral effort to obtain a certain bargaining goal, but subjecting the union to antitrust sanction if management agreed to implement labor's demands. The Supreme Court therefore decided to expand the congressional exemption to unilateral union activity by creating a nonstatutory exemption that also would immunize qualifying collective bargaining agreements from antitrust liability.

The Supreme Court established the principles for extending antitrust immunity to bilateral, collectively bargained restraints in *Allen Bradley Co.* v. *Local Union 13, IBEW*[11] and the companion cases of *UMW* v. *Pennington*[12] and *Local Union No. 189, Amalgamated Meat Cutters* v. *Jewel Tea Co.*[13] The Court did not grant the collective bargaining process the same absolute exemption Congress had granted unilateral union activity. Not every provision obtained from an employer as a result of good-faith bargaining was exempt from the antitrust laws. The nonstatutory exemption was instead founded upon weighting the competing policies of antitrust and labor law.

Antitrust considerations balanced in the nonstatutory exemption dictate that management-labor agreements that restrain a product market will not be granted immunity if the agreement can be characterized as either a management conspiracy to monopolize commerce or as a restraint of trade furthering management's competitive interests in the activities of entities not party to the agreement.[14] This liability attached to both management and union, even if the product-market restraint produced benefits for the labor force.[15] However, if a collective agreement did not exhibit such tendencies, the restraint could qualify for the nonstatutory exemption.[16] The nonstatutory exemption reflects the policy underlying the statutory immunity—the agreement must substantially embody the unilateral interest of labor. If the collective agreement primarily embodies the competitive interest of management, it does not qualify for the nonstatutory exemption.

Philadelphia World Hockey Club, Inc. v. _Philadelphia Hockey Club, Inc._[17] and _Robertson_ v. _National Basketball Association_[18] are two of the first cases to consider extensively the exemption's application to professional sports. _Philadelphia Hockey_ was a lawsuit initiated by teams of the new World Hockey Association against the established National Hockey League (NHL). The new league claimed that the NHL, primarily through its reserve clause and contractual arrangements with minor league teams, restrained and monopolized the professional hockey market. _Robertson_ was a class action filed on behalf of all professional basketball players, contending that a variety of National Basketball Association practices violated the Sherman Act. Both of these decisions applied the principles established by the Supreme Court and rejected the defendant league's claim for the nonstatutory exemption. Although the exemption was created to benefit unions, both courts noted that employers can assert the immunity derivatively when they have participated in bargaining and are sued for provisions encompassing union activity.[19] However, not all agreements on mandatory subjects of bargaining were entitled to the exemption.[20] Labor policy only mandated an antitrust exemption if the provision at issue was a result of union self-interest and the product of extensive good-faith bargaining. The record in both cases failed to satisfy this standard. However, even good-faith bargaining could not exempt a provision that restrained the outside competitors of a defendant league and therefore embodied a management-labor conspiracy proscribed by the Supreme Court.[21]

Philadelphia Hockey and _Robertson_ established the framework for the application of the exemption to professional sports. Two subsequent Court of Appeals cases, _Mackey_ v. _National Football League_[22] and _McCourt_ v. _California Sports, Inc._,[23] delineate the current exemption standards employed by courts in this context. _Mackey_ was a lawsuit brought by players against the NFL, challenging the validity of the league's free agent compensation system, the so-called Rozelle Rule. The players claimed that a system whereby the commissioner had sole discretion to award a club compensation for losing a player inhibited player movement and restrained trade. The Eighth Circuit reinforced the holdings of *Philadelphia Hockey* and *Robertson* and rejected the NFL's claim for the nonstatutory exemption. After noting that employers, as well as employees, could assert an exemption that attached to the collective agreement, the court formulated a three-part test for granting immunity:

> First, the labor policy favoring collective bargaining may potentially be given pre-eminence over the antitrust laws where the restraint on trade primarily affects only the parties to the collective bargaining relationship. Second, federal labor policy is implicated sufficiently to prevail only where the agreement sought to be exempted concerns a mandatory subject of collective bargaining. Finally, the policy favoring collective bargaining is furthered to the degree necessary to override the antitrust laws only where the agreement sought to be exempted is the product of bona fide arm's-length bargaining.[24]

Although the NFL's evidence had satisfied the first two requirements, the district court record did not reveal any good-faith bargaining concerning the Rozelle Rule. The compensation provision was created by the league and then imposed by the NFL on a weak union in the first two bargaining agreements. The circuit court used its interpretation of good-faith bargaining to fortify the union by giving it increased bargaining leverage through the imposition of antitrust liability. If the NFL wanted to insulate its compensation system from antitrust attack, the league must legitimately engage in meaningful bargaining with the union. The Eighth Circuit, however, expanded the exemption by suggesting that evidence of a *quid pro quo*—union agreement to the unmodified rule in exchange for other benefits—might satisfy this requirement. *Mackey* also subtly extended the scope of the exemption by concluding that the Rozelle Rule was incorporated sufficiently in the bargaining process to qualify for an exemption claim.[25]

McCourt is the most recent sports case to deal with the exemption issue. This case also involved a player's antitrust challenge to the free agent compensation system of the National Hockey League.[26] The Sixth Circuit began its exemption analysis by adopting the three-part test established by Eighth Circuit in *Mackey*. As in the earlier football case, the court quickly noted that the first two aspects of the test were satisfied. A compensation plan affected only veteran players and clearly involved the terms and conditions of their employment. The issue in the case therefore was narrowed to the question of good-faith bargaining. After reviewing the bargaining history of the league in detail, the Sixth Circuit concluded that good-faith bargaining had occurred. The circuit court cited traditional labor law principles in the nonexemption context to support its two-part analysis of the bargaining obligation. The inclusion of the bylaw in the exact form of management's previously imposed rule did not evidence a lack of bargaining, but rather the union's failure, after intense negotiations, to keep "an unwanted provision out of the contract."[27] Good-faith bargaining does not require either side to make a concession or yield on a particular point. Labor law does not mandate substantive terms of agreement, and the duty to bargain in good faith permits a party to stand firmly on a proposal if its "insistence is genuinely and sincerely held."[28] Second, the opinion noted that the union had applied bargaining pressure to keep the compensation plan out and, when unsuccessful in that effort, obtained considerable benefits from the league as the price of inclusion. The incorporated bylaw therefore was entitled to the exemption and judgment was entered for the defendants.

The three-part test enunicated in *Mackey* appears to be the appropriate standard for application of the exemption in professional sports cases. The first part of the test clearly embodies the Supreme Court's concept of an Allen Bradley conspiracy and the appropriate primacy of antitrust concepts over labor law rules when the restraint significantly affects groups not party to the collective bargaining relationship. The second part correctly implies that labor law policy is not sufficiently implicated in management-labor agreements on nonmandatory subjects of bargaining to justify overriding antitrust concerns. The final part of the *Mackey* test looks at the source of the restraint and its treatment by the parties in their bargaining. Although labor law rules should dominate the conduct of a mature management-labor relationship, this inquiry is required to recognize the prounion orientation of the exemption and to give antitrust concerns their proper weight in the balancing process. If the questioned provision was initiated by the union in substantially the form finally adopted, employer acquiescence to the union demand should be protected by the exemption. If, however, the term at issue was initiated by management or if it significantly reflects management interests, the exemption will be granted only if there has been adequate union participation in the structuring of the final proposal. Adequate union participation in this sense means that the management proposal has undergone some significant modification by the union prior to acceptance or that the union has received a specific, significant *quid pro quo* in exchange for inclusion of the term. The judicial inquiry, in the case of non labor-initiated proposals, would thereby be focused on the integrity of the union as exclusive employee representative.

The exemption should be granted when labor law considerations indicate that an individual employee should not be allowed to "second-guess" the wisdom of the union in making concessions or modifications.[29] The integrity of the bargaining process also dictates that a union should not be free to second-guess itself regarding a provision where bargaining history indicated union involvement in shaping or "selling" the provision. In such situations, the derived employer immunity can be justified by the need to preserve the integrity of the union and the bargaining process, and by management's reliance upon the exclusive nature of the union's collective representation. Courts can police application of this aspect of the test by searching for a specific *quid pro quo* for unmodified management proposals. The National Basketball Association's salary caps, for example, seemingly would qualify for the nonstatutory exemption on both rationales if it were challenged by an NBA player. The basketball union shaped the final form of the system and received some other benefits, mainly in the job security area, in exchange for their agreement. Such an analysis differs slightly from the reasoning in *McCourt*. The Sixth Circuit should eliminate its initial emphasis on the traditional labor law interpretation of good-faith bargaining and the unilateral insistence of management permitted thereby. Instead, the circuit court should focus on the degree of union participation in the structuring of Bylaw 9–A after the labor group accepted financial benefits specifically offered by the league as *quid pro quo* for the inclusion of the compensation system. If the benefits granted by management were related directly to the acceptance of Bylaw 9–A, the exemption should apply.[30]

Future application of the nonstatutory exemption could occur in a variety of professional sports contexts. New leagues with no collective bargaining agreement in force face potential antitrust action regarding their player restraint and other league rules. The league needs to embody its practices, such as player drafts or territorial drafts, in a collective agreement reflecting union participation in order to insulate those practices from antitrust liability. In this sense, the exemption, as it did in the earlier sports cases, provides the union with additional bargaining leverage in collective negotiations. A new league needs a bona fide union and a creditable bargaining agreement in order to possess even a minimal claim on the exemption.

The nature of the labor law exemption leaves all team owners with a difficult decision: Should a league contend that a particular practice is a management perogative, not collectively bargain over it, and risk antitrust liability regarding its implementation, or, should management agree that a topic is a mandatory subject of bargaining and obtain an arguable immunity at the price of permitting a union to bargain over the practice and refashion its form? Many established leagues have tried to resolve this dilemma by having the league's constitution and bylaws, management's unilaterally adopted practices, incorporated or referenced in the collective bargaining agreement with the union. Professional football provides a convenient context for examining problems in this area. The football collective bargaining agreement states that any terms of the NFL constitution and bylaws that are not inconsistent with the agreement are to remain in full force and effect and all parties agree to be bound by such terms.[31] *Mackey*'s inclusion of such an incorporated term within the exemption's scope arguably allows a league to shelter a unilaterally imposed restraint in this manner. However, this reference combined with management's assertion that general economic benefits (such as pension payments, minimal salaries) to labor were the *quid pro quo* for its inclusion, should not by itself be sufficient to justify granting the exemption. Courts should require a specific *quid pro quo* for inclusion of a practice or direct evidence of union participation in the shaping of the rule.

A bylaw provision likely to be challenged in the future is the term regulating eligibility for the football draft. NFL teams cannot draft or sign a player unless (1) all college eligibility of the player has expired, (2) five years have passed since the player would have entered college, or (3) the player has received a diploma from a recognized university or college.[32] This eligibility system is now limited to football. Baseball and hockey traditionally have drafted athletes without reference to collegiate competition.[33] Basketball had eligibility provisions similar to football. Those restrictions were declared in violation of the antitrust laws in a suit brought against the league by a college superstar, Spencer Haywood.[34] Following the Haywood litigation, the NBA modified its eligibility requirements to permit the drafting of underclassmen through the hardship process.[35] Significantly, the opinion in *Haywood* did not consider the applicability of the exemption. In addition to the question of an underclassman being a party to the bargainig relationship, the union has not meaningfully participated in the adoption of this rule. Therefore, the suit should proceed to the issue of substantive antitrust liability.

Other provisions in the NFL constitution and bylaws directly affect player movement and salaries. If a veteran player performs his contract obligation to an NFL team and then signs with a different league, the collective bargaining agreement does not deal with the issue of the former team's player rights if that player returns to the NFL following the termination of the other league's contract. NFL teams have maintained that the former club retains the exclusive rights to such a player because, on his departure from the NFL, the player was placed on a reserve or retired status list provided for by the bylaws. A player in such a position should be able to litigate the antitrust validity of the rule restricting his freedom if in fact it has been imposed unilaterally by management.

Additionally, NFL owners split television revenues equally.[36] This method of revenue sharing arguably allows the owners to control player salaries and eliminate the economic incentive for owners to bid on free agents. Players or the union should be free to challenge this practice and its price/salary-fixing effects if in fact the system has not been the product of active union participation.[37]

Another problem in the future application of the exemption is posed by potential litigation initiated by nonbargaining unit players (either college seniors or players of another league) over the entry-level barriers (such as player draft, territorial schools, or veteran allocation) of a particular league. An entry barrier likely to be challenged in the near future by basketball draftees is the NBA salary cap provision contained in the NBA collective bargaining agreement, which restricts the salary offers that teams over the cap can make to their draftees. Assuming that the entry barriers are a mandatory subject of bargaining and that unions have participated to some extent in forming the entry rules, a question remains as to whether prospective players are parties to the bargaining relationship. The primary issue in such a challenge to entry barriers would therefore be the first requirement of the *Mackey* test: Does the restraint primarily affect only parties to the bargaining relationship? Players are not members of the league until they have gone through the entry process, signed contracts, and made the team. If a nonunit athlete brought suit against a league challenging an entry barrier on antitrust grounds, a court would have difficulty characterizing the player as a party to even the bargaining "relationship" prior to his signing a contract.

A district court opinion, *Smith* v. *Pro-Football, Inc.*,[38] speculated on the exemption's application to the professional football draft. The court commenced its examination by noting that, considering labor law precedent regarding bargaining over hiring halls and seniority benefits, the draft would be considered a term or condition of employment and therefore a mandatory subject of bargaining. The first two requirements of the *Mackey* test could be satisfied. Regarding the nonunit effect of the draft, the court observed that a player draft differs from traditional restraints in that the draft produced a detrimental effect, not on the employer's competitors, but on potential employees—"persons neither party to the agreement nor members of a union which is party to the agreement."[39] Protection of such a group is less central to the purposes of antitrust laws than the prohibition of product-market restraints. Since labor law is deeply concerned with allowing unions freely to negotiate bargains they consider best for their members, the district court concluded that the draft should be immune from antitrust liability if a union, in pursuit of its own interests, agreed to the procedure.

As noted in *Smith*, the arguments supporting the inclusion of prospective union members as parties to the relationship have been based on an analogy to nonsports cases that assert that union hiring halls are a mandatory subject for bargaining.[40] Although this comparison seems relevant for the determination that the draft is a mandatory subject of bargaining, the argument does not apply with equal force to the nonunit effects of the restraint. The use of the analogy in both contexts implies that the first two requirements of *Mackey* are actually one—whether the draft is a mandatory subject of bargaining. This single-issue analysis has been rejected by the Supreme Court. The hiring-hall analogy is a particularly inappropriate vehicle for extending the exemption beyond the parties to the bargaining agreement. Hiring halls are perceived as enhancing union security and increasing employee salaries. The hiring hall is limited to unique occupations, and an employee is free to reject any assignment he obtains from the hall. Since these job assignments tend to be short-term, there can be no long-term prejudicial effect of the procedures.

Hiring halls therefore have been characterized as mandatory subjects because, like the exemption, they concern the integrity of the union itself.[41] Conversely, entry barriers depress player salaries and frequently force the individual player to sign a long-term contract with a club not of his choosing. A series of decisions meant to enhance union status and employee interests should not be used to extend the insulation of an antilabor practice. Requiring the union to bargain over terms of entry should not imply that future employees are parties to the bargaining relationship. This is particularly true in sports, where the union often is hostile to the interests of draftees because of their ability to command large salaries. The union therefore may not truly represent the interests of prospective players.

A final potential problem is that a bargaining agreement might not be in force during the period after a current agreement expires and before a new one can be negotiated.[42] If management continues to enforce player restrictions during such an interval, the issue becomes whether such practices should receive immunity from the antitrust laws. The resolution of this dilemma should focus on the source of the restraint and the extent of the union's participation in shaping it. The clearest case for granting immunity would be that in which management simply continued the exact practices contained in the now-expired agreement. If the restraints are identical, the same principles governing the exemption during the life of the agreement should control the impasse period. If the union participated in the creation of the rule, protection of the bargaining process and labor law interests dictate that the exemption should continue during impasse.[43] If, however, an employer significantly modifies a rule and then seeks to impose it during an impasse period, courts should be reluctant to grant the exemption. Some commentators have argued that, if the employer proposed the modified rule to the union and an impasse is produced, unilateral employer change consistent with past offers to the union satisfies the employer's duty to bargain in good faith and should receive the exemption. The application of good-faith bargaining principles to the granting of immunity distorts the origin and purposes of the exemption. Employer restraints unilaterally imposed should not derive benefit from a labor-oriented exemption. If the union has participated in the molding of the modified practice, the exemption should be granted. If the union has not participated, the employer's unilateral imposition should run the risk of antitrust liability.[44]

The Single-Entity Exemption

Most sports litigation to date has focused on alleged violations of Section One of the Sherman Act, which renders illegal any contract, combination, or conspiracy in restraint of trade or commerce.[45] A necessary predicate for the application of Section One is therefore that the challenged restraint involve two or more distinct entities, since, by definition, a single entity cannot contract, combine, or conspire with itself.[46] In the nonsports context, the single-entity issue is litigated most frequently in the parent-subsidiary or intraenterprise fact pattern. If the subsidiaries are incorporated separately, the First, Third, and Fifth circuits of the Federal Courts of Appeals have held that the fact of separate incorporation by itself renders the corporations multiple entities.[47] The Second Circuit renders the corporations multiple entities if the corporations hold themselves out as competitors.[48] Finally, the Seventh, Eighth, and Ninth circuits have enunciated an "all the facts and circumstances" test whereby the court in any particular case must make the multiple-entity conclusion on a particular analysis of the corporate entities before it.[49] Decisions in this area are rendered difficult because of the opposing factors of separate incorporation and common ownership. The Supreme Court has recently rejected the multiple-entity theory in the context of parents and wholly owned subsidiaries.[50] The Court decided that separately incorporated, wholly owned subsidiaries, like unincorporated divisions, were parts of the parent and therefore a single enterprise. A legally single entity—a corporation with multiple divisions or a partnership with many partners—is incapable of violating Section One, since it is considered one entity in the eyes of the law.

Sports leagues have not presented the single-entity defense in cases initiated by plaintiffs who were either players or unions. The leagues have conceded that, in such situations, each team within the league is acting on its own behalf in competition with each other team in the league in the acquisition of playing talent. As such, each team is itself a separate entity, and any league agreement embodying a player restraint is an agreement between separate multiple entities.[51] In addition, the defendant leagues may have not raised the single-entity defense because they preferred to rely instead on the application of the nonstatutory labor law exemption. However, in cases instituted by nonlabor plaintiffs, the defendant leagues have raised the single-entity defense. In such suits, the labor law exemption is not available because either the challenged practice is embodied in the league's constitution and bylaws rather than in the collective bargaining agreement (frequently the case when an individual team owner sues his own league), or the challenged practice has a competitive effect outside the bargaining unit (frequently the case when one league sues a rival league).

The National Football League has been the most frequent advocate of the single-entity defense. In such a posture, the league has claimed that it is, in effect, a partnership that shares revenues and produces a unitary product that no individual team could produce by itself. Thus the NFL has argued that it should be entitled to a functional immunity from Section One liability, since, as a single entity, it cannot contract, conspire, or combine with itself. This position also finds support in some of the economic theories that provide a framework for the enunciation of the goals of antitrust enforcement. If the goals of the antitrust laws are to maximize consumer wealth and promote producer efficiency, the law should encourage a seller to maximize his profits by producing as much of his product as he can at the lowest possible price. This will keep prices down and provide enough of the product to satisfy the entire consumer demand for the good or service. Thus a consumer-wealth economist would argue that the antitrust laws should encourage practices that increase the output of any given product and proscribe those practices that restrict the output. Since the NFL's restraints do not reduce the output of its alleged product—the number of football games—the league can argue that granting it a single-entity exemption is consistent with an economic goal of the antitrust laws.

The NFL claim for single-entity status has been rejected by the Second Circuit in *North American Soccer League* v. *National Football League*[52] and by the Ninth Circuit in *Los Angeles Memorial Coliseum Commission* v. *National Football League*.[53] *North American Soccer League* (NASL) involved a suit in which the newer soccer league challenged an NFL constitution and bylaws provision that prohibited NFL owners from owning a team in another professional sport.[54] The district court in NASL agreed with the single-entity analysis, but the Second Circuit reversed by noting that the Supreme Court has never favored a "joint venture" antitrust exemption.[55] The single-entity immunity is rarely, if ever, granted when the separate corporations involved in a combination are not commonly owned.[56] The Second Circuit looked to prior Supreme Court cases and the decisions of other circuits (including player restraint cases) that had applied Section One to sports leagues and determined that the case at bar was indistinguishable from that precedent. Additionally, the cross-ownership ban not only protected the league from other league competition but also shielded individual teams from home-territory competition by local teams of another league. The Second Circuit therefore reasoned that the team nature of the restraint precluded any single-entity exemption for the league as a whole.[57]

The Los Angeles Coliseum Commission, which desired a professional football tenant, and Al Davis, owner of the Oakland Raiders, challenged the NFL constitution and bylaw provision that prohibited an owner from relocating his franchise without the approval of three-fourths of the league's owners.[58] The Ninth Circuit began its rejection of the NFL's claim for single-entity immunity by citing the extensive precedent that has applied Section One of the Sherman Act to a sports league, including the Second Circuit's opinion in NASL.[59] The court also noted that, unlike cases in which single-entity status was granted, the individual clubs did not have any common ownership, nor were the policies of the NFL set by one individual or a parent corporation. League decisions were more appropriately characterized as action by separate entities acting jointly.[60] Although the NFL did produce a unitary product that required some cooperation among other teams, the teams were individually owned, made separate decisions on numerous business matters, and competed with each other for personnel, fan support, and media attention. Although league revenues were divided equally to a significant extent, profits and losses were not shared and in fact varied significantly from club to club. The NFL therefore was a combination of twenty-eight entities subject to the full force of Section One proscription.[61]

Both the Second and Ninth circuits realized that the allowance of the single-entity defense would in effect have granted all of professional sports an exemption from Section One of the Sherman Act. Both courts were properly reluctant to grant such an industrywide immunity in the absence of Supreme Court or congressional guidance. The single most influential factor in finding a single entity in the nonsports precedent—common ownership—is absent in the case of a professional sports league. To that extent, the Supreme Court's opinion in *Copperweld Corporation* v. *Independence Tube Corporation*,[62] which is limited to the wholly owned subsidiary context, does not support a league's claim for single-entity status. The individual ownership of teams and the independent function of clubs in the business decisions noted by both opinions should preclude a characterization of a sports league as a single entity. The rejection of the NFL's defense also implied that the economic goals of consumer wealth and producer efficiency were not the only goals of the antitrust laws.[63] The courts did not consider directly the argument that the league's restraints did not restrict output. However, the Ninth Circuit clearly indicated that although such considerations did not justify an immunity from Section One, they were relevant in determining whether the restraints were reasonable pursuant to the rule of reason analysis.[64] In so doing, the Ninth Circuit reflected some of the arguments noted by Justice Rehnquist in his dissent from the denial of *certiorari* in NASL.[65]

The rejection of the single-entity defense reflects a policy decision that restraints embodied in a league's constitution and bylaws, or that produce competitive effects upon another league, are still subject to antitrust scrutiny. The continued antitrust exposure of professional sports in this regard is consistent with the newer judicial policy of treating sports as a normal profit-making industry. One bylaw provision that is a candidate for antitrust challenge in the future is the NFL's provision dictating that television or cable revenue generated by NFL teams be shared equally by all member clubs.[66] If a cable channel were willing to offer NFL games on a pay-per-view basis, an owner in a cable market with many customers and fans (such as Los Angeles) might be reluctant to share those revenues with clubs in smaller television markets. Although such a suit might not satisfy the standards for substantive liability, the rejection of the single-entity defense implies that such an allegation would at least be the subject of a lengthy trial. A league facing such a prospect might well consider bargaining with the league's union regarding the revenue split in order to obtain at least the arguable defense of the nonstatutory labor law exemption.

Congressional Grants of Immunity

Congress has been willing to entertain the request of professional sports leagues for specific statutory exemption of a league practice from the effects of the antitrust laws. For example, Congress did grant an exemption for the American Football League to merge with the National Football League and produce the modern NFL. Such legislation also allows the teams of a sports league to combine together and negotiate jointly as a league with the members of the broadcast industry.[67] When Congress grants such a specific legislation exemption, the judicial function is limited to interpreting the statute and defining the intended reach of immunity. No suit or litigation would be permitted if the plaintiff's claim or cause of action were determined to be included within the ambit of the congressional immunity.

In light of the judicial rejection of its single-entity defense claims, the NFL has supported legislation that would exempt from antitrust liability (a) any league rule "authorizing the membership of the league to decide that a member club of such league should not be relocated" and (b) any league rule relating to "division of league or member club revenues that tend to promote comparable economic opportunities for the member clubs of such a league."[68] The bill states that it is not intended to exempt any provision relating to player employment within a league. Of course, the nonstatutory labor law exemption already provides immunity for most such practices. Having failed to attain the single-entity exemption in the judicial system, professional sports leagues are attempting to insulate the rules governing the subjects they presumably deem most important to their survival—franchise distribution and revenue sharing—from the stringent sanctions of antitrust law by petitioning Congress for appropriate remedial legislation. The granting of such a congressional immunity would appear to be a return to the old policy of granting professional sports favored treatment. Consistent with the modern judicial perception of the sports industry as a commercially oriented business, Congress should reject any proposed legislation that would only protect the unilateral economic interests of the leagues.

Congressional policy in the immunity setting should incorporate protection of the interests of sports' consumers—the fans. Players are able to safeguard their concerns through individual and collective bargaining. Rival leagues, under most congressional action, will retain their ability to use the antitrust laws to preserve their ability to compete in the marketplace. Fans and the local community, however, are powerless to preserve their "investment" in a franchise. The granting of a congressional immunity to particular league practices is extraordinary and seemingly inconsistent with congressional distaste for antitrust immunity requests by traditional business organizations. Therefore, if Congress seriously considers such a request, the final statute should not reflect only the narrow concerns of the team owners. Such legislation would be a return to the outmoded policy perspective that government should protect management to preserve the "game." A special grant of immunity should safeguard the interest of the fans in keeping a team they have supported, or in ensuring that the revenue distribution of a particular league does not destroy the owner's economic incentive to win. If the leagues dislike this interference in the management of their business, they should be treated like a traditional business and be denied the antitrust immunity. If the leagues ask for a special exemption not normally available to an industry, they should expect a certain amount of governmental "interference" inappropriate for mainstream commerce.

SUBSTANTIVE ANTITRUST LIABILITY IN THE SPORTS CONTEXT

A court's refusal to grant an exemption should not imply that any particular contract term or market restraint is a violation of the antitrust laws. If a plaintiff successfully has rebuffed a league's defense of immunity, he must still litigate and win the separate and distinct issue of antitrust liability prior to recovery. Many of the professional sports cases to date have alleged a violation of Section One of the Sherman Act.[69] This section, as written, seems to condemn all agreements in restraint of trade. Since every business contract restrains trade to some extent, a literal interpretation of this section would stifle the economy. To prevent such economic chaos, the Supreme Court, in *Standard Oil Co. of N.J.* v. *United States*,[70] adopted the policy that only *unreasonable* restraints of trade were proscribed by the statute. Courts were required to conduct a lengthy analysis, pursuant to this rule of reason logic, to determine if a challenged practice unreasonably restrained trade in its particular business context. As antitrust law developed, however, certain practices were found to be inherently unreasonable, so an exhaustive inquiry on their reasonableness was no longer required. Typical examples of such categories of *per se* liability under Section One of the Sherman Act are price fixing, division of markets, tying arrangements, and concerted refusals to deal.[71] Most league restraints have been challenged as concerted refusals to deal or as group boycotts.

  Denver Rockets v. *All-Pro Management, Inc.*[72] and *Robertson* v. *National Basketball Association*,[73] two early district court decisions in modern sports law litigation, declared that certain league player restraints (such as draft, refusal to draft undergraduates, and free agent compensation) were group boycotts of individual players and therefore *per se* violations of Section One of the Sherman Act. However, later decisions by the Federal Circuit Court of Appeals have held that the *per se* standard of liability of Section One is inappropriate for the imposition of antitrust liability in the professional sports context.[74] The superior courts reasoned that the defendant professional leagues should not be subject to the harsh *per se* substantive criteria, since some league-imposed restraints were at least implicitly encouraged by the judicial attitude of the first half of the 20th century, intimating that sports were not subject to the antitrust laws. Additionally, sports leagues are unique in that each team has a business need for intraleague cooperation (a variant of group boycott) in order to produce an effective on-the-field product. The teams of a given league, while competitors on the field, are not economic competitors in the traditional business use of the term.[75] Finally, the *per se* standard is inappropriate when either the nonstatutory labor law or the single-entity exemption and the complex issues inherent therein are present in a case.[76] A finding of substantive antitrust liability in the professional sports context must be predicated on a rule of reason analysis and on a full judicial inquiry into the reasonableness of the practice and its effects and the history of its origin and implementation mandated thereby. The rule of reason requires the court to evaluate the reasonableness of the restraint within the context of the industry in which the alleged antitrust violation occurs. As explained by the District of Columbia Court of Appeals:

> Under the rule of reason, a restraint must be evaluated to determine whether it is significantly anticompetitive in purpose of effect. In making this evaluation, a court generally will be required to analyze "the facts peculiar to the business, the history of the restraint, and the reasons why it was imposed." If, on analysis, the restraint is found to have legitimate business purposes whose realization serves to promote competition, the "anticompetitive evils" of the challenged practice must be carefully balanced against its "procompetitive virtues" to ascertain whether the former outweigh the latter. A restraint is unreasonable if it has the "new effect" of substantially impeding competition.[77]

The Eighth Circuit employs a slightly different formulation of the required analysis: "The focus of an inquiry under the Rule of Reason is whether the restraint imposed is justified by legitimate business purposes, and is no more restrictive than necessary."[78]

In the sports context, management frequently has tried to avoid substantive antitrust liability under this standard by claiming that, although players were harmed and trade restrained to a certain extent, the challenged restraints were reasonable and necessary to maintain competitive balance on the field. This argument has been rejected as support for the anticompetitive effect of most restraints. Competitive equality among teams—even with significant player or income restraints—appears illusory, since the same teams have dominated their respective leagues every season. Other business justifications offered by the leagues to support the "reasonableness" of their practices have included recapturing of player costs, loyalty to the league, protection of capital investment, and regional balance. The restraints, however, have been declared unreasonable and therefore illegal because (a) some of the business rationales advanced have, under judicial scrutiny, been declared insubstantial and (b) the anticompetitive impact of the restraint sweeps more broadly than the proposed rationales for their adoption would justify.[79]

Most courts have suggested that revised procedures would survive the rule of reason inquiry if they were less restrictive on the rights of players and owners, if they were more closely related to a substantial business purpose, and if they contained procedural safeguards to protect the restrained party's interests from arbitrary and capricious decisionmaking. A professional sports league therefore could reasonably contain some restraints so that arguable parity of talent would exist within the league and those franchises in geographically disadvantageous locations would receive assistance in fielding teams. However, practices that have the effect of unduly depressing player salaries, restricting player or franchise freedom of movement for a significant period of time, or vesting unrestricted control over a player or a team to league management seem suspect under the rule of reason standard of substantive antitrust liability.

Section Two of the Sherman Act also has been used in the sports litigation context. This section sanctions every person who monopolizes, attempts to monopolize, or combines or conspires with another to monopolize any part of trade or commerce.[80] The Supreme Court in *United States* v. *Grinnel Corporation* has stated: "The offense of monopoly under § 2 of the Sherman Act has two elements: (1) the possession of monopoly power in the relevant market and (2) the willful acquisition or maintenance of that power as distinguished from growth or development as a consequence of a superior product, business acrument or historic accident."[81] The relevant market consists of a product market and a geographic market. Products in the same market are those whose uses are reasonably interchangeable and whose demand is cross-elastic.

Philadelphia World Hockey Club v. *Philadelphia Hockey Club*[82] and *Mid-South Grizzlies* v. *National Football League*[83] are the prime examples of Section Two analysis in the professional sports context. *Philadelphia Hockey* determined that the relevant market was major league hockey as is played in the NHL. Of course, with that definition of the market, the NHL possessed monopoly power. *Mid-South Grizzlies* also found that the NFL had a monopoly in the United States in major league football. Courts in the professional sports setting have been willing to accept a narrow market definition that usually coincides with the major sport at issue. Indeed, a market definition also can be conducted in assessing whether a restraint of trade is unreasonable in a Section One litigation. *NASL* (a special submarket in sports capital)[84] and *Los Angeles Memorial Coliseum* (the unique nature of NFL football)[85] support the conclusion that a narrow sports-market definition also is appropriate in that context. However, a narrow market definition and the existence of monopoly power does not, by itself, mean that Section Two has been violated. *Philadelphia Hockey* found such a violation by concluding that the NHL had willfully and intentionally maintained its monopoly status through the use of numerous predatory practices directed against the World Hockey Association.[86] However, *Mid-South Grizzles* held that the NFL had not abused its monopoly power in denying plaintiff an NFL franchise. The NFL had done nothing to prevent plaintiff from forming a rival team or playing football in Memphis.[87]

Antitrust plaintiffs usually prefer to bring a cause of action pursuant to Section One of the Sherman Act rather than Section Two. A Section One suit usually avoids the difficult questions of relevant market and abuse of monopoly power. However, Section Two frequently is the basis for a lawsuit by a new league against an established league in a similar sport. If the older organization has taken action beyond its own league activities to make operations more difficult for the new league, the charge of at least attempted monopolization has some facial validity. A Section Two violation does not require multiple entities for a finding of substantive violation. However, with the apparent rejection of the single-entity defense, Section One will continue to be the preferred antitrust cause of action in the professional sports context.

CONCLUSION

The nonbaseball sports leagues have tried to achieve the immune status of baseball by obtaining some form of antitrust exemption. The nonstatutory labor law exemption seems to be the most effective exemption achieved by the leagues in that provisions embodied within a legitimate collective bargaining agreement will not be subject to antitrust attack by members of the bargaining relationship. As such, federal labor law rather than antitrust law will be the appropriate legal context for resolving management-labor disputes in a professional league where the two parties possess roughly equal strength. This exemption, however, has two serious drawbacks from the perspective of a professional league: (1) the price of the exemption is allowing a union to bargain over the practice, thereby forfeiting potential unilateral control over what could arguably be considered a management prerogative, and (2) practices with extra-unit effects are not within the scope of the exemption.

The single-entity defense has proved to be less useful to sports management, since the Second and Ninth circuits, the only courts to hear the defense in a sports context, have both rejected its applicability to professional leagues. Specific statutory immunities are totally effective once written into law, but getting a bill through Congress is, at best, a long and unpredictable process. The leagues will continue to face antitrust liability, generally under the substantive standard of the rule of reason of Section One of the Sherman Act. This antitrust exposure will not destroy professional sports in America. However, league practices will need to be reformed to comply more closely with the business purpose that motivated the restraint and to protect the restrained party from arbitrary decisions.

Antitrust liability will lessen the ability of the established leagues' management to maintain unilateral control of the sports industry. Such a result is consistent with the public policy determination, made by the judicial system in the 1970s, that professional sports should be subject to the same legal restraints and liabilities as any other profit-making industry.

NOTES

1. 259 U.S. 200 (1922).

2. 15 U.S.C. SS 1 and 2 (1976).

3. See Toolson v. New York Yankees, Inc., 346 U.S. 356 (1953); American League Baseball Club of Chicago v. Chase, 86 Misc. 411, 149 N.Y.S. 6 (Sup. Ct. 1914); Philadelphia Base Ball Club, Ltd. v. Lajoie, 10 Pa. Dist. Rpts. 309 (1901), rev'd, 202 Pa. 210, 51 A. 973 (1902).

4. See Sports Broadcasting Act, and Merger Addition thereto, 15 U.S.C. SS 1291–95 (1976).

5. Flood v. Kuhn, 309 F. Supp. 793, 797 (SDNY 1970), aff'd 407 U.S. 258 (1972).

6. See Radovich v. National Football League, 352 U.S. 445 (1957) and United States v. International Boxing Club of N.Y., 348 U.S. 236 (1955).

7. 407 U.S. 258 (1972). The baseball players union achieved its bargainig leverage by gaining free agency for players through the arbitration process. See Professional Baseball Clubs, 66 LAB. & DISP. SETTL. 101 (1975) (Seitz, Arb.), aff'd sub nom., Kansas City Royals Baseball Corp. v. Major League Baseball Players Ass'n, 409 F. Supp. 233 (W.D. Mo. 1976), aff'd, 532 F.2d 615 (8th Cir. 1976).

8. Clayton Act of 1914 S 6, 15 U.S.C. SS 17, 20; 29 U.S.C. S 52 (1976). See also Norris-LaGuardia Act of 1932 SS 1–15, 29 U.S.C. SS 101–15 (1976).

9. See Apex Hosiery Co. v. Leader, 310 U.S. 469 (1940).

10. United States v. Hutcheson, 312 U.S. 219, 232 (1941).

11. 325 U.S. 797 (1945).

12. 381 U.S. 657 (1965).

13. 381 U.S. 676 (1965).

14. See Allen Bradley v. Local Union No. 13, IBEW, 325 U.S. 797, 811 (1945) (the origin of the phrase "Allen Bradley conspiracy"), and UMW v. Pennington, 381 U.S. 657, 665–66 (1965).

15. Local Union No. 189, Amalgamated Meat Cutters v. Jewel Tea Co., 381 U.S. 676, 707 (1965).

16. For a more extensive discussion of Supreme Court and other non sports cases analyzing the exemption, see Phillip J. Closius, "Not at the Behest of Non-Labor Groups: A Revised Prognosis for a Maturing Sports Industry," *Boston College Law Review* 24 (1983): 348–62.

17. 351 F. Supp. 462 (E.D. Pa. 1972).

18. 389 F. Supp. 867 (S.D.N.Y. 1975).

19. Ibid., pp. 885–86; see also Philadelphia World Hockey Club, Inc. v. Philadelphia Hockey Club, Inc., 351 F. Supp. 462, 497–98 (E.D. Pa. 1972).

20. Ibid., p. 888. This result was dictated by the Supreme Court's opinion in UMW v.

Pennington, 381 U.S. 657, 664–65 (1965) and Local Union No. 189, Amalgamated Meat Cutters v. Jewel Tea Co., 381 U.S. 676, 691 (1965).

21. Philadelphia World Hockey Club, Inc. v. Philadelphia Hockey Club Inc., 351 F. Supp. 462, 498–99 (E.D. Pa. 1972).

22. 543 F.2d 606 (8th Cir. 1976), cert. dismissed, 434 U.S. 801 (1977).

23. 600 F.2d 1193 (6th Cir. 1979).

24. Mackey v. National Football League, 543 F.2d 606, 610–11 (8th Cir. 1976) p. 614.

25. Ibid., p. 615. The 1970 NFL agreement also contained a "zipper clause," which read: "[T]his Agreement represents a complete and final understanding of all bargainable subjects of negotiation among the parties during the term of this Agreement." Ibid., p. 613. This agreement had expired in 1974 and the union, seeking the elimination of the Rozelle Rule, had been unable to produce an agreement with the league.

26. McCourt v. California Sports, Inc., 600 F.2d 1193, 1196 (6th Cir. 1979).

27. Ibid., p. 1203.

28. Ibid., p. 1201.

29. Such employee-union disputes are best settled through the union election process or through enforcement of the union's duty of fair representation.

30. For a more detailed discussion of this interpretation of the exemption, see Closius, "Non-Labor Groups," pp. 372–77.

31. NFL-NFLPA Collective Bargaining Agreement, Art. I, S2.

32. NFL Constitution and By laws, S 12.1 (A)

33. Baseball traditionally drafts players after their senior year of high school or their junior year of college. Hockey traditionally drafts players of post-high school years from the junior hockey leagues. Neither baseball nor hockey provide for their draft in a collective bargaining agreement. Robert C. Berry and William B. Gould, "A Long Deep Drive to Collective Bargaining: Of Players, Owners, Brawls and Strikes, "*Case Western Reserve Law Review* 31 (1981): 790–91.

34. Denver Rockets v. All-Pro Management, Inc., 325 F. Supp. 1049 (C.D. Cal. 1971).

35. National Basketball Players Association Agreement, Art. XXII, S 1 (f) (1980–82).

36. NFL Constitution and By laws, S 17.6.

37. The federal statute granting NFL teams an antitrust exemption for the purpose of bargaining as a single group with the broadcast industry does not appear to immunize the method by which the fruits of such negotiations are distributed. See Sports Broadcasting Act, 15 U.S.C.S. 1291 (1976). For a possible challenge to this shared-revenue system by an NFL owner, see note 85.

38. 420 F. Supp. 738, 743–44 (D.C.C. 1976), aff'd in part, rev'd in part, 593 F.2d 1173 (D.C. Cir. 1978). The appellate court did not consider the exemption issue. The actual holding of the district court was that the exemption did not shield the draft at issue, since, at the time Smith was drafted, it was embodied in the league's constitution and bylaws and not in a bargained agreement.

39. Ibid., p. 743.

40. See Smith v. Pro-Football, Inc., 420 F. Supp. 738, 743–44 (D.C.C. 1976), aff'd in part, rev'd in part, 593 F.2d 1173 (D.C.C. 1978); John Weistart and Cym Lowell, *The Law of Sports* (Charlottesville, Va.: Bobbs-Merrill, 1979); S 5.05, pp. 552–54; Michael S. Jacobs and Ralph K. Winter. "Antitrust Principles and Collective Bargaining by Athletes: Of Superstars in Peonage," *Yale Law Journal* 81 (1971): 16. Hiring halls are in effect a job referral service provided by unions. In certain industries, usually maritime and construction, employers have short-lived and irregular employment needs. In these areas, prospective employees register with a union hall. The employer, when the need for employees arises, goes to the hall and obtains a qualified and available labor force. The union supplies workers based on "neutral" or "objective" criteria. See Robert Gorman, *Basic Text on Labor Law* (St. Paul, Minn.: West Publishing Co., 1976).

41. See Local 357, International Bhd. of Teamsters v. National Labor Relations Board, 365 U.S. 667, 675 (1961); National Labor Relations Board v. Associated Gen. Contractors of America, Inc., 349 F.2d 449, 452 (5th Cir. 1965), and Gorman, *Basic Text on Labor Law*, pp. 664–65.

42. The NFL-NFLPA Collective Bargaining Agreement expired on July 12, 1982. When the last agreement expired in 1974, management and labor did not conclude a new agreement until

the settlement of the Alexander case in August 1977. Alexander v. National Football League, 1977–2 Trade Cases (CCH), s 61, 730 (D. Minn. 1977).

43. A contrary rule would give the players' unions unwarranted bargaining power in that management could not run its business without fear of antitrust liability unless it produced an agreement with the union. This might unduly force employers to make substantive concessions. Comment, "Application of the Labor Exemption After the Expiration of Collective Bargaining Agreement in Professional Sports," *New York University Law Review*, 57 (1982): 197.

44. Weistart and Lowell, *The Law of Sports*, S 5.06, at 588–90.

45. Section 1 of the Sherman Act, 15 U.S.C. S 1 (1976), states in relevant part: "Every contract, combination in the form of trust or otherwise, or conspiracy, in restraint of trade or commerce among the several states, or with foreign nations, is declared to be illegal."

46. United States v. Addyston Pipe and Steel Co., 85 F. 271 (6th Cir. 1898), modified and aff'd, 175 U.S. 211 (1899).

47. Milton Handler and Thomas A. Smart, "The Present Status of the Intracorporate Conspiracy Doctrine," *Cardozo* 3 (1981): 40.

48. Ibid., p. 52.

49. Ibid., pp. 40 and 56.

50. Copperweld Corporation v. Independence Tube Corporation, 52 U.S. Law Week 4821 (1984).

51. For a critical view of this analysis in player-restraint cases, see Myron C. Grauer, "Recognition of the National Football League as a Single Entity Under Section 1 of the Sherman Act: Implications of the Consumer Welfare Model," *Michigan Law Review* 82 (1983): 35–49.

52. 670 F.2d 1249 (2d Cir. 1982), cert. denied, 103 S. Ct. 499 (1982).

53. 726 F.2d 1381 (9th Cir. 1984).

54. NFL Constitution and By laws, Art. IX, S 4, quoted in NASL v. NFL, 670 F.2d 1249, 1255 (2d Cir. 1982).

55. NASL v. NFL, 670 F.2d 1249, 1257 (2d Cir. 1982).

56. See Copperweld Corp. v. Independence Tube Corp., 52 U.S. Law Week 4821 (1984); Los Angeles Memorial Coliseum Commission v. National Football League, 726 F.2d 1381, 1388 (9th Cir. 1984).

57. NASL v. NFL, 670 F.2d 1249, 1257 (2d Cir. 1982).

58. NFL Constitution and Bylaws, Art. IV, S 3, quoted in Los Angeles Memorial Coliseum Commission v. National Football League, 726 F.2d 1381, 1385 n.1 (9th Cir. 1984).

59. Los Angeles Memorial Coliseum Commission v. National Football League, 726 F.2d 1381, 1388 (9th Cir. 1984).

60. Ibid., p. 1389.

61. Ibid.,p. 1390.

62. 52 *U.S. Law Week* 4821 (1984).

63. Lawrence A. Sullivan, *Handbook of the Law of Antitrust* (St. Paul, Minn.: West Publishing Co., 1977) p. 11.

64. Los Angeles Memorial Coliseum Commission v. National Football League, 726 F.2d 1381, 1390, fn.4 (9th Cir. 1984).

65. NASL v. National Football League, 103 S. Ct. 499, 500 (1982).

66. NFL Constitution and By-Laws, S 10.3.

67. Sports Broadcasting Act, and Merger Addition thereto, 15 U.S.C. SS 1291–95 (1976). This statute does not, on its face, immunize the manner in which broadcast revenue is distributed by a league after it has been negotiated and received.

68. Sports Antitrust Bill, S.2784, 97th Cong., 2d sess. (1982), 128 *Congressional Record*, S. 9330–31 (daily ed., July 28, 1982).

69. See note 58.

70. 221 U.S. 1, 63–70 (1911).

71. See Sullivan, *Hardbook of the Law of Antitrust*; Robertson v. National Basketball Ass'n, 389 F. Supp. 867, 893 (S.D.N.Y. 1975).

72. 325 F. Supp. 1049 (C.D. Cal. 1971).

73. 389 F. Supp. 867 (S.D.N.Y. 1975).

74. See Los Angeles Memorial Coliseum Commission v. National Football League, 726 f.2d 1381 (9th Cir, 1984); NASL v. National Football League, 670 F.2d 1249 (2d Cir. 1982); Mackey

v. National Football League, 543 F.2d 606 (8th Cir. 1976), and Smith v. Pro-Football, Inc., 593 F.2d 1173 (D.C. Cir. 1978).

75. Los Angeles Memorial Coliseum Commission v. National Football League, 726 F.2d 1381, 1389 (9th Cir. 1984); Mackey v. National Football League, 543 F.2d 606, 619 (8th Cir. 1976).

76. See Milton Handler and William Zifchak, "Collective Bargaining and the Antitrust Laws: The Emasculation of the Labor Law Exemption," *Columbia Law Review* 81, (1981): 510–13.

77. Smith v. Pro-Football, Inc. 593 F.2d 1173, 1183 (D.C. Cir. 1978).

78. Mackey v. National Football League, 543 F.2d 606, 620 (8th Cir. 1976).

79. See Los Angeles Memorial Coliseum Commission v. National Football League, 726 F.2d 1381, 1396–98 (9th Cir. 1984); NASL v. National Football League, 670, F.2d 1249, 1261 (2d Cir. 1982), and Mackey v. National Football League, 543 F.2d 606, 621–22 (8th Cir. 1976).

80. Section 2 of the Sherman Act, 15 U.S.C. S 2 (1976), states, in relevant part: "Every person who shall monopolize, or attempt to monopolize or combine or conspire with any other person or persons, to monopolize any part of the trade or commerce among the several States . . ."

81. 384 U.S. 563, 570–71 (1966).

82. Philadelphia World Hockey Club v. Philadelphia Hockey Club, 351 F. Supp. 462, 501 (E.D. Pa. 1972).

83. Mid-South Grizzlies v. National Football League, 550 F. Supp. 558, 571 (E.D. Pa. 1982).

84. NASL v. National Football League, 670 F.2d 11249, 1259–61 (2d Cir 1982).

85. Los Angeles Memorial Coliseum Commission v. National Football League, 726 F.2d 1381, 1392–94 (9th Cir. 1984).

86. Philadelphia World Hockey Club v. Philadelphia Hockey Club, 351 F. Supp. 462, 510–13 (E.D. Pa. 1972).

87. Mid-South Grizzlies v. National Football League, 550 F. Supp. 558, 571 (E.D. Pa. 1982).

9

Property Rights in Sports Broadcasting: The Fundamental Issue

Philip R. Hochberg

As the world of communications became ever more complex in the 1970s and first half of the 1980s—cable television, pay television, pay cable, satellites, "superstations," signal piracy, home taping—so too did the world of sports broadcasting. Indeed, in virtually every aspect, sports broadcasting "tracked" the new developments: For every unique consideration that television broadcasting as a whole had, sports had much the same problems and even some unique problems of its own. For example, in television, the owners of a program like "M★A★S★H" would be concerned that if they sold telecasting rights to WTBS Atlanta, WGN-TV Chicago, or WOR-TV New York, the telecast by that station (which would then be retransmitted by satellite to cable systems around the country) would injure possible sales in other markets. "M★A★S★H" would be competing against itself. The sports interests had the same sort of concern. If the Braves or Cubs or Mets were playing at Pittsburgh and the Pirates didn't want to televise their home game, it might still come back into Pittsburgh via the superstation transmission of the visiting team's away game. Not only might this injure the home attendance for those very games, but it could hurt other home games or the entire local television package or simply offer too much baseball for the success of the Pittsburgh club.

The threshold questions, however, have to be addressed before moving to complex, new areas. And in so doing, one first has to identify who owned those very telecasts that were at the heart of the problem.

---

*The arguments presented in this chapter elaborate on those presented in Philip R. Hochberg and Robert A. Garrett, "Sports Broadcasting and the Law," *Indiana Law Journal* 59 (May 1984): 155–93.

ESTABLISHING THE PROPERTY RIGHT

The law of sports broadcasting had its origin some five years before the first major sports event was ever televised, when A. E. Newton, who operated radio station WOCL from the basement of his Jamestown, New York, home, decided to go into the sports broadcasting business. Since 1921, Major League Baseball had entered into contracts authorizing the broadcast of World Series games by various radio stations. Newton, however, conceived of a way to broadcast the 1934 World Series between the Cardinals and Tigers without negotiating (that is, paying) for the right to do so. He simply provided his audience with "running accounts" of the games based upon information that he had received while listening to authorized radio broadcasts.

Newton's "play-by-play" subsequently formed the basis of a challenge to his license renewal before the Federal Communications Commission. The claim was that such conduct violated section 325(a) of the Communications Act of 1934, which prohibits one station from rebroadcasting, without consent, another station's programming. The FCC considered Newton's conduct to be "inconsistent with fair dealing," "dishonest in nature," "unfair utilization of the results of another's labor," and "deceptive to the public upon the whole, and contrary to the interests thereof"—but not violative of section 325. Emphasizing that he had confined his sportscasting career to the 1934 World Series, the FCC renewed Newton's license.[1]

Newton's was the first in a series of reported decisions involving the right of sports clubs to control the dissemination of the accounts of their games. The forum, however, soon shifted from the FCC to the state and federal courts, where the sports clubs were more effective than they had been before the commission. Those who sought to follow in Newton's footsteps argued that the accounts of sports events constituted news in the public domain and that any person had the right to disseminate the news. The courts took a different view.

The leading case is *Pittsburgh Athletic Co.* v. *KQV Broadcasting Co.* (1939).[2] The defendant in that case was Pittsburgh radio station KQV, which had broadcast play-by-play descriptions of the Pirates' baseball games without the consent of the Pirates. The KQV announcers obtained their information about the games from station employees positioned at vantage points outside the Pirates' Forbes Field. The Pirates, who had licensed their radio rights to NBC, sued to enjoin the unauthorized KQV broadcasts.

The 1938 Pirates had the rare distinction of losing the National League pennant to the Chicago Cubs, but they were victorious against station KQV. The court enjoined KQV's activities, concluding that the ball club "by reason of its creation of the game, its control of the park, and its restriction of the dissemination of news therefrom, has a property right in such news, and the right to control the use thereof for a reasonable time following the games." The court held that KQV had misappropriated the property rights of the Pirates in the "news, reports, descriptions or accounts" of the Pirates' games; that such misappropriation resulted in KQV's "unjust enrichment" to the detriment of the Pirates; and that KQV's actions constituted "unfair competition," a "fraud on the public," and a violation of unspecified provisions of the Communications Act.

A similar result obtained seventeen years later in *National Exhibition Co.* v. *Fass* (1954).[3] The defendant in that case, an "independent newsgatherer" named Martin Fass, listened to authorized radio and television broadcasts of the 1953 and 1954 New York Giants. Without securing the Giants' consent, Fass simultaneously teletyped reports of their games to radio stations across the country for immediate rebroadcast. The Giants made it to the World Series in 1954; Fass did not. Some three months before Willie Mays turned his back on the celebrated Vic Wertz fly ball, the court enjoined Fass's activities and awarded the Giants damages, concluding:

> Plaintiff is the owner of the professional baseball exhibitions which it produces; and its property rights, as owner of such exhibitions, include the proprietary right to sell to others, who desire to purchase and to whom plaintiff desires to sell, licenses or rights under which the purchasers are authorized to [broadcast the games] in such geographical area or areas as may be agreed upon between plaintiff and such purchasers. . . .
>
> In creating the games, the competing clubs not only create an exhibition for the spectators at the game but also create, as the game unfolds, a drama consisting of the sequence of plays, which is valuable program material for radio and television stations and for which licensees have paid and are paying plaintiff substantial sums.[4]

In a similar fashion, other courts have protected the sports clubs' property rights to the accounts and descriptions of their games by preventing the unauthorized exploitation of these rights.

The sports property right concept was strengthened by the U.S. Supreme Court in *Zacchini* v. *Scripps-Howard Broadcasting Co.* (1977).[5] There, an Ohio television station broadcast a fifteen-second tape of the celebrated "Flying" Zacchini's "human cannonball" performance without obtaining his consent. In response to Zacchini's claim that the station had unlawfully misappropriated his professional property, the station responded that its broadcast was protected as free speech. A 5–4 majority of the Supreme Court sided with the Flying Zacchini. Citing the *Pittsburgh Athletic* decision and other authority, the Court concluded:

> Wherever the line in particular situations is to be drawn between media reports that are protected and those that are not, we are quite sure that the First and Fourteenth Amendments do not immunize the media when they broadcast a performer's entire act without his consent. *The Constitution no more prevents a*

State from requiring respondent to compensate petitioner for broadcasting his act on television than it would privilege respondent to film and broadcast a copyrighted dramatic work without liability to the copyright owner . . . *a prize fight . . . or a baseball game,* where the promoters or the participants had other plans for publicizing the event.[6][emphasis added]

Congress added a new dimension to the sports property-right concept when it enacted the Copyright Act of 1976.[7] At the urging of the professional sports leagues, Congress extended federal copyright protection to live sports broadcasts, thereby vesting the owners of these telecasts with the exclusive right to "perform" them "publicly." To be eligible for copyright protection, the broadcast must be "fixed" (recorded) simultaneously with its transmission. The remedies afforded by the Copyright Act are particularly valuable because they permit the copyright owner to recover statutory damages of between $250 and $50,000 for each act of infringement without regard to actual damages suffered.

IDENTIFYING THE BENEFICIARIES OF THE PROPERTY RIGHT

Given the increasingly valuable nature of the property right that the sports clubs established in the accounts and descriptions of their games, it is not surprising that two other groups—broadcasters and players—have argued that they also are beneficiaries of this right. A somewhat related question, which has become important to colleges in particular, is which of the two teams involved in a game owns the rights to disseminate the accounts and descriptions of that game?

The Broadcasters' Claims

The legislative history of the Copyright Act of 1976 is replete with instances where the sports clubs assumed they would own the copyright that they urged Congress to create.[8] Not once during the decade-long debates did the broadcasters assert anything to the contrary; on occasion, they even testified that the clubs would be the copyright holders. Nevertheless, when it came time to claim a share of the royalties paid by cable systems for retransmitting copyrighted television programming, the broadcasters' principal trade association—the National Association of Broadcasters (NAB)—argued that broadcasters have a copyrightable interest in sports telecasts that they produce, and that this interest entitles them to a share of royalties.

The Copyright Royalty Tribunal, the federal agency responsible for allocating the cable royalties among copyright owners, rejected the NAB's claims in the 1978 royalty-distribution proceeding (the first such proceeding under the Copyright Act of 1976). Relying primarily on the legislative history of the act, the tribunal concluded that the sports clubs are the copyright owners of the telecasts of their games and are entitled to all of the cable royalties attributable to these telecasts—unless the broadcaster and club have a contractual agreement "specifically" to the contrary. The U.S. Court of Appeals for the District of Columbia Circuit did not find the legislative history to be quite so dispositive of the question. Nevertheless, it affirmed the tribunal's decision to award to the sports interests all of the 1978 royalties for sports programming.[9]

The Copyright Act provides that cable royalties may be awarded only to copyright owners.[10] Thus the court's decision to affirm the tribunal's sports award leaves no doubt that the sports clubs are copyright owners of the telecasts of their games. The decision, however, suggests that the broadcasters also may have a copyrightable interest in sports telecasts that they produce, and that the mission of the tribunal is to evaluate the broadcasters' interest in these telecasts vis-à-vis that of the sports clubs.

In the appeal of the 1978 cable royalty proceeding, the court observed that the broadcasters' interest was "quantitively de minimis"; thus it upheld the tribunal's decision not to award any sports royalties to the broadcasters. In the subsequent appeal of the 1979 proceeding, however, the court determined that the valuation issue was one to be decided on the basis of the particular record before the tribunal. Because the NAB had introduced new evidence in the 1979 proceeding on broadcasters' contributions to sports telecasts and because the tribunal had not evaluated this evidence, the court remanded the sports award to the tribunal for such an evaluation. The court did make it clear, however, that the tribunal need not award the broadcasters any royalties whatsoever for their contributions to sports telecasts.

Before the Court of Appeals had ruled in the 1979 case, the Tribunal, in the 1980 cable royalty proceeding, appeared to make the very evaluation of the record subsequently ordered by the court. The tribunal concluded that the broadcasters' contributions are indeed de minimis and do not warrant any increase in the broadcasters' royalty award:

> [T]he contribution of the broadcaster as compared with that of the teams is minimal. . . .
>
> We find no evidence in our record, including that of the NAB sports witnesses, establishing that the contribution of the broadcaster in any significant respect contributes to a cable operator's interest in sports programming, or the decision of an individual to subscribe to cable television. . . .
>
> Proceeding from the broadcaster use of ratings to judge the value of programs, [a witness for the sports interests] testified that the factors that affect the ratings all relate to the sports teams, and that the quality of the production does not affect the ratings. We concur in this testimony. We do not find it creditable that a cable subscriber would pass up viewing a game involving

teams competing for the pennant to watch a Chicago Cubs game because of the quality of the production of the Cubs telecast.[11]

The broadcasters and sports interests ultimately resolved their differences before the tribunal. The settlement provides that the sports interests will continue to receive all of the royalties attributable to sports telecasts; individual broadcasters can seek to enter into negotiations with their clubs as to how, if at all, these royalties might be shared. In adopting the settlement agreement, the tribunal noted:

> As we and the Court of Appeals have previously recognized, it is clear that a sports club owns a copyright in the telecasts of its games if simultaneously "fixed"; it is equaly [sic] clear that a broadcaster who produces the telecasts of such games also owns a copyright in such telecasts. These copyrightable interests have relative market values, the determination of which may be addressed in any royalty distribution proceedings. By adopting the approach of [the broadcasters and sports interests], it is not necessary that we make such a valuation; rather, we are simply allowing the parties themselves to do so in the context of their private negotiations.[12]

The Players' Claims

In May 1982 the Major League Baseball Players Association (MLBPA) sent a form letter to a number of the television stations, national television networks, and cable networks broadcasting professional baseball games. The MLBPA claimed that the players possess the property rights to the televised performances of baseball games; that there can be no broadcast of these performances without the players' consent; and that the Major League Baseball clubs, the leagues, and the Commissioner of Baseball have no authority to grant such consent—although they have been doing so for nearly forty years.

The response of the Major League Baseball clubs was to seek a declaratory judgment that the players have no rights to broadcast revenues. In *Baltimore Orioles, Inc.* v. *Major League Baseball Players Assn*, the clubs sought a ruling that they, as the employers of the players, possess all rights in the telecasts of their games based upon (a) the "works made for hire" doctrine in the 1976 Copyright Act; (b) the common law master-servant doctrine; (c) the Uniform Players's Contract; and (d) the doctrines of waiver and estoppel and implied and express consent. Three years later, in May 1985, Major League Baseball was granted Summary Judgment on the copyright and master-servant theories.[13] Nevertheless, the issue of whether players may receive a direct share of the increasingly important broadcast revenues (over and above their current salaries) surely will surface during collective bargaining sessions.

Interclub Claims

Sports clubs have confronted challenges not only from broadcasters and players, but from other clubs as well. Because a game cannot be played without two teams, the question has arisen: Which team owns the right to distribute the accounts and descriptions of that game? Typically, this question is resolved by agreement.

One interesting case, where no contractual resolution had been reached, was *Wichita State University Intercollegiate Athletic Ass'n, Inc.* v. *Swanson Broadcasting Co.*, a 1981 Kansas case. This case involved a radio station in Wichita, Kansas, which had contracted with opponents of the Wichita State University (WSU) football and basketball teams to broadcast WSU's away games (that is, the opponents' home games). WSU, which itself had entered into a broadcasting contract with another Wichita radio station, sought to enjoin the other broadcasts in its home city of Wichita. It relied upon common-law principles of misappropriation and contractual interference. The court granted a preliminary injunction, concluding:

> Wichita State University has the right to broadcast the sports events into their home territory, be it a "home game" or "away game." They do not have the right to make a determination who will broadcast that game to New York, Los Angeles, or Moose Jaw, Montana, but they do have a right to make a determination as to who they will contract with to broadcast that game into the Wichita area. It is an exclusive right and it is a right exclusive even of the opponent of Wichita State University; they cannot make that determination.[14]

In the famed litigation between the universities of Oklahoma and Georgia and the NCAA—which started in 1981 and ended with a Supreme Court decision in June 1984 in *Board of Regents of the University of Oklahoma* v. *National Collegiate Athletic Association*[15]—the ownership question was at the very heart of the issue. The Supreme Court affirmed the lower courts' opinions that the actions of the NCAA reduced output and fixed prices in a joint sale of collegiate football telecasting rights.

The *NCAA* litigation was brought by Oklahoma and Georgia in substantial part because the NCAA had prohibited the schools and other member institutions from selling games on their own to the networks or the news media. The College Football Association (CFA), of which Oklahoma and Georgia are members, had sought to negotiate a television package outside the NCAA contracts, believing that the property rights belonged to individual institutions unless specifically relinquished by those institutions. In response, the NCAA adopted the following "Official Interpretation" of an NCAA bylaw:

> The Association shall control all forms of televising of the intercollegiate football games of member institutions during the traditional football season.
> . . . Any commitment by a member institution with respect to the televising or

cablecasting of its football games in future seasons necessarily would be subject to the terms of the NCAA Football Television Plan applicable to such season.

According to the district court, this was the NCAA's "first clear statement" that mere membership in the NCAA was a grant by the member to the NCAA of the right to act as the school's agent for televising football. As the district court also found, it was "NCAA's first specific statement that it controlled 'cablecasting' as well as broadcasting." The district court concluded that while the NCAA "has a valid role to play in the regulation of college athletics, it has gone far beyond the pale of this legitimate purpose in commandeering the rights of its members to sell their games for television broadcast."[16] While the Supreme Court did not address the ownership question directly, it appeared clear that between the NCAA and the schools, the NCAA could not usurp ownership or complete control, absent an exemption from the antitrust law.

The ownership question almost came up in one of *Board of Regents'* progeny. A subsequent lawsuit came up in Los Angeles, where UCLA and USC wanted to sell their games against Nebraska and Notre Dame, respectively, to CBS. Nebraska and Notre Dame objected, stating that the CFA contract with ABC prohibited the CBS agreements. In seeking a preliminary injunction, UCLA and USC claimed, among other things, that as home teams they had exclusive sale rights. Although the preliminary injunction was granted (and affirmed),[17] UCLA and USC had withdrawn their ownership claim. The court, perhaps much relieved, did not have to face the question, leaving it unanswered—and maybe unanswerable.

CONCLUSION

There would be no broadcast revenues if the law had not recognized certain property rights in the accounts and descriptions of sports events. The size of these revenues is itself a function of the way in which the law has defined and restricted such property rights. The relationship between sports and television has been, and will continue to be, defined in large measure by a multitude of judicial, legislative, and administrative pronouncements.

Clearly, the communications industry is undergoing a dramatic revolution; the sports industry has a substantial stake in this changing technology. As the stakes get even higher, there will be increasing pressure for litigation, legislation, and regulation affecting sports broadcasting. The courts, legislative bodies, and regulatory agencies will have to make decisions on cable rights, royalty payments, home video recording, the use of satellite transmissions (that is, piracy), pay telecasts, superstation telecasting, and even the right to broadcast game highlights. The fundamental question in each case is who owns the broadcast rights. Is it the players, the leagues, or the owners? In resolving these complex problems, it is necessary to draw upon four decades of legal history, which have produced principles and guidelines of significance.

NOTES

1. In re A. E. Newton, 2 FCC 2d 281 (1936).
2. 24 F. Supp. 490 (W. D. Pa. 1938).
3. 133 N.Y.S. 2d 379 (Sup. Ct. 1954).
4. 143 N.Y.S. 2d 767, 770 (Sup. Ct. 1955).
5. 433 U.S. 562 (1977).
6. Ibid., pp. 574–75.
7. 17 U.S.C. 101 *et seq.* (effective January 1, 1978).
8. See, for example, hearings on S. 1361 before the Subcommittee on Patents, Trademarks, and Copyrights of the Senate Committee on the Judiciary, 93d Cong., 1st sess. (1973), pp. 526–33.
9. National Association of Broadcasters v. Copyright Royalty Tribunal, 675 F. 367 (D.C. Cir. 1982).
10. 17 U.S.C. 111(d) (4).
11. 48 Fed. Reg. (1983), 9552, 9565–66.
12. *1979 Cable Royalty Distribution,* 49 Fed. Reg. 3899 (1984).
13. Case No. 82-C-3710, N.D. Ill., May 23, 1985.
14. Transcript of Bench Ruling (January 23, 1981), p. 5. But see Kelly Communications Corp. v. Westinghouse Broadcasting Corp., Case No. 83–377 Civil (Supreme Judicial Court for Suffolk Cty., Massachusetts). After Kelly had purchased the rights to Boston College football and sold them to one Boston radio station, Westinghouse's Boston station joined the Penn State radio network for a single game, Penn State at Boston College. In a bench ruling the day before the game, the appeals court dissolved a preliminary injunction that would have prevented Westinghouse from presenting the broadcast. Language in the *Pittsburgh Athletic* decision suggests that the home club has exclusive broadcasting rights absent agreement to the contrary. Of course, the court was not called upon in that case to adjudicate the conflicting rights of the two clubs.
15. —U.S.—, 104 S.C. & 2948 (1984). This litigation illustrates the significance of the Sports Broadcast Act of 1961 (15 U.S.C. pp. 1291–95, as amended by Public Law 89–800, enacted November 8, 1966) to professional sports leagues. That law exempts the professional leagues from antitrust liability for the pooled sales of their telecasting rights. The colleges were not covered by this act and, thus, the antitrust status of these broadcasting arrangements remain uncertain.
16. See Board of Regents v. National Collegiate Athletic Ass'n, 546 F. Supp. 1276 (W.D. Okla. 1982).
17. Regents of University of California v. ABC, 747 F. 2d. 511 (9th Cir. 1984).

10

The Impact of Tax Policy on Sports

James F. Ambrose

In the view of John W. Reynolds, Chief Judge of the United States District Court for the Eastern District of Wisconsin, "Baseball is good for Americans."[1] Whether or not this is true, it does not necessarily follow that the Internal Revenue Code will then treat professional baseball in any particular way.

The federal income tax treatment of certain industries is intended more for purposes of regulation or for their encouragement than merely to raise revenue. For example, charitable contributions and the interest portion of a person's home-mortgage payment are deductible. Because you can pay such amounts with dollars that are not subject to income tax, it is easier to make such a payment. A $600 mortgage payment is cheaper than a $600 rent payment. It costs someone in the 50 percent tax bracket only $500 to give $1,000 to charity. The rationale for making such payments deductible is that it will stimulate gift giving and home buying. Other tax legislation is intended to regulate negatively or discourage such activity. Examples of this are the taxes on alcohol and tobacco.

These principles of taxation policy also apply to analysis of the federal tax treatment of the ownership and operation of professional sports franchises. If the federal government is interested primarily in raising revenues, then the most direct approach would be to impose a special tax on ticket proceeds or gross television revenues. If the primary purpose is something other than raising revenues, the threshold question is whether federal tax treatment should encourage, discourage, or be neutral on the operation of professional sports franchises. If the treatment is to be favorable, then the question is how to implement such a policy.

Historically, the federal attitude of neglecting professional sports had been favorable for the owners.[2] However, in 1976 the first major piece of tax legislation aimed specifically at the ownership and operation of professional sports franchises was restrictive from the standpoint of the franchise owners. That legislation is an excellent illustration of the fact that not all federal tax legislation is designed to implement a clearly specified objective. It is difficult to draft legislation affecting an industry as a whole when the motivation may be to force the placement of a major league baseball team in the nation's capital, or, in the alternative, to penalize the owners for moving the Washington, D.C., franchise to Texas.[3]

The tax policy of the federal government toward professional sports is the end product of the efforts of a large number of people with different interests. Therefore, it is difficult, if not impossible, to achieve a clear consensus on even the threshold question, much less on the question of how to implement the policy. Furthermore, the impact of tax policy cannot be completely ascertained until the judiciary imparts its own impressions and prejudices that then become a part of the federal tax policy. What is clear is that tax policy frequently has many consequences, direct and indirect. The 1976 legislation was aimed at those who own the teams. More specifically, it was intended to have a direct impact at the time when these individuals would sell or purchase a sports franchise. Consequently, this legislation should have had an indirect influence on how they operated those franchises.

BACKGROUND AND PRE-1976 TAX TREATMENT

The implementation of any tax policy almost invariably centers around the classification of expenditures as either current expenses, capital assets, or nondepreciable (nonamortizable) assets. For example, a company buys paper clips to be used in the office and it deducts the cost of those paper clips as a current expense. The same company buys a drill press for $50,000. It "depreciates" that $50,000 cost or payment over five years (or roughly $10,000 per year). Whatever amount is depreciated in a particular year is an expense on the company's income tax return. The same company also buys land for $100,000 that does not have any buildings on it. That is a nondepreciable asset and the company does not get to classify any of that $100,000 cost as a deduction on its income tax return. Thus to the extent that an expenditure is a current expense, the taxpayer will receive the most favorable tax treatment the government can provide. The next best thing is a capital asset, while the least favorable is a nondepreciable asset.

The other focus of tax policy is whether the gain realized on a particular transaction is taxed at capital gain rates or ordinary income rates. Normally, it has been better for the taxpayer to have an item treated as a capital gain, since the effective tax rate on capital gains is lower.

One of the essential assets of a professional sports franchise is the player contract. This is the contract by which the franchise obligates the professional athlete to render his services for and on behalf of only that particular franchise. Initially, the cost of all player contracts was expensed by the owners in the year of purchase as a cost of doing business.[4] The Internal Revenue Service distinguished in 1954 between the purchase of a single-player contract and a transaction or a series of transactions where an entire, or substantially entire, roster of a baseball club's player contracts is acquired at one time. In the former case it would be proper to expense the cost, while in the latter case the aggregate amount assignable to player contracts is to be capitalized and recovered (depreciated) over the useful life of the asset being acquired.[5]

In 1967 the IRS reconsidered its position with regard to the purchase of a single-player contract and held that a single-player contract also constituted a capital asset to be depreciated over the useful life of the asset. Straight-line depreciation was held to be the only method of depreciation available.[6] In the same year another ruling provided that player contracts held for a sufficient length of time were eligible for capital gain treatment upon the sale thereof.[7]

Further rulings in 1971 expanded the different types of receipts by owners of professional sports franchises that qualify for capital gain treatment as opposed to ordinary income.[8] These receipts included the sale proceeds for expansion franchises and the surrender of exclusive territorial rights in exchange for money. The IRS expanded the availability of the use of Subchapter S Corporations, thus enabling the taxpayers to utilize the vehicle of a corporation (and its limited liability) while at the same time obtaining the advantage of having any tax benefit (that is, losses) the business incurred flow directly to the taxpayers to offset their income.[9]

The combination of these factors made it possible for certain persons to regard their ownership of a professional sports franchise as a tax shelter. For example, assume Mr. Smith purchases a franchise for $10.8 million and allocates $10.2 million of the purchase price to player contracts (of the expansion draftees if an expansion franchise or of the players already on the team if an established franchise). The franchise receives an allocation of $500,000 and $100,000 is allocated to miscellaneous equipment and other tangible personal property. Next, assume a net operating income of $100,000 before depreciation of the tangible personal property and before the depreciation (normally referred to as "amortization" when dealing with intangible personal property) of player contracts. Using the Accelerated Cost Recovering System (ACRS) method of depreciation, there is a 15 percent cost recovery for the first year of property with a five-year useful life. This means that the owner will have a $100,000 positive cash flow but a loss for tax purposes in the amount of $1,545,000. In the second year, assuming the same positive cash flow, the loss is even greater and amounts to $2,166,000. Mr. Smith is then able to offset his income from other sources, provided the franchise is held as either a sole proprietorship, partnership, Subchapter S Corporation, or a subsidiary of a privately held corporation.

It is this ability to offset other income, upon which the taxpayer might otherwise be paying a marginal federal income tax of 50 percent, that makes the ownership of a professional sports franchise a promising tax shelter. The losses as illustrated above would exist for five years, after which Mr. Smith, if he was in the professional sports business primarily for the purposes of obtaining a tax shelter (as opposed to owning and operating a professional sports team), would sell the franchise. At that time most of the players who were on the team at the time of the original acquisition would have retired or been released and the contracts of the players who were presently on the team would have been only minimally depreciated. Therefore, the bulk of the sale proceeds, even if allocated to player contracts, would be taxed at capital gain rates, as opposed to depreciation recapture, which is taxed at ordinary income rates.

After one owns a sports franchise for five years, the tax-shelter aspects begin to lose their appeal. The player contracts initially acquired when the franchise was purchased have been fully depreciated at that point. Whether prospective owners approach the decision to purchase a franchise as primarily a tax shelter is debatable.[10] Those owners with a long family history as owners, such as Walter O'Malley of the Los Angeles Dodgers, Calvin Griffith of the Minnesota Twins, and Phillip Wrigley of the Chicago Cubs, clearly operated their franchises as personal businesses. For the new indiviuals and companies who purchased franchises in the 1960s, 70s, and 80s, the jury is still out. Turnover has been substantial, but so has been the number of franchise failures and league failures. More time has to be given to see if owners like Larry Weinberg with the Portland Trailblazers, Gulf-Western with the New York Knicks, George Steinbrenner with the New York Yankees, and the Chicago Tribune with the Chicago Cubs have real staying power.

If there was a great potential for recapture upon the sale of the franchise, the seller could allocate most of the purchase price to the franchise assets and little to the player contracts. This would ensure the treatment of the sale proceeds as capital gain. The buyer, on the other hand, would allocate whatever portion of the purchase price that he wanted to the depreciable player contracts. This practice of using different allocations for the same transaction is known as "whipsawing." The only check on this practice was the threat of an adjustment by the Internal Revenue Service. However, until the mid-1970s the probability of the IRS requesting an allocation had been low, and the amounts of the adjustments made were for the most part minimal. History has shown that the owners had allocated, prior to 1976, a vast majority of the purchase price to player contracts.[11]

Tax shelters generally have a negative connotation to the public because it is felt that the losses generated for tax purposes are really only paper losses as opposed to true economic losses. If so, then a truly profitable operation can appear on paper to be most unprofitable. The claim constantly is made by all professional sports leagues that most teams operate in the red. The teams actually may be in the red only because of sizable amortization deductions. It is difficult, at best, to ascertain whether the teams truly are losing money when the books of the franchises are not open to inspection. Obtaining information from the teams and league offices is next to impossible. Despite their claims of fiscal woe and their appeals for protection (both from the Treasury's taxing power and their own practices of paying outlandish sums to star performers), owners have not felt obliged to release financial information.

THE 1976 TAX REFORM ACT

Congress's interest in and awareness of the ownership of sports franchises and the accompanying tax treatment increased dramatically during congressional hearings over the professional basketball merger in the early 1970s. It reached its zenith when baseball's Washington Senators relocated from Washington, D.C., to Texas. At the time of this writing, congressional interest has been stirred again as a result of the relocation of the National Football League's Baltimore franchise to Indianapolis. One proposed bill would deny certain tax benefits to owners who relocate their franchise, another would require expansion and the placement of an NFL franchise in Baltimore, and another would require some sort of public approval before a franchise could be relocated.

In any event, the Tax Reform Act of 1976 classified professional sports as a tax shelter and made it subject to special tax treatment that was far more restrictive than the pre-1976 practices. Congress evidently felt either (a) that the scheme of federal taxation should not encourage the opportunity to use professional sports franchises as tax shelter vehicles or (b) that professional sports should be penalized for moving the Senators. The IRS did not request the legislation and in fact felt that it was unnecessary.[12] The IRS was of the opinion that it already had the tools to curb this type of an approach to the ownership of sports franchises. Congress, though, evidently felt that the IRS needed some help.

The major provisions of the 1976 Tax Reform Act as it applied to only sports franchise ownership included the following:

1. When the sale or exchange of a franchise occurred, the buyer and the seller of the franchise are forced to agree on an allocation that would be binding on both (thereby eliminating the "whipsaw" effect).

2. A rebuttable presumption was placed into the law that no more than 50 percent of the purchase price of a franchise would be allocable to player contracts. There is no reverse presumption if the taxpayer merely wants to

settle for the 50 percent allocation. The rebuttable presumption means that the IRS is given the benefit of the doubt if it says that no more than 50 percent of the purchase price should be allocated to depreciable player contracts. If there is no conclusive evidence one way or the other, the IRS wins. If the taxpayer wants to allocate anything more to player contracts, he must present affirmative evidence to show this. He or she has the burden of proof. In theory, this is only an affirmation of existing practice, since the IRS's position in tax matters is presumed correct until shown otherwise. The actual impact is to minimize the argument by the taxpayer that the allocation agreed to by the parties is correct, since it reflects an arm's-length negotiation between two independent parties.

3. A special recapture provision exclusively for sports franchises has become part of the Internal Revenue Code. This provision denies the owner the tax benefits of stocking the franchise with new players (possessing contracts that have not been substantially depreciated) just before selling the franchise. That gain attributable to those player contracts will now be ordinary income in lieu of capital gain.

The treatment of these three areas in the legislation is consistent with a disapproving view of the professional sports industry as a tax shelter. Whether this treatment is appropriate and whether it is effective remains open to debate. As to its appropriateness, not all owners treat their franchises as tax shelters, and other types of tax shelters do not have special rules such as these regarding allocations and recapture. As to effectiveness, the trafficking in franchises has not abated in recent years. The number of franchises being sold and the purchase prices continue to escalate. What tax strategies are being used in these new transfers is unknown.

THREE COURT DECISIONS

The IRS did not feel it needed statutory changes to address the tax treatment regarding purchase-price allocations in sports franchise transfers. The IRS already had started to challenge the allocations set by the purchasers and sellers of professional sports franchises. Three attempts by the IRS to challenge the taxpayer's allocations have resulted in judicial opinions on the subject. These cases involve football's Atlanta Falcons in 1974 (*Laird*),[13] basketball's Seattle Supersonics in 1978 (*First Northwest*),[14] and baseball's Milwaukee Brewers in 1983 (*Selig*).[15] There has been some consistency of thought in all three decisions. However, the most important lesson of the cases is that the courts are still feeling their way in this area, and, with so few cases having been decided, each case adds an essential element that ultimately will determine federal tax policy and its impact on the owners, affecting how they manage their ownership interests.

Laird v. United States (1974)

The Atlanta Falcons was an expansion team in which the owners, through a Subchapter S Corporation, paid a purchase price of $8,500,000. Only $50,000 was allocated to the franchise right. Over 90 percent was allocated to player contracts. The IRS originally argued that only 12 percent of the purchase price should be allocated to player contracts, but it changed tactics at trial, contending that all assets purchased constituted a bundle of inextricably related assets, none of which has a reasonably ascertainable value on its own, but each of which has value. Under that theory it follows that no depreciation deductions were to be allowed at all. This position is known as the "Mass Asset Theory." The acceptance by the court of the Mass Asset Theory would have eliminated the possibility of paper losses and ended all negative references to professional sports franchises as tax shelter vehicles. Countering the government's Mass Asset Theory, the taxpayer argued that if its proposed allocation to player contracts was not to be sustained, then a portion of the purchase price should be allocated to the network television contract and depreciated over its four-year term.

While *Laird* is not governed by the special provisions of the Tax Reform Act of 1976 delineated earlier,[16] it is important to be aware that the Court of Appeals decision and its opinion in the case came after that legislation had been passed. The decision in *Laird* rejected the Mass Asset Theory. It allowed $3,035,000 (35.7 percent of the purchase price) to be allocated to player contracts based on the expert testimony presented by the taxpayer.[17] The alternative position of the taxpayer in that case—to allocate a portion of the purchase price to the network television contract—backfired. An allocation to the network television contract was permitted, but the asset was then determined to be nondepreciable because it had no readily ascertainable useful life (held to be just one contract in a line of many television contracts that will extend over an indefinite period). With the exception of some prepaid interest, the only amount allocated to depreciable assets was the $3,035,000 for player contracts. The balance was allocated to nondepreciable assets.

First Northwest Industries of America, Inc. (1978)

First Northwest involved a purchase price of $1,750,000 for a basketball expansion team. In this case the Tax Court rejected the Mass Asset Theory and the sophisticated economic theories put forth by the economist used by the IRS.[18] The Tax Court relied on the expert testimony of the taxpayer presented at trial. In this case the taxpayer had problems with the qualifications and independence of its experts. As a result of these problems, the expert testimony, with regard to the value of the player contracts, was discounted. The finding was a player-contract allocation of $500,000

(28.5 percent of the purchase price). The court examined all the different assets that are involved with a professional franchise, separating them into thirteen categories. However, the bottom line was that with the exception of player contracts, equipment, and the right to the following year's expansion proceeds (which was allocated $250,000), all of the other assets were lumped together and considered nondepreciable. The rationale for this holding was that the assets had no "readily ascertainable useful life."

Selig v. United States (1983)

The most interesting opinion is found in *Selig*. Judge Reynolds, in the opinion, begins by listing the assumptions (that is, legal conclusions) upon which he based his ultimate decisions. The assumptions include the depreciability of player contracts and the rejection of the Mass Asset Theory. The court cites *Laird* and *First Northwest* as its basis for the rejection of the Mass Asset Theory. Judge Reynolds then goes on to state that the assets are to be allocated based on general accounting principles and that appraisals are the appropriate vehicle in determining that allocation. While coming to that conclusion about the use of appraisals and the use of generally accepted accounting principles, he notes that any attempt to allocate separately a portion of the purchase price to any particular asset is economically arbitrary because all the assets are intertwined with one another as components of the overall asset, which does have value. Under this reasoning, since any allocation among the assets is essentially arbitrary, the economic theories posed by the IRS—a regression analysis and an income sensitivity analysis—were considered inappropriate. In this case the court found the expert testimony presented by the taxpayer to be fairly persuasive and concluded that an allocation of $10.2 million to the player contracts (94.4 percent of the purchase price) was appropriate and thus held for the taxpayer.

Based on the opinions in the three court cases, the following conclusions can be drawn: (1) the Mass Asset Theory is not applicable to the ownership and tax treatment of professional sports franchises, (2) an allocation of the purchase price among the assets is the appropriate method in determining the tax treatment, (3) use of expert testimony and other related statistical information regarding the valuation of the separate assets is appropriate, (4) sophisticated economic theory is not necessarily helpful in ascertaining the value of various assets, and (5) most, if not all, of the assets other than player contracts and tangible personal property are nondepreciable. All three of the cases ruled in favor of these conclusions. The difference between the cases is the importance or emphasis placed on each of the conclusions and the weight given to expert testimony. *Selig* does not overrule *Laird* or *First Northwest;* it merely considered a different factual situation—professional baseball and not an expansion franchise—additional factors, and more credible expert witnesses.

It is acknowledged that a legitimate purpose of tax policy is to encourage certain types of activity and to discourage other types of activities. If one type of activity to be encouraged is the long-term, stable operation of professional sports franchises, one could argue that the application of the Mass Asset Theory is a step in the right direction. However, the Mass Asset Theory probably goes too far. It assumes that there are individuals or companies who are willing to enter into the business of the ownership of sports franchises without *any* attendant tax benefits or even without the aid of the general tax treatment that is available to all other businesses that are operated for profit.

The Mass Asset Theory is one extreme. The other extreme is the allocation of virtually all of the purchase price to depreciable assets that have a relatively short useful life, such as player contracts. The rejection of the Mass Asset Theory properly puts the focus in this area on the appropriate percentage that should be allocated to the depreciable assets. When the percentage is greater than 90 percent of the purchase price, then tax policy becomes so lenient that it arguably encourages trafficking in sports franchises (as opposed to encouraging long-term, stable relationships between the owner of the franchise, the city in which it is located, and the fans in that locale).

Both the District Court and the Court of Appeals in *Laird* rejected the Mass Asset Theory. This rejection was continued in *First Northwest* and in *Selig*. This would appear to be the appropriate position to take, especially in light of the 1976 Tax Reform Act legislation, which implicitly rejects the Mass Asset Theory in favor of an allocation of a portion of the purchase price to depreciable player contracts.

Consequently, the courts have been forced to wrestle with the problems of allocating the purchase price. Consistency in the courts' decisions will go a long way toward formulating an established tax policy. It is only when a tax policy is established firmly that the true impact on the business of owning a professional sports franchise can be determined. In early years, when the tax policy was consistently liberal, this unwittingly encouraged the operation of sports franchises as tax shelter vehicles. This undoubtedly was one of the factors in the proliferation of sports franchises in various professional sports and the heavy trafficking of sports franchises that has occurred in professional sports.[19]

Federal tax policy has changed, as evidenced by the restrictive provisions in the 1976 Tax Reform Act, the IRS intention to challenge allocations, and the judiciary's willingness to reduce player-contract allocations. It should be only a matter of time until that change is firmly established and the extent of the impact on the business of owning and operating professional sports franchises will be known. The problem is that the process is a slow one. None of the three cases has dealt with a factual situation that occurred subsequent to the passage of the 1976 legislation. The three court cases, resulting in allocations to player contracts ranging from 28.57 to 94.44 percent, do not really narrow the options available to the owner of a sports franchise. Also, there is the secrecy of financial information prevalent in the sports industry, thus making it difficult to ascertain what impact there has been. The only certainty is that the frequency of sports franchise transfers of ownership has not abated.[20] Changing the tax policy has not seemed to dampen the demand for franchises. How much of this can be attributed to the desire to be a part of a glamourous enterprise, regardless of tax consequences and/or profitability, is questionable.

PRESENT TAX POLICY

Whatever the impact, federal tax policy should, and frequently does, accommodate the peculiarities or inconsistencies within a particular industry. The rejection of the Mass Asset Theory is a step forward in this regard. The three court decisions that have been discussed illustrate that distinctions between the various professional sports are significant and, in and of themselves, warrant a difference in tax treatment that reflects the differences in the economic realities faced by each sport. It is not surprising that baseball, in the *Selig* case, approved the highest allocation to player contracts. The following is an analysis of those variables that are relevant to valuation with respect to player contracts and the issue of franchise rights. The latter issue is the primary focus of the current federal tax policy toward professional sports.

A combination of factors convinces one that uniform financial stability is more closely achieved among franchises in the National Football League (NFL) than in any other sport. National television revenues, which were the subject of much discussion in the *Laird* case, have become even more important.[21] Another major factor is the policy regarding the sharing of gate receipts. Gate receipts in the NFL are split 60 percent for the home team and 40 percent for the visiting team.[22] This gate-receipt policy goes hand in hand with the fact that variance in attendance among teams in the NFL was at one time only about 6.5 percent. The uniformity of success that NFL teams have at gate attendance is illustrated by the fact that one expansion club presold 59,000 season tickets before it had even played one game.[23] When the Baltimore Colts moved to Indianapolis, despite its poor showing on the field in the years immediately prior to the move, the franchise had to cut off sales of season tickets because of excess demand. Figures presented to the Senate Finance Committee in 1976 estimated that in 1975 the network television contract money and gate receipts totaled more than 89 percent of each team's revenues.[24]

Such guaranteed eveness of financial pictures among NFL teams illustrates the fact that the right to hold and operate an NFL franchise in an exclusive territory constitutes a relatively large value compared to the other rights involved. However, this type of analysis has been clouded by recent developments in the cable and pay television area. For example, many believe the move by the Oakland Raiders to Los Angeles was motivated primarily by the greater potential in the Los Angeles metropolitan area for cable and pay television revenues, which are not shared among all franchises in the NFL. Whether this distinction among franchises should or will affect the tax treatment upon the purchase of a franchise is still unknown. Such a distinction might be attributable solely to the area in which the franchise is located as opposed to the quality of the player contracts that the franchise owns. For example, the New York Yankees can afford to pay a Dave Winfield more than the San Diego Padres can, because of the former's greater potential for gate receipts and media contracts.

The situation in the National Basketball Association differs considerably from the NFL. Gate receipts are not shared at all with the visiting team: The home team takes 100 percent.[25] The dollar amounts attributable to those receipts show tremendous disparity between the teams. The Portland Trail-blazers, for example, consistently sell out all of their home games, whereas other teams in the league, such as the Phoenix Suns and Chicago Bulls, have or have had severe attendance problems. Other factors that come into play include: (a) the relatively small number of players on a team, so that the impact of one or two specific player contracts on attendance and athletic competitiveness can be more easily documented;[26] (b) the longer season—82 games compared to football's 16—makes attendance figures and the value of local broadcasting rights far more susceptible to the competitiveness, in terms of wins and losses, of the franchise; and (c) the relative value of the network television contracts, which recently have cut back the exposure given to the National Basketball Association as a result of low ratings.

Major league baseball is very different from basketball or football. National television revenues also exist for baseball owners, but they are of relatively lesser importance despite the increase in spectatorship.[27] The revenues available for major league baseball show a tremendous potential for fluctuation when compared to the NFL. The gate-receipt policy of major league baseball calls for sharing, but not to the extent existing in the NFL.[28] Nor is there the widespread phenomenon of constant sellouts for most franchises that is found in professional football. The fact that the season for professional baseball is the longest of all (162 games) tends to support the theory that attendance figures and the overall profitability of a franchise is more dependent upon the quality of the team on the field rather than the supply of contests.[29] The attendance figures thus affect revenues from concessions, parking, and advertising.[30] A major factor in baseball is the right to local broadcasting revenues.[31] Cable and pay television are just wild cards thrown into the system affecting the valuation of different assets that comprise the franchise as well as the overall total value of the franchise.[32] The exact impact of the existence of the minor league farm system for development of talent in major league baseball on the valuation is uncertain. However, it is undoubtedly a factor in crediting more value to the player contracts than is the case in professional basketball or football, where player development is conducted primarily by the colleges and individuals step right out of college and onto the major league rosters.[33]

Professional hockey is probably at the opposite end of the spectrum from professional football. The gate receipt policy is identical to that of professional basketball, and the length of season and its attendance discrepancies compare more closely with professional baseball.[34] The sport has no national network television contract, and local broadcasting rights range in value from nothing to substantial sums.[35] A minor league system of player development is an integral part of professional hockey. In addition, the National Hockey League has had a history of relative ownership stability when compared to other sports.[36]

CONCLUSION

The peculiarities within the professional sports industry militate against any set percentage rule for allocating a portion of the total sale price to player contracts in the purchase of a professional sports franchise. Three court decisions that have been rendered based on pre-1976 factual situations resulted in allocations to depreciable player contracts ranging from 28.57 percent to 94.44 percent. Two of those cases involved expansion franchises as opposed to the sale of an established franchise, wherein one would expect the valuation of player contracts to be greater.[37] The impact of the 1976 Tax Reform Act on this issue has yet to be determined. We do not know what allocations are being proposed in the recent sales of sports franchises—and the number of sales seems to be increasing—but it is probably safe to say that the taxpayers are *not* being conservative in the allocations.

Other factors that have not manifested themselves in the various court decisions because they are relatively recent phenomena, but which undoubtedly affect the valuation of player contracts and the nonamortizable franchise right, include (a) congressional developments regarding the applicability of antitrust legislation to professional sports (to the extent there is an antitrust exemption, the value of the franchise right in and of itself is more valuable); (b) attempts by public organizations to seize the ownership of a professional sports franchise under the power of eminent domain (theoretically having a severe negative impact on the value of a franchise right); (c) proposed congressional legislation requiring professional sports to expand into certain cities and/or limit the ability of franchises to transfer location from one city to the next; (d) the lack of sharing of cable and pay television revenues among teams within a single professional sport and the growing amount of dollars that are involved in these cable and pay television rights;[38] and (e) the erosion of the contractual relationship between the players and the franchise (free agency and the various compensation programs with the use of salary caps).[39]

The entire structure of player compensation is changing dramatically. Witness the proposal by the players association in professional football for a request for a percentage of the team's gross receipts as the basis for the players' compensation, which was rejected by the owners.[40] Compare that to the owners' proposal in professional basketball to give the players a percentage of the gross receipts, letting that be the limit on player compensation. That proposal was accepted in modified form by the players, but initially it was opposed by the players and is seen as a detriment for players who could otherwise command higher compensation.[41]

Federal tax policy toward the professional sports industry is an extremely complex area, and one in which myriad factors come into play. The Detroit Tigers baseball franchise was sold in 1983. How would the purchase price then compare to the value in November 1984, after the team won the World Series? The value is undoubtedly greater, but how much of that increase is attributable to player contracts? Other than any general increase in franchise-right values experienced throughout major league baseball, the total increase should be attributed to player contracts, since the players' success on the field has been the key to the increase in the franchise's profitability.

Tax law should and does have the ability to accommodate distinguishing characteristics while affording the appropriate tax treatment to sellers and purchasers of professional sports franchises. Federal tax policy can in a number of ways have an effect on how an owner views and manages a particular franchise, by either encouraging or discouraging expansion. While the goal of tax policy arguably should be to encourage stability of professional sports franchises, especially in light of the public interest involved,[42] such tax policy should provide the owners a reasonable opportunity to recover a fair portion of their investment in the assets during their term of ownership. This merely is asking for treatment similar to that afforded to a manufacturing business that recoups a portion of its investment in plant and equipment through depreciation deductions. The sports industry should not be singled out for special treatment; it does not deserve a unique status for tax purposes.

Lenient tax treatment encourages short-term ownership. Unrealistically harsh treatment is punitive and will eliminate responsible prospective owners from entering the industry. By treating owners fairly—and this means allowing them to demonstrate and prove the values of their respective assets—perhaps the industry will attract owners who have the financial ability to invest the monies that are appropriate and necessary to operate a franchise.[43] This will continue the "return" to the public, which is inherent in the public's enjoyment of a local sports franchise.

NOTES

1. Alan H. Selig v. United States, 565 F. Supp. 524, 528 (1983).

2. On this lenient attitude, Bill Veeck, twice former owner of the Chicago White Sox, commented in his 1965 book, *The Hustler's Handbook:* "Look, we play The Star Spangled Banner before every game. You want us to pay income taxes, too?" "Monopoly Pays Off in the Business of Sports," *Business Week*, October 13, 1980, pp. 146–47 (hereafter cited as "Monopoly").

3. The following exchange between the Chairman of the Senate Finance Committee and Bowie Kuhn, who was then the Commissioner of major-league baseball, occurred during the Senate hearings on the Tax Reform Act of 1976.

Chairman: Mr. Kuhn, my Uncle Earl used to like to refer to the bug under the chip; what the thing was really about. I want to see what your reaction is to this: I have heard the rumor that the purpose of all this, some of which for a ridiculous tax law, is to cause you people to put a baseball team back here in Washington, D.C. Have you heard that? Has that thought ever occurred to you?
Mr. Kuhn: I have heard the rumor and the thought has occurred to me.
Chairman: All I can say is, it is one hell of a way to write a tax law.

Hearings on H.R. 10612 before the Senate Finance Committee, 94th Cong., 2d sess. (1976), p. 630 (hereafter cited as *Finance*).

4. Commissioner v. Pittsburgh Athletic Co., 4 USTC R1338, 72 F. 2d 883 (CA–3, 1934); Commissioner v. Chicago National League Ball Club, 35–1 USTC R 9089, 74 F.2d 1010 (CA–7); Helvering v. Kansas City American Association Baseball Co., 35–1 USTC R9148, 75 F2d 600 (CA–8).

5. Rev. Rul. 54–441, 1954–2 CB 101.

6. Rev. Rul. 67–379, 1967–2 CB 127.

7. Rev. Rul. 67–380, 1967–2 CB 291.

8. Rev. Rul. 71–123, 1971–1 CB 227; and Rev. Rul. 71–583, 1971–2 CB 312.

9. Rev. Rul. 71–407, 1971–2 CB 318.

10. San Francisco Giants' owner, Robert Lurie: "Tax benefits 'are not the primary reason to get into baseball.' " And Lamar Hunt, owner of the Kansas City Chiefs: "I've always believed you don't go into any venture unless you can make a profit." "Monopoly," p. 146.

11. Benjamin A. Okner, "Taxation and Sports Enterprises," in Roger G. Noll, ed., *Government and the Sports Business* (Washington, D.C.: Brookings Institution, 1974), Table 1, p. 163.

12. *Final Report of the House Select Committee on Professional Sports*, 94th Cong., 2d sess., p. 97. "The Deputy Assistant Secretary of the Treasury for Tax Policy had no strong objection to this new tax provision, but considered it unnecessary to add any special legislation to curb any abuses which might arise. His position was that any abuse can be dealt with administratively by the IRS as is done in cases of misallocation in any other business."

13. Laird v. United States, 75–1, USTC 9274 391 F. Supp. 656 (N.D. Ga., 1975); 77–2 USTC 9569 566 F.2d 1224 (CA–5, 1977).

14. *First Northwest Industries of America, Inc.*,CCH Dec. 35, 384, 70 TC 817 (1978).

15. Selig v. United States, 565 F. Supp. 524 (1983).

16. The transaction regarding the purchase of the franchise itself occurred years before the legislation and consequently it is not governed by the legislation.

17. *Laird*, p. 1242.

18. *First Northwest Industries of America, Inc.*, 70 TC 817.

19. Ownership changes, expansion teams, and new leagues proliferated. In the seven-year history of the ABA, only one team had stayed with its original owner. "Upheaval in Pro Sports," *U.S. News and World Report*, August 12, 1974, p. 54. In a twelve-year period, there were 44 ownership changes in the NBA. In 1969 there were 42 teams in 5 professional leagues, while in 1974 that number had expanded to 114 teams in 8 professional leagues. Richard A. Koch, *The Professional Sports Team as a Tax-Shelter—A Case Study: The Utah Stars* (1974) *Utah Law Review* 3 556, 557.

20. From 1982 to 1984 the movement in ownership has maintained a relatively hectic pace.

Six NBA teams have changed hands, at least partially; in baseball, eight teams have changed hands. At the winter meetings in Houston in December 1984, the new Commissioner of Baseball, Peter Ueberroth, commented that seven franchises were contemplating ownership changes.

21. The current contract between the NFL and the networks is set at $2.1 billion, which works out to $14.2 million per team per year. *New York Times*, March 2, 1983, p. B11. The United States Football League's ability to get off the ground has been attributed to its national television contracts, valued at $33 million for its first two years. "USFL and TV Rights: How Bad Can You Hurt?" *Forbes*, February 14, 1983, p. 42. "The $31 Million Kickoff: TV Pacts Give the USFL a Sporting Chance," *Barrons*, May 16, 1983.

22. Howard Zaritsky, "Taxation of Professional Sports Teams After 1976: A Whole New Ballgame," *William and Mary Law Review* 679 (Summer 1977): 685 (hereafter cited as "Ballgame").

23. *Finance*, p. 637.

24. Ibid., p. 643; "Monopoly," p. 146.

25. Ambrose, "Recent Tax Developments Regarding Purchases of Sports Franchises—The Game Isn't Over Yet," *Taxes, The Tax Magazine*, November 1981, pp. 739, 757.

26. Ray Kennedy and Nancy Williamson, "Money, The Monster Threatening Sports," *Sports Illustrated* 49 (July 17, 1978), p. 51. The San Francisco Warriors' loss of Rick Barry was worth $404,000 in gate receipts over a single season. Lemat Corp. v. Barry, 80 Cal. Rptr. 240, 243 (1969). Kareem Abdul Jabbar's presence on the Milwaukee Bucks team was considered directly responsible for an increase of $700,000 in profits to the franchise. As a result of the acquisition of Julius Erving by the Philadelphia 76ers, ticket sales doubled, the value of radio advertising more than doubled and souvenir sales increased threefold. Kennedy and Williamson, "Money, the Monster," p. 51.

27. *Finance*, p. 642. The broadcasting revenue figures for the 1975 seasons show that major league baseball had national revenues of $9.6 million and local revenues of $26.495 million, while the NFL had national revenues of $50.1 million and local revenues of $2.948 million. "Ballgame," p. 682. The new baseball contract calls for $1 billion over five years.

28. "Ballgame," p. 685.

29. In 1966 the home attendance of the Boston Red Sox was 811,172. The next year, because of a pennant race, attendance was 1,727,832. *Finance*, p. 635; see also "Investing in Billy Ball," *Forbes*, February 14, 1983, p. 41.

30. In baseball these sources of revenue in recent years accounted for 11 to 13 percent of a team's revenues, while in football they accounted for only about 2 percent. *Finance*, pp. 637, 642.

31. "Baseball's '75 Opening Line-up: The Money, Stations, Games' Sponsors," *Broadcasting* (March 3, 1975) pp. 38–39; "Baseball—1983 Pay TV Spurs 29% Increase in Baseball Rights" *Broadcasting* (February 28, 1983), pp. 51–70; "Monopoly," p. 148; *Finance*, p. 637.

32. "Baseball, 1983: Pay Television Spurs 29% Increase in Baseball Rights," *Broadcasting*, February 28, 1983, pp. 51–70; "Monopoly," pp. 146–49.

33. *Monthly Labor Review* 104, no. 10 (October 1981): 49.

34. "Ballgame," p. 685.

35. *Finance*, pp. 617,647.

36. Ibid.

37. Lynn Adkins, "Appraising the Sports Game," *Dun's Review*, August 1979, pp. 54, 57.

38. "Baseball, 1983," p. 51.

39. James R. Hill and William Spellman, "Professional Baseball: The Reserve Clause and Salary Structure," *Industrial Relations* 22 (Winter 1983): 1–19. This is contrasted to the current lack of movement by the free agents in the NFL. *New York Times*, April 13, 1983, p. B8.

40. *Wall Street Journal*, September 8, 1982, pp. 1, 25.

41. *New York Times*, March 2, 1983, p. B12.

42. A large number of pro franchises use municipally owned facilities. The rents and increased business activities resulting from sporting events are extremely important to local governments.

43. Too restrictive a tax policy might limit the ownership and operation of sports franchises to large diversified companies such as Gulf-Western, Ralston Purina (which recently dropped out

of the sports business), *The Chicago Tribune,* or Anheuser-Busch. This is not necessarily the most desired result. Family owned franchises have been sucessful and good for professional sports; for example, the O'Malley's of the Los Angeles Dodgers; see "The Most Valuable Executive in Either League," *Forbes,* April 12, 1982, pp. 129–35. Without the attendant tax benefits, the market may become too limited. All businesses have some tax incentives, and it would be inappropriate to penalize professional sports. Since it is an industry where appreciation is essential to an investor's rate of return, substantial investment in terms of operating capital is imperative. As one banking publication put it: "To a certain extent, investing in a team is like investing in certain areas of real estate; the investor really hopes only for an even cash flow, and then counts on the profits to come from capital appreciation." *Sporting News,* December 6, 1980, p. 16.

PART III

Public Policy, Sports, and the Public Interest

The final chapters are devoted to three policy areas that directly relate to the public interest. The popularity of gambling, coupled with a general trend toward the legalization of forms of gambling other than sports betting and the desire to raise revenue, has prompted public officials to look to the legalization of wagering on sports events. James Frey reviews the various models of legalization that exist, from "benign prohibition" to absolute state control. He analyzes the prospects for raising revenue and for controlling organized crime by legalizing sports betting, and evaluates the professional sports leagues' opposition to the legalization of sports betting.

Recent court rulings have made it possible for professional sports franchises to move with ease from one community to another. The threat of relocation commonly accompanies a team owner's demand for new playing facilities or greater tax subsidies. Arthur Johnson reviews the dynamics of the team-city relationship which lead communities to offer escalating subsidies in an effort to retain or acquire a franchise. He also describes and evaluates several policy options designed to resolve the franchise relocation problem.

Recent Olympic Games have highlighted the role of sport in international relations. The 1980 boycott by the United States and more than thirty nations was stimulated by a desire on the part of President Carter to dramatize the Afghanistan situation and to reassert America's leadership in the free world. The 1984 boycott by the Soviet Union represented a retaliation. Thus the Olympics became the setting for the major powers to play out their conflicts without seriously damaging existing economic or political arrangements. James Nafziger discusses the use of sport as a vehicle for international diplomacy. In some countries, such as the Soviet Union and some in eastern Europe, sport is subsidized heavily by government and is deliberately used as a form of propaganda to promote these countries' political systems. In America, sport is not significantly subsidized by government, but it can be used for the same purposes. Nafziger discusses the levels of government involvement in international sport and relates international law to the practices of diplomacy through sport.

These essays illustrate the fact that the public has a significant interest in the sports-government relationship. Sports policy decisions have consequences beyond the athletes' and administrators' interests. The authors assert that the public's interest should be recognized whenever policy issues in sport are debated.

11

Gambling, Sports, and Public Policy

James H. Frey

Governments at all levels are being challenged to develop a public policy position on gambling. Gambling, or the deliberate wager of a possession of some value on a future event, the outcome of which is uncertain and determined to a large extent by chance, is an ubiquitous activity with a long and somewhat unglorious tradition.[1] There probably is not any member of the American population who has not gambled in one form or another during his or her lifetime. Perhaps we pitched pennies against a schoolyard wall, wagered a dime on a World Series pool in fifth grade, played poker with friends on Friday nights, or traveled to the gambling mecca of Las Vegas to try our hand at blackjack or roulette. The mass appeal of gambling plus the attraction of its revenue potential have forced state and local governments to reevaluate what heretofore has been a prosecutorial or "prohibition" orientation to gambling control and to adopt a regulatory stance that emphasizes legalization within state established guidelines.[2] This trend, which is consistent with a general tendency in American public policy and law to decriminalize victimless crimes, such as gambling, prostitution, and drugs,[3] is dramatized by the recent legalization of casinos in Atlantic City and by the rapid increase in the number of states that permit lotteries. Another form of gambling that is now drawing considerable attention from gambling entrepreneurs and public officials for the purposes of legalization is betting on sports events.

When any sports event occurs, whether amateur or professional, football or horse racing, there will be legal or illegal wagering on the outcome of that event. Most of the bets are friendly wagers among friends for relatively small amounts, but a few are for significant dollars. No one really knows how many people bet on the outcome of sports events, but the most comprehensive study on gambling indicated that 40.4 million people bet on sports events and this did not include horse or dog racing.[4] Until recently, parimutuel wagering on horse racing, dog racing, and jai alai was the only legal sports betting available. In a parimutuel system the players wager against each other rather than against a bookmaker. Of the total amount wagered, a percentage, usually 15 to 17 percent, called "takeout" is extracted and paid to the track, horse owners, and state or local tax collectors. The remainder is distributed to the winners either by win, place, or show bets or by exotic bets (such as quinella). The odds and potential payout varies dramatically before each race. All betting was to take place at the track until recently, when New York State legalized Off-Track Betting (OTB), and states like Delaware and Connecticut permitted telephone betting and Nevada legalized simulcasting of races. Illegal horse-race betting developed around a "wire service," which networked bookmakers and bettors, with neither required to be at the track. In addition, illegal betting was attractive because the bookmakers' takeout was considerably less than that of the track. It is this situation that has stirred the most significant policy controversy over state regulation of horse-race gambling, and it is best illustrated by the New York OTB case, which will be discussed later in this chapter.

The most popular form of illegal gambling is betting on sports events. Ordinarily, one might include both race betting and wagering on nonracing sports events such as football under the generic phrase "sports betting." However, popular usage of the term restricts its application to wagering on sports events such as football, basketball, and baseball games. In fact, betting establishments in Nevada now distinguish between "Sports Books" and "Race Books." Even though this chapter will address sports betting, it is necessary to discuss race betting when appropriate to certain public policy issues.

In recent years the most dramatic increase in wagering handle—the total amount of dollars bet—and revenue has occurred with legal bookmaking. The largest portion of this increase has come from sports betting or wagering on football, basketball, boxing, baseball, and other sporting events. Several factors have contributed to this increased interest in sports betting. First, the media saturation of sporting events has brought more and different events to the public and thus enhanced their familiarity with the sport. Evidence indicates that more than 70 percent of the population watch a television sports event each week; if they are not watching an event, they are participating in a sport, talking about athletics, or reading the sport pages. Professional football, basketball, and baseball draw the largest television audience and attract the greatest gambling action. The single most popular spectator events—the Super Bowl, Kentucky Derby, and the World Series— are also the year's major betting events. The Super Bowl alone attracts an estimated $50 to 60 million in wagers.[5]

A second phenomenon that promotes sports betting is the weakened stigma associated with gambling in general and gambling on sport in particular. The moral indignation against gambling seems to have virtually dissolved. More than two-thirds of the population gambles in any one year, and most would support some legalization for revenue purposes.[6] Third, legitimation of sports gambling in the eyes of the public has also been promoted by the popularization of a gambling orientation to sports events, particularly as represented in the media. Every newspaper carries a betting line; national television commentators such as Jimmy the Greek and Pete Axthelm are featured for their gambling prowess rather than commentating skill. Fourth, the volume of information available to the bettor, via newspaper stories or advertisements, by Sports Service newsletters, phone services, and other publications, is enormous. The bet can now be made without a distraught feeling that all is left to chance.[7] Fifth, not only is it easier to make an informed bet, it is also easier to place a bet, legal or illegal. In the past, the requirement that the bettor place his or her bet at the bookie's location and that results could only be obtained from a telegraph-wire-service apparatus at that same location probably kept many from betting. Telephone technology now permits betting transactions to be made with considerable ease and with little fear of law enforcement reprisal.[8] Finally, there always has been a high demand for sports betting, but a large portion of the public who wanted to bet, but not illegally, did not know where to place their bets. The opening of OTB outlets in New York for race betting and the installation of sport and racebooks in the popular Nevada casinos provided this. As a result, many sports bettors switched from illegal to legal betting, or they were motivated to place their legal first bets with a bookmaker rather than with friends.

Sports bookmaking originated as a sideline. Horse-race bookmakers would accept wagers on a sports event as a courtesy to their special customers.[9] Today, the reverse is true. Betting on sports events usually takes one of two forms, each placed through a bookmaking operation. The first is a direct wager on an event such as a boxing match or football game. The bookmaker's role is that of a broker between those who bet on one team and those who want to bet on another. For this service he takes a commission, or "vigorish," on the total amount wagered. His goal is to equalize the amount bet on each side so that the losses of one set of customers are offset by the winnings, less vigorish, of the other bet. A point spread, or handicap to the stronger team, is used to equalize the teams and to attract wagers on both sides. The point spread or "line" is adjusted up to nearly game time in order to achieve the balance.[10] Generally, the bookmaker's takeout is around 4 to 6 percent of the total amount wagered or "handle." Sports-card wagering, the second form of betting, is also known as pool-card or parley-card wagering. A pool card lists games scheduled for the upcoming weekend with point spreads. These spreads are fixed and do not change before game time. This type of betting is attractive to the small bettor, and it relies more on chance and less on skill for the outcome. The defunct Canadian Sports Select Baseball and Delaware's "Football Bonus" and "Touchdown" games were sports pools.

There is considerable pressure for states and local governmental jurisdictions to consider legalizing sports betting. This pressure stems from the fact that sports betting is popular with the general public, that the state could go a long way to controlling organized crime if it took away the criminal syndicate's principal source of income, and that the state could capture additional revenue without having to raise taxes or add new taxes. I will review the data on participation in gambling in America and follow that with discussion of the policy implications associated with the state entering the gambling business and with the government using gaming revenues in lieu of taxes.

PARTICIPATION AND POPULARITY

Almost every state in the union and virtually every country in the world has some form of legalized gambling. This suggests that gambling is overwhelmingly a legal business and is not restricted to the shady underworld. This means that most of the world has the opportunity to place a bet, and many do.

The most comprehensive study of gambling behavior was conducted in 1974 under the auspices of the Commission on the Review of the National Policy Toward Gambling. This study reported that 61 percent of Americans had gambled in 1974, and 11 percent of the gamblers bet illegally. Those most likely to gamble were from the Northeast, male, single, white, in higher income brackets, of British, Irish, and African extraction, who had attended college and lived in suburban communities. Card games with friends and lotteries were the most popular gambling activities. Betting on professional football was the third most popular form of gambling. A major conclusion of the study was that gambling was universal. In only a few groups (such as those over 55) did gambling participation drop below 50 percent.[11] Most bettors wagered less than $200 a year and their characteristics matched those of the general population. Heavy bettors of more than $200 tended to be white males, divorced, age 25 to 44, and from the Northeast. Most non-gamblers came from rural areas and had been taught that gambling was sinful.

The study concludes that the "factors that most consistently differentiate gamblers from non-gamblers are the degree of an individual's exposure to gambling and the availability of that activity."[12] A person is more likely to gamble if he or she was exposed to gambling early in life, such as seeing parents play or participate in a World Series pool, if one knows persons who gamble, and if opportunities to gamble are available and gambling is legal.[13] Thus the widespread legalization of gambling, the increasing popularization of gambling in the media, and the declining moral resistance to gambling are forces that will create an even higher portion of gamblers in the population in the future. The newly created gamblers will bet both legally and illegally.

The commission study found that 36 percent of Americans have bet on sports (not including race betting) during their lifetime; 28 percent, or 40.4 million people, bet on sports in 1974. Also, 4 percent of the total population bet illegally. Most of the betting took place among friends rather than with bookies, particularly among light and moderate bettors. The typical illegal sports bettor was from the Northeast or North Central United States, white, male, with some college education, and with an annual income over $10,000. Only 50 percent of those betting illegally with a bookmaker would drop the illegal wagering system in favor of a legal arrangement. Income tax considerations were given as the major reason for their lack of willingness to shift.[14] Most illegal bets were placed by phone from home or work. The most popular sports bets were professional football and baseball, followed by college football and professional basketball.

The study also found that the majority of sports bettors have a realistic view of their probability of winning since they see chance as a big element in sports betting success. Illegal bettors left less to chance and put more faith in their skill. Most respondents agreed that professional sports were more likely to be "fixed" than were college or amateur athletic events. Finally, sports bettors had a higher rate of illegal betting than did gambling in any other type of game. Those who were motivated by recreational reasons were more likely to bet with friends and in legal settings; those oriented to make money were more likely to bet with bookies under illegal conditions,[15] probably to avoid the tax takeouts on wagers.

The findings of the commission have been supported to some extent by several recent studies conducted by the Gallup organization for *Gaming Business* magazine. For example, the latest Gallup survey showed that 17 percent of the population or 28.4 million persons bet on a sports event in 1983; 23 percent of all males over 18 and 12 percent of all females bet on sports during this time. These studies also noted a high awareness of gambling, a factor necessary to increased participation. The research demonstrated that legalization has shown increased public acceptance since the 1974 Gambling Commission Study, particularly for lotteries and sports betting.[16] In 1974 the commission study showed that 31 percent of the population favored legalization; in 1982 the Gallup survey demonstrated that 51 percent favored legalization. This represented the most dramatic increase in approval rating of all other types of gaming. However, the impetus for legalization does not come from a relaxed moral stance. Rather, Americans take a somewhat pragmatic view: If they want services but no additional taxes, then legalized gambling seems reasonable. However, the public is reluctant to support legalized betting, particularly in their state, if the latter would attract organized crime or stimulate compulsive gambling.[17] This also means that the public will not support decriminalization, which would mean almost no regulatory role for governments. Despite these views on legalization, it is safe to say that the rates of sports betting, including racetrack betting, will increase in the future, and more governments will look to obtain a piece of the gambling revenue pie.

The revenue potential for governments from gambling has been demonstrated to be significant. Legal gross wagering (also called "handle") for 1983 was $132.09 billion; illegal wagering reached $28.9 billion for a total handle in 1983 of $160.99 billion. This represented an increase of $9.5 billion, or 6.7 percent, from 1982.[18] Most of this growth occurred in state lotteries, slot machines, legal bookmaking (race and sports), and, interestingly enough, in illegal gambling. The only decline in handle occurred in parimutuel betting, once the dominant form of legal gambling. The largest handle gain, 58 percent, was recorded by legal bookmaking; this was attributed to the increase in the number of legal operators in Nevada.[19] It also did not hurt the legal bookmaking business to have the federal wagering excise tax reduced from 2 percent to 0.25 percent on January 1, 1983. Legal sports betting experienced a significant increase of 33 percent in handle from 1982 to 1983. Table 11.1 demonstrates the growth in the legal sports betting in Nevada on a number of dimensions.

In order to clearly understand the income potential of gambling, it is necessary to analyze the net revenue or the amount of money that is realized after expenses have been charged.

In 1983 the gross revenues from legal and illegal commercial gambling in the United States totaled $16.9 billion. This represents an increase of $1.9 billion, or 13.1 percent, over 1982.[20] Total illegal revenue was estimated at $5.03 billion, up 13.1 percent from 1982.[21] Sports bookmaking (race and sports) totaled $2.5 billion; illegal numbers totaled $2.49 billion. So gambling is big business, but it is fragmented. No single gambling enterprise would rank among the top 500 businesses in America. Yet, when all gambling businesses are combined, they are a formidable entity.

Table 11.2 summarizes the wagering profile of all gambling activity. This economic overview suggests that parimutuel gambling (horse racing, dog

Table 11.1   Nevada Sports Book Analysis

	1974	1975	1976	1977	1978
Handle($)	8,039,000	41,044,000	92,120,000	88,900,000	118,600,000
Win($)	694,000	3,010,000	2,627,000	3,300,000	4,100,000
Percentage win	8.63	7.33	2.85	3.73	3.45
Number of books	9	12	15	19	22
Percent increase over previous year handle		411%	125%	4%	34%

racing, jai alai) is a suffering component of the gambling industry. All other gambling experienced growth; parimutuel did not. Since governments have granted geographic monopolies to racetracks, which has influenced the government's portion of the parimutuel takeout, public bodies need to be concerned about the extent to which they invest in parimutuel gambling in the future. According to the recent *Gaming Business Magazine* survey, government revenues from horse racing declined to $641.4 million, their lowest since 1976.[22] The picture is not as dismal for other games, however. Lotteries, for example, generated net revenues of $2 billion for the states in 1983.[23] Another estimate suggests that states could receive just over $8 billion in revenue from all forms of gambling.[24]

It is no wonder that states are looking to the legalization of gambling as a way to relieve the fiscal pressure they are experiencing. However, the policy concerns are not easily resolved. First, the state must determine what form of gambling to legalize and then analyze systematically the economic potential. The latter must be weighed against the administrative costs of being in the gambling business, the regressivity of the particular game or tax assigned to the game, and the extent to which legal gaming reduces the illegal competition. Finally, states have to resolve the dilemma of going into the business of promoting an activity that is, if no longer viewed as immoral by the public, at least of questionable social value, and which brings with it a history of criminal association. This may be the most significant policy question to emerge with the states' association with gambling and, more specifically, with sports betting.

THE TENDENCY TO LEGALIZATION

Governments, particularly at the local and state levels, have an intimate relationship with gambling activity. Only four states do not officially permit some form of gambling. Forty-five states allow some form of bingo or

1979	1980	1981	1982	(Fiscal) 1983	(Calendar) 1983
188,200,000	257,800,000	359,114,000	415,162,000	521,040,000	692,020,000
7,700,000	11,300,000	14,311,000	7,725,000	11,463,000	19,251,000
4.10	4.40	3.99	1.86	2.2	2.78
25	26	32	44	64	64
59%	37%	40%	16%	26%	33%

Table 11.2   Gambling Economic Profile, 1983

	1983 Handle (Billion)	% Change from 1982	1983 Revenue (Billion)	% Change from 1983	Retention Percentage
Legal Gambling					
Casino[a]	$105.95	+4.4	4.61	+10.3	
State lotteries	5.17	+26.5	3.04	+40	54
Horse racing	9.93	−0.6	1.86	−0.9	18.7
Off-track Betting					
(OTB)	1.72	+0.5	0.40	+0.6	23.4
Greyhounds	2.33	+6.7	0.45	+6.8	19.5
Jai alai	0.62	−0.5	0.11	−0.5	18.0
Total parimutuel	14.6	+0.7	2.82	+0.5	—
Legal bookmaking	0.85	+58.4	0.04	+68.9	5.11
Card rooms[b]	1.05	+5.2	0.05	+5.2	5.0
Bingo	3.07	+2.3	0.79	+2.3	26
Charitable					
gaming[c]	1.40	+17.2	0.46	+17.0	33
Total	132.09	+5.0	11.84	+13.8	
Illegal Gambling					
Bookmaking[d]	23.9	+21.7	2.52	+11.3	17/4.5[f]
Numbers	4.89	+18.4	2.49	+11.8	51
Other illegal	0.10	NA	0.17	NA	
Total	28.9	+21.2	5.03	+11.5	
Grand total	160.99	+6.7			

[a]Includes table games (such as black jack) and slot machines.
[b]Excluding Nevada.
[c]Excluding bingo. An example of charitable gambling is "Las Vegas Night" sponsored by service clubs to raise money for a worthy cause.
[d]Includes pool cards, sports, and race betting.
[e]Takeouts vary from game to game. It is well known, however, that the house has the advantage on all games. The expected win for Craps is 1.4 percent of handle and 5.2 percent for American Roulette.
[f]Legal race-book takeout is 17 percent and sport-book takeout is 4.5 percent. Sports cards retain 50 percent of wager.

Source: Christiansen (June 1984), pp. 50–51, and Christiansen (May 1984), pp. 30–31.

charitable gambling; thirty-three states permit parimutuel betting at race-tracks, dog tracks, or jai alai; twenty-one states and Washington, D.C., operate lotteries; eight states have card rooms; two have casino gambling; and two permit sports betting.

Table 11.3 profiles the range of legal gambling found in the various states. The proliferation of legal gambling is not restricted to the United States. Almost every country in the world permits some form of gambling. For example, forty-one nations have legal sport, and all of Canada's provinces or territories have lotteries, bingo, horse racing, and legal telephone betting.[25]

The profile of the distribution of gambling in America suggests that it is indeed a popular, and essentially legal, activity. Interesting policy questions are posed by this tendency to legalize gambling. First, is legalization with state regulation just the next step in the general trend in American public policy and law to decriminalize victimless crimes? Second, can the traditional corruption of law enforcement by criminal elements be stopped? And third, with the increased financial stake of the state in gambling revenue, can the regulators prevent the tendency of the industry being regulated from "capturing" or "co-opting" the regulators?[26] These issues are associated with gambling and they reflect a change in the dominant model of state control of gambling. That is, because of revenue needs and declining public support for enforcement, states have abandoned the prosecutorial model that emphasized prohibition and punishment in favor of a regulatory model that emphasizes control while encouraging the activity in question. The federal government, while retaining the prosecutorial model, is essentially out of the gambling-enforcement business.[27] Gambling enforcement is a "states' rights" issue; it is a low priority with federal authorities unless the gambling violations can be associated with criminal activity of a larger magnitude, such as the use of gambling establishments to "launder" profit from illicit narcotics transactions to legitimate financial institutions.[28]

The increased popularity of gambling and the declining view of moral approbation associated with gambling has had an impact on public policy. These factors have made it possible for states to look at gambling from more than a public protection or prohibition model. The doors are open for governments to consider the options of legalization or decriminalization in order to use gambling to their own ends. The mounting fiscal pressures on state and local budgets have forced these governments to look for new sources of revenue in lieu of additional taxes. Revenue from gambling, also called a voluntary tax, is one of the alternatives many are considering, and one many have adopted. The government also feels that if it enters the gambling arena it can garner funds for housing, social services, and other critical needs areas that otherwise would fill the coffers of organized crime or be used to corrupt public officials. Finally, states are revising their views of gambling simply because law enforcement resources assigned to gambling seem misplaced when the enforcement needs for more serious crimes are considered. Changing the government's stance vis-à-vis gambling does not come without public policy controversy, however.

The government, by legalizing some form of gambling, places itself in a rather hypocritical position. First, is it appropriate for the government to regulate what are called "victimless crimes" in order to protect citizens from themselves? If it is the proper role of government to do so, then how can it sanction one form of gambling and prohibit others? By legalizing gambling the government is in effect dangling temptation before the public and is depending on these same persons to give in to their weaknesses. Second, despite the popularity of gambling, it is difficult to generate enthusiasm

Table 11.3 Legal Gambling in America

STATE	Bingo	Card Rooms	Casinos	Greyhounds	Harness	Quarterhorse	Thoroughbred	Jai alai	Lottery	Numbers	Lotto	VLTs	Interstate intertrack	Intrastate intertrack	Pari-theatre	Parlors	Telephone betting	Sports betting
Alabama	●			●														
Alaska	●	●																
Arizona	●			●		●	●		●		x		●	x	*			
Arkansas				●			●											
California	●	●		●		●	●		x				*					
Colorado	●			●	○	●	●						●	●				
Connecticut	●			●				●	●	●	*					●	●	●
Delaware	●			●			●		●	●	●		*					
Florida	●			●		●	●	●					*					●
Georgia	●																	
Hawaii																		
Idaho	●					●	●											
Illinois	●				●	○	●		●	●	●	*	●	*				
Indiana																		
Iowa	●	●		x	x	x	x											
Kansas	●																	
Kentucky	●				●	x	●						●	x			●	
Louisiana	●				○	●	●						●	x				
Maine	●				●				●	●	x							
Maryland	●				●		●		●	●	*		*				●	
Massachusetts	●			●	●		●		●	●	●		●					
Michigan	●				●	●	●		●	●	*							
Minnesota	●				x	x	x		x					x				
Mississippi																		
Missouri	●						x		x									
Montana	●	●				●	●											●
Nebraska	●					●	●							*				
Nevada	●	●	●	x	x	●	x	○									●	●
New Hampshire	●				●	●	●		●	●	x							
New Jersey	●		●			●	●		●	●	●				*			
New Mexico	●					●	●											
New York	●				●	○	●		●	●	●						●	●
North Carolina	●																	
North Dakota	●	●																
Ohio	●				●	●	●		●	●	●		●					
Oklahoma	●					x	x											
Oregon	●	●		●		●	●		x									●
Pennsylvania	●				●		●		●	●	●		●				●	
Rhode Island	●			●	○		○	●	●	●	●							
South Carolina	●																	
South Dakota	●				●		●	●										
Tennessee	●																	
Texas	●																	
Utah																		

Table 11.3 Legal Gambling in America (Continued)

STATE	Bingo	Card Rooms	Casinos	Greyhounds	Horses			Jai alai	Lottery				– OTB –					
					Harness	Quarterhorse	Thoroughbred		Lottery	Numbers	Lotto	VLTs	Interstate intertrack	Intrastate intertrack	Pari-theatre	Parlors	Telephone betting	Sports betting
Vermont	●				●	●	○		●	●	x							
Virginia	●																	
Washington	●	●			x	●	●		●	✻	x		●					
West Virginia	●			●	○		●		x				●	x				
Wisconsin	●																	
Wyoming	●					●	●											
Puerto Rico	●		●				●		●									
Virgin Islands									●									
Washington, D.C.	●								●	✻	✻							

Key: ● Legal and operative.
  ○ Previously operative, currently inactive.
  ✻ Implemented 1983–84
  x Authorized but not yet implemented.

Source: "U.S. and Canadian Gaming-at-a-Glance," *Gaming Business Magazine,* August 1984, p. 53. Updated to include results of votes in November 1984 general election.

among the public for its legalization in any form other than lotteries. This has meant that the major social impetus for the government's involvement in gambling has come from public officials. This raises the question of how adequately these officials represent the public interest. This hypocrisy may be the most significant policy issue facing governments as they consider legalization of gambling of any type. Jerome Skolnick notes this in his discussion of casino gambling:

> Ultimately, the public policy issue may not rest on whether gambling is moral as such, but on whether the government ought to promote an activity that is, if not immoral, at least not exemplary.
>
> Is it consistent for the same government that promotes literacy, public health, the environment and other conventionally salutary activities also to endorse gambling? Thus, the most fundamental criticism of any form of legal gambling has to do with the government's role in promoting what is often justified as a voluntary tax.[29]

With respect to gambling, the government is caught between the proverbial rock and a hard place. It is faced with the need to raise revenue and to deliver services, yet there is no support for increased taxation. If government suggests gambling as an alternative, it compromises its role as moral leader even in the face of high public demand for that activity. These dilemmas pose difficult problems for policy alternatives that depend upon legalized gambling.

Models of Control

The control of gambling puts the state in a precarious position. If it adopts a model of prohibition, the state is faced with public disfavor and symbolic law enforcement. Prohibition has other consequences of significance. Christiansen and Skagan assert that with prohibition:

1. Vast markets for commercial gambling services exist, in most cases, with no legal supplier. This stimulates the illegal entry of suppliers to meet the high inelastic demand. Certainly illegal sport and race bookmakers have taken advantage of this situation.

2. The diversion of law enforcement and judicial resources have to be equally determined to keep existing and lucrative, but forbidden, gambling markets from being supplied.

3. Suppliers who succeed in entering gambling markets illegally become criminal organizations which must resort to the corruption of police and judges in order to stay in business.

4. The resulting ineffectual law enforcement permits criminal organizations to stay in business and to establish relatively secure positions in the gambling market.[30]

Advocates for reform of the prohibition model suggest that a legalization or decriminalization approach would eliminate the monopoly enjoyed by organized crime, scarce law enforcement resources could be applied to more pressing problems, public officials would not be corrupted and the status of government would be raised in the eyes of the citizens because it no longer will be applying criminal law to private behavior, and to behavior in which the participants do not see themselves as victims. Those against reform suggest that legalization will result in a dramatic increase in the illicit activity, corruption will not be eliminated, citizens will lose faith in government if the latter is viewed as promoting an activity that does not have any redeeming social value, and, even with legislation, organized crime will exist and in a profitable way.[31] The experience of legalization suggests that both sides are correct, which does not make the policy issues associated with gambling any easier to resolve.

It seems that the era of gambling prohibition is behind us. The number of gambling arrests is down and there is little or no public or police support for enforcement.[32] In addition, there is no evidence that corruption goes away with legalization, as recent cases with the New Jersey Gaming Commission demonstrate.[33] Finally, law enforcement policy places a low priority on gambling because the investigation and adjudication required for such enforcement places a considerable burden on the justice system and detracts from this system's ability to deal with more serious crime. The end result of all this has been the second model of control—*decriminalization* of a number of gambling activities, including sports betting. However, it has been *de facto* rather than *de jure*. The state could adopt a formal model of decriminalization that provides for the removal of all criminal sanctions for a given activity. In some cases citations could be issued. However, for the most part, the government is not involved in regulation, which is now left to nonpublic institutions such as the family and church. This model is probably consistent with the public desire on enforcement, but it does suggest some public interest irresponsibility on the part of the state, since it is not taking advantage of the revenue potential or leaving itself the option of protecting the public from its excesses. *De facto* decriminalization is the current federal pattern and it exists where any form of gambling is found, even in states that have legalized gaming.

A third model is for the state to *legalize gambling by holding the operators license* and, in effect, to transfer the monopoly on the gaming activity to itself. The state will operate the gambling activity by creating an agency within the existing government apparatus, by leasing the operation to a private entity, or it will create a separate government corporation specifically designed to operate the gambling enterprise. OTB in New York is an example of the latter. State-run lotteries are examples of the implementation of this model. This approach has been tried with sports betting, but with little or no success. The cases of Canada's Sport Select Baseball and Delaware's football pools illustrate the difficulty states have with this model of gaming control.

Sport Select Baseball. In the spring of 1984 the Canadian Government created Sport Select Baseball (SSB), a betting pool that would take wagers on major league baseball games. The government expected a $200 million handle and a $50 million profit. The bulk of the net revenue would be used to finance the 1988 Winter Olympic Games to be held in Calgary. Major league baseball and the Canadian provinces reacted immediately. Major league baseball said that Sport Select Baseball violated league copyrights and would potentially damage the integrity of baseball. In its lawsuit to stop the implementation of Sport Select Baseball, the well-known position of major league baseball on gambling was anticipated:"It (baseball) is a wholesome family event with a world-wide audience drawn to the game because of its unblemished record of integrity. These values are too important to permit erosion through lotteries or pool betting."[34] Major league baseball asserted that SSB was in violation of the copyrights the league held on schedules and trademarks. SSB also threatened baseball's goodwill with the public.

The provinces also filed a breach-of-contract suit charging that the pool was a lottery and contravened the 1979 agreement between the federal and provincial governments that gave the provinces the sole right to run lotteries.[35] The federal government claimed that the pool was in fact not a lottery, but a game of skill based on the accurate prediction of baseball scores on some thirteen games. The provinces also felt that this new game would infringe on a very profitable $1.5 billion lottery business, particulary if the sports cards would be sold by lottery vendors.

After two months of operation the federal government folded Sport Select Baseball. The enterprise was losing $700,000 a week and quickly eating into the $10 million starting appropriation and $20 million line of credit granted by the federal government. The demise of Sport Select Baseball can be attributed to the complicated nature of the game, the lack of competent administrative experience, and the resistence of lottery vendors (25,000 throughout the provinces) to selling the cards. The provinces did inform many of their vendors that if they sold SSB cards they would lose their lottery contract; 7,000 vendors proceeded to cancel their SSB agreements. The lottery was too lucrative not to be involved.

Instead of deciding the matter in the courts, the federal and provincial governments reached an agreement that has been called a "sweetheart deal." The provinces will give the federal government $25 million a year for four years to help pay for the Winter Olympics and 3 percent of gross lottery sales from 1986 to 2000. In return, the federal government agrees to stay out of the lottery or sports-betting business for the next sixteen years.[36]

The reduction of revenue to illegal gambling was never an issue in the Canadian sports-betting enterprise. The federal government saw the income potential of a betting pool based on its observations of public interest and of the provincial lottery profits. It did not want to raise or create taxes to finance the Olympics because that would surely mean a serious challenge to the Conservative Party's control of government; Canadian citizens did not want a repeat of the 1976 Montreal financial debacle. Thus governments placed themselves in competition with each other, and a jurisdictional dispute was the result.

Delaware Football Pool. Two weekly sports-betting games were begun by the Delaware State Lottery on September 12, 1976. One game was entitled "Football Bonus" and the other "Touchdown." Each represented a pool where several games were selected, with a parimutuel payout schedule of 55 percent to the state and 45 percent to the players.[37] The Office of the Attorney General of the State of Delaware had interpreted Delaware statutes to allow that these games were a lottery and not dependent on skill.[38] The National Football League immediately filed a suit, and its arguments were similar to those used by baseball officials in the Canadian case.[39] The NFL claimed misuse of property rights to team names, schedules, and game scores, damage to the integrity of football, and violation of state lottery laws. On November 20, 1976, Delaware's football-betting venture was terminated.

The demise of the Delaware pool can be attributed in part to the NFL suit, which eventually was denied in U.S. District Court of Delaware when the judge ruled that the copyright claim was questionable, since all of the game-related information (such as schedules) also was available to the general public through the press. The NFL did not appeal this decision, but its threat of continued litigation added to the apprehension of Delaware lottery officials. The closing also took place because of low interest on the part of the general public, the inability of pool officials to establish correct or "balancing" odds, and the lack of sufficient computerization to handle a large volume of wagers. It is the lack of expertise on the part of state officials who operate government-sponsored sports betting that is a major factor in their ability to operate efficiently and with a profit.

A fourth model of gaming legalization is the Nevada prototype, which calls for the state to grant licenses to private entrepreneurs who provide the public with gambling services under the state's guidelines. Parimutuel racetracks, Nevada's casinos and race/sports books, Atlantic City's casinos, and some state lotteries operate on this basis. The state collects revenue in the form of license fees, direct taxation of the operators' revenues or facilities, and indirect taxation in the form of excise and sales taxes obtained from the consumer.

This model is what Skolnick calls the "qualification model," where persons desiring to operate a gambling business must apply and submit to an extensive background investigation.[40] If found suitable, the person is allowed to operate the business as long as the state's guidelines are followed. Thus, under this model, the gambling industry is viewed as a "privileged" industry rather than an activity that can be undertaken as a matter of constitutional "right." The privileged status of the gaming industry has been upheld in court in the face of constitutional challenges; the courts have even permitted the existence of an exclusive "Black Book" of persons who cannot enter any type of gambling establishment.[41] The rationale for judicial support arises out of gambling's nefarious past and the need for the state to have every means of control at its disposal.

Sports and race betting has been subject to each of these approaches to legalization. Where such gambling is officially legalized, the model of privileged licensure is followed. In most other jurisdictions, however, race and sports betting is prohibited, or it is allowed to operate under de facto decriminalization. The mood of the country suggests a change in this situation; there seems to be a move to legalize sports betting officially under the models of private licensing or state monopoly. Many public policy issues need to be addressed before this trend can be actualized.

LEGALIZING SPORTS BETTING

Revenue and Taxation. In 1983 legalized gambling generated $3.1 billion in state and local taxes.[42] This fact, combined with the significant popularity of sport spectatorship and the well-known phenomenon of illegal sports betting, has stimulated the movement to legalize the betting on sports events. The betting volume at the Nevada sports books also suggests that the state takeout from legal betting could produce significant dollars.

In 1974 Nevada sports books handled approximately $8 million. In 1983 the handle had grown over 900 percent, to nearly $700 million. Add nearly $160 million for race-book betting in 1983 (see Table 11.1). The incredible increase in the handle is the result of the reduction of the federal wagering tax from 10 percent to 2 percent in 1974 and to 0.25 percent in 1983.[43] Thus the bettor can now obtain a return on his bet nearly equal to what would be possible with an illegal bet. The increase in betting volume was also the result of the State of Nevada's decision to allow sport and race books in the casino in 1975. There were twelve operations in 1975 and sixty-four in 1983. It became easier to handle the larger volume of betting by the installation of an automated procedure for handling bets, called Nevada Automated Betting System (NABS). Finally, the sports bet is more attractive to the average bettor because it is taken at "fixed odds" rather than at a parimutuel's floating odds. Thus sports betting represents one of the best possibilities for a player to win when compared to other games. Simulcast racing and intrastate telephone betting also stimulated betting volume.

The most significant revenue figure for policy consideration is not the total wager figure; it is in the percent win or net profit. In 1983 the percent win for Nevada books was 2.78 percent; a figure that leaves a significant amount of money for taxable purposes. In fact, sports betting has the smallest retention percentage of any form of commercial gambling. It produces the lowest net state revenue per capita of all games.[44] It also means that sports betting gives the player the greatest chance of winning, and the implication is that sports betting is not a significant revenue producer. If other states were to legalize sports betting and install themselves as the operator, they would stand a good chance of not making much money or, in fact, losing money. The Canadian Sports Select Basketball and the defunct Delaware football pool illustrate the problem. Neither entity had the expertise or talent to run a profitable sports-betting operation. If the state wants to be the gambler, operating its own betting operation with its own people, it had better be prepared to take a loss.

Lotteries with takeouts of up to 50 percent and parimutuel betting (with takeouts of 15 to 17 percent) guarantee the state's share, but no guarantee can be made with sports betting. However, if the state could legalize some form of a sports pool that has lotterylike features, including a high takeout, and operated by qualified personnel, the public entity could generate substantial revenue.

Off-Track Betting (OTB) of New York illustrates how a state can make money from a form of sports betting that depends on parimutuel wagering. Table 11.4 demonstrates that OTB has realized its revenue potential.[45] This is the result of the "revenue imperative" of the New York legislature when it developed the 1970 OTB-enabling legislation. The current takeout for OTB is 22 percent, compared to 17 percent for on-track betting. The legalization not only had the effect of raising revenue, but it initially reduced the handle of the pre-OTB suppliers and it did not affect the rate of illegal gambling.

OTB raises two policy questions. The first is one of jurisdiction. That is, should state or local governments run gambling? The second is to what extent should the state be in competition with private commercial enterprises? The legalization of OTB was in large part the result of local governments being dissatisfied with state government's financial attention to local problems. While OTB did enhance local revenue, it detracted from state revenue and private profit.

In addition, if the state adopts gambling as a revenue producer, consideration must be given to the extent to which the legalized form of gambling is regressive; that is, to what extent is the tax burden born disproportionately by low income households. The few analyses available suggest that gambling tends to be a regressive form of taxation, even though it may be classified as a "voluntary tax."[46] Based on the percent of total income wagered, numbers, lotteries, bingo, sport pools, and racetrack betting tend to be the most regressive; casinos and sports betting are the least regressive.[47] For example, families with incomes of $30,000 or less have 77 percent of the total income, but these families account for 92 percent of lottery revenue.[48] The most regressive games have the highest takeout and the worst odds of winning but also the highest pay-out potential. These are just the type of games that governments implement, thereby shifting a disproportionate tax burden to low income persons who are attracted to these types of bets.

In the case of nonparimutuel sports betting, a paradox exists. Sports betting provides the lowest revenue potential, but it is the least regressive. If state policy is guided by regressivity, legalized sports betting is attractive; if the policy is to raise revenue, sports betting is not a viable alternative. These problems suggest that it might be cheaper to raise an existing tax a small percentage to produce the desired income rather than legalize a sports-betting operation that has the potential of producing a small amount of revenue at a substantial cost of implementation, administration, and control.

Table 11.4 New York City Off-Track Betting Corporation

Revenue in Support of Government (Calendar years) (in millions)

	1971	1972	1973	1974	1975	1976	1977	1978	1979	Total
Handle	$118.6	$450.3	$691.3	$786.7	$773.6	$785.9	$777.4	$791.9	$835.8	$6,011.5
To New York State	$ 1.8	$ 0.0	$ 16.3	$ 18.2	$ 18.4	$ 18.2	$ 17.8	$ 17.5	$ 17.9	$ 135.1
To local government (surcharge)				4.7	9.4	9.5	8.9	8.8	8.7	50.0
To New York City	2.7	16.5	39.2	54.0	64.1	64.3	63.1	59.1[a]	62.9[a]	425.9
Total	$ 4.5	$ 25.5	$ 55.5	$ 76.9	$ 91.9	$ 92.0	$ 89.8	$ 85.4	$ 89.5	$ 611.0

Revenue in Support of the Racing Industry (calendar years) (in millions)

	1971	1972	1973	1974	1975	1976	1977	1978	1979	Total
To racetracks and horsemen (purse money)	$ 1.8	$ 12.1	$ 18.2	$ 30.7	$ 30.9	$ 31.4	$ 33.0	$ 36.8	$ 42.0	$ 236.9
To breeding funds			$ .3	$ .7	$ .7	$ .6	$ 1.3	$ 2.5	$ 2.8	$ 8.9
Total	$ 1.8	$ 12.1	$ 18.5	$ 31.4	$ 31.6	$ 32.0	$ 34.3	$ 39.3	$ 44.8	$ 245.8

[a]Includes surcharge revenues from other communities.

Source: Eugene M. Christiansen and Michael D. Shagan, "The New York Off-Track Betting Law: An Exercise in Selective Decriminalization," Connecticut Law Review 12 (1980): 863.

In other words, why create a new bureaucracy when for virtually no additional cost the state can use an organizational apparatus that is already in place?

Reduction of Illegal Gambling. If revenue production is not a realistic goal for legalized sports betting, then the control of organized crime and political corruption by reducing illegal wagering becomes the policy orientation of legalization. Now that a major obstacle to operating a legal sports-betting scheme has been removed with the reduction of wagering taxes from 10 percent to 0.25 percent, it is possible for the legal version to be competitive with the illegal variety (that is, with similar takeout rates).

It must be kept in mind that all commercial gambling has a built-in operator edge or advantage. This house advantage must provide a sufficient operator return to cover costs of the game, including insurance, loan amortization, payroll, and of course profit. The edge also must be large enough to cover gambling taxes. Thus the legal industry needs a higher edge than what is required by the illegal enterprise. This will be a problem as long as the states view gaming as a revenue source. Finally, the taxes extracted from legal commercial gambling must (1) be sufficient to cover any costs associated with supervising, operating, or controlling the gaming enterprise; (2) provide enough dollars to cover losses of tax revenue from similar legal games (such as OTB versus on-track), and (3) generate enough monies to have an impact on the social maladies that were used to promote the implementation of the legal game in the first place. Lotteries, casinos, and some forms of parimutuel betting may satisfy these revenue needs, but sports betting, particularly if the state is the operator, will not.[49] If states adopted a parimutuel system of sports betting, as some have suggested, the states' takeout percentage would be guaranteed, but the game would not be competitive with its illegal counterparts.[50] Thus the state is confronted with an interesting set of paradoxes. These are described by one economist in his analysis of national commission data:

> When the state steps into the picture and provides gambling or other services banned to private producers, it places itself into a peculiar position. By offering the service itself, the state announces that the activity is not, *per se*, contrary to the public interest; rather the state has merely attempted to transfer to itself the monopoly of the product by continuation of the prohibition of private production. To the degree that this monopoly is profitable to the state, however, it remains potentially profitable to the private operator. The only way for the state to deprive the illegal operation of its demand is by the competition in price, but this erodes the revenue available from the service. In other words, if gambling is to be a revenue source, the state must maintain a situation in which illegal gambling is likewise profitable.[51]

If the purpose is to drive out illegal operations, price competition is necessary; if its purpose is raising revenue, illegal operations will continue to exist even if a state's game is attractive. Thus there is a significant conflict between the objective of law enforcement and revenue production. To raise money, the state must operate a game with a high takeout rate, but this will mean that the illegal game will be more attractive to bettors. A game that matches the price and payout schedule of the illegal game will affect the illegal operation but will not generate revenue. Sports betting appears to be a poor candidate for legalization because it cannot help the state meet either goal.

A major argument promoting legalization is that legalization will direct gamblers from illegal to legal channels. This results in depriving illegal operators of revenues that allegedly are used to finance other illegal activities, such as narcotics and prostitution, and to finance political corruption. Since both the National Advisory Commission on Organized Crime (1967) and the National Commission on a National Policy on Gambling (1976) assert that illegal sports betting produces the most income for organized crime, this argument has more credence. However, as noted, sports betting is the most difficult to legalize because it is difficult for the state to match the costs and services provided by the illegal operation. In addition, recent studies indicate that the potential for legal gambling to reduce the illegal variety has not been demonstrated.[52] In fact, legal gambling may increase the number of illegal bettors because the bettor's gambling education is enhanced as the result of participating in legal games and because of the state's sanction of what was once a deviant activity. In addition, the illegal operation can offer the incentives of no income tax on winnings (also called a "crime tariff," which permits an illegal operator to offer higher returns on bets), credit betting, telephone betting, personal service, and usually better payouts. The risk of offering these services by the illegal bookmaker are not great, since the public generally demands them and gambling control is a low enforcement priority. In addition, Reuter's study observes that "organized crime" is not the benefactor of illegal bookmaking revenues. Rather, organized crime helps to mediate disputes among gamblers and to protect illegal operations from police harassment.[53] This means that the legalization of sports betting would not have an impact on organized crime as it is traditionally defined. Rather, the impact would be on small-time bookmakers who cater to a local and regular clientele.

The state would be confronted with an interesting dilemma if it were to legalize sports betting. It is obvious that organized crime or the illegal entrepreneurs have the expertise to operate bookmaking. Either the state would have to hire former illegal operators to run its game or it would have to eliminate the competition completely if it wanted to legalize sports betting. The latter, of course, is a virtual impossibility, and the former would be political suicide for any government.

The widespread support for legalization also has been an outcome of the lowered enforcement policy and the general public acceptance of gambling. The high rate of participation as documented by the National Commission suggests that moral resistance has all but dissipated. Recent opinion polls show that four-fifths of the population support legalization in one form or another. Two-thirds of the population agreed that legal gambling attracts criminal elements, but this does not seem to dampen approval.[54] In most cases, OTB being the exception, the approval rating improved between 1976 and 1982. Sports betting approval improved to the greater extent—twenty points. This generally favorable attitude, despite knowledge of personal or social costs, suggests that citizens feel that the government has no right to prevent a person from gambling.

Sports betting legalization garnered more approval in 1982 than in 1976. However, it has the lowest overall approval rating when compared to other types of gambling. For example, 48 percent approved of sports betting, but 74 percent approved of legalizing Bingo, 72 percent of lotteries, and 62 perent of casinos.[55] A more recent national survey by Gallup showed that only 41 percent approved of legalizing betting on professional football, baseball, or football, whereas 53.5 percent disapproved.[56] The major reasons for resistance were a fear of organized-crime involvement and the stimulus to cumpulsive gambling. The public is not overly concerned about the corruption of athletes, even though one-fourth feel games are fixed occasionally.[57] However, convictions under the Federal Sports Bribery Act of 1964 (18 USC 224) have been rare. Since 1970 only seven persons have been convicted and only two of these were related to sports betting. Actually, the sports betting industry, illegal or not, does a good job of policing itself. The bookmaker can detect a "fix" by watching the ebb and flow of bets. Since his bottom line depends on a balanced bet, he will withdraw any game from the betting cycle if he feels a fix is in. Bookmakers, rather than law enforcement agencies, have done the most to expose corruption in sports.

The resistance to approving legal sports betting can be explained by an ideological association of sports with revered and traditional American values, such as competition, fair play, courage, teamwork, and loyalty. Sport betting carries more ideological baggage than other types of betting and therefore is a poor candidate for legalization. This is particularly true for college sports. If betting were restricted to professional sports, the approval rate might be considerably higher.

Legal sports betting is aggressively resisted by college and professional sports organizations. In the college ranks, coaches and administrators do not feel that illegal sports betting affects their programs. But they do feel that this will change if legalization occurs.[58] Since most betting on college games seems to be a casual activity among friends rather than an activity restricted to well-known, big-time gamblers, the existence of illegal gambling is not viewed as a threat. However, if legalization did take place, these same individuals felt that the incidence of fixing games would increase, the public confidence in the college game would decrease, coaches and players might make decisions based on the betting line and not on the context of the game, and more extensive—and costly—security measures would be required.[59] Despite the fear of the effect of gambling on the college game and the efforts of coaches and administrators to educate players about the dangers of gambling, coaches admit that they are aware of point spreads and that they often refer to the betting line when talking with their players. Coaches view these contingencies as minor irritations that could be converted to major problems should wagering on college sports events be legalized.

The position of the professional sports leagues on gambling is well know. They are against it. This position asserts that wagering, legal or illegal, on professional sports events is bad for the game, since it will compromise the integrity of competition. That is, there will always be the suspicion that the outcome of the event may not be the result of the natural struggle of adversaries; but that it could be the result of contrived action designed to meet the betting line. The competitive value of the contest would no longer be of interest to the fan. Rather, the fan's focus would be on the outcome as it relates to his financial investment in that outcome. The industry's position is represented by the following statements from its representatives:

> Walter Kennedy, former Commissioner of the National Basketball Association: The potential abuses are endless and would lead to the destruction of professional sports in this country because of the irreplaceable loss of confidence in the integrity of competition.[60]

> Pete Rozelle, Commissioner of the National Football League: Professional football depends for its survival on the public's perception of the integrity of the games, owners, and players. . . . The pressure on players and club and league personnel from increased numbers of people seeking inside information would quickly become intolerable. . . . Legal sports betting would seriously erode public confidence in the games. It would create a generation of cynical fans, obsessed with point spreads and parimutuel tickets and constantly suspicious of the movies [sic] of players and workers. . . . A State-run monopoly on team sports betting would be administratively burdensome and extremely expensive to oversee, with only dubious prospects of ultimate financial reward. There is serious doubt that State-run gambling could compete effectively with illegal gambling.[61]

> Bowie Kuhn, former Commissioner of Baseball: Legislation of sports gambling would make every adult citizen a potential gambler—rather than just a fan. For if legalized sports betting will not win over those who are dealing with neighborhood bookmakers, then it must depend upon and create *new* gamblers from among sports fans, concerned not so much with who wins, but by what amount one team or another beats the point spread. . . . Every missed basket,

bad pass, substitution or strategy move would become an economic factor; cynicism would replace family fun. The potential abuses are endless, but they all lead in the end to the destruction of professional athletic leagues because of the consequent loss of confidence in the integrity of the game.[62]

In sum, the professional leagues resist the legalization of sports because they feel it will jeopardize public confidence in the sport, increase the danger of scandal, create new gamblers, and otherwise compromise the public interest in one of America's significant traditions. In other words, sports are intertwined in the American social fabric that holds society together. Any policy that would undermine that fabric can only do a disservice to the public interest.

More recently, this position has been challenged by the newly organized Major Indoor Soccer League (MISL). League representatives feel that legalized sports wagering will benefit their game rather than detract from it. Betting would stimulate interest, enhance visibility, and attract television viewers to the indoor game. In fact, the former commissioner of the MISL, Earl Foreman, feels that it is time to acknowledge the natural association of wagering and sports.

But I would say we should be very realistic and honest about the situation. Wagering on prospects is a part of the American sports scene. If you don't believe that, then turn on the pro football pregame shows on the television networks and listen to their prognosticators.

If you don't think gambling is not part and parcel with sports in this country, then you are playing an ostrich, sticking your head in the sand. Gambling and sports are first cousins.[63]

An MISL general manager comments: "Betting is like free advertising. It gets conversation going and it might get extra people into the arena. Let's face it, television sponsors know that people who bet have a lot of disposable income. The networks know what is going on."[64]

The position of the leagues also was challenged by the House of Representatives Select Committee on Professional Sport. Taking a stance at odds with the National Commission on the Review of a National Policy Toward Gambling, this group recommended that wagering on professional sports, not college sports, be legalized. The committee felt that legalization would produce revenue for the state, reduce the incidence of illegal betting, detract from the profits of organized crime, induce better control because of licensing, conform to the public's wishes, and eliminate the hypocrisy of having unenforcible gambling laws in the codes. Finally, the committee concluded that gambling is a legitimate recreational outlet. It is here to stay, and it has not seemed to affect the integrity of sports even under illegal auspices. The committee's recommendations were not implemented.

It is not likely that the leagues will change their stance on gambling. However, these statements draw some attention to the hypocrisy of the major leagues' position. Despite being against wagering, the leagues, and the media who sponsor and finance these sports, contribute to the gamblers' interest by providing injury data, personnel information, and betting lines. The official media justification for publishing point spreads is that they serve a valid "journalistic function" related to the accurate assessment of a team's chances. The leagues state that if they did not publish injury reports or related information they would be even more susceptible to charges of conspiring with gamblers because someone might accuse the leagues of selectively releasing this information, thereby giving someone the "edge" in gambling wagers. The leagues and the media are aware that betting promotes interest in their product. On the one hand, the leagues can take a moral and prohibitive public stance, but privately they do all they can to promote the gambler's interest in their events.

The integrity of the game is not the only reason sports leagues, both college and professional, resist the legalization of sports betting. These entities also fear the intrusion of government into their private enterprise. Their concern is that with legalization comes regulation; that regulation could affect scheduling, outcomes, and even qualification for participation.

> But what really has the sport establishment on edge is the possibility of government regulators invading their private fiefdoms. The scenario goes like this: What if a heavily bet playoff game were won on what was later shown to be an incorrect call by an official? As long as betting is illegal, the losers have to hold their peace. Inevitably, state sponsored betting would require state sponsored regulation of the competition, just like at the race track.[65]

It is possible, under legalization, for teams to have to share property rights with the state without compensation.[66] The approval and licensing of owners, mandatory drug testing, background investigation of players, and takeout on gate receipts are potential consequences of legalization. For these reasons, in addition to the integrity issue, professional leagues will resist the legalization of sports betting. Their position will be prominent, since they hold the right to assign a valuable and desired product—franchise locations. Thus states and cities will resist legalization if they know that it will mean not being considered for a major league franchise if and when one is available. Finally, the leagues' stance is reinforced by the current tendency to reduce the influence of government in private life and to reduce the financial outlay of government. Legalization would only have the opposite effect in both cases. The fact that league owners, in agreement with media counterparts, form a powerful interest group makes it possible for leagues to marshal significant political and economic resources to resist efforts at legalization of gambling on sports.

CONCLUSION

Even though wagering on sports is a popular activity, it is not likely that sports betting will be legalized. This is true for several reasons. First, the potential for revenue is much lower when compared to other games. This is because of the low takeout rates. If takeout rates are raised above those used by the illegal bookmakers, the legal game will be priced out of the competition. Second, the state's competitive position is further compromised by its inability to match the illegal bookmakers' options of offering credit and of taking bets by telephone. Third, legalized sports wagering could only mean more government involvement in what is essentially a self-regulatory industry. There is considerable ideological resistance to this possibility. Fourth, many states are not ready to absorb the costs of regulation and control, or the expanded bureaucracy, that legalization would produce. Fifth, the public still holds sport on some kind of value pedestal; sport, for many, represents what is good and virtuous about society. In combination with the public's residual moral abhorrence of gambling, this view works successfully as a force resisting the legalization of sports wagering. Finally, the states do not have the expertise to run sports-betting operations. The comments of G. Robert Blakey, noted authority on gambling, have merit on this issue:

> But I worry that government will succumb to the illusion that there's a lot of money to be made by legalizing sports gambling. Government would put in charge 8-to-5 types who won't care whether they get stung or not, and the wise guys would take the government to the cleaners. Government lacks the imagination, the flexibility and the savvy to run gambling.[67]

This lack of expertise, plus an economic dependence on gaming revenue, will make it easier for the regulators to be co-opted by the industry. Taking the side of the industry subsequently reduces the effectiveness of control efforts. Thus, states may consider sports wagering, but they will legalize other forms of gambling that are not so problematic.[68]

The states' most likely policy option with respect to wagering on sports events is the adoption of a model of *de facto decriminalization* or "benign prohibition." In reality, this approach seems to be consistent with the public interest. That is, the public enjoys gambling and participates at a high rate; however, it still holds sports gambling, particularly where it is excessive and where it potentially corrupts the amateur game, as morally objectionable. By retaining gambling's illegal status, the state retains the option of enforcing gambling laws when excesses are discovered. In the meantime, the federal government will have virtually nothing to do with gambling law enforcement, and the local jurisdictions will ignore gambling activity as long as other enforcement priorities exist and as long as no major political or economic problems arise with this generally illegal activity.

NOTES

1. Agreement on the definition of gambling has not been reached. However, a review of the literature suggests that gambling entails three basic factors: (1) the placement of a wager is a matter of deliberate choice and not coercion or unusual pressure; (2) the outcome of the event on which the wager is placed is uncertain or subject to chance; and (3) persons entering the gambling transaction wager something of value. Ordinarily we translate this as money, but the possession of value could be almost anything. In addition, these definitions are not inclusive or speculative but "legitimate" financial transactions, such as the purchase of grain futures or common stocks. In fact, the Commission on the Review of the National Policy Toward Gambling reinforces this point by defining gambling as "financial risk-taking that is viewed by the bulk of the participants as a form of recreation." See *Gambling in America*, Final Report of the Commission on the Review of a National Policy Toward Gambling, Washington, D.C., 1976.

2. Decriminalization and legalization often are suggested as two alternatives to deal with victimless crimes or those entered into by mutual consent. Both terms suggest some kind of reform in the approach of law enforcement to these types of crimes. Reform is viewed as necessary because there is high public demand for the goods and services provided by those who participate in these activities, and the public also does not support enforcement of these violations. In addition, reform in legal outlook would relieve the burden of the criminal justice system and perhaps put a dent in the rewards garnered by organized crime. According to the 1976 Task Force on Organized Crime, *decriminalization* refers to the removal of all criminal sanctions for an activity. Governmental regulators would be replaced by the churches, the family, or other nonlegal institutions. Government's only involvement is to provide treatment for abusers. *Legalization* involves making an activity or aspect of it legal, but within certain guidelines or regulations. The government is the regulator; violation of the regulations could be either a civil or a criminal offense. Legalization is usually the preferred alternative. This approach still permits the government to combat abuse, and it preserves a climate of disapprobation around an activity. The final regulatory result, however, is some mix of decriminalization and legalization. Little or no law enforcement is directed at private behavior, such as the friendly poker game at home or the use of controlled substance in a private dwelling. Enforcement attention, rather, is focused on the organizers or purveyors of the activity in question. See National Advisory Commission on Criminal Justice Standards and Goals, *Organized Crime: Report of the Task Force on Organized Crime* (Washington, D.C.: Law Enforcement Assistance Administration, 1976), pp. 229–30.

3. Jerome H. Skolnick and John Dombrink, "The Limits of Gaming Control," *Connecticut Law Review* 12 (Summer 1980): 762–84.

4. *Gambling in America*, p. 297.

5. Estimate provided by Mr. Sonny Reizner, manager of the Castaways Sports Book, Las Vegas, Nevada.

6. *Gambling in America*.

7. The popularity of betting, particularly on football, was enhanced when line makers went from a money line that emphasized odds such as 8 to 1 or 3 to 1 to a system of point spreads that adds and/or subtracts from the final outcome. In addition, the exciting nature of the bet is embellished by the prospect of an uncertain outcome. Sports information call-in services received 80 million calls in 1983.

8. Peter Reuter, *Disorganized Crime: The Economics of the Invisible Hand* (Boston, Mass.: MIT Press, 1983), pp. 14–44.

9. *Gambling in America*, p. 174.

10. Another method to balance the wagers besides moving the line is to "lay off" bets. If the bookmaker has an overabundance of bets on one team, he can place the excess wager with another bookmaker. Federal statutes prohibiting interstate wagering [18 U.S.C. 1081, 1084 (1961) (1970)] interfered to a great extent with telephone transmission of layoff bets.

11. Maureen Kallick-Kaufman, "The Micro and Macro Dimensions of Gambling in the United States," *Journal of Social Issues* 35 (1979): 7–26. See also *Gambling in Amerca*.

12. Ibid., p. 24.

13. James H. Frey, "Gambling: A Sociological Review," *Annals of the American Academy of Political and Social Science* 474 (July 1984): 107–21.

14. *Gambling in America*.

15. Studies on motivations to gamble show that the nonfinancial benefits of gambling, such as "excitement," "recreation," "new experience," and "relief of boredom," outweigh financial consideration for most bettors. Ronald W. Smith and Frederick W. Preston, "Vocabularies of Motives for Gambling Behavior," *Sociological Perspectives* 27 (July 1984): 325–48; Daniel B. Suits, "Economic Background for Gambling Policy," *Journal of Social Issues* 35 (1979): 43–61.

16. Howard J. Klein, "Gallup Poll: Landslide for Gaming," *Gaming Business Magazine*, July 1983, pp. 19–21; Robert Bezilla, "Legalized Sports Betting Faces Strong Opposition," *Gaming Business Magazine*, vol. 5 (August 1984), pp. 14–17. All references to sports betting in these articles are to bets on professional sports events. It is likely that the approval ratings and the participation rates for bets on college and amateur events would be much lower.

17. Ibid.

18. Eugene M. Christiansen, "The Gross Annual Wager of the United States: 1983" (Part I: Handle Trends), *Gaming Business Magazine*, August 1984, pp. 47–54, 84–85. "Handle," or total amount of money wagered, of course includes multiple bets of variable amounts. The estimates for the legal and illegal amounts are based on figures provided by the commercial gambling industry, the state-operated gambling entities, and by Internal Revenue Service and other concerned federal agencies. Illegal gambling wagers are based on the IRS's estimates on unreported income and illegal wagers attributed to the "underground economy"—the nonreporting of income for tax evasion purposes. For a more detailed discussion of the underground economy and the estimates of its dollar value, see Carl P. Simon and Ann D. Witter, *Beating the System: The Underground Economy* (Boston, Mass.: Auburn House, 1982).

19. Ibid., p. 47.

20. Eugene M. Christiansen, "The Gross Annual Wager in the United States: 1983" Part II: Revenues, *Gaming Business Magazine*, 5 (September 1984) pp. 29–33, 36. "Handle" means different things to different people. For example, not all of the money handled on a bookmaking operation is accounted for because of credit betting; however, parimutuel and lottery wagers are completely accounted for. Thus, for comparative purposes, handle is not valuable. Revenue from any game, whether it is a parimutuel takeout or a casino win, is easily identifiable as the price gamblers pay for wagering. It provides comparative data among games and with other industries.

21. These estimates are based on applying industry-generated retention percentages, also called takeout. These represent amounts deducted from total wagers, but before deductions for taxes and operating expenses. The takeout rate for race books is 17 percent; for sports books, 4.5 percent; for numbers, 51 percent; and for lotteries, 54 percent. Ibid., pp. 30–31.

22. Christiansen, "Gross Annual Wager," p. 32. The government takeout on a parimutuel system averages between 15 and 25 percent after about 2 to 3 percent has been taken out by the track. The remainder is spent among the bettors.

23. H. Roy Kaplan, "The Social and Economic Impact of State Lotteries," *Annals of the American Academy of Political and Social Science* 474 (July 1984): 94. The $2 billion represents 3 percent of the total budgets for the states with lotteries.

24. Daniel B. Suits, "Economic Background for Gambling Policy," *Journal of Social Issues* 35 (1979): 60.

25. "World Gaming at a Glance," *Gaming Business Magazine*, August 1983, pp. 28–30: 103 countries have lotteries, 75 have casinos, 69 permit horse racing, and 11 sanction cockfighting.

26. Skolnick and Dombrink, "Limits of Gaming Control." States are finding it increasingly difficult to "legislate morality" and as a result have removed criminal sanctions from the traditional vices of sexual relations, pornography, and gambling. It is also suggested that the greater a state's economic investment in gaming, the more likely regulatory decisions will favor the industry. These points are reinforced by the views of a former member of the Connecticut Gaming Commission. He asserts that while regulators give the appearance of being tough, they actually remain pawns of the industry. Enforcement personnel are unsophisticated when compared to their counterparts in the industry; if arrests are made, it is underlings who suffer, not the industry's policymakers. And the regulatory function is complicated by jurisdictional disputes among enforcement agencies and by the influx of corporate entities accompanied by complex business practices. Lester Snyder, "Regulation of Legalized Gambling: An Inside View," *Connecticut Law Review* 12 (1980): 665–726.

27. The federal government has by virtue of this stance decriminalized gambling in a de facto manner. Federal laws against the interstate transmission of wagering information (18 USC 1081,

1084) or the interstate transportation of wagering paraphernalia (18 USC 1953) are implemented on a selective fashion. Rarely, if ever, are they directed at a player or a consumer. For a more complete discussion of federal law as it relates to gambling enforcement, see G. Robert Blakey, "Legal Gambling Since 1950," *Annals of the American Academy of Political and Social Science* 474 (July 1984): 12–22; Kier T. Boyd, *Gambling Technology* (Washington, D.C.: Federal Bureau of Investigation, 1977); Cornell Law School, *The Development of the Law of Gambling* (Ithaca, N.Y.: Cornell University, 1977).

28. Money laundering is the process by which one conceals the existence, illegal source, or illegal application of income and then disguises that income to make it appear legitimate. Under the Bank Secrecy Act (31 USC 5311–22) and the federal Currency and Foreign Transactions Reporting Act, financial institutions must report domestic transactions valued at $10,000 or more. The President's commission recently recommended that this legislation be expanded to apply to casinos. See President's Commission on Organized Crime, *The Cash Connection: Organized Crime, Financial Institutions, and Money Laundering*, Interim Report to the President and the Attorney General, October 1984.

29. Jerome H. Skolnick, "A Zoning-Merit Model for Casino Gambling," *Annals of the American Academy of Political and Social Science* 474 (July 1984): 49.

30. Eugene M. Christiansen and Michael D. Shagan, "The New York Off-Track Betting Law: An Exercise in Selective Decriminalization," *Connecticut Law Review* 12 (1980): 868–69.

31. These arguments are summarized in greater detail by the National Advisory Committee on Criminal Justice Standards and Goals, *Organized Crime: Report of the Task Force on Organized Crime* (Washington, D.C., 1976). This report reflects the general tendency of the federal government to withdraw from gambling enforcement.

32. Reuter, *Disorganized Crime;* Floyd J. Fowler, Thomas W. Mangione, and Frederick E. Pratter, *Gambling Law Enforcement in Major American Cities* (Washington, D.C.: Department of Justice, 1978). This approach also has been called "benign prohibition" or the imposition of minimal legal sanctions on illegal gambling by law enforcement agencies. This occurs largely because gambling is a low-priority crime and the state does not want to devote the resources required for full-scale investigations and prosecutions of gambling activity. See I. Nelson Rose, "The Legalization and Control of Casino Gambling," *Fordham Urban Law Journal* 8 (1980): 245–300.

33. Dennis P. Hickman, "Should Gambling Be Legalized for Major Sports Events?" *Journal of Police Science and Administration* 4 (June 1976): 203–12.

34. "Kuhn, Majors Seek to Halt Canadian Betting Plan," *Baltimore Sun* (April 5, 1984). D–2.

35. Len Butcher, "A Quick Demise for Sport Select Baseball," *Gaming Business Magazine*, 5 August 1984, 50–51.

36. Ibid., p. 50.

37. John Merwin and David Whitford, "Betting Football," *Sport* 75 (November 1984): 26–43.

38. Relevant Delaware statutes included Delaware Code Ann. tit. 29 4803 (b) (1979). Interestingly, the same approach was taken when New York proposed a sports lottery in 1984. If sports betting is viewed as dependent on chance, it comes under state lottery laws, so new legislation or a constitutional amendment, as in the case of New York, is not required. The lack of sufficient statewide support prevented a wholesale move to establish the sports lottery in New York. The Delaware Football Lottery was aided by two federal actions directed at lotteries in general. President Ford signed Public Law 93–583 and 94–525 in January 1975 and October 1976, respectively. These laws legalized the interstate transportation of lottery tickets or materials into other states, the use of mails to send lottery tickets or materials into a lottery state, and the publication or broadcast of lottery information, price lists, and other information by the media.

39. National Football League v. Governor of Delaware, 435 F. Supp. 1372 (D. Delaware, 1977).

40. Skolnick, "Zoning-Merit Model for Casino Gambling." The applicant finances the investigation, which has the major purpose of making a determination that the applicant has the financial qualifications to operate the business and that the applicant shows a record of no involvement in criminal activity or no association with representatives of organized crime.

41. Constitutional challenges have been based on the due process clause of the Fourteenth Amendment. See State of Nevada v. Rosenthal, 93 Nev. 36 559 P.2d 830 (1977). Nevada's Black

Book contains the names and descriptions of fifteen persons who cannot use gaming facilities. License revocation is the penalty for any operator found hosting or associating with any of these listed individuals.

42. Christiansen, "Gross Annual Wager" (Handle Trends).

43. IRC 440 (a) as amended by Section 109(a) (1) of Public Law 97–362 (October 25, 1983). The wagering occupational tax was reduced from $500 to $50 per employee. These costs, being so small, are absorbed by the bookmaker and not charged back to the player. Such was not the case when the wagering tax was at 10 and 2 percent.

44. Suits, "Economic Background for Gambling Policy," p. 59. Numbers, if legalized, produces the highest return at $22.50 per capita, horse tracks generate $16.28 per capita, and casinos generate $1.73.

45. Christiansen and Shagan, "New York Off-Track Betting Law," p. 865. Initially, OTB and on-track betting had the same takeout rate of 17 percent. In 1975, a 5 percent surcharge for municipalities was permitted by the legislature (NY UNCONSOL LAW 8077). New York City did implement this surcharge. This stimulated on-track betting and reduced some of the animosity of racetrack operators to OTB, which was now more expensive for the bettor.

46. Suits, "Economic Background for Gambling Policy."

47. Ibid.

48. Ibid., p. 54.

49. George Sternlieb and James W. Hughes, "The Atlantic City Gamble" (Cambridge, Mass.: Harvard University Press, 1983), pointed out that net revenue from casinos in Atlantic City has not sufficiently met these three criteria. One analysis of lotteries points out that the revenue generated represents only 2 to 3 percent of state budgets. Many states, such as Pennsylvania and Connecticut, make a considerable amount of money on these lotteries, but they had to create new taxes anyway. State sales or income taxes have been shown to generate more dollars over time than lotteries. Lotteries also are viewed to be regressive. See also Kaplan, "Social and Economic Impact of State Lotteries," David Weinstein and Lillian Deitch, The Impact of Legalized Gambling: The Socioeconomic Consequences of Lotteries and Off-Track Betting (New York: Praeger, 1974).

50. John Boddie, "Parimutuel Sports Betting," Gaming Business Magazine, July 1983, pp. 52–55.

51. Suits, "Economic Background for Gambling Policy," p. 52.

52. Reuter, Disorganized Crime; Fowler, Mangione, and Pratter, Gambling Law Enforcement.

53. Reuter, Disorganized Crime. The decline of the dependence on a centralized wire service and the rise in sophistication of telephone technology has fragmented and decentralized the illegal bookmaking industry. It could be categorized as a low-capital cottage industry. This makes control more difficult either by police or a criminal hierarchy. It follows that police corruption via payoffs and protection by organized crime are no longer required to the extent they once were.

54. Klein, "Gallup Poll: Landslide for Gaming." The National Advisory Commission Study (1936) showed an approval rate of 80 percent.

55. Ibid., p. 20.

56. Robert Bezilla, "Legalized Sports Betting Faces Strong Opposition," Gaming and Wagering Business, (January 1985), p. 46. Legal racetrack betting draws a 60 percent approval; OTB is approved by only 41 percent of the population. Robert Bezilla, "The Public Doesn't Believe in the Traditional Myths of the Race Track," Gaming Business Magazine, July 1984, pp. 4–8, 37–44.

57. Ibid.

58. James H. Frey, "Gambling and College Sports: Views of Coaches and Athletic Directors," Sociology of Sport Journal 1 (1984): 36–45.

59. Ibid., p. 39.

60. Select Committee on Professional Sports, Inquiry into Professional Sports, Final Report of the Select Committee on Professional Sports, United States House of Representatives (January 1977), p. 137.

61. Ibid., p. 135.

62. Hickman, "Should Gambling Be Legalized?" p. 211.

63. "MISL Pushes for Legalized Betting on Its Games," Baltimore Sun, November 16, 1984, p. 10.

64. Ibid. Early in January 1985 a Las Vegas casino Sports Book announced that it would

accept wagers on an upcoming Professional Bowling Association (PBA) event in that city. Representatives of the PBA did not resist this action. When the United States Football League (USFL) started operations in 1983, officials of the new league were concerned that Las Vegas oddsmakers *would not* put up a line on the league's games. They knew that posting a betting line would stimulate interest in their league.

65. Merwin and Whitford, "Betting Football," p. 30.

66. Snyder, "Regulation of Legalized Gambling: An Inside View," *Connecticut Law Review* 12 (1980): 665–726.

67. G. Robert Blakey, "Legalizing Gambling Would Ruin Football," *USA Today*, May 17, 1983, p. A10.

68. Space does not permit a comparative analysis of the types of gambling that can be legalized. Some are more problematic for legalization than others. Lotteries, for example, are a more likely candidate for legalization since there is a high takeout rate, its control requirements are simpler, and large payouts are possible. For such a comparison, see Weinstein and Deitch, *The Impact of Legalized Gambling* (New York: Praeger, 1974).

12

The Sports Franchise Relocation Issue and Public Policy Responses

Arthur T. Johnson

In 1984 nearly fifty American cities hosted professional sports franchises in baseball, basketball, football, hockey, and indoor and outdoor soccer.[1] Each of these cities provided public subsidies that benefited their sports franchises. Nevertheless, since 1980, more than half of these cities have been confronted by the owners of one or more sports franchises with demands for increased public subsidies. The most common of these demands are reduced rent for the use of publicly owned stadiums and arenas, improvements to those facilities, the construction of new facilities at public expense, and tax abatements for privately owned sports facilities. Almost without exception, removal of the sports franchise from the host community is an implied, if not explicit, threat underlying the demands of sports franchise owners.

The relocation threat is built into the negotiating relationship between a team owner and local officials because there is always one or more cities willing to meet an owner's demands if officials of a team's host community are unwilling to do so. The excessive demand for sports franchises relative to their supply is a result of two factors: (1) the perception by municipal officials and local business interests that a sports franchise brings to a city net economic and social benefits, and (2) the cautious control of the supply of franchises by sports leagues. Professional sports franchise owners are able to extract financial concessions from their host communities by exploiting their bargaining advantage during lease negotiations and at other opportune times. If such concessions are not forthcoming, or if another city offers a more advantageous arrangement, owners are free to abandon a city despite the community's sustained economic and psychological investment in the team.[2]

The abandonment of Oakland by the National Football League's Raiders in 1982, despite league objections and a history of community support, stimulated public debate over the right of a sports franchise owner to relocate at will. Legislative interest in and the amount of litigation related to the

Table 12.1 Professional Sports Teams Within Standard Metropolitan Statistical Areas, 1984

SMSA	1980 RANK	Baseball	Basketball	Football	Hockey	Indoor & Outdoor Soccer
New York City[a]	1	2	X	3(U)	X	[h]
East Rutherford, N.J.[a]	1		X	2(U)	X	O[d]
Los Angeles–Long Beach	2	X	X[c]	2(U)	X	I—O[d]
Chicago	3	2	X	2(U)	X	
Philadelphia	4	X	X	2(U)	X	
Detroit	5	X	X	X	X	
San Francisco[a]	6	X		X	X	O
Oakland[a]	6	X		U		
Washington, D.C.–Md.–Va.	7		X	2(U)[e]	X	
Dallas–Ft. Worth	8	X	X	X		
Houston	9	X	X	2(U)		
Boston	10	X	X	X	X	
Nassau-Suffolk, N.Y.	11				X	I
St. Louis	12	X		X	X	
Pittsburgh	13	X		2(U)	X	
Baltimore	14	X				
Minneapolis–St. Paul	15	X		X	X	
Atlanta	16	X	X	X		U[n]
Newark, N.J.	17					
Anaheim–Santa Ana–Garden Grove	18	X				
Cleveland	19	X	X	X		
San Diego	20	X	X[c]	X		O[d]
Miami	21			X		
Denver–Boulder	22		X	2(U)		
Seattle–Everett	23	X	X	X		
Tampa–St. Petersburg	24			2(U)		
Riverside–San Bernadino–Ontario, Calif.	25					
Phoenix	26		X	U		O
Cincinnati–Ky.–Ind.	27	X		X		
Milwaukee	28	X	X	X[f]		[h]

City	(24/21)	(23/23)	(46/33)	(14/13)	(18/18)
Kansas City, Mo.–Kan. (29)	X		X		I
San Jose (30)	X		X	X	f,h
Buffalo (31)		X		X	
Portland (32)		X	2(U)		
New Orleans (33)		X	X		
Indianapolis (34)		X			
Columbus, Ohio (35)		X	U		
San Antonio (36)					
Ft. Lauderdale–Hollywood, Fla. (37)					
Sacramento (38)					
Rochester, N.Y. (39)					
Salt Lake City–Ogden, Utah (40)		X	U		j
Memphis, Tenn.–Ark.–Mis. (42)			U		
Birmingham (45)			U		
Jacksonville, Fla. (53)			U	X	
Hartford (54)			U[g]		
Tulsa (56)					O
Tacoma (81)					—
Wichita (94)					—
Total Teams/SMSA[b]	24/21	23/23	46/33	14/13	18/18

[a] Belongs to same SMSA.
[b] Excludes Canadian teams.
[c] San Diego franchise will play in Los Angeles in 1985.
[d] Has moved to the MISL from the NASL for the 1985 season.
[e] Will not play in Washington in 1985; future location unknown.
[f] Green Bay Packers play part of home schedule at Milwaukee.
[g] Expected to merge with another USFL franchise in 1985.
[h] New York franchise will not exist in 1985; Phoenix and Buffalo franchises have been given leaves of absence for 1985.

I. Major Indoor Soccer League franchise.
j. Memphis franchise will play in Las Vegas in 1985.
O. North American Soccer League franchise.
(U) Includes a United States Football League franchise.
X. One franchise. Numbers signify the number of franchises in a particular SMSA.
Un. This franchise will join the MISL in 1985. It formerly was an NASL franchise in 1983 and a United Soccer League franchise in 1984.

sports franchise relocation issue increased dramatically in 1984 as a result of subsequent relocations of the Baltimore Colts to Indianapolis, the New York Jets to East Rutherford, New Jersey, the San Diego Clippers to Los Angeles, and the potential departures of the Saints from New Orleans, the Twins from Minneapolis, the Indians from Cleveland, and the Mariners from Seattle. In fact, the sports franchise relocation issue promises to be the most important public policy issue in professional sports in the 1980s and 90s.

The issue brings into direct conflict the private property interests of team owners, the public interest of their host communities, and the sports leagues' interest in maintaining self-regulation. Franchise location is of economic and social significance to sports fans and their communities, and it is one of the few sports policy issues that directly involves policymakers at each level of government. In the future the franchise relocation issue will define the status of sports leagues for antitrust purposes, and it threatens to transform privately owned sports franchises into objects of public ownership.

The basic elements of the relocation problem must be understood before one can evaluate proposals to resolve it. This chapter first explores the causes of the excessive demand for professional sports teams relative to their supply. It then describes and evaluates public policy proposals and strategies designed to respond to the relocation issue. Finally, it notes the significance of this issue in terms of broader public policy considerations.

THE POLITICAL ECONOMY OF HOSTING SPORTS FRANCHISES

Cities continue to pursue professional sports franchises despite the owners' escalating demands and continuing franchise instability. In order to make a judgment as to the wisdom of such pursuit, it is necessary to distinguish between the actual and perceived benefits and costs of hosting professional sports teams. Civic boosters tend to inflate a team's benefits, while critics and muckrackers tend to underestimate or discount entirely their value. In fact, it is nearly impossible to measure accurately the net benefit or cost of a sports team to its host community.

Benefits of Having a Franchise

Commentators usually limit their attention to the amount of economic and social benefits a city derives from its sports teams. Direct economic benefits take the form of rental income, tax revenues, franchise expenditures in the community, and increased jobs. Indirect economic benefits include the additional business generated by fans and participants in related industries such as food, hotel, and transportation; the increased convention business a city attracts as a result of a team's presence; and the additional jobs produced by the secondary effects of a team's presence.

The overall economic impact of a sports team is estimated to be in the tens of millions of dollars. For example, the Green Bay Packers are said to produce $20–25 million annually for their community of 90,000 citizens; the Pittsburgh Pirates have been credited with more than $21 million worth of benefits; the Raiders accounted for $36 million in direct benefits and an additional $100 million in indirect economic benefits according to testimony of Oakland officials; the Jets infused $33 million annually into New York City's revenues; and the Colts generated approximately $30 million in direct and indirect revenue, Maryland officials estimate.[3] Disruptions in the playing seasons by players' strikes or owners' lockouts allegedly cost cities millions of dollars.[4] Alternatively, special sporting events such as the Super Bowl, league championship series, and All-Star games infuse millions of dollars into the local host economy.

Noneconomic or social benefits are more difficult to measure than a team's indirect economic impact. Social benefits include additional entertainment and recreational opportunities for citizens that improve a city's quality of life. More often cited, however, are the civic pride, community spirit, and prestige that a team brings to a city. Buffalo's widely praised "Talking Proud" civic campaign had as its centerpiece the Buffalo Bills football team. It is common journalistic lore that the Detroit Tigers' 1968 championship season helped heal the wounds of that city's racial riots that occurred a year earlier, just as the 1984 Tigers restored pride and spirit in a recession-scarred community. The following statements typify assertions of sports teams' social benefits:

> [Oakland] is a poor community. It has severe unemployment; it has had auto plant closings. But the one thing that has helped Oakland rebuild since its real demise began after the Second World War has been its professional sports franchises. It has been a unifying factor between labor and management and between poor and rich.[5]

> When we won the Super Bowl, we had a parade and a million people turned out. They represented every age group, every racial background, every economic and social value on earth. And they climbed on top of the Stock Exchange Building and they stood out on ledges of high rise buildings and they said one thing—thank you. And this is the public interest that exists in major league sports and football.[6]

Costs of Having a Franchise

The literature is consistent in that little attention is given to the costs associated with hosting a sports franchise.[7] Discussion of costs, when such does occur, usually is limited to facility construction costs or annual deficits of facilities. Costs, however, may take forms other than operational expenditures and bonded indebtedness. Opportunity costs of land use and foregone tax revenues are not analyzed. Costs for additional police protection, traffic control, and sanitation rarely are calculated.

Just as there are noneconomic benefits, noneconomic costs accompany a sports franchise. If a winning team can boost civic pride and enhance community prestige, it is logical to believe that a losing team can harm a city's image and reduce citizen morale. Pittsburgh was not always the "city of champions," but once was known equally for its losing teams and dirty smokestacks. Philadelphia and Boston have suffered in image because of their losing sports teams and surly fans. Buffalo is noted most for its fierce weather, thanks, in part, to nationally televised football games played in rain, snow, and mud.

Also, it can be questioned whether sports franchises are in fact accepted by an entire community. Historically, racism has been a part of sports, and it lingers still in some cities. The Pittsburgh Pirates consistently have trouble attracting fans despite fielding championship teams. Some believe Pittsburgh fans are reluctant to watch a team heavily populated by blacks and Hispanics.[8] The Phoenix Suns long remained a white team in a black-dominated league. Minority fans are harassed in the bleacher section of some ballparks. The move to the suburbs by several NFL clubs reflects the fact that the price of football tickets is beyond the reach of the poor. In such cases, sport can exacerbate rather than alleviate a community's racial tensions. If true, sports then will represent an unwanted cost rather than a desirable benefit.

Benjamin Okner concluded from his analysis of subsidies of sports facilities that the answer to the question of a sports franchise's community worth is arguable and that the answer hinges on the valuation of indirect and intangible benefits and costs.[9] In a study of Baltimore's support of the Colts and Orioles from 1977 to 1983, Johnson found that the city did receive financial benefits in excess of its direct expenditures in four of the seven years examined (see Table 12.2).[10] In one other year the net direct costs were minimal. Echoing Okner, Johnson concluded:

> Sports teams can be "worth it" if a sports facility can boast more than one major tenant (or is multi-purpose) and if negotiated concessions and/or bonded indebtedness do not exceed a certain point. . . . The question of worth becomes more debatable when only one tenant exists and/or concessions and/or debt service become excessive. . . . In all such instances, the worth of hosting sports teams can only be determined by the valuation of their net intangible and indirect benefits.[11]

Estimating a franchise's economic and social value to a community is therefore a subjective act. Not only must difficult-to-measure economic benefits and costs be calculated, but intangibles need to be evaluated as well.

Table 12.2 Public Revenue and Expenditures Attributable to Professional Baseball and Football in Baltimore, 1977–1983

Revenue source	1977[a]	1978	1979[b]	1980	1981[c]	1982[d]	1983[b]
Team rent	323,154	128,078[e]	835,001	623,975[e]	737,424	150,179	681,199[f]
Concessions, parking, and scoreboard advertising	106,382	105,664	461,009	403,577	402,369	287,296	453,030
Other stadium revenue	8,131	9,198	10,454	9,757	117,457	8,517	22,144
Admission tax from baseball	390,000	384,000	928,000	751,000	516,000	854,041	1,513,433
Admission tax from football	483,000[h]	437,000	367,000	428,000	439,000	178,100	479,241[g]
Total revenue	1,310,667[h]	1,063,940	2,601,464	2,216,309	2,212,250	1,478,133	3,149,047
Expenditures							
Memorial stadium	948,372	1,111,020	1,304,567	1,300,036	1,467,894	1,516,020	1,617,256
Police	364,923	395,450	498,244	522,032	441,681	567,017[g]	714,334[g]
Capital expenditures[i]	—	—	—	556	211,484	169,139	16,212
Debt Service	—	—	—	—	—	—	—
Total expenditures	1,313,295[h]	1,506,470	1,802,811	1,822,624	2,121,059	1,151,176	1,347,951
Net revenue	(2,628)	(442,530)	798,653	393,685	91,191	(774,043)	801,096

[a]All figures are based on the calendar year and include the full baseball and football seasons.
[b]Includes baseball playoffs and World Series.
[c]Baseball strike.
[d]Football strike, four home games played.
[e]Colts' rent due this year paid in succeeding year.
[f]Does not include Colts' rent, which was not paid as of April 1, 1984.
[g]Estimated by author.
[h]Includes seven regular season football games and one playoff game.
[i]City General Funds only. The state of Maryland has committed $1,000,000 annually since 1979 to capital improvements at Memorial Stadium.

Sources: City of Baltimore Accounting Operations Detail Register and Fiscal Division, City of Baltimore Police Department.

Further, the distribution of benefits and costs must be assessed in terms of political acceptability.[12] This process ultimately reflects political ideology and goals more than economic theory and calculation. Even when costs do exceed benefits, acquisition or retention of a team still can be justified. For example, if a new stadium can anchor an important redevelopment project and symbolize downtown rejuvenation, local officials will view the costs of a new stadium as acceptable when compared to those of continuing downtown deterioration.

Politically, local officials understand that the net cost of a franchise represents a very small fraction of the city's budget. Baltimore's budget in 1982, when the sports deficit was $774,000, was $1.6 billion. A net loss of even a million dollars has a negligible impact on taxpayers of a large city.[13] Local officials realize that the public's intense identity with its sports teams for the most part leads it to ignore or remain insensitive to the financial aspects of the teams' relationship to the city.

Cities pursue sports franchises for their perceived benefits, which, correctly or not, are believed to exceed public costs. In doing so, cities will subsidize franchise owners in many ways. Most often, these subsidies are provided through the lease arrangements for playing facilities. The actual dollars involved in lease negotiations will be of much greater importance to a team owner than to public officials who take into consideration a team's intangible net benefits. Thus we should not be surprised to find owners driving harder bargains and public officials making concessions in their pursuit of professional sports franchises.

THE MUNICIPAL PURSUIT OF PROFESSIONAL SPORTS FRANCHISES

A city that obtains a sports franchise can do so in one of three ways: (1) it can obtain an expansion franchise from an existing league; (2) it can be assigned a franchise in a newly formed league; or (3) it can seduce another city's franchise. These three municipal options are reviewed in this section.

If the initial option is adequate to provide a city capable of supporting a team with a franchise whenever it desires one, no reason exists to steal away another city's team. The balance of power at the negotiating table will be either equalized or tilted in the favor of municipalities. On the other hand, if the first two options are not adequate, seduction as a means of acquiring a sports franchise, with consequent intense intercity competition, is an understandable and common policy for cities that want to obtain a sports team.

If no reason exists to justify the courting of another city's sports team, legislation protecting a community's sports interests and restricting team movement can be justified. However, if it is agreed that professional sports events should be available to citizens on as broad a basis as is practical, and if league expansion or new league formation are not reasonable means of achieving that policy goal, then either intercity competition for teams and franchise relocation should be permitted or changes in professional sports league operations should be mandated.

It is argued that neither league expansion nor new league formation has proven to be practical means for cities to acquire sports teams. Although municipal officials will pursue any one of the three strategies, in reality the third option is the most practical means for acquiring a sports franchise.

New League Formation and League Expansion

New sports leagues have a checkered past. Before 1960 new leagues were relatively rare and not very successful. Since 1960, six new leagues have been attempted. In their first years none was accepted by the media or the public as being equivalent to established leagues. Franchises in each new league were viewed as "minor league." Acquiring a sports franchise in a new league therefore does not grant a community the "major league" status it seeks in terms of public image.

Each of the new leagues also experienced various degrees of instability. Two leagues, the American Basketball League (ABL) (1961–62) and the World Football League (WFL) (1974–75), did not survive longer than two years. During the leagues' brief existence, the locations, names, and ownership of franchises in these leagues changed frequently. In the remaining four leagues, approximately fifty franchise failures and/or relocations occurred.[14]

Despite their instability, three of the leagues—the American Football League (AFL), the World Hockey Association (WHA), and the American Basketball Association (ABA)—were able to mount a credible challenge to their existing competitors. This eventually led to either a merger with or an absorption by the older league. Only the AFL survived merger without losing franchises, which was a condition for receiving congressional approval of the NFL-AFL merger.[15] The fate of the recently formed United States Football League (USFL) is unclear at this writing. Several of its franchises are displaying signs of financial weakness and instability. Many predict that a small number of USFL franchises will be absorbed eventually by the NFL and the remaining USFL franchises will be dissolved.

A city with a sports franchise in a new league therefore cannot be certain of the permanency of its franchise as a result of the instability of new leagues. It should not be surprising that cities, when faced with a choice, have preferred an expansion team in the established league to that of a franchise in a newly created league. This explains in part the expansion strategy of the established leagues. Expansion has coincided closely with the announcement of new leagues and has brought expansion franchises into the potential markets of the new leagues.

Cities that desire an expansion franchise actively lobby the leagues to expand to their locale. In addition to traditional lobbying tactics, which become most visible at annual league meetings, cities have staged specific sports events, such as exhibition or old-timers games, for the purpose of demonstrating fan interest and support.

The problem of course is that leagues carefully limit the number of franchises. League officials assert that this is necessary to maintain a certain quality of on-the-field play and to avoid losing fan interest through oversaturation. The more important consequence of limiting the supply of teams is to increase the dollar value of existing franchises. Between 1975 and 1984 only six expansion franchises were granted by the four major leagues combined.

Once an expansion team is acquired, a string of losing seasons is nearly certain. Depending on the competitive progress of the team, declining fan support may threaten its financial viability, thus tempting the franchise owner to look for a new location. Since 1970, two of five NBA expansion franchises and two of six NHL expansion franchises have relocated, and one of these moved twice. Not one of the WHA or ABA expansion franchises survived merger or league absorption.

Thus, if a city depends on league expansion to acquire a sports team, it faces keen competiton for a very limited number of franchises. It has no control over when expansion franchises become available. Also, it is important to note that a city competing for an expansion franchise must persuade at least a majority of team owners, each with their own biases and favorites, that it is worthy, whereas a city seeking a team by relocation has to convince only one owner of its worth. For these reasons, it is not surprising that cities more often seek to attract an existing franchise from another city rather than wait for an expansion franchise, and that opportunities to do so present themselves more frequently than do league-expansion opportunities.

Intercity Competition for Sports Franchises

A city seeking a franchise cannot target for relocatioin any team it desires. Many owners are loyal to their host communities and view their teams as integral to the cities' identities.[16] The teams of these civic-minded owners therefore are unavailable for relocation. Also, teams are tied to cities for a specific number of years by their leases to use playing facilities.

Nevertheless, in any given year it appears that one or more teams in each league are entering their final year of a lease or entering an option year, after which an owner no longer legally is bound to remain in the community. For example, as reported in Table 12.3, from 1985 to the year 2012, in every two-year period except two at least one baseball team's lease expires, giving its owners the right to consider relocation. Also, a few owners have negotiated "buy-out" clauses, which permit them to relocate at will with the payment to the city of a specified amount of money, or they have negotiated terms that permit relocation during the lease under specific conditions, such as failure to meet a certain attendance level.[17]

It is difficult to generalize as to why an owner desires to relocate. A variety of reasons motivate franchise owners, including inadequate, deteriorating, or outmoded facilities in the present community, poor public relations or acrimonious relations with the local media, a relatively small television

Table 12.3   Stadium Lease Expiration Dates for Major League Baseball Franchises

Year Lease Expires	Team
1985	Cleveland (currently under negotiations)
1986	Baltimore
1988	San Diego, Oakland
1990	Atlanta
1991	Toronto
1994	Montreal, San Francisco
1995	Milwaukee
1997	Seattle
2001	Philadelphia, Anaheim
2002	New York Yankees
2004	Houston
2007	Detroit, Cincinnati
2008	Kansas City
2009	New York Mets
2011	Pittsburgh
2012	Minneapolis

Teams playing in privately owned stadiums: Chicago White Sox and Cubs, Boston, Texas, Los Angeles, and St. Louis.

market that limits the team's profit potential, lack of fan support, or the necessity to share facilities with other tenants.

Suitor cities seek to exploit whatever appears to be an owner's disincentive for staying put. They also offer a wide array of incentives beyond low rent and generous shares of parking and concession revenues. These have included free use of training facilities built with public funds, lucrative real estate arrangements, absorption of a team's debt, loans at interest rates well below the market rate, profitable broadcasting agreements, and guaranteed ticket sales. The competiton for teams has become so intense that cities are investing tens of millions of dollars in new sports complexes with only a hope—no promises—of a tenant to help repay their costs.[18]

In sum, cities seek sports franchises as a matter of public policy because of the perceived economic and social benefits derived from hosting a sports team. The inadequacy of either expansion or new league formation as a means of acquiring a team forces cities into competition with one another for existing teams. The means of competition have become various kinds of public subsidies, including large public investments in modern playing facilities. The excessive demand for sports teams relative to their supply makes it possible for owners to escalate their demands for subsidies and to threaten to relocate if the host community resists. The owner's threats are made credible by the willingness of other cities to meet the owner's demands. Thus, in the absence of external intervention, the balance of power in the city-team relationship rests in favor of sports franchise owners.

POLICY OPTIONS TO THE RELOCATION PROBLEM

If a sports team owner exploits his or her advantage to force a city to make financial concessions that are unwise economically, any concept of partnership between the city and its team becomes meaningless, and the local public interest is threatened. In such cases, cities will seek to alter the basis for their teams' advantage. It will be less expensive and potentially more profitable for cities to seek legislative or judicial means to modify the negotiating balance of power and thereby resolve to their advantage the relocation problem. In this section, five policy options to the relocation problem are described and evaluated.

Congress: Self-Regulation and Antitrust Immunity

Professional sports leagues historically have controlled franchise relocation decisions. Each league requires the approval by a significant percentage of its member franchises of proposals to relocate.[19] The federal courts have found that the NFL relocation rule fails to meet the test of the "rule of reason" and therefore violates federal antitrust law. The district court suggested that requirement of a simple majority vote rather than three-fourths approval might meet the rule of reason.[20] The Court of Appeals of the Ninth Circuit suggested:

> To withstand anti-trust scrutiny, restrictions on team movement should be more closely tailored to serve the needs inherent in producing the NFL "product". . . . An express recognition and consideration of those objective factors espoused by the NFL as important, such as population, economic projections, facilities, regional balance, etc. would be well advised.[21]

The refusal, in November 1984, by the United State Supreme Court to accept the NFL appeal of the decision of the Ninth Circuit Court leaves unanswered the question whether a more reasonable percentage approval requirement in fact would be accepted by the courts. That question will be answered in the NBA's suit initiated in June 1984 to nullify the San Diego Clippers move to Los Angeles. The NBA case should apply to all sports leagues except professional baseball, which enjoys judicially granted immunity from federal antitrust laws.[22]

Sports leagues have been sued or threatened with legal action by abandoned cities for permitting a franchise to relocate, as well as by cities and owners for opposing relocation.[23]Thus the leagues argue that they need a clear affirmation of their right to determine francise location so that they can conduct their business in an orderly manner. The leagues, led by the NFL, have sought antitrust immunity from Congress so that relocation rules can be implemented without fear of costly litigation.

In an attempt to head off the Raiders' move to Los Angeles, the NFL in 1981 sought legislation that would have defined sports leagues as "de facto single economic entities." If accepted as a single economic entity, a sports league would enjoy blanket immunity from the antitrust laws, since a "contract, combination or conspiracy" between at least two independent enterprises is necessary to violate Section One of the Sherman Act. The NFL's legislative efforts in 1981 failed.

Since 1981, the NFL's legislative efforts have sought more narrowly defined protection. In 1982, even as the Raiders were playing in Los Angeles, the league vigorously lobbied for legislation—the Professional Sports Community Protection Act of 1982 (S.2784)—that would have made league franchise relocation rules and revenue sharing practices immune from antitrust laws. The proposed legislation would have applied retroactively to the Raiders' move to Los Angeles. The NFL continued in 1984, to no avail, to seek such protection and retroactive authority.

The leagues argue not only that they must have clear authority to determine franchise location in order to avoid chaos, but that they are the only parties that can protect municipal interests in their dealings with franchise owners. Senate Bill 2784 and its subsequent versions would protect community interests from *ownership* desires to relocate, but permit *league* decisions approving relocation. League officials in their congressional testimony supporting S.2784, however, did not reveal any criteria used to evaluate relocation proposals, nor did they propose such criteria.

History suggests that no sports league has protected its host communities adequately. For example, between 1950 and 1982 eleven relocations occurred in baseball, forty in basketball, fourteen in hockey, and thirteen in football.[24] When the rare league rejections of proposed moves have occurred, they were directed at owners who were labeled as "mavericks" (such as Charles O. Finley and Al Davis). In addition, there is no evidence that the sports leagues have attempted to dampen owner demands for increased public subsidies. Thus, if a sports community is to be protected, not only must its team be retained, but the city's treasury must be defended as well.

Professional sports leagues are composed of franchise owners. It is naive to believe that relocation proposals will be rejected by the league with much frequency, since the owners voting on another's request may someday have a request of their own on the table. However, if the relocation rule allows one or a small number of owners to veto requests, and if a proposed relocation threatens an owner's interests, then that owner may be expected to attempt to block the move. Even so, when this situation has arisen, owners often have worked out arrangements like indemnification payments that permit the move. Such a settlement, for example, permitted the Nets to move to New Jersey. League commissioners, who are hired and fired by the franchise owners, are of little help on these matters. The commissioners are perceived correctly as representatives of the owners, not of the players or host communities. They might take action against a single owner, but rarely will they defy owner consensus on an issue.

Sports leagues will not support restrictive legislation or judicial action designed to protect municipal interests. To do so would endanger the value of each owner's franchise as well as an owner's right to do with the franchise whatever he or she pleased. This is illustrated by the NFL's opposition in 1982 and 1984 to congressional legislation that would establish criteria that must be met before relocation would be permitted (S.2821 and S.2505, respectively).[25]

In sum, sports leagues argue for self-regulation and assert their willingness and ability to protect community interests. History and logic suggest that this policy option will not protect those interests. Nevertheless, definitive clarification of the leagues' status under antitrust laws should be made so that all interests understand what the leagues may and may not do with regard to relocation.

Congress: Restrictive Legislation

In 1982, mayors of the several professional sports communities supported the NFL's position on S.2784.[26] Since then, however, several of these mayors have sought legislative relief in proposals that go beyond the leagues' desire for self-regulation. A variety of options has been suggested. The most popular have been those that would force owners to demonstrate that one or more conditions have been met before they are allowed to relocate[27] and those that require that, before relocation is permitted, officials in a community threatened with the loss of its team be given the "right of first refusal" to match or better whatever offers might be luring the franchise away. Legislation incorporating both requirements was reported favorably from the Senate's Commerce Committee in June 1984, but it was not acted upon.[28]

Such restrictive legislation will be much more effective than self-regulation in protecting community interests. It will solve the relocation problem to the extent that owners will not be able to move their franchises at will, and it will tilt the balance of power in the negotiating relationship between city officials and team owners to the advantage of the former. As a result, public subsidies likely would decline, with a consequent decline in the value of sports franchises.

Passage of restrictive legislation, however, will be difficult. The sports leagues will oppose any legislation that threatens the financial value of franchises. It is unlikely that the players' unions will support the legislation, since a decline in public subsidies eventually will translate into less money available for players' salaries.[29] Combined opposition of players and owners usually is enough to kill any sports legislation.[30]

A second problem in gaining the adoption of restrictive legislation is that it has been designed to regain the Raiders for Oakland and, more recently, the Colts for Baltimore. That is, the legislation either has been retroactive or, as with one amended version of S.2505, has provided the NFL with an incentive—exemption from the law's restrictions—to place a team in Baltimore by league expansion before 1987. Giving favor to any city will attract opposition from representatives of communities that also are seeking franchises. Additionally, opposition will continue out of concern for potential constitutional problems related to the retroactive nature of the legislative proposals.

The relevant question, however, is whether such restrictive legislation is good public policy. The argument of this analysis is that congressional intervention to restrict franchise relocation is not good public policy. The argument for rejection can be made on several grounds.

First, it is arguable that the public interest dictates the need for such legislation. Two premises of restrictive legislation are that a sports team is essential to a city's well-being and that all sports teams should be treated alike. Clearly, however, not all sports franchises within a community are essential to that community's well-being, nor are they of equal importance. An indoor-soccer team that attracts an average of 8,000 fans to its games is of doubtful importance to a city's fiscal condition. It is debatable whether or not a football team that attracts 50,000 fans for eight home dates is as imporant as a baseball team that attracts an average of 20,000 fans for 82 home games.

Some who assert the necessity of sports to a community argue that sports franchises are analogous to public utilities. Lowell and Weistart, however, argue that general principles of law reject the sport as public utility argument:

> It would be difficult to argue that a local sports franchise has the characteristics of a public utility as that term has been historically applied. While the services it offers may be of economic importance, that fact alone has not traditionally provided a reason for judicial control. Any firm with a large payroll or significant sales may be important to the local economy. The element missing from a sports operation, and from most other significant local enterprises, is the presence of an activity affecting the basic public need for food, shelter, and sanitation. Even if the concept of "public welfare" were expanded to include emotional well-being, it would require a quantum leap to find that privately-run forms of entertainment were of vital importance. In short, there is little law to support the application of public utility concepts to sports enterprises.[31]

Further, the public utility argument misses the point that the public financial investment is in the playing facility (stadium or arena) and not the team as such. The facility remains after the team's departure and, theoretically, can prove profitable without the team. It is possible that a facility could have more frequent and more profitable bookings when the sports team is not a primary tenant.[32] Adoption of legislation based on the premises of the public utility argument will lead to inconsistent treatment of franchises, since not all teams make use of public facilities (especially in basketball and hockey). Finally, acceptance of the public utility argument also would make vulnerable to the same government action, by analogy, other users of public facilities.

More important, professional sports is not a unique industry either in terms of receiving public subsidies or in terms of being able to locate its operations wherever entrepreneurs desire. Public subsidies from local governments commonly are targeted to individual businesses (for example, by the use of Industrial Revenue Bonds and local tax abatements and exemptions).[33] Cities that are anxious about their economic future are in a vulnerable situation vis-à-vis entrepreneurs of all types. The leverage exerted on and benefits received from city governments by sports entrepreneurs are not unusual. Nonsports businesses are free to locate new operations where they please, as well as to shut down operations in one locale in favor of another whenever it is deemed appropriate.

Neither the 95th (H.R. 76) nor the 96th (S.1609) Congress chose to adopt the National Employment Priorities Act, which was designed to respond to the economic and social impacts of plant closings and relocations. Thus it is necessary for supporters of restrictive legislation to demonstrate conclusively how sports operations are different from other business ventures. If Congress is convinced to act, it then will be necessary to explain why other industries should not be treated similarly in achieving community protection.

A further objection to restrictive legislation is that Congress is responsible for the "public interest" in a broader sense than that represented by fifty cities. The restrictive options, in essence, propose to freeze the status quo with regard to the distribution of professional sports franchises, to the disadvantage of those cities without sports franchises but that desire a team. This is contrary to past congressional concerns with making professional sports available to as broad a geographical area as possible.[34]

If legislation is to be based on the policy assumption that it is desirable and beneficial for communities to host sports teams, it is logical that the broad public interest dictates that any city capable of supporting a team should be permitted the opportunity to do so. There should be no need to entice another city's team if cities reasonably can expect to acquire a sports franchise either by league expansion or by the creation of a new league. In such a case, restrictive legislation is reasonable to promote league stability and to minimize public expenditure. However, since neither league expansion nor new league formation has proven to be satisfactory options for teamless cities, intercity competition should be permitted (certainly not restricted) until league operations are modified so that the public policy goal of having the broadest possible access to live professional sports can be achieved.

Finally, it is clear that restrictive policy proposals abridge the franchise owners' property rights. It is beyond the scope of this chapter to analyze in detail the constitutional arguments that would be raised in the aftermath of restrictive legislation. Suffice it to note that significant litigation challenging such legislation is certain.[35]

In sum, legislation that restricts the right of team owners to relocate is poor public policy. However, restrictive legislation will resolve the sports franchise relocation problem in that the legislation proposes to make it more difficult, if not impossible, to relocate a franchise and thereby radically alter the balance of power to the city's advantage. Support for such legislation primarily comes from representatives of those cities that have been abandoned recently by teams. Most such proposals therefore are designed to return the teams to the abandoned cities, and they tend to be retroactive. With or without the retroactive conditions, Congress faces the difficult task of balancing community interests against significant private property interests of franchise owners.

Judicial Relief: The Issue of Eminent Domain

Abandoned sports communities have not placed their hopes for regaining their teams solely on congressional intervention. In the past, they have sought judicial rulings that proposed that relocations violated antitrust laws. Lowell and Weistart, however, demonstrate that use of federal antitrust laws by municipalities to prevent relocations is difficult and unlikely to succeed.[36] For example, even though Milwaukee was successful in its effort to block the Braves' move to Atlanta in its lower state courts, the state supreme court ruled that the franchise relocation did not violate federal antitrust law.[37]

A more interesting and significant approach being tested by the cities of Oakland and Baltimore is the use of state and local eminent domain laws in the struggle to force the return of their teams.[38] The Oakland and Baltimore cases differ in several ways. The former involves an intrastate move, while the latter challenges an interstate relocation. Oakland is basing its actions on an interpretation of a liberally revised state eminent domain law that does not refer specifically to the "taking" of a sports franchise. Baltimore, on the other hand, bases its actions on specific legislation that authorizes the "taking" of sports franchises. Questions about the legal location of both franchises (necessary to know in order to determine the cities' right to take the franchises) complicate both cases, but they are much more complex in the Baltimore case.[39] At issue is whether or not the Colts franchise had already relocated—that is, was beyond the state's jurisdiction—at the time the legislation was signed into law.

Baltimore and Oakland argue that their states' eminent domain laws permit the "taking" of intangible property such as sports franchises. They argue that the large sums of public money invested to support the Colts and Raiders put the teams in the public domain. Their success hinges on the argument that sports franchises serve a public purpose and constitute a public use that is important, if not essential, to the communities' economic and social well-being. In essence, they rely upon the "sport as public utility" argument.

The cities intend to pay the teams' owners fair compensation and to resell the teams to local interests who will pledge not to remove the franchises from their cities.[40] It is assumed that individuals can be found who are willing to buy the franchises at their court-determined value. However, if this does not occur, and the resale takes place at a level below the court's determination of the teams' value, the cities will have to make up the difference from their tax funds. The resale tactic is necessary at this point because league rules that forbid municipal ownership have not been challenged.

Team owners, on the other hand, argue that the franchises are intangible property and therefore not subject to eminent domain laws. They contend that their teams neither constitute a valid municipal use nor serve a public purpose in the legal sense. Finally, they argue that the eminent domain laws do not permit resale of condemned property to private interests for their use and profit.[41] These cases are expected to reach the Supreme Court. They raise two questions: (1) Will the Supreme Court permit the condemnation of sports franchises under state eminent domain laws? (2) Is eminent domain a practical solution to the relocation issue?

Obviously, it is difficult to predict the outcome of cases that are in their early stages. The 1984 Supreme Court decision, *Hawaii Housing Authority et al.* v. *Midkiff et al.*,[42] however, provides a precedent favoring the cities' position. In an 8–0 decision, the court ruled that eminent domain powers are a matter for state legislators to define. Since local and state governments know best what constitutes public use within their borders, the federal courts should refuse to second-guess their decisions. The court did not object to the resale of land to private parties.

Whether the court will use this decision as precedent in the Oakland and Baltimore cases is debatable. Intangible property is at stake in the cities' cases. The taking of such property suggests that there is no limit to a state's eminent domain powers. The retention of a sports team is of less obvious social significance than the goals of land reform. Eminent domain actions that obstruct relocation to another state may be seen as interfering with interstate commerce, the protection of which may be determined to be more important than a locality's need for a sports franchise. Further, the arguments advanced in the previous section suggest the weakness of a public utility rationale to justify the taking of a sports franchise.

If the court permitted the condemnation of sports franchises, it would be difficult not to permit the taking of businesses—banks, manufacturing plants, hospitals, virtually any commercial or cultural entity—that threaten to relocate.[43] It remains arguable whether or not the court will risk an epidemic of attacks on private property by fiscally distressed cities that must compete for the presence of industry and commerce within their borders. Thus, assuming no early settlement and no legislative intervention, the conservative Burger Court will be asked to resolve a conflict between states' rights and private property interests.

Without judging the merits of either city's case, and regardless of what the court decides, the eminent domain strategy can lead to broader difficulties if it is utilized. First, it requires states to enact legislation either broad enough to permit a taking of sports franchises or specific enough so as to identify sports franchises as eligible for condemnation. If the former approach is pursued, all types of property become vulnerable to taking—a consequence that will not be received well by various interests within the state. If the latter approach is followed, the legislature may appear to be excluding other similar types of property not identified in the legislation. This would make other eminent domain actions more difficult. Further, if a state independently makes sports franchises subject to eminent domain action, it will cause owners of new franchises and those seeking to relocate to avoid any city within the state.[44] Thus, unless a state's cities have all the franchises they desire, the legislation is likely to be self-defeating.

Nevertheless, such legislation, if upheld by the courts, is a solution to the relocation problem and alters the balance of power to the city's advantage. State legislators therefore must decide whether or not to attempt to keep existing sports franchises within their state by the threat of eminent domain at the risk of frightening away potential new sports franchises (and possibly other businesses) and opening a Pandora's box with regard to eminent domain in general. The fact that no other state has moved in this direction suggests that this is not a practical solution to the relocation problem.

Reduced Barriers to League Entry

A fourth option, which few have been willing to support, is to force leagues to reduce the barriers to membership. If, as was argued earlier, the essence of the relocation problem is the limited supply of league franchises, then easier league entry would allow a city to replace a lost franchise without much difficulty. If this is possible, the impact of the loss of a franchise on a city would not be great. This possibility creates a more equitable balance of power between local officials and team owners. At the same time, the property rights of franchise owners would be preserved. Owners argue, however, that if easier entry is mandated, playing quality will decline, since there is a limited number of quality players. If player quality declines, it is asserted, fan interest and attendance also will decrease, with a consequent loss of gate receipts and television revenues. League stability will descend into chaos, further dampening fan interest and team revenues.

Similar arguments were raised in the past in opposition to league expansion. Although player quality may have declined after expansion, it cannot be demonstrated that professional sports have suffered. In fact, the relationship between player quality and fan interest is unclear. Many believe that the spectator is merely interested in a sports contest where the outcome is uncertain. According to this view, fan interest and attendance will be maintained as long as competing teams are relatively equal in ability and the outcomes of individual contests and season-long campaigns are somewhat uncertain. Weistart and Lowell, however, argue that unlimited league entry will result in such competitive imbalance that fan interest will decline and owners' investments in their teams will be endangered.

> A legal rule mandating unrestrained entry of new franchises without regard to their potential profitability would seemingly have one of two effects, neither of which is desirable from the perspective of investors, fans, nor the cities housing the clubs. If there were complete freedom of entry, leagues would either have to extend their subsidization to all new entrants, and face the risk that the shared-

resources would be severely diluted, or eliminate the subsidy arrangements and require that each franchise stand on its own financial feet. In either case, it is likely that the degree of competitive imbalance within the league would be greatly increased, and the quality of the league's product would diminish, with a resultant loss of fan and investor enthusiasm.[45]

While these arguments appear to be reasonable, it also is true that the case for reducing barriers to league entry has not been given serious study, especially as a means for resolving the franchise relocation problem.[46] Without a doubt, professional sports as we know them will be transformed radically if an unlimited entry option is forced upon the leagues. However, there is little reason to believe that adequate arrangements could not be found to allow rational operation of sports leagues with reduced barriers to league entry.

Neither this proposal nor others that have been advanced suggests that league entry should be completely without restraints. For example, cities seeking franchises could be required to meet a minimum population requirement and have adequate playing facilities in place. Prospective team owners could be required to demonstrate a minimal level of financial solvency, perhaps posting a bond of a substantial amount to protect the league against a team's financial failure. Cities in which franchises fail financially might be required to wait five years or longer before reentry into the league. Once interest in a franchise is announced and all entry requirements are met, a two-year waiting period could be imposed to permit the franchise's management team to organize itself, to learn about league operations, to promote the new team, and to prepare facilities. This also would allow the league sufficient time to schedule. New teams could be stocked by drafts of unprotected players from existing teams (with payment of reasonable compensation), from the amateur ranks, or from the minor leagues.

It is doubtful that a reduction of league entry barriers will intensify the competitive imbalance that already exists under current league arrangements. Table 12.4 reveals that no league is free from such imbalance. Revenue could be shared more equally among teams with easier league entry than is done at present in order to equalize opportunity for on-the-field success. A reduction in the barriers to league entry therefore does not imply that competition will be uninteresting or less attractive to sports fans.

It is uncertain to what degree government is able to mandate an economic association to open its membership. Since unlimited membership would likely devalue existing franchises, adequate compensation from new franchises might be ordered. If compensation requirements were excessive, however, new franchises would be placed at a serious disadvantage, perhaps ensuring prophecies of failure. But without adequate compensation, judicial challenges to easier league entry that was mandated legislatively might succeed.

Although the players' associations would welcome the increase in the number of new jobs that easier league entry would bring, they would not welcome the probable drop in salaries and greater mobility that would be forced on athletes. If salaries declined as a result of lower team revenues, it is unlikely that the decline would reach an unacceptably low level. Indeed, if one believes that athletes' salaries are grossly inflated today, their decline may be a socially acceptable consequence of easier league entry. On the other hand, it could occur that easier league entry will increase the bidding for players' talents and further inflate salaries.

Facilitating league entry therefore is a potential solution to the franchise

Table 12.4   Distance Between First Place and Last Place Teams, 1984

	Games behind
Major League Baseball (162-game season)	
American League – East	36.5
American League – West	14.5
National League – East	21.5
National League – West	26
National Basketball Association (82-game season)	
Atlantic Division	27
Central Division	24
Midwest Division	16
Pacific Division	24
National Football League (1983, 16-game season)	
AFC – Eastern Division	5
AFC – Central Division	8
AFC – Western Division	6
NFC – Eastern Division	10.5
NFC – Central Division	3
NFC – Western Division	7
United States Football League (18-game season)	
Eastern Conference – Atlantic Division	13
Eastern Conference – Southern Division	8
Western Conference – Central Division	8
Western Conference – Pacific Division	3
North American Soccer League (32-game season)	11
Major Indoor Soccer League (48-game season)	
Eastern Division	19
Western Division	8

	Points behind
National Hockey League (80-game season)	
Patrick Division	66
Adams Division	38
Norris Division	27
Smythe Division	60

relocation problem in that it attacks the issue from the supply side rather than imposing regulatory mechanisms on present league arrangements. It protects community interests, while minimally affecting team owners' property interests. However, proposals to reduce the barriers to league entry contradict the traditional cartel arrangements of sports leagues. Adoption of legislation mandating easier entry thus is unlikely because of its radical nature. League interests likely would be successful in mobilizing public sentiment against such a proposal. It will require a strong coalition of franchiseless communities and much public education to provide a serious hearing for this policy option.

Local Self-Help Strategies

Without a resolution of the relocation problem by means of government intervention, city officials must seek their own local means of protecting their treasuries while retaining their teams. Local officials must develop political strategies and local policy responses, since they negotiate with team owners from a position of weakness. It is essential that municipal officials perceive their relationship with team owners as being a consequence of local public policy decisions and accept as a policy option the possibility of permitting their teams to relocate. Not only must the public be made to understand that providing excessive subsidies to team owners undermines the local public interest, but officials must remain free from the control of those interests, especially the business community and media, which favor retention of sports franchises at whatever cost.

The policy goal of sports communities should be to lock a team into an ironclad long-term lease containing few options and a clause giving local interests a right of first refusal to purchase the team before relocation is permitted. Since there is little reason to expect owners to accept such a lease, officials must employ tough negotiation tactics as well as incentives. Local officials should not feel that they lack incentives to offer, since most cities with teams are attractive locations with a desirable market and existing facilities. If modern facilities are in place, an owner will be reluctant to abandon the city.

It will be more difficult for an owner to use public opinion as leverage against a city's negotiators if the public is educated about the degree to which a team costs a city money. Even though public sentiment initially may favor a team owner, poor public relations as a result of bitter lease negotiations (with their implicit threats of relocation) can prove more harmful financially to a team owner than the concessions he or she must make to avoid protracted negotiations.

Special incentives can be a device to convince an owner to sign a lease that is advantageous to a city. For example, favorable terms early in the lease's life may be an incentive, as might other financial arrangements that play to an owner's tax needs. Each negotiating situation will be different. What is crucial is that city negotiators be equal to the task, and that mayors and other political leaders provide the policy direction and support necessary to signal the owner and the public that the negotiators have their unified backing. Without professional negotiators and unified support, owners will maintain their bargaining advantage.

It also is necessary that a host community's state and neighboring jurisdictions assist the city in supporting a team. The benefits of a team's presence flow beyond a city's boundaries, much more so than its costs. In today's economic climate, the desirability of regional support for cultural and recreational activities is increasingly necessary and logical. The loss of a team will hurt the state and neighboring jurisdictions as well as the host city. It is in their interests therefore, as well as the host community's, that the latter retains its teams with the strongest lease possible.

Similarly, private sector interests who benefit economically from a team's presence should be expected to share in the cost of retaining the team. This is especially true when the construction of a new sports facility is under consideration. The financing of modern sports facilities should be a joint effort of those interests who will benefit from use of the facility—the team owner, the local business community, and the public (that is, a city, its neighboring jurisdictions, and the state). Funding a multimillion dollar sports facility strictly with general obligation bonds is no longer practical financially and is likely to lead to political conflict. A team owner can contribute financially by agreeing to a lease that is of sufficient duration to allow amortization of the facility's debt and sufficiently rewarding to the city to provide coverage of the team's fair share of the facility's operating costs. Refusal of these conditions on the part of an owner should lead city officials to resist all demands for a new facility.

Maintaining the status quo obviously preserves the owner's property rights and keeps in place the existing bargaining relationship between a team and city. It is suggested that local officials do have the means of altering that relationship more to the city's favor. The risk in attempting to do so is the loss of a city's team. To take that risk is a policy decision, the viability of which only local officials can judge.

SUMMARY AND CONCLUSIONS

The sports relocation issue is a complex public policy issue with implications for the future of professional sports. It presents policymakers with many of the same dilemmas and quandaries that other public policy issues do.

Essentially, the issue brings into conflict with one another the property interests of the owners, the public interest of communities and their states, and the management interests of the sports leagues.

There is little to suggest that the option of self-regulation will protect the interests of municipalities. It also is arguable that self-regulation protects the property interests of individual owners, especially if they tend to be mavericks. It is unlikely that the leagues will be able to use this issue to obtain a broad antitrust immunity either from Congress or the courts. The cynic, however, does recognize the possibility that the NFL will be able to receive from Congress the power over franchise relocation that it seeks in exchange for expansion franchises in the home territories of key congressmen.

The options of restrictive legislation, which virtually freezes teams where they are at present, and condemnation of franchises through the use of eminent domain resolve the issue to the advantage of local communities at the expense of team owners and the leagues. Restrictive legislation is unlikely to succeed as long as the owners and leagues oppose it. If a rash of relocations occur over a short time, however, their opposition may not be sufficient to neutralize congressional reaction, especially if franchises within the constituencies of key congressmen are lost. Ironically, if the legislation is not retroactive, those communities that have lost a team may be frozen out of professional sports by its adoption. The potential success of the eminent domain strategy strikes at the heart of the sacredness of private property and has radical implications beyond professional sports. For that reason, it will not be surprising to see the Supreme Court find reasons to reject or ignore the cities' eminent domain arguments. However, if the Court accepts those arguments, professional sports legally will be in the public domain, providing the necessary justification for further government regulation of the industry.

It is noteworthy that the least discussed option, that of reducing barriers to league entry, appears to protect the interests of all parties. Although the leagues will have lost control over the membership process, the remaining elements of their operating procedures remain untouched. If sport is as vital to economic and social well-being as the cities suggest, it appears equitable and good public policy to permit all communities with the resources to support sports teams to do so. Rejection of this proposal should occur only either when league expansion or league creation becomes a realistic means for a city to acquire a professional sports franchise or when convincing evidence is presented to support the league officials' and team owners' prophecies of doom. Both are absent at present.

Finally, the status quo as policy option emphasizes the property interests of team owners. This chapter has suggested that it is necessary for local officials to determine how important a sports team is to their community, and as a matter of explicit policy to act on that determination. The analysis suggests that the balance of power between a city and its team may be modified in many instances with professionals negotiating for the cities, and that permitting a team to depart is an acceptable policy option.

The sports relocation issue makes clear that the relationship between a city and its team is a tenuous and uneasy partnership. It brings to the fore questions of empirical fact (what is a team's impact upon a community?), values (should wealthy team owners receive public subsidies when there are others in greater need?), and policy (to what extent should the federal government interfere in a local issue?). More important, the sports relocation problem makes explicit three issues that will affect public policy debates for the remainder of this century.

First, the relocation problem emphasizes the increasingly amorphous nature of the distinction between public and private. Clearly, privately owned sports teams have achieved the success they enjoy because of their owners' ability to exploit the public's coffers and goodwill. There is little difference between professional sports and those industries that owe their success to protective trade policies, public bailouts, leasebacks, Industrial Revenue Bonds, Urban Development Action Grants, and beneficial tax policies. Government largess and regulation so permeate the private sector that it is nearly impossible to delineate public from private.

Second, the issue forces team owners to accept or deny a moral obligation to their host communities. Advocates of restrictive legislation are seeking to transform a moral obligation on the part of some owners into a legal obligation for all. The dynamics of the franchise relocation issue are analogous to those of the plant closing and relocation issue and other debates of corporate social responsibility. Critics of corporate behavior increasingly are supporting public policies that mandate companies to meet what many believe to be their moral obligations.

Finally, the relocation issue joins a debate over the appropriate role of government regulation. The issue invites the classic alignment of liberal-conservative principles, which confront one another in other areas of public policy. It is arguable whether we can learn anything of general usefulness from sport's experience with self-regulation or whether increased government intervention in sport will protect the public interest. It is ironic that at a time when the trend is to privatize government functions there are strong efforts to define the sports industry as being in the public domain, especially since the industry's leaders consciously have attempted to symbolize and promote in many ways the values of capitalism and free enterprise.

The resolution of the franchise relocation issue may say as much about the future direction of American public policy as it does about the future of professional sports in America.

NOTES

1. This includes cities with franchises in the United States Football League (USFL), the North American Soccer League (NASL), and the Major Indoor Soccer League (MISL). In addition, 110 cities hosted minor league baseball teams in classes A–AAA in 1984. The relocation issue and intercity competition also are problems for minor league cities. See "2 La. Cities, Vying for Same Team, May Sell Bonds to Build Stadiums," *The Weekly Bond Buyer*, September 16, 1983, and "Greenville, S.C. Plans $1.6 Million Revenue Issue for Baseball Stadium," *The Weekly Bond Buyer*, August 22, 1983. Competition for preseason training camps also exists. See "Fla. Unit May Woo Houston Astros with Bonds for Training Camp," *The Weekly Bond Buyer*, July 25, 1983.

2. Los Angeles Memorial Coliseum Commission v. National Football League, et al., 726 F. 2d 1381 (1984), permits unhampered relocation of sports franchises. For background information and analysis of the Raiders case, see Jeffrey Glick, "Professional Sports Franchise Movements and the Sherman Act: When and Where Teams Should be Able to Move," *Santa Clara Law Review* 23 (Winter 1983): 55–94, and Lewis S. Kurlantzick, "Thoughts on Professional Sports and the Antitrust Laws: Los Angeles Memorial Coliseum Commission v. National Football League," *Connecticut Law Review* 15 (Winter 1983): 183–208.

3. See the testimony of the mayors of Green Bay, Pittsburgh, and Oakland, as well as other cities, for a recitation of the benefits sports teams bring to a city and estimates of their financial impact in *Professional Sports Antitrust Immunity*, Hearings Before the Committee on the Judiciary, U. S. Senate, 97 Cong., 2d sess. (1982), pp. 134–80, 221–31, and 352–68 (hereafter referred to as *Professional Sports*). See also Michael Goodwin, "Jets to Make Jersey Move, Koch Asserts," *New York Times*, September 29, 1983, p. B20. The estimate of the Colts' worth was produced by the Bureau of Revenue Estimates, State of Maryland.

4. For example, it was estimated that for each game not played because of the 1981 baseball players' strike, Boston lost $18,000 in taxes and $650,000 in spending near the stadium. See Joseph Durso, "Mayors Cheer—and Count the Gate," *New York Times*, April 10, 1983. This assumes that money not spent at baseball games will not be spent at all in the city—a questionable assumption.

5. Fortney H. Stark (D–Cal.), *Professional Sports*, p. 23.

6. Diane Feinstein, *Professional Sports*, p. 135.

7. For a rare discussion of costs, see Benjamin Okner, "Subsidies of Stadiums and Arenas," pp. 325–47 in Roger Noll, ed., *Government and the Sports Business* (Washington, D.C.: The Brookings Institution, 1974).

8. Jeff Samuels, "Pirate Attendance: Why Seats Are Empty," *Pittsburgh Post Gazette*, August 22, 1978, p. 1.

9. Okner, "Subsidies," pp. 346–47.

10. Arthur T. Johnson, "Economic and Policy Implications of Hosting Sports Franchises: Lessons from Baltimore," *Urban Affairs Quarterly* (March 1986).

11. Ibid., p. 12.

12. For a discussion of political considerations in deciding to attract a sports franchise, see Arthur T. Johnson, "The Uneasy Partnership of Cities and Professional Sport: Public Policy Considerations," pp. 210–27 in Nancy Theberge and Peter Donnelly, eds., *Sport and the Sociological Imagination* (Fort Worth: Texas Christian University Press, 1984).

13. See Robert Baade and James Chessen, "The Sports Tax," Paper presented at the Eastern Economic Association Meetings, New York (March 15–17, 1984), pp. 5, 11.

14. The history of franchise movement, creation, and failure for the period 1950–82 in baseball, basketball, football, and hockey is detailed in Arthur T. Johnson, "Municipal Administration and the Sports Franchise Relocation Issue," *Public Administration Review* 43 (November/December 1983): 519–23. See also Joseph Coniglio, *The Names in the Game: A History of the Movement of Sports Franchises* (New York: Vantage, 1978).

15. See *Professional Football League Merger*, Hearings Before Antitrust Subcommittee of the Committee on the Judiciary House of Representatives 89th Cong., 2d, sess. (1966), pp. 80–83, and reprinted in *Professional Sports*, pp. 305–309.

16. See, for example, the discussion of baseball team owners' motives in Jesse Markham and

Paul Teplitz, *Baseball, Economics and Public Policy* (Lexington, Mass.: Lexington Books, 1982), pp. 25–31.

17. Such a clause was in the Minnesota Twins' lease. A public campaign to purchase the required number of tickets was conducted in 1984 to prevent the clause from taking effect. Sale of the Twins, however, aborted any relocation. Note also that cities cannot violate terms of the lease as Seattle did by scheduling an NFL Seahawks game the same day that baseball's Mariners were to play in the Kingdome.

18. Indianapolis and New Orleans took such a gamble and have been able to acquire only football franchises to play in their domed stadiums. Other cities may not even be this lucky. See Howard Kurtz, "Cities Building New Stadiums to Lure Major Teams, Money," *The Washington Post*, January 25, 1984, p. A3; John Helyar, "More Cities Plan Domed Stadiums But Return May Prove to Be Small," *Wall Street Journal*, May 17, 1984; and Paul Attner, "For Many Cities, There's No Place Like a Dome," *The Washington Post*, June 8, 1984, p. C3.

19. Professional baseball leagues require the consent of three-fourths of the members of a team's league and a majority of the members in the other league before a team can relocate. The NFL and the USFL require consent of three-fourths of their members. This is the rule struck down by the Raiders case. The NHL requires unanimous consent. The NBA requires the support of a majority of its members.

20. Los Angeles Memorial Coliseum Commission v. National Football League, 484 F. Supp. 1274, 1277 (C.D. Cal. 1980).

21. Los Angeles Memorial Coliseum Commission v. National Football League, 726 F. 2d 1397 (1984).

22. Curtis C. Flood v. Bowie K. Kuhn et al., 407 US 258 (1972), reaffirmed the baseball anomaly that was established by the court in Federal Baseball Club of Baltimore v. National League, 259 U.S. 200 (1922), and initially reaffirmed in Toolson v. New York Yankees, 346 U.S. 356 (1953).

23. The NHL has been sued by Ralston Purina Company, former owner of the St. Louis Blues, for rejecting the company's application to sell and transfer the team to Canada. The NHL successfully defended its right to control relocations in 1974 in San Francisco Seals, Ltd. v. National Hockey League, 379 F. Supp. 966 (Cent. D. Cal. 1974), which was precedent until the Raiders case. The NBA was sued in 1982 for reviewing a proposed move of the San Diego franchise to Los Angeles and by season ticket holders in the event that the move was permitted. It also faced potential suits by the City of San Diego. The owners of the New York Nets threatened suit if the league prevented the team's move to New Jersey. In 1974 the World Football League threatened to sue the NFL if it expanded into Memphis. After the World Football League folded, the owner of the Memphis franchise did sue the NFL for refusing to permit him entry into the league.

24. Johnson, "Municipal Administration," pp. 520–23.

25. *Professional Sports*, pp. 63–66, and *Professional Sports Team Community Protection Act*, Hearings Before the Committee on Commerce, Science and Transportation, U. S. Senate, 98th Cong., 2d sess. (1984), pp. 58–63.

26. See *Professional Sports*, pp. 134–80, 221–31, and 352–68.

27. Such conditions are likely to be continued financial losses, inadequacy of a city's stadium, or a city's failure to comply with terms of the lease. S.2505 as amended, however, identifies nine criteria.

28. Senate Report 98–592.

29. The NFL Players Association and the Major League Baseball Players Association gave qualified support to S.2821 in 1982 and S.2505 in 1984, but they did not endorse either as written. Their intent at this point clearly is to limit any expansion or strengthening of the leagues' antitrust exemptions.

30. See Arthur T. Johnson, "Congress and Professional Sports: 1951–1978," *Annals of the American Academy of Political and Social Science* 445 (September 1979): 102–15.

31. John Weistart and Cym Lowell, *The Law of Sports* (Charlottesville, Va.: Bobbs-Merrill, 1979), pp. 742–43.

32. For example, even without the Raiders, the Oakland Coliseum may be producing a surplus. See Los Angeles Memorial Coliseum Commission v. National Football League, reporters' transcript of proceedings reprinted in *Professional Sports*, pp. 212–13.

33. See, for example, Dennis Judd, *The Politics of American Cities* (Boston: Little, Brown, 1979), pp. 359–85; J. Allen Whitt, *Urban Elites and Mass Transportation* (Princeton, N.J.: Princeton University Press, 1982). Between 1975 and 1982 private-purpose bonds such as IRBs grew 300 percent to $44 billion. See Neal Peirce, "Congress Curbs 'Free Lunch' IRB's," *PA Times*, August 1, 1984, p. 2.

34. See *Organized Baseball*, Report of the Subcommittee on the Study of Monopoly Power. House Report 2002, 82d Cong., 2d sess. (1952). Congress again voiced its concerns with this issue in the late 1950s, when baseball proved reluctant to expand, in 1965–66 during hearings on the AFL–NFL merger, and in the mid–1970s during hearings on the ABA–NBA merger.

35. Pete Rozelle, Commissioner of the NFL, in fact cited potential litigation as one reason not to support S.2821. See *Professional Sports*, p. 64.

36. Weistart and Lowell, *Law of Sports*, pp. 733–53.

37. See 31 Wis. 2d 730–731, 144 N.W. 2d 17–18.

38. See City of Oakland v. Oakland Raiders, 32 Cal. 3d 60, 646 p. 2d 835, 183 Cal. Rptr. 673 (1982), and Mayor and City Council of Baltimore v. Baltimore Football Club Inc., Civil Action B84–1294.

39. The Baltimore Colts are incorporated in Delaware, had their offices and training camp in Baltimore County, not Baltimore City, and moved their physical property (uniforms, equipment, office furniture, and papers) out of Maryland the night before the city council voted to condemn the franchise.

40. Determination of a just compensation for the teams will prove most difficult. For example, should a team's value be that which the local government can resell it for with relocation restrictions placed on new owners, or is it the value of the team in its new location with presumably a higher profit potential and no relocation restrictions? Even if the cities win their cases, they will be in the courts several years debating the appropriate value of their teams.

41. Law review commentators thus far agree with the owners' positions. See Michael Schiano, "Eminent Domain Exercised—*Stare Decisis* or a Warning: City of Oakland v. Oakland Raiders," *Pace Law Review* 4 (Fall 1983): 169–93, and Julius Sackman, "Public Use—Updated (City of Oakland v. Oakland Raiders)," *Institute on Planning, Zoning and Eminent Domain* (1983): 203–35.

42. 52 LW 4673.

43. Shortly after the Hawaii Housing Authority decision, the mayor of New Bedford, Massachusetts, announced his intention to use eminent domain laws to prevent Morse Cutting Tools, a 120-year-old company owned by Gulf and Western Industries, from closing its operations.

44. Another possibility is that an owner and city officials would negotiate a lease with the proviso that the city will not exercise its eminent domain rights. Such a clause of course defeats the purpose of the legislation and is of dubious legality.

45. Weistart and Lowell, *Law of Sports*, p. 737. League officials, especially those of the NFL, also argue that an uncontrolled increase in new teams will provide an oversaturation of sports that will dampen the public's interest in professional sports. Evidence supporting this argument is unclear.

46. Exceptions to this statement include Demmert, who provides an economic analysis that supports the theoretical validity of such a policy response to the relocation problem, and Noll, who suggests this option in combination with greater revenue sharing among teams and certain tax reforms. See Henry Demmert, *The Economics of Professional Team Sports* (Lexington, Mass.: Lexington Books, 1973), pp. 77–92, and Roger Noll, "Alternatives in Sports Policy," pp. 414–15 in Roger Noll, ed., *Government and the Sports Business* (Washington, D.C.: The Brookings Institution, 1974).

13

Foreign Policy in the Sports Arena

James A. R. Nafziger

The international sports arena is also a political arena. The ancient Greeks, Hitler, pro-Palestinian terrorists, Canadian wheat lobbyists, antiapartheid forces, President Carter, and President Chernenko have all known this to be true and have used sport as an instrument of foreign policy. The intervention of governments in the sports arena raises several policy issues. First, what is the proper role of government—promoter or facilitator? Second, what are or should be the political objectives—for example, to establish diplomatic relations? Third, what are the legal constraints on political intervention in the sports arena? Fourth, in order to accomplish political objectives, how much and what kind of power is necessary?

THE PROPER ROLE OF GOVERNMENT

There are three levels of governmental intervention in the sports arena:

Level I. Simple governmental financial assistance by direct appropriations, by the use of revenue from governmental lotteries, or by other means. Such assistance is not only acceptable, but encouraged, as an international practice. Among the few examples of this practice in the United States at the federal level is official support of exchanges or clinics. States and local jurisdictions subsidize athletics in making appropriations to educational institutions.

Level II. Indirect or direct governmental authorization, supervision, or control over the administration of sport is a widespread practice in most countries. The activity of sport is often supervised by a Ministry of Sports, but sometimes, as in the United States, by a chosen instrument of the government, such as a National Olympic Committee.

Level III. Diplomatic exploitation of sports in the external affairs of the government. Boycotts, sports propagandizing, refusal of visas, hosting the Olympics, and sports exchanges are examples of how governments can use or abuse sport to fulfill foreign policy purposes.

Level III, which stirs up most of the controversy in international sport, will be the primary focus of this chapter.

In the United States, a coherent foreign sports policy did not emerge until the 1970s. Since then, sport has become a controversial and very visible part, though only a minor part, of United States foreign policy. The sources of the new attention to sport during the 1970s lay in a gradually accepted awareness that governmental involvement in sports helps promote the national interest and that political adversaries score points in the international sports arena. A more immediate interest in federal sports policy was provoked by public disenchantment with the management and quality of American participation in the 1972 (Munich) Olympic Games and the shock of witnessing terrorism there. The spectacular expansions in media coverage of transnational athletic competition brought all the excitement, glory, humanity, administrative bungles, and ultimate horror of the 1972 Games into living rooms so graphically as to confirm the important role of sports in global affairs. The involvement of this country's athletes in global competition came to be of major public interest, if not concern. The terrorist nightmare in Munich prompted the State Department to introduce a Draft Convention for the Prevention and Punishment of Certain Acts of International Terrorism[1] and generated legislative proposals to govern internationally related aspects of amateur athletics. More generally, it was apparent after the Munich Games that responses to political problems in the sports arena could not arise strictly from the private sector.

The early 1970s brought an articulation of a foreign policy interest "in furthering mutual understanding and communication through sports."[2] Accordingly, the federal government initially strengthened its role in sports by committing further resources to facilitate people-to-people communication and public diplomacy conducted by private individuals and groups.[3] The federal government became more involved in supporting technical athletic assistance abroad and in helping procure athletic equipment for programs in developing countries. The government recognized that transnational athletic exchange could help improve international relations. Even limited athletic exchange could serve to make foreign policy more "human."

A study undertaken for the Department of State in 1971, which is still useful to policy planners, observed that sports had largely been ignored in diplomacy and suggested two policy options besides the existing role of the department as a *facilitator* of international athletic exchange and competition. Alternatively, the department could work (a) as an active *promoter* to increase the stature of United States participation in international sports programs as a primary means of achieving the objectives of the Fulbright-Hays Act; or (b) as a *programmer* of United States participation in international sports—sport would become a foreign affairs resource that, when balanced with other such resources, might be important to the achievement of foreign policy objectives.[4]

The study recommended that the government's choice among these options should be made by balancing the attendant risks and benefits. As to risks, the facilitative role seemed the safest. The promoter role was slightly riskier because it depends on the vagaries of congressional funding. The programmer role seemed even riskier, since foreign affairs officials might not know how to employ sports skillfully as a diplomatic tool and athletes might dislike the political implications. As to benefits, the promoter and programmer roles offered greater assurance of effective and more visible participation in international competition, in which the United States had been poorly represented in the past. The programmer role would recharacterize the government as a partner rather than a handmaiden of sports activities, and it would therefore tend to encourage a more positive role for sports and physical fitness in public life.[5] In considering which option to pursue, the study concluded that "the Department must first decide the objective of its sports activities and have a cogent plan for achieving that objective before very strong feelings, either way, emerge."[6] Clearly, some form of foreign sports policy was an idea whose time had come.

Criteria for judging the efficacy of a foreign sports effort under governmental auspices may vary according to the intensity of governmental involvement. Low-level policies will be concerned with more or less immediate returns on each dollar invested. For example: What works at a clinic in a particular country? What doesn't? Should a government send a basketball coach to Mauretania after his visit in Dakar? If a government sees itself as simply a facilitator at Level I, the exposure it receives abroad and the contacts the activity generates will be critical. If, however, a government's role extends to that of a promoter or programmer, then the success of its athletes in competition abroad, the degree to which a foreign country adopts a newly introduced sport, or the accomplishment of some other major objective will likely dominate an evaluation of governmental performance.

On Level I of governmental intervention, the State Department's former Bureau of Educational and Cultural Affairs, which was absorbed into the United States Information Agency in 1978, established three objectives that have shaped official programs of athletic exchange: (a) to enlarge the circle of those able to serve as influential interpreters between the United States and other nations, (b) to stimulate institutional development in directions that favorably affect mutual comprehension, and (c) to reduce structural and technical impediments to the exchange of ideas and information. Within this framework the government has conducted programs of athletic exchange while often eschewing direct sponsorship.

The Amateur Sports Act of 1978. The relationships between "nationalism and sports" and "politics and sports" often have been viewed as disjunctive or antagonistic. Until recently, for example, any acknowledgment of an official United States intervention into the sports arena was shunned. Now, however, there is a recognition of the inevitability of athletic realpolitik and of governmental involvement in sports.

After years of discussion and preliminary bills, Congress confirmed its commitment to a federal sports policy and to the supremacy of the Olympic Movement by passing the Amateur Sports Act of 1978. That act largely defines the scope and nature of involvement by the federal government in sports, at least on Levels I and II. The act establishes the United States Olympic Committee (USOC) as a chosen instrument to "promote and support amateur athletic activities involving the United States and foreign nations" (§ 374[5]), and to "establish national goals for amateur athletic activities and encourage the attainment of those goals" (§ 374[1]). Among other provisions, the act instructs the USOC to "coordinate and develop amateur athletic activity in the United States directly relating to international amateur athletic competition, so as to foster productive working relationships among sport-related organizations" (§ 374[2]). With specific references to the Olympic and Pan-American Games, the Amateur Sports Act expresses a public determination to "obtain for the United States, either directly or by delegation to the appropriate national governing body, the most competent amateur representation possible in each competition and event." (§ 374[4]).

An "exclusive jurisdiction" provision in the 1978 act is of particular significance in defining options for using sport as an instrument of foreign policy. Accordingly, the USOC shall

> exercise exclusive jurisdiction, either directly or through its constituent members of committees, over all matters pertaining to the participation of the United States in the Olympic Games and in the Pan-American Games, including the representation of the United States in such Games, and over the organization of the Olympic Games and the Pan-American Games when held in the United States.[7]

Although this provision cannot in itself constrain federal action that is otherwise legitimate, it nevertheless does establish an expectation that the decisions of the USOC, within a larger international framework, will shape the implementation of foreign sports policy.

Soon after the Amateur Sports Act became law, the boycott of the 1980 (Moscow) Olympic Games confirmed the Carter Administration's willingness to politicize the sports arena by raising federal intervention to the highest level of policymaking. The Reagan Administration generally maintained a low profile, limiting its actions to Levels I and II. In sum, the intensity of United States foreign sports policy peaked at Level III (full governmental intervention) in 1980.

POLITICAL OBJECTIVES

What should be the objectives of a foreign sports policy? At which of the three levels of governmental intervention should it operate? Perhaps a government should look upon sport simply as a diplomatic tool to serve immediate purposes, or perhaps it should view sport more ambitiously as a tool to promote world order.[8] If a government acts unilaterally, either perspective may be deficient because of the degree of ambiguity and complexity inherent in unilateral decisions and policy. A government is therefore ill-advised to "go it alone." Rather, governments are well advised to develop comprehensive and coherent foreign sports policies consistent with international sports law. Good policy can mean an end to bad politics. What is important is not the quarantine of governments and politics from the international sports arena, but the channeling of governmental decisions and politics along acknowledged lines of world ordering. A government can best establish constructive policy, not on the basis of bureaucratic interplay, political expediency, ideological constraints, and pluralistic pressures, but on the basis of accepted international practice. Foreign sports policy consistent with international law seems to be the best means of protecting individual athletes from political injury and promoting athletic values in global society.

In considering the policy options, it may be useful first to identify six political uses of international sports competition: international cooperation, national ideology and propaganda, official prestige, diplomatic recognition and nonrecognition, protest, and conflict.[9] Of these, only diplomatic nonrecognition and conflict are improper official uses of sports competition according to international law, although variations on the other uses may constitute unfriendly acts. Within this margin of discretion, it is necessary for governments to clarify their objectives. The Carter Administration's demand for a boycott by the USOC of the Moscow Games was based on what appeared to be unclear policy concerns.[10] The Administration variously argued principles of diplomatic protection of its nationals, deterrence and retribution. The President first justified the boycott on the grounds of a presumed danger to American athletes and spectators, which was the rationale parroted by the Soviet Union to justify its boycott of the 1984 Games.[11] After having advanced this rationale for the compelled boycott, the White House later changed its mind by asserting that the real reason for the boycott was to deter future aggression and to send the Soviets "a signal of world outrage."[12] To add to the confusion, the Secretary of State, however, appeared to disagree by viewing the boycott as retribution for the Soviet violation of what he thought was a principle against contemporaneous involvement by a sovereign host in open warfare.[13] It became clear that the Carter Administration was indecisive in establishing a rationale for the boycott.

In 1984 the Reagan Administration's quiet handling of the Soviet retaliatory boycott of the Los Angeles Games implicitly acknowledged the futility of distinguishing between the 1980 and 1984 cases. President Reagan's response was particularly apt because not only did he acknowledge, quite correctly, that there was no "prudent" action within his discretion, but he correctly pledged to work through "citizens groups and our people," to encourage the Soviet Union and its allies to reverse their decision not to compete in the Los Angeles Games. By responding carefully within the ambit of its authority under the Amateur Sports Act of 1978, the Reagan Administration deferred at Level II to the authority of the Olympic movement.

United States foreign policy objectives are limited not only by specific law—in particular, the Amateur Sports Act of 1978 and international law—but also by the federal constitutional structure. The federal government could do nothing to override a decision by Colorado voters not to host the 1976 Winter Games. Similarly, the financing structure of the 1984 Games in Los Angeles was beyond direct federal supervision. In 1978 the citizens of Los Angeles overwhelmingly approved an amendment to the city charter that prohibited the city from spending any tax revenue on the Games that would not be reimbursed by binding, legal contract. This meant that the Los Angeles Olympic Organizing Committee (LAOOC) had to break with Olympic tradition. While previous organizing committees had been part of the municipal government of the host city, the LAOOC by necessity was formed as a private, nonprofit corporation under California laws.

Aside from these limitations on policy options, policy failures sometimes result from ineffective implementation. For example, when the Australian government compensated those athletes and sports bodies that had stayed home from the 1980 Games, it did so for the express purpose of financing their involvement in alternative sports events. Later, to the chagrin of the public and the delight of the media, it was determined that Canberra had failed to supervise or at least monitor the use of the payments. Hence, to the embarrassment of the policymakers, the public came to view the compensation payments as a questionable use of tax revenue.

LEGAL CONSTRAINTS

Unfortunately, commentaries about sports policy too often overlook the legal constraints. Sometimes social observers view law not as prescription, but as just another datum. Thus "[t]he cumulated sociological research on the Olympics may broadly be classified into descriptive investigations, studies on the Olympic Movement as a formal organization, examinations of the relationship between the Olympic Games and various societal subsystems, and analyses of the Olympics as a cultural system."[14] A legal framework seems to be missing in much of the empirical inquiry.

Under the United States Constitution the Executive may, under its foreign relations power or under delegated congressional authority,[15] intervene in the arena of international sports. Generally, the Amateur Sports Act of 1978 defines the government's policy options and related private options even to some extent on Level III of governmental intervention. For example, a study of the boycott of the Moscow Games concluded that "the Act did not authorize the USOC to boycott the Games in order to effect national policy objectives."[16] There are, however, gaps and uncertainties in the supervision of amateur sports under the 1978 act. Whenever the act is silent or ambiguous—as, for example, in providing rather cryptically for the "exclusive jurisdiction" of the USOC—the federal legislation has less force.

Foreign sports policy must comply with international law, including that governing nation groups such as the Commonwealth of Nations. Although a full discussion of international legal constraints lies beyond the scope of this chapter and has been undertaken elsewhere,[17] a brief summary of some important aspects will at least indicate the framework.

The Olympic Charter best evidences international custom pertaining to sports competition, Olympic or not. The Rules of the Charter are administered by a "supreme authority,"[18] the International Olympic Committee (IOC). The IOC is a corporate body having juridical status and perpetual succession.[19] Rule 9 of the Olympic Charter provides that "[e]very person or organization that plays any part whatsoever in the Olympic movement shall accept the supreme authority of the IOC and shall be bound by its rules and submit to its jurisdiction."[20] Although the IOC is a nongovernmental organization[21] that cannot in itself compel state obedience, its rules best evidence current international practice and therefore have legal significance.[22]

Three of the IOC rules are particularly instructive. Rule 3, one of the cornerstones of international sports law, provides that "[n]o discrimination . . . is allowed against any country or person on grounds of race, religion, or politics."[23] Rule 9 states that "[t]he Games are contests between individuals and teams and not between countries."[24] Rule 24 obligates National Olympic Committees (NOCs) to be autonomous, to resist all political pressures, and to enforce the Rules and Bylaws of the IOC; "NOCs shall be the sole authorities responsible for the representation of their respective countries at the Olympic Games."[25] Bylaw 8 to Rule 24 defines the term "representation" to cover a decision to participate or not.[26] Violations of the rules, such as yielding to political pressures, expose NOCs to penalties.[27] Thus governmental intrusion into these rules of custom is abusive. The Draft Declaration Relating to the Protection of the Olympic Games,[28] although still under study, would confirm the binding force of these rules, especially Rules 3 and 24, on members of the United Nations.

In interpreting these and other provisions, a line may be drawn between governmental support of individual athletes, teams, and events on the one hand, and governmental interference in the sports arena on the other. The IOC has long emphasized "the importance and desirability of government aid, and reconfirmed the dangers of government interference of a political nature in the running of sport in any country."[29] Also, as a matter of textual interpretation, the validity of political intervention in the sports arena is generally acceptable when it furthers specific provisions of international law. Thus boycotts to combat apartheid and other forms of official racism are valid, whereas geopolitically motivated boycotts must be evaluated on a case-by-case basis.[30]

Given the weakness of the international legal system, a government's perception of the strength of international norms and institutions may influence its decisions. For example, rightly or wrongly, the Dutch government compelled a boycott of the 1980 Games, but later it drew only passing attention to human rights problems in Uruguay when the issue arose of whether to disallow participation by the Royal Dutch Football Federation in a tournament in politically controversial Uruguay: "It is not for the Government to say in a case like this: you may not go."[31] The Minister of Foreign Affairs justified the distinction between the two situations largely on the basis of the strength and transcendental purposes of the Olympics, "unlike a series of football matches."[32]

Remedies for the rights accorded by international sports law take many forms, including adjudication and diplomacy. The Amateur Sports Act of 1978 prescribes that

> the United States Olympic Committee shall "provide for the swift resolution of conflicts and disputes involving amateur athletes, national governing bodies, and amateur sports organizations, and protect the opportunity of any amateur athlete, coach, trainer, manager, administrator, or official to participate in amateur athletic competition."[33]

The act requires that the USOC constitution and bylaws establish and maintain provisions for the swift and equitable resolution of disputes involving any of its members and relating to the opportunity of an amateur athlete, coach, trainer, manager, administrator, or official to participate in the Olympic Games, the Pan-American Games, world championship competition, or other such protected competition as defined in such constitution and bylaws. The act also specifies procedures for settling two common types of conflicts: (1) those that arise when an amateur sports organization or eligible person attempts to compel an NGB to comply with the organizational and sanctioning criteria in the act, and (2) those generated when an amateur sports organization seeks to replace an incumbent NGB.[34] Although these procedures may address issues of international consequence, they primarily are concerned with such technical issues as organization, team recruitment, and financing.

A new international institution, the Court of Arbitration for Sport (CAS), is designed to help settle "disputes of a private nature arising out of the practice or development of sport, and in a general way, *all* activities pertaining to sport."[35] Although the CAS may have limited impact in itself, it evidences the gradual institutionalization of international sports law and therefore is relevant to policy planning. Article 4 of its statute provides that "[s]uch disputes may bear on questions of principle relating to sport or on pecuniary or other interests affected on the occasion of the practice or the development of sport, and in a general way, all activities pertaining to sport."[36] The following parties have the standing to submit a case to the CAS "provided they have an interest in so doing":[37] the IOC, National Olympic Committees, Organizing Committees of the Olympic Games, sports association, national federations, "and, in a general way, any natural person or corporate body having the capacity or power to compromise."[38] The statute of the CAS provides for a discretionary procedure of conciliation in addition to arbitration.[39]

ASSESSMENT OF POWER TO EFFECT RESULTS

A foreign sports policy will be unproductive if it is not realistic; power is a driving force of policy. Thus the Carter Administration's failure to assess its limited power to encourage a global boycott of the 1980 Games led to diplomatic embarrassment. The boycott divided athletes, threatened to destabilize the international Olympic movement, aggravated a global public, worried persons with a business stake in the Moscow Games, and threatened to isolate the United States from some of its most important allies. "The boycott policy was long on risks and short on assurances."[40]

Although the deficiencies of the 1980 boycott policy were numerous, the "power failure" was prominent. The Carter Administration incorrectly assessed the power of the International Olympic Committee and the various sports federations to control their members, ward off government intervention, and thereby defy governmental pressures. In addition, the United States could not rely on a total commitment from its allies because sport is really symbolic of relationships and is not worth hard-core persuasive efforts—for example, a denial of economic aid or political support. Vital interests were not at stake in this situation. The president of the IOC emphasized that reality, as did another observer when he wrote:

> In the final analysis, the policy posed too stern a test for the Western alliance over a non-crucial matter. While sports can certainly be used as a political weapon, the Administration was ill-equipped to employ it effectively as a sanction of the Afghanistan invasion. Participation in Moscow would have been less harmful to U.S. interests than the boycott . . . The Administration gave very little thought to the Olympics prior to Afghanistan. There had been some

discussion of the Moscow Games during consideration of the Amateur Sports Act in 1978, but nothing was sustained. Possibly, some Administration members were familiar with amateur sports, but only one or two had had personal contact with amateur sports officials. This lack of knowledge caused the government to underestimate the USOC's independence and to overestimate the USOC's status in international amateur sports.[41]

Most seriously of all, the Administration failed to understand that unilateral boycotts, by and large, are of doubtful legality, do not work very well, and are almost guaranteed not to work in a geopolitical context. Generally, boycotts do not seem to change or eliminate the condition at which they are directed. Examples of the futility of boycotts outside the sports arena are legion. They did not work against Italy in the 1930s (after that country's occupation of Ethiopia), Rhodesia in the 1960s (after the marshaling of global opinion against the segregationist regime of Ian Smith), or Cuba from 1960 on (after the establishment of the Cold War between the new Castro regime and the United States government). In sum, the United States government, and this applies as well to other governments, "must be better equipped to deal with the Olympic movement should the U.S. attempt to make the Games an instrument of U.S. policy again in the future."[42] If sport is to be a meaningful instrument of policy in the geopolitical scene, any government that uses it must be prepared to follow up with strong, decisive measures. It is easier for the Soviets to coerce its allies. The United States, on the other hand, has more of a "partnership" relation with its allies and therefore can seldom resort effectively to anything but persuasive tactics. The Carter Administration was unwilling or unable to use more forceful tactics in order to obtain boycott cooperation. If a foreign sports policy is to work, a government must have sufficient power, including expertise and supervisory personnel, and it must be willing to risk its power. Also, a government's actions must be acceptable under international law and to pertinent international bodies, such as the IOC, to achieve success.

CONCLUSION

Politics is apparently in the sports arena to stay, but playing politics in the sports arena can turn out to be futile. Recent boycotts of the Olympic Games confirm that they generally do not work well and may even work against the implementing governments.

For the future, governments are well advised to develop comprehensive and coherent foreign sports policy, rooted not in geopolitics but in international law, including the accepted rules of the Olympic movement. Good policy can mean an end to bad politics. What is imporant is the channeling of governmental decisions and politics along acknowledged lines of world ordering rather than on the basis of bureaucratic interplay, political expediency, ideological constraints, and pluralistic pressures. Legitimate foreign sports policies consistent with international norms and rules are the best means of protecting individual athletes from political injury, while guiding governmental and nongovernmental decisionmaking along appropriate lines. At the very least, internationally acceptable policies will help keep governments running on the same track.

NOTES

1. John F. Murphy, *The United Nations and the Control of International Violence: A Legal and Political Analysis* (Totowa, N.J.: Rowman & Allanheld, 1982), p. 181.

2. See transcript of the speech delivered by Alan A. Reich, Deputy Assistant Secretary of State for Educational and Cultural Affairs, before the General Assembly of International Sports Federations, in 119 *Congressional Record* 95 (daily ed., June 19, 1973); remarks of Walter Boehm, in R. Singer, *Multidisciplinary Symposium on Sport and the Means of Furthering Mutual International Understanding*, U.S. Department of State, Bureau of Educational and Cultural Affairs, December 4, 1973, (1974).

3. See Alan A. Reich, *New Role for Associations in Promoting World Understanding*, *Association Management* (February 1973), p. 32.

4. Harris/Ragan Management Corporation, International Sports Policies for the Department of State: A Presentation of Options 25, 7, unpublished (September 24, 1971) [hereafter cited as Harris/Ragan Report].

5. Ibid. at 25–26.

6. Ibid. at 28.

7. 36 U.S.C. §§ 371–396 (Supp. IV 1980).

8. The press frequently reported on international politics in sports. See, for example, *New York Times*, October 25, 1974, p. 49, col. 4; *The Washington Post*, October 30, 1974, p. F1, col. 8 (refusal of India to participate against South Africa in Davis Cup competition); *The Washington Post*, February 7, 1975, p. A14, col. 1; and *Sports Illustrated* (February 24, 1975), p. 18 (refusal of India, contrary to its prior commitment, to allow participation by South Africa and Israel in world table-tennis championships held in Calcutta, together with a simultaneous invitation to the Palestinian Liberation Organization). Indian teams in particular appeared to be "guided by the rules and regulations of the State." *The Washington Post*, February 7, 1975, p. A14, cols. 1, 5; *The Washington Post*, March 20, 1975, p. E4, col. 5 (refusal of the Mexican government to grant visas to a South African Davis Cup tennis team to play in Mexico and a directive to Mexicans not to compete with South Africans elsewhere); *Sports Illustrated* (May 12, 1975), p. 15 (same with respect to World Championship Tennis Competition in Mexico); *The Washington Post*, May 7, 1975, p. D2, col. 3 (French exclusion of Rhodesian tennis team). On the politicization of the International Chess Federation, see *The Oregonian*, March 20, 1975, p. A10, col. 1 (on rule-changing proposals by the United States Chess Federation): "The voting Wednesday went generally by blocs, with East and West European and Arab federations siding with the Russians, and Asian and Latin American federations lining up with the United States." Public and professional opinion on this subject was ambiguous. A 1971 sampling of forty-four sports administrators, government administrators, sports commentators, government observers, and sports participants revealed mixed attitudes toward expansions of the government's role in sports, including federal financial support for sports and questions about the efficacy of a sports policy. Most of these surveyed did, however, agree on what they then saw as a need to keep "politics" aloof from sports and to improve the program administered by the Department of State. Harris/Ragan Report. This survey was taken prior to the Munich Olympic Games and the demise of plans for the Denver Winter Games. A Harris sports survey taken after the Munich Games disclosed considerable public disenchantment with both the administration and particularly the enforcement of the Olympic Rules, and it indicated considerable public support for

official protection by the government of U.S. interests in the Games. "Sports Fans Assess '72 Olympics," *The Harris Survey* (October 5, 1972).

9. James A. R. Nafziger and Andrew Strenk, "The Political Uses and Abuses of Sports," *Connecticut Law Review* 10 (1978): 280–89.

10. See James A. R. Nafziger, "Diplomatic Fun and the Games: A Commentary on the United States Boycott of the 1980 Summer Olympics," *Willamette Law Review* 17 (1980): 67.

11. *Department of State Bulletin* 80 (January 1980): Special-B.

12. *Department of State Bulletin* 80 (March 1980): 51.

13. Ibid., p. 50.

14. Jeffrey Segrave and Donald Chu, *Olympism* (Champaign, Il: Human Kinetics, 1982), p. 201.

15. U.S. Constitution article II, pp. 1–3; United States v. Curtiss-Wright Export Corp., 299 U.S. 304 (1936).

16. Comment, "Political Abuse of Olympic Sport: DeFrantz v. United States Olympic Committee," *New York University Journal International and Politics* 14 (1982): 155, 178.

17. James A. R. Nafziger, "Nonaggressive Sanctions in the International Sports Arena," *Case Western Reserve Journal of International Law* 15 (1983): 329.

18. Olympic Charter (1984), at Rule 4. Rule 23 of the Olympic Charter provides also that "[t]he IOC is the final authority on all questions concerning the Olympic Games and the Olympic movement."

19. Ibid., at Rule 11.

20. Ibid., Rule 9.

21. Ibid., at Rule 11.
The IOC is a permanent organization. It selects such persons as it considers qualified to be members, provided that they speak French or English and are citizens of and reside in a country which possesses an NOC recognized by the IOC. The IOC welcomes them into membership with a brief ceremony during which they accept the required obligations and responsibilities. There shall be only one member in any country except in the largest and most active countries in the Olympic movement, and in those where the Olympic Games have been held, where there may be a maximum of two. Members of the IOC are representatives of the IOC in their countries and not their delegates to the IOC. They may not accept from governments or from any organizations or individuals instructions which shall in any way bind them or interfere with the independence of their vote. [ibid., at Rule 12]

22. A 1977 Belgian court decision, confirming the position of the French courts, the Council of Europe, and the High Court of Justice of the European Communities, ruled that the international rules of sport supersede conflicting national policies and laws. The Second Conference of European Sports Ministers adopted a resolution that explicitly confirmed the authority of the Olympic Charter. Furthermore, leading publicists have established the authority of the Olympic Rules in the international sports arena.

23. Olympic Charter, note 18, Rule 3 (emphasis added).

24. Ibid., Rule 9.

25. Ibid., Rule 24.

26. Ibid., Bylaw 8 to Rule 24.

27. Ibid., Rule 25.

28. *Olympic Review* (1982): 481–82.

29. *Olympic Review* (1974): 490. See also Letter from Lord Killanin to President Gerald Ford in *Sports Illustrated* (September 2, 1974), p. 12.

30. See note 17.

31. The Netherlands participation in the mini-world football championship in Uruguay, *Netherlands Yearbook of International Law* 13 (1982): 268.

32. Ibid.

33. 39 U.S.C. 374(8). On related issues, see James A. R. Nafziger, "The Amateur Sports Act of 1978," *Brigham Young University Law Review* (1983): 86–94.

34. Ibid.

35. Article 1., Statutes *[sic]* of the Court of Arbitration for Sport, *Olympic Review* (1983): 763 (emphasis added).

36. Ibid., Article 4.

37. Ibid., Article 5.
38. Ibid.
39. Ibid., Article 29, p. 766.
40. Adam Goldstein, "The 1980 Olympic Boycott: The Role of National Olympic Committees and of the International Olympic Committee" (May 19, 1981), unpublished, p. 86.
41. Ibid., p. 84.
42. Ibid., p. 92.

14

Conclusion: Sports, Regulation, and the Public Interest

James H. Frey
Arthur T. Johnson

A review of the chapters of this book discloses an underlying consensus that the sports industry should not receive special treatment by policymakers that would place sport outside existing law. This position, for example, rejects the arguments of representatives of professional and intercollegiate sports that sport is unique and needs immunity from antitrust laws to operate effectively.

Rejection of the idea that the sports industry deserves special treatment not only rejects pleas for favorable consideration, but it denies demands by the industry's critics for increased regulatory oversight. The contributors to this book are close to a consensus that existing law applied fairly is adequate in dealing with most industry issues.

Those authors who do call for government intervention do so to end such abuses as discrimination, violence, and exploitation of college athletes. They acknowledge that ideally self-regulation is best, but they find that sports officials have failed to pursue the public interest when given the opportunity. Therefore, they call for legislators and judges either to prod sports organizations to reform their members' behavior or to impose regulatory policy on them to achieve the desired change in behavior.

The conflict between the public interest and industry self-interest raises the specter of government regulation and ensures that politics will remain an important part of the future of sport. The conflict's significance is of sports officials' own making. On the one hand, sports officials have led the way in seeking government favor by consciously fostering an identification of sport with the public interest. On the symbolic plane, for example, sport has been credited with promoting democratic values of justice, equality, and rules obedience as well as symbolizing in general the American way of life. Instrumentally, sport offers athletes from poor and disadvantaged families a means of acquiring an education and an opportunity for upward mobility, and it serves in many communities as an instrument of economic development.

On the other hand, sports officials—amateur and professional, and athletes as well—have emphasized the commercial aspects of sports, relentlessly pursuing profit maximization. With regard to several issues, expectations that sports officials would follow other than their self-interest have proven to be false hopes. This has generated intense skepticism that sports officials are willing and able to serve the public interest. Nevertheless, the belief—or perhaps the hope—that sport and the public interest are one lingers. Therefore, proposals for government intervention are put forth that seek to force upon sports officials socially responsible action, regardless of financial consequences.

Whether such proposals or other proposals generated by conflicts between and among athletes and sports officials are translated into public policy mandates is determined ultimately by the political process. Although some theorists argue that economics determines regulatory policy, it is our contention that politics is the more important factor in determining the existence and nature of regulation.[1]

James Q. Wilson offers an explanation of the politics of regulation that permits the prediction of the probability of a regulatory proposal's success.[2] Such a prediction can be based upon the degree to which a proposal concentrates or diffuses the distribution of benefits and costs. Oversimplifying, if benefits or costs are concentrated, organized interests to be affected by the proposed policy will intensely support or resist it. Alternatively, a proposal promising diffuse benefits or costs will elicit a much weaker reaction from those who would be affected. In all cases, interests must be organized if they are to be represented effectively in policy debates.

Figure 14.1 arrays specific sports policy proposals according to the degree to which groups might expect benefits and costs to be concentrated or diffused. Note that no proposal promises diffuse costs. Thus, because of the concentration of costs, active opposition to each proposal is to be expected.

The issues for which our authors call for increased government action—sports violence, rights of scholarship athletes, and possibly agent regulation—promise diffuse benefits and concentrated costs. According to Wilson, it is likely that political effort in support of this type of proposal will be nonexistent or weak, while opposition will be strong. Thus it is probable that these proposals will not be successful in the face of political action on the part of those organized interests who perceive themselves to be threatened by the proposals. This partly explains why such proposals have a greater probability of success in arenas less political—principally the courts and, to a lesser extent, the bureaucracy—than legislative bodies like the United States Congress.

If a policy proposal with diffuse benefits and concentrated costs is to be

FIGURE 14.1
Distribution of Benefits and Costs of Various Sports Policies

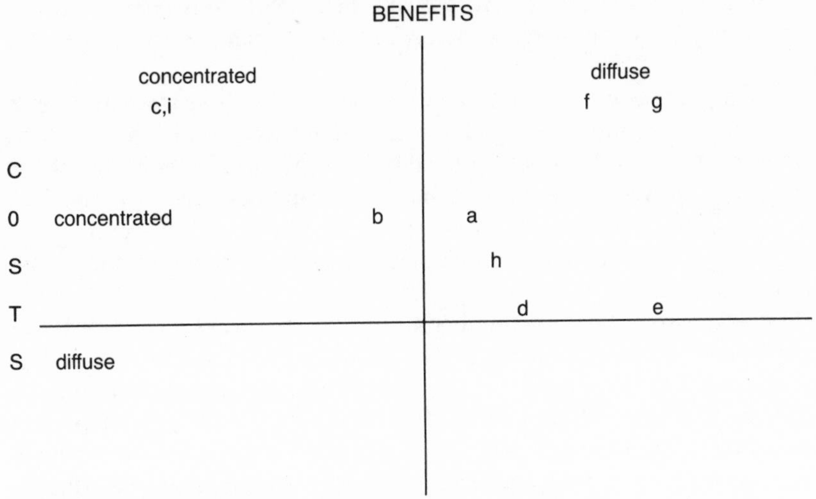

BENEFITS

```
                concentrated                        diffuse
                   c,i                            f        g


  C

  O    concentrated                 b        a

  S                                      h

  T  _____|____d_____e_____

  S    diffuse
```

Legend:
[a]Legal recognition of college scholarship athletes as employees
[b]Acceptance of program-specific interpretation of Title IX
[c]Grant professional sports leagues antitrust immunity
[d]Regulation of agents
[e]Regulate sports violence
[f]Apply antitrust laws to NCAA operations
[g]Stricter tax policy for professional sports team owners
[h]Legalize sports betting
[i]Regulate sports franchise relocation

---

legislated, societal conditions must be such that a public demand for action arises. For example, a crisis that can be personified in villainous terms might appear suddenly or evolve over time.[3] Increased regulation of intercollegiate athletics might occur by dramatizing the corrupting effect of college athletics on the educational mission of universities and student athletes. It appears that scattered reports, no matter how frequent, are insufficient in themselves to bring action. A triggering event leading to a perceived or actual crisis is needed.

Intense political conflict can be expected over those proposals that promise concentrated benefits and costs for different organized interests. Both sides will seek actively to influence the policy process, with a minimal goal of preventing the opposition from winning. The conflict itself will be highly visible. The outcome of such contests is difficult to predict, since neither side will dominate. Labor relations and franchise relocation proposals in professional sports are excellent examples of such issues at present. It is noteworthy that Title IX proponents have broadened the gender discrimination issue to include other forms of discrimination and thereby have attracted various allies, principally civil rights advocates, in their efforts to reverse the *Grove City* decision. This will increase the probability of their success in the 99th Congress.

Wilson argues, as we have in Chapter 1, that the "decisive stage in the ebb and flow of social conflict is control over the public agenda; what government may or may not do is chiefly determined by what people have come to believe is properly a 'private' or a 'public' matter."[4] Sport has become a "public" issue. The focus now is on specific issues within sports, and the conflict now is being fought at the policy formulation and adoption stages rather than that of agenda setting.

The basic assumptions of this book are that sport and government are closely related and that public policy has a profound impact on sports. The authors were free to respond to the questions posed in the introductory chapter as they saw fit. Although a full range of postures was adopted, a consensus emerged that sport—both amateur and professional—must remain within the reach of existing law. Even those who seek minimal government intervention into sports hint that regulation may be necessary if abuses continue or if sports officials flaunt the public interest.

The free market is not perfect, but neither are our regulatory mechanisms. Public policies commonly are followed by unintended consequences. Prescriptively, the basic question for the policymaker today is which is the least likely to be harmful to the public good—the imperfections of the free market or the imperfections of government regulation?

NOTES

1. For a comprehensive review of the theories of regulatory origin and a thorough discussion of the "creation, design and removal of regulatory forms," see Barry M. Mitnick, *The Political Economy of Regulation* (New York: Columbia University Press, 1980), especially chap. 3, pp. 79–240.

2. James Q. Wilson, "The Politics of Regulation," pp. 135–68 in James W. McKie, ed., *Social Responsibility and the Business Predicament* (Washington, D.C.: The Brookings Institution, 1974). See also his "The Politics of Regulation," pp. 357–94 in James Q. Wilson, ed., *The Politics of Regulation* (New York: Basic Books, 1980), and James Q. Wilson, *American Government: Institutions and Policies* (Lexington, Mass.: D. C. Heath, 1980), pt. IV.

3. The sports antiblackout issue in 1973 met these conditions. See Harry Shooshan, "Confrontation with Congress: Professional Sports and the Television Anti-blackout Law," *Syracuse Law Review* 25 (Summer 1974), 713–45. In many cases, the targeted interests will negotiate a *quid pro quo* that permits them to escape the regulation or to receive the desired benefits. Thus in 1975 the antiblackout legislation was withdrawn in exchange for a promise from the league to adhere voluntarily to the temporary antiblackout regulations and possibly for an NFL franchise in Seattle. See Arthur T. Johnson, "Congress and Professional Sports: 1951–1978, *Annals of the American Academy of Political and Social Sciences* 445 (September 1979), 112.

4. Wilson "Politics of Regulation," p. 166.

Indexes

SUBJECT INDEX

Age Discrimination Act of 1975, 62
Agenda setting, 10–12, 264
Amateur athletes, 9, 13
  legal rights of, 44, 50, 57
Amateur Athletic Act of 1978, 10, 13, 58, 251, 254–55
Amateur Athletic Union (AAU), 8
Amateur sport, 8–9, 41
  as work, 43–44
  as leisure, 43–44
American Baseball Guild, 26
American Basketball Association, 27, 227
American Basketball League, 227
American Council on Education (ACE), 9, 120, 134–35
American Football League, 79, 227
Association for Intercollegiate Athletics for Women (AIAW), 62
Association of Representatives of Professional Athletes (ARPA), 93
Atlanta Falcons, 177

Baltimore, 224, 236–37
Baltimore Colts, 180, 223, 233, 236
Baseball Players Fraternity, 26
Black Sox Scandal of 1919, 5
Broadcasting property rights, 163–70

California, 85–87
Canada, 52–57, 196, 201–2
Canadian carded-athlete system, 52–57
Collective bargaining, 28–36, 142–49
College Football Association, 9, 118, 168
Columbia Broadcasting System, 8, 169
Commission on Civil Rights, 72
Commission on the Review of the National Policy Toward Gambling, 192
Communications Act of 1934, 163
Conflict theory of sport, 3
Copyright Act of 1976, 165–67
Copyright Royalty Tribunal, 165–67
Court of Arbitration for Sport, 255–56

Delaware, 202–3
Department of Education, 70, 72, 73
Department of Health, Education, and Welfare, 11, 12, 64, 119
Department of State, 249–50

East Germany, 8
Educational Testing Service, 120
Elite class interests, 2–3
Eminent domain, 236–38

Fans, 13
Federal Communication Commission, 11, 163
Fitness and Amateur Sport Act, 52
Foreign policy, 248–58
Franchise relocation, 175, 219, 228–44
Free agent, 80
Free agent compensation
  in baseball, 30, 34
  in basketball, 30–31, 34
  in football, 31, 34–35, 143–44
  in hockey, 32, 35–36, 144–45

Gambling, 189–92
  attitude of professional leagues toward, 201, 210–12
  control of, 200–204
  gross revenues from, 194–95, 204
  legalization of, 195–212
  public participation in, 192–95
Grove City College, 70–71

Indiana State University, 47, 124
International Olympic Committee, 51–52, 254

Judicial policymaking, 10, 121–24, 133–34

Labor law exemption, 142–49
League entry, 227, 238–41
League expansion, 227–28

League Protective Players' Association, 26
Liberal-pluralist theory of sport, 3

Major League Baseball, 167, 181–82, 201–2
Major League Baseball Players' Association, 26, 29, 90, 167
Mass asset Theory, 177–79
Mexican League, 27
Milwaukee Braves, 11, 236

National Basketball Association, 31, 34, 143, 181, 231
  merger with American Basketball Association, 8
National Basketball Players' Association, 26
National Brotherhood of Professional Ball Players, 25
National Collegiate Athletic Association, (NCAA), 6, 9, 10, 12, 41, 51, 58, 83, 133–36
  and AIAW, 63–66, 118
  feud with AAU, 8
  legal challenges to, 51, 117–21, 168–69
  registration of sports agents, 90–92
  and women's athletics, 9, 63–66, 75–76
National Employment Priorities Act, 235
National Football League (NFL), 11, 27, 79, 143–44, 146–47, 150–53, 156–57, 180–81, 203, 231
National Football League Players' Association (NFLPA), 26, 28, 79, 84, 87–90
National Hockey League, 26, 29, 37, 90
National Hockey League Players' Association, 26
National Labor Relations Act, 26, 29, 37, 90
National League, 22, 26
New York Giants, 164
New York off-track betting, 190, 205
New York Yankees, 8

Oakland, 223, 233, 236–37
Oakland Raiders, 11, 231, 233, 236
Olympic boycotts, 8, 13, 251–53, 256
Olympic Games, 8, 79, 249, 253

Pittsburgh Pirates, 163, 223–24
Players' League, 26
Players' salaries, 36–38, 89
Players' strikes, 7–8, 33, 35
Portland Trailblazers, 90
President's Commission on Olympic Sports, 10
Professional sports, as tax shelter, 173–74
Professional Sports Community Protection Act, 231
Property rights of athletes, 44, 119, 128–30
Property rights of coaches, 119
Proposition 48, 118
Public interest, 261–64

Rehabilitation Act of 1973, 62
Reserve rule
  in baseball, 22–24, 32–33
  in basketball, 24
  in football, 24
  in hockey, 24
Revenue sharing, 35
Rival leagues, 26–27, 80
Rozelle Rule, 11, 31, 143–44
Rule of reason, 131, 155–56

Salary cap, 34, 146, 148
San Diego Chargers, 81, 82
Scholarship athletes, as employees, 44–51, 124–28
Select Committee on Professional Sports, 9, 211
Self-regulation of sport, 230–32, 261–64
Sherman Act, 28, 37, 131, 140, 149–53, 155–56
Single-entity exemption, 149–53
Soviet Union, 4, 8
Sports
  and anti-trust law, 140–58, 231
  as business, 2, 8–9, 141
  changing perceptions of, 5–10, 140–41
  as fun and games, 5–6
  idyllic image of, 5–10
  as public trust, 2
  and the state, 1–4
  as transmitter of values, 1–2
  and violence, 99–112
Sport Canada, 53–57
Sport Select Baseball (SSB), 201–2

Sports agents, 79–97
  and amateur athletes, 83
  regulation of, 83–97
  services provided by, 80–81
Sports Assistance Fund, 52
Sports betting, 190–92, 201–12
Sports franchises
  benefits derived from, 222–26
  costs attributed to, 223–26
  municipal demand for, 226–30
  as public utilities, 234, 236
  subsidies of, 219
  supply of, 226–27
Sports injuries, 100–101
Sports Lawyers Association, 93–95

Tampa Bay Bandits, 81, 82
Tax policy, 171–83
Tax Reform Act of 1976, 172, 175–76
Television rights and NCAA, 130–32
Temple University, 70
Title IX of the Higher Education Act of
  1972, 9, 11, 12, 62–76, 119
Tower Amendment, 64

Unionism, 25–26
United States Congress, 10, 13, 262
  and amateur athletics, 6, 12, 251
  and professional sports, 6, 140, 153–
    54, 230–36
  and sports agents, 93–96
  and sports violence, 109–11
  and women's athletics, 73, 74

United States Football League (USFL),
  27, 227
United States Olympic Committee
  (USOC), 12, 251, 255
United States Supreme Court
  and amateur athletics, 41, 49
  and professional sports, 6, 28, 140,
    237
  and television rights, 49, 132, 168–69
  and women's intercollegiate athletics,
    68–73
University of Georgia, 168
University of Maryland, 73
University of Minnesota, 128
University of Oklahoma, 168

Violence
  commercial value of, 104
  and criminal prosecution, 105–6
  illegitimate, 101
  league control of, 102–5
  and public opinion, 112
  and tort suits, 106–9

Washington Senators, 11, 175
Western Michigan University, 45, 125–
  28
Wichita State University, 168
Women's Intercollegiate Athletics, 62–76
Worker's compensation, 44–51, 124–28
World Football League, 27, 227
World Hockey Association (WHA), 27,
  32, 52, 143, 227

NAME INDEX

Acosta, R. Vivian, 67
Ambrose, James F., 116, 117
Anderson, Gary, 81–82
Argovitz, Jerry, 81–82
Atkinson, Mark Alan, 48

Barrett, James D., 131, 132
Berger, Bennett, 42
Blakey, G. Robert, 213
Boucha, Henry, 105
Brighthill, Charles, 42
Brohm, Jean-Marie, 3
Bulaich, Norm, 99
Bunzel, John H., 72
Butz, Dave, 80
Byers, Walter, 63

Carlson, Chris, 108, 110–11
Carpenter, Linda J., 19, 62, 67
Carter, Jimmy, 13
Chambers, Ernie, 58
Chayes, Abram, 122
Cheevers, Gerry, 32
Christiansen, Eugene M., 200
Clark, Charles "Booby", 107
Closius, Phillip J., 115, 140
Coleman, Willie, 45–49, 125–28

Daschle, Tom, 110
Davis, Al, 232
Decker, Mary, 80
DeGrazia, Sebastian, 42
Dumazedier, Joffre, 42
Dworkin, James B., 19, 21

Eitzen, D. Stanley, 20, 99
Etzioni, Amitai, 42
Ewing, Pat, 90

Fairbanks, Chuck, 81
Fass, Martin, 164
Finley, Charles O., 232
Forbes, David, 105

Ford, Gerald, 10
Frey, James, 187, 189, 261

Grange, Red, 5, 79
Green, Ted, 99
Gregory, Gwen, 63–64

Hackbart, Dale, 107
Hall, Mark, 128–29
Hamel, Jean, 99
Haywood, Spencer, 147
Hoch, Paul, 2
Hochberg, Philip R., 115, 162
Horner, Bob, 80
Horowitz, Donald, 123
Horrow, Richard, 101, 106, 108–09, 111

Johnson, Arthur, 187, 219, 224, 261
Johnson, Edwin, 5

Kapp, Joe, 31
Kennedy, Robert, 10
Kennedy, Walter, 210
Kheel, Theodore, 10
Kidd, Bruce, 19, 41
Kraus, Richard, 42
Kuhn, Bowie, 210
Kunnert, Kevin, 34

Leonard, Margaret, 86
Lewis, Carl, 41, 80
Lord, Miles, 129
Lowell, Cym, 49–50, 234, 236, 238
Luke, Steve, 99

Mac-Arthur, Douglas, 10
Mackey, John, 28–29, 31
Maki, Wayne, 99
Manton, Jack, 80
Marichal, Juan, 99, 101
McCormack, Mark, 80
McNally, Dave, 29
Messersmith, Andy, 29

Metzenbaum, Howard, 135
Moses, Edwin, 41
Mosier, James, 46
Mottl, Ronald M., 109
Mulvey, Paul, 101
Mulvoy, Mark, 104

Nader, Ralph, 13
Nafziger, James, 187, 248
Neinas, Charles, 46
Newton, A. E., 163
Noll, Roger, ix

O'Brien, Larry, 34
Okner, Benjamin, 224
Owens, R. C., 31

Paterno, Joe, 92
Pieper, Joseph, 42
Porto, Brian, 51, 115, 117
Powell, William, 70
Pyle, C. C., 79

Reagan, Ronald, 253
Rehnquist, William, 132
Rensing, Fred, 47–51, 124–28
Reynolds, John, 171, 178
Robertson, Oscar, 30
Roche, George, 74
Roseboro, John, 99, 101
Rozelle, Pete, 31, 210
Russo, Ronald, 86

Ruth, Babe, 5
Ruxin, Robert, 79

Sack, Allen, 19, 41
Sanderson, Derek, 32
Seitz, Peter, 30
Shefsky, Lloyd, 94
Shuck, Donald, 44
Skagan, Michael, 200
Skolnick, Jerome, 199, 203
Sleigher, Louis, 99
Stevens, John Paul, 132

Tarkanian, Jerry, 133
Thomas, Carolyn, 46
Thompson, John, 90

Upshaw, Gene, 86

van der Merve, Marina, 55

Walker, Herschel, 80
Walker, Matthew, 108, 110
Walton, Bill, 34
Washington, Kermit, 34, 107
Weistart, John, 49–50, 234, 236, 238
Wells, Lloyd C. A., 82
Wendel, John, 94
White, Byron, 49, 132
Wilson, James, 262, 264
Winfield, David, 80

Ziegler, John, 103

INDEX OF CASES

Alan H. Selig v. United States, 178–79

Albach v. Odle, 137n

Alexander v. Jenning, 73

Alexander v. National Football League, 160n

Allen Bradley Company v. Local Union 13, IBEW, 142

American Federation of Musicians of U.S. and Canada v. Carroll, 97n

American League Baseball Club of Chicago v. Chase, 158n

American League of Professional Baseball Clubs and Association of National Baseball League Umpires, 40n

Apex Hosiery Company v. Leader, 158n

Askew v. Macomber, 45

Baltimore Orioles Inc. v. Major League Baseball Players' Association, 167

Behagen v. Intercollegiate Conference (Big Ten), 137n

Board of Public Instruction of Taylor County v. Finch, 70

Board of Regents of the University of Oklahoma v. NCAA, 59n, 60n, 130–32, 168–69

Board of Regents v. Roth, 138n

Bob Jones University v. Johnson, 70

Boris v. USFL, 98

Boston Professional Hockey Club v. Cheevers, 40n

City of Oakland v. Oakland Raiders, 247n

Coleman v. Western Michigan, 45–51, 124–28

Colorado Seminary (University of Denver) v. NCAA, 137n

Commissioner v. Chicago National League Ball Club, 184n

Commissioner v. Pittsburgh Athletic Company, 184n

Copperweld Corporation v. Independence Tube Corporation, 152

Curtis C. Flood v. Bowie K. Kuhn, et.al., 16n, 39n, 141, 246n

Denver Rockets v. All-Pro Management, 154

Federal Baseball Club v. National League, 6, 39n, 140, 246n

First Northwest Industries of America Inc., 177–78

Goldfarb v. Virginia State Bar, 138n

Grove City v. Bell, 17n, 68–75, 136n

H. A. Artists and Associates v. Actors' Equity Association, 97n

Hackbart v. Cincinnati Bengals, 107, 109

Haffer v. Temple University, 70

Hall v. University of Minnesota, 128, 129

Hawaii Housing Authority et al. v. Midkiff et al., 237

Helvering v. Kansas City American Association Baseball Company, 184n

Hillsdale v. Department of Health, Education and Welfare, 69

Howard University v. NCAA, 138n

International Brotherhood of Teamsters v. National Labor Relations Board, 159n

James McCoy (Yazoo) Smith v. Pro Football et al., 17n

Kansas City Royals Baseball Corporation v. Major League Baseball Players' Association, 158*n*

Kapp v. National Football League, 40*n*

Kelly Communications Corporation v. Westinghouse Broadcasting Corporation, 170*n*

Laird v. United States, 177

Lemat Corporation v. Barry, 185*n*

Local Union No. 189, Amalgamated Meat Cutters v. Jewel Tea Company, 142

Los Angeles Memorial Coliseum and Oakland Raiders v. National Football League, 17*n*, 151, 157, 245*n*

McCourt v. California Sports Inc., 143–44

McDonald v. NCAA, 137*n*

Mackey v. NFL, 39*n*, 40*n*, 143–44

Marine Pipeline and Dredging Ltd. v. Canadian Oil Ltd., 60*n*

Mayor and City Council of Baltimore v. Baltimore Football Club Inc., 247*n*

Mid-South Grizzlies v. National Football League, 156

Mitchell v. Louisiana High School, 137*n*

Morgan v. Winschuler's Restaurant, 47

NCAA v. Califano, 16n, 17n, 65

Nabozny v. Barnhill, 107

Nassau Sports v. Hampson, 40*n*

National Association of Broadcasters v. Copyright Royalty Tribunal, 170*n*

National Exhibition Company v. Foss, 164

National Football League v. Governor of Delaware, 216*n*

National Labor Relations Board v. Associated General Contractors of America, 159*n*

North American Soccer League v. National Football League, 151, 157

North Haven Board of Education v. Bell, 68

Othen v. Ann Arbor School Board, 69

Philadelphia Baseball Club Ltd v. La-joie, 158*n*

Philadelphia World Hockey Club v. Philadelphia Hockey Club, 35, 143, 156

Pittsburgh Athletic Company v. KQV Broadcasting Company, 163

Public Instruction of Taylor City v. Finch, 70

Radovich v. National Football League, 39n, 158*n*

Regents of University of California v. ABC, 170*n*

Regents of the University of Minnesota v. NCAA, 137*n*

Regina v. Green, 113*n*

Regina v. Maki, 113*n*

Regina v. Maloney, 113*n*

Rensing v. Indiana State University Board of Trustees, 47–51, 124–28

Robertson v. National Basketball Association, 40*n*, 143, 154

San Francisco Seals, Ltd. v. National Hockey League, 246*n*

Smith v. Pro Football Inc., 148

Standard Oil Company of New Jersey v. United States, 154

State v. Forbes, 105

State of Nevada v. Rosenthal, 216*n*

Tarkanian v. University of Nevada et al., 137*n*

Toolson v. New York Yankees, 6, 39*n*, 158*n*, 246*n*

Tomjanovich v. California Sports, Inc., 107

TWA v. Thurston, 73

UMW v. Pennington, 142

United States v. Addyston Pipe and Steel Company, 158*n*

United States v. Grinnel Corporation, 156

United States v. Hutcheson, 158*n*

United States v. International Boxing of New York, 158*n*

University of Nevada v. Tarkanian, 137n

University of Richmond v. Bell, 69

Wichita State University Inter-Collegiate Athletic Association Inc. v. Swanson Broadcasting Company, 168

Zacchini v. Scripps-Howard Broadcasting Company, 164

Zinn v. Parish, 97n

Contributors

JAMES H. FREY is professor of sociology at the University of Nevada, Las Vegas. His research interests include organizational effectiveness, corporate deviance, sport sociology, and the sociology of work and leisure. He is the author of *The Governance of Intercollegiate Athletics* (1982) and *Survey Research by Telephone* (1983). He was formerly editor of the *Journal of Sport and Social Issues*.

ARTHUR T. JOHNSON is associate professor of political science at the University of Maryland Baltimore County. His research interests relate to issues of municipal administration. He has written several articles on the relationship between sports and government, which have appeared in various social science journals, including *Public Administration Review, Annals of the American Academy of Political and Social Sciences,* and *American Behavioral Scientist.*

JAMES F. AMBROSE is a partner in the firm of Bullivant, Houser, Bailey, Pendergrass, Hoffman, O'Connell, and Goyak in Portland, Oregon. His areas of specialty include corporate and personal tax, qualified employee benefits, executive compensation, and general corporate and real-estate law. Mr. Ambrose was admitted to the Oregon Bar in 1979 and to the California Bar in 1980. He is the author of "Recent Tax Developments Regarding Purchases of Sports Franchises—The Game Isn't Over Yet," *Taxes, The Tax Magazine* (November 1981). He is a graduate of the University of Notre Dame and Loyola University School of Law.

LINDA J. CARPENTER, professor of physical education at Brooklyn College, City University of New York, holds a doctorate in physical education from the University of Southern California and a Juris Doctor from Fordham University. Her current research interests are the administration of women's sports and sports law.

PHILIP J. CLOSIUS is a graduate of the University of Notre Dame and of the Columbia University School of Law, where he was a three-year Stone Scholar. After practicing law for several years, Mr. Closius joined the faculty of the University of Toledo College of Law, where he is associate professor of law. He has represented several football players in the negotiation of their professional contracts.

JAMES B. DWORKIN is associate professor of industrial relations in the Krannert Graduate School of Management, Purdue University. His teaching and research interests are in the areas of labor relations and collective bargaining. He has published *Owners Versus Players: Baseball and Collective Bargaining* (1981) and has authored more than twenty articles for professional journals. He is an active arbitrator, mediator, and factfinder in labor disputes and serves on labor panels maintained by the American Arbitration Association, National Mediation Board, Iowa Public Employment Relations Board, and Indiana Education Employment Relations Board.

D. STANLEY EITZEN is professor of sociology at Colorado State University. His areas of specialty are social stratification, political sociology, criminology, social problems, and the sociology of sport. He has written eight books, including two on sport: *Sociology of American Sport* (1982) and *Sport in Contemporary America* (1984). He recently completed a six-year term as editor of *Social Science Journal*, and he has served as an associate or advisory editor for several sport-related journals: *International Review of Sport Sociology, Review of Sport and Leisure, Journal of Sport Behavior,* and *Journal of Sport Psychology.*

PHILIP R. HOCHBERG is a partner in the law firm of Baraff, Koerner, Olender, and Hochberg in Washington, D.C. Mr. Hochberg and his firm have represented the National Basketball Association, National Hockey League, North American Soccer League, Major Indoor Soccer League, and the College Football Association. He has authored many papers on sports law and media practice.

BRUCE KIDD is associate professor of physical and health education at the University of Toronto. His publications include *The Death of Hockey* (1972), *The Political Economy of Sport* (1979), and *Athletes' Rights in Canada,* with Mary Eberts (1982). In the 1960s he won Canadian, American, British, and Commonwealth championships in track and field and was twice selected Canada's Athlete of the Year. In 1983 he was appointed chairman of a government task force investigating amateur boxing. He is also chairman of the Olympic Academy of Canada.

JAMES A. R. NAFZIGER is professor of law at the Willamette University College of Law. His degrees are from the University of Wisconsin and Harvard. He was an editor of *Harvard International Law Journal.* Professor Nafziger was administrative director of the American Society of International Law and has taught at Catholic University, the University of Oregon, the National Autonomous University of Mexico (as a Fulbright lecturer), and the University of Thessaloniki. He is chairman of the International Law Section of the Association of American Law Schools, chairman of the Human Rights Section of the International Law Association (American Branch), and member of the Executive Council of the American Society of International Law. Professor Nafziger has published numerous articles on international sports law.

BRIAN L. PORTO is formerly an assistant professor of political science at Macalester College in St. Paul, Minnesota. He is currently enrolled in the School of Law at the University of Indiana. Dr. Porto's articles concerning the legal status and constitutional rights of college athletes have appeared in *Journal of Sport and Social Issues* and Herb Appenzeller, ed., *Law and Sports: Some Contemporary Issues* (1985).

ROBERT H. RUXIN, the author of *An Athlete's Guide to Agents*, is a vice-president of the Sports Lawyers Association. An honors graduate of Princeton University and Harvard Law School, Mr. Ruxin practices communications and sports law in the Washington, D.C., office of Preston, Thorgrimson, Ellis, and Holman. He chaired the Sports Legislation Subcommittee of the American Bar Assocation's Forum Committee on Entertainment and Sports Industries from 1982 to 1984.

ALLEN SACK is associate professor of sociology and chairman of the Sociology and Social Welfare Department of the University of New Haven. His articles on sport have appeared in the *New York Times, Sporting News,* and *Sociology of Education.* He is also a contributing editor to the *Journal of Sport and Social Issues.* Dr. Sack was a defensive end on Notre Dame's 1966 National Championship Football Team and was drafted by the Los Angeles Rams. From 1981 to 1983 he was director of the federally funded Center for Athletes' Rights and Education.